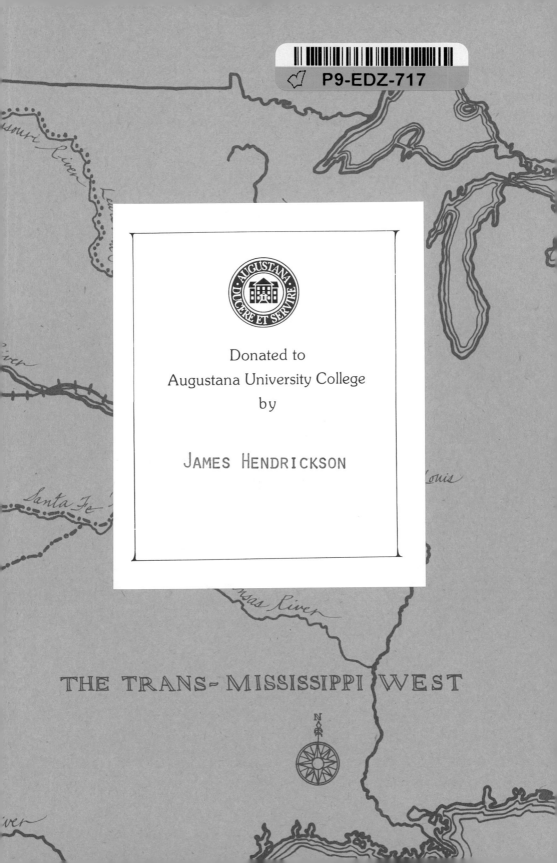

THE TRANS-MISSISSIPPI WEST

THE
FRONTIER
EXPERIENCE

THE
FRONTIER
EXPERIENCE
Readings in the Trans-Mississippi West

Edited by ROBERT V. HINE, University
of California, Riverside

and EDWIN R. BINGHAM, University
of Oregon

WADSWORTH PUBLISHING
COMPANY
Belmont, California

Library of Congress Catalog Card Number : 63-18663
Printed in the United States of America

PREFACE

No aspect of the American West has proved more interesting or more significant than the effect of the frontier on American life and character. "From the conditions of frontier life," wrote Frederick Jackson Turner (and no one has disputed him on this point), "came intellectual traits of profound importance." The themes and hypotheses of this book of readings are based on two such traits—and their opposites: the individualistic and the innovative threads of frontier experience, versus the cooperative and the traditional threads.

Turner, for all his insight and sagacity, was never one to define his terms carefully, so that the exact meaning of his reference to the West as a catalyst for American individualism is nebulous. Generally, however, "individualism" means a belief in the value and dignity of the individual man: in the social sphere, the individual above the group; in political theory, the individual above the state; in religion, the individual above the church. As such, its roots are certainly as deep as the ideas of Socrates or Martin Luther or John Stuart Mill. If the ideal of the individualist is a man unfettered by restrictions, be they of government, of church, or of moral code, then Voltaire and Adam Smith have contributed more to the ideal than any fur trapper or cowhand ever did. Perhaps the latter were only practitioners of a long tradition in Western civilization. Perhaps, on the other hand, the environment in which they lived (the "free land" of Turner or the "man-land ratio" of Walter Prescott Webb) made possible the shaping of the tradition into a particularly interesting pattern.

Individualism implies freedom, but what kind of freedom? Unrestrained license, or conformity to perfect law? The American frontier may well have been a force toward license, an abuse of freedom, a perversion of individualism. Such would be one extreme. Or it may have been no more than a push toward that self-sufficient, self-reliant condition that Emerson proclaimed and nineteenth-century Americans cherished as their chief virtue.

But for those who with Wordsworth found "unchartered freedom" tiring, the frontier was something else again. For them it might well have been a challenge to cooperation, a lesson in the inadequacy of individualism. The loneliness of the frontier mocked the individualist; it tore at his heart and his mind. Often the individual stood aside while the group took over:

raising a cabin or a barn, husking the corn, threshing the wheat. Sometimes the group assumed the guise of a corporation or company, and the lonely trapper gladly trekked to the organized rendezvous, the tired prospector resignedly surrendered to the large-scale investor.

If the free individual is one who will not tolerate restrictions, then he will tend to deviate from accustomed habits, experiment, try different customs or ideas that he finds in his new environment. The miner joined the Vigilance Committee and took law into his own hands; the Texan devised the Texas Rangers; the Spaniard adapted his mission system to a wild borderland; the trapper turned his back on civilization and became himself a savage. Such was the innovative impact of the frontier.

Yet how strong was the pull of habit, how persistent was the need to hold to the old culture! Louis Wright has cautioned against an undue emphasis on the lawlessness of the frontier, overlooking "the unspectacular efforts of godly and law-abiding folk to establish old patterns of behavior." The pressures for church and school were strong and early; the reliance on older models in shaping new state constitutions was often slavish; the massing of frontiersmen at Shakespearian productions was not solely the result of extra change in the pocket; it also reflected a desire to keep old and familiar traditions alive in a rough world. Jenny Lind singing to the miners was a cultural hoop of steel. The woman and her song held before the men something they feared to lose.

So we must admit at the outset that the frontier experience was complex and protean and diverse. All of the subsequent chapters will illustrate that point. But they will not demonstrate, at first sight or superficially, the complexity of individualism itself. If we take the guidance of such modern writers as Erich Fromm and David Riesman, individualism as it grew out of the Enlightenment was already subject to some grave disappointments by the end of the nineteenth century. What had begun hopefully as a freeing of the human spirit had produced first loneliness and insecurity, and then a frightening level of conformity. As Riesman points out, the "inner-directedness" of the nineteenth-century man had given way to an "other-directedness," an anxious turning toward the group for guidance. But since every other individual turned likewise, the group was a hollow source. Human society became the measure of all things. At the same time, says Fromm, men become alienated from one another. With some men, society becomes intolerable; with others, submersion into mass conformity is the only escape. Man's roots become shallow; he moves aimlessly from place to place. He lives without a meaningful tradition and tries to convince himself that all he needs is more and more freedom to bring order into his life. But apathy and confusion have spawned impotence. Individualism reaches the bitter irony of its own destruction.

What, then, of the cooperative strain? Here again some rather funda-

mental distinctions must be made. What basically brings men to cooperate
with one another? It can be, as Locke and the liberal tradition would have
it, that cooperation is the result of a contract between men, motivated by
self-interest, and that the contract can be voided if its terms are in any way
broken. If there is no further context for the contract than the individuals
composing it—if, in short, God ceases to be a third party—then the contract
will be nullified at any time it ceases to serve the egocentric purposes of the
individuals involved. Individualism thus enters the picture again, potentially
destructive of the idea of cooperation as based on human contract.

But cooperation may be based on other concepts—for example, the organic community (which grows from natural relationships like the family)
or the society that comes together to accomplish a particular job—ridding
the range of rustlers or banding into a wagon train for Indian protection;
when the ends are achieved, the society disbands. Both the organic community and the specific society may also involve a third element in their
group relationship, theism, thus becoming communities in which the brotherhood of man rests upon the fatherhood of God. In this type of community
the individual is not relieved of his responsibility simply because the relationship no longer pleases him. Most of the societies that were based upon
some religious idea, like Amana in Iowa or the Mormons in Utah, had long
lives—in contrast with a welter of secular groups, whose average life would
probably not exceed three years. Thus it would seem that the society that
most denied the individual as a supreme test of the good was the community
that had the power to last.

One final distinction should be made: the difference between imitation
and tradition. Tradition is a part of a man; it surrounds him from the
cradle, or it slowly develops within him during his lifetime; it emerges from
or seeps into his unconscious. He may come into a new land and try to
imitate the traditions of a foreign people, but those imitations do not easily
become a part of his tradition. Tradition in this sense is nearer to what the
anthropologists would call culture, and imitation results in a conflict of cultures. In the process of conflict some things are lost, others retained, others
modified. A man does not imitate his own tradition; he brings it with him
and he has no choice.

The frontiersman, then, had a tradition, and he could no more have
left it behind than he could have left his nose. It should also be pointed
out that tradition itself, although consistent, is not static; it can involve
the progressive unfolding of an idea, as any Burkean conservative would
contend. But it cannot involve mere imitation of another's tradition, and
it cannot involve violent or sudden change—especially beyond the banks
of the stream within which the tradition runs.

So the question is posed: What was the nature of the frontier experience and how did it relate to those parts of the American character

called individualism, cooperation, innovation, and tradition? Is the trapper or the lone prospector the antisocial individualist who has alienated himself from society so thoroughly that he is no longer capable of deeper human attachments? Is the restless Western movement from city to city evidence of that contractual community which binds only as long as it serves; if conditions are better elsewhere, is there any responsibility to stay and improve them where you are? Do the Oregon "wolf meetings" or the miners' assemblies to settle claim disputes exemplify the community that exists for the particular job at hand but cannot be counted on any further? Do the Mormons represent an experience with theistic community which pervades all aspects of life and has an uncanny ability to persist? Does the Roman Catholicism of the Protestant settlers in Texas represent an imitation which simply did not take? And, conversely, does Sarah Royce's religion, carried across scorching deserts to the California mines, picture a tradition so deep that it cannot be abrogated? Do the new legal patterns for water rights in Mormon Utah and Spanish California illustrate the way in which traditions can be modified by new conditions and in contact with new cultures? These and a thousand similar questions may be asked, and the reader is invited to seek their answers in the selections that follow, with only the one warning that there will be no simple answers in the lot.

We realize, of course, that the American West is much broader than the boundaries here drawn. The time span is limited substantially to the nineteenth century; yet no fewer than twelve generations of Americans— that is, from the beginning of settlement on the Atlantic Coast—have lived under the frontier influence. And although we concern ourselves with an area beyond the Mississippi, we are nevertheless aware that the Hudson and the Alleghenies and the Ohio River were also frontiers, however dissimilar. The limitations are for purposes of deeper probing; let no one consider them bounds to the experience. Just as we have been deliberately selective in time and area, we know that the themes are only a few of many possibilities. The West as a source of homogeneity, of nationalism, of scientific interest, of economic wealth (to mention but a few) will be little treated here; the logger, for example, is scarcely mentioned. There will, in a few areas, be a small number of selections that do not contribute to the themes; but these will occur only when it is felt that the West cannot be understood without them. We hope that a keener grasp of a few key ideas will compensate for the omissions. To appreciate the complexity of a limited number of generalizations is, we believe, more valuable than the uncritical exposure to many.

RVH
ERB

CONTENTS

UNDERSTANDING THE AMERICAN WEST

At mid-twentieth century the West belongs to the nation. The most popular image springs from the cow country and involves the six-gun and the spur, the Stetson and the star. To others, the West is first of all a wonderland of physical phenomena—the deep canyons of the Colorado and the Snake, the redwoods of Northern California, the wind-riven pinnacles of Bryce, or the tortured lava lands of the Columbia Plateau. The sportsman sees the West primarily as playground. The conservationist fights to keep the land primitive and whole, while the promoter works to subdivide it. When sophisticate and *bon vivant* meet to reminisce, their West is generally San Francisco or Hollywood or Las Vegas. Some look westward with a jaundiced eye, seeing the region as culturally retarded, blindly provincial, and handicapped by a heritage of brutality and violence. The historically inclined recall Lewis and Clark, Frémont, the retreat of Chief Joseph, the Donner disaster, or the Mormon exodus; while professional historians argue over the significance of the frontier in American history or protest the prominence of antiquarians and sensationalists in the field. One zealot defined as West anywhere far enough toward the setting sun to be "out from under." Some insist that the West is more process than direction or locality. One thing is certain—whatever the angle of vision, the West is firmly fixed in the collective mind and imagination. To what extent and why the West has become a kind of national fixation constitutes a complex problem, one that can be only suggested here and in the four selections to follow.

For more than a century, from the Northwest Ordinance of 1787 to the Carey Act of 1894, the moving frontier was one of the irreducible facts of national life. Because Americans were so thoroughly involved in westward expansion, there was little disposition to make any kind of general inquiry into the meaning of the Western experience. The West as frontier had virtually to disappear before it could be properly appreciated as a formative factor in our national development and acknowledged as a persistent pressure on our national character. However, this is not to say that the Western or frontier experience (they were not always synonymous) was ignored in the nineteenth century. Obviously it was not. On the one hand, a documentary and largely realistic version of the Western advance was taking shape in the form of letters, diaries, reports, account books, statistical records, and legislation—along with occasional creative efforts that bore the stamp of authenticity, such as Hamlin Garland's short stories of the "Middle Border." On the other hand, highly unreliable conceptions about the West came from sources as disparate as promotional literature, dime novels, newspapers, and the tall tales of frontier humorists. Over most of the century American writers—Timothy Flint, James Fenimore Cooper, Washington Irving, Walt Whitman, and Mark Twain, to name the most obvious—were intrigued by frontier themes that they rendered with varying degrees of fidelity. Even Henry Thoreau from his relatively cozy wilderness around Walden Pond confessed that his walking tours invariably veered toward the West. As for history, Francis Parkman and his admirer Theodore Roosevelt wrote popular and compelling narratives of the struggle to possess two of the earlier Wests, and on the Pacific Slope Hubert Howe Bancroft and his assistants produced a fast-selling historical series dealing with the Far Western states and territories as well as Mexico and Central America. Clearly, then, on the practical plane of participation and in the vicarious spheres of legend, fiction, and narrative history, the nineteenth-century American was aware of the West.

However, it took a young professional historian from Wisconsin reading a paper on "The Significance of the Frontier in American History" at the meeting of the American Historical Association in Chicago in 1893 to block out the lines for a more comprehensive and systematic search into the meanings of the frontier and of the West. Through this seminal essay and others to follow, along with more methodical and exacting monographic work, Frederick Jackson Turner converted a generation of American historians to frontier history. With some who came after Turner (not necessarily his followers), the focus was narrow and local; but others were stimulated to examine his affirmations and test his insights; to investigate other frontier regions; or, like Frederick L. Paxson, Walter P. Webb, Louis B. Wright, and Henry Nash Smith, to advance broad interpretations of their own concerning the frontier and the West.

Turner did not end the dualism of romance and realism that characterized nineteenth-century treatments of the West. The antiquarian and the narrative historian could draw encouragement from the master's emphases and enthusiasm from his rhetoric; the social scientist and institutional historian could profit from his method. Writing about the American West, then, still reflects two moods. The dominant one remains romantic. The Indian is a tragic and noble figure; the free trapper is splendidly barbaric or a self-appointed leader of the people; the moving frontier democratizes and revivifies the American character; wide-open spaces expand emotional and spiritual horizons—all these are romantic ideas. But the West of tall tale and fantasy and sweeping assertion evokes a response that seeks to test heady generalizations, to examine the commonplace and typical as well as the bizarre and unique, to get at the factual as well as the fanciful.

The selections that follow represent four attempts to measure the meaning of the frontier and the West. Indeed, within the confines of the themes of individualism, cooperation, innovation, and tradition, this book is simply one more approach to an understanding of the Western experience. The search goes on.

Frederick Jackson Turner

Frederick Jackson Turner (1861–1932) has long since ceased to be the last word in frontier history, but it is eminently appropriate that he have the first word in a book concerned with the Western experience. His essay on the significance of the frontier is undoubtedly the most provocative piece of writing in American historiography; the excerpt reprinted here suggests some of the more conspicuous and familiar facets of his frontier thesis and demonstrates the literary style that helped make Turner's prose so persuasive. A word of caution: this is the more romantic and rhetorical Turner. The analytical Turner, the student of institutions and statistics, the more enduring—though perhaps less compelling—Turner is much more in evidence in his monographic works. The student ought to read in their entirety the essays from which the following selections are drawn and, perhaps, Turner's "The West and American Ideals" and "Social Forces in American History" as well.

The Significance
of the
Frontier in America*

Up to our own day American history has been in a large degree the history of the colonization of the Great West. The existence of an area of free land, its continuous recession, and the advance of American settlement westward, explain American development. . . .

American social development has been continually beginning over again on the frontier. This perennial rebirth, this fluidity of American life, this expansion westward with its new opportunities, its continuous touch with the simplicity of primitive society, furnish the forces dominating American character. The true point of view in the history of this nation is not the Atlantic coast, it is the Great West. . . .

The most significant thing about the American frontier is, that it lies at the hither edge of free land. In the census reports it is treated as the margin of that settlement which has a density of two or more to the square mile. The term is an elastic one, and for our purposes does not need sharp definition. We shall consider the whole frontier belt, including the Indian country and the outer margin of the "settled area" of the census reports. This paper will make no attempt to treat the subject exhaustively; its aim is simply to call attention to the frontier as a fertile field for investigation, and to suggest some of the problems which arise in connection with it.

. . . Our early history is the study of European germs developing in an American environment. Too exclusive attention has been paid by institutional students to the Germanic origins, too little to the American factors. The frontier is the line of most rapid and effective Americanization. The wilderness masters the colonist. It finds him a European in dress, industries, tools, modes of travel, and thought. It takes him from the railroad car and puts him in the birch canoe. It strips off the garments of civilization and arrays him in the hunting shirt and the moccasin. It puts him in the log cabin of the Cherokee and Iroquois and runs an Indian palisade around him. Before long he has gone to planting Indian corn and plowing with a sharp stick; he shouts the war cry and takes the scalp in orthodox Indian fashion. In short, at the frontier the environment is at first too strong for

---

* From Frederick Jackson Turner, "The Significance of the Frontier in American History," American Historical Association, *Annual Report for 1893* (Washington, 1894), pp. 199 ff.

the man. He must accept the conditions which it furnishes, or perish, and so he fits himself into the Indian clearings and follows the Indian trails. Little by little he transforms the wilderness, but the outcome is not the old Europe, not simply the development of Germanic germs . . . The fact is, that here is a new product that is American. At first, the frontier was the Atlantic coast. It was the frontier of Europe in a very real sense. Moving westward, the frontier became more and more American. As successive terminal moraines result from successive glaciations, so each frontier leaves its traces behind it, and when it becomes a settled area the region still partakes of the frontier characteristics. Thus the advance of the frontier has meant a steady movement away from the influence of Europe, a steady growth of independence on American lines. And to study this advance, the men who grew up under these conditions, and the political, economic, and social results of it, is to study the really American part of our history. . . .

The United States lies like a huge page in the history of society. Line by line as we read this continental page from West to East we find the record of social evolution. It begins with the Indian and the hunter; it goes on to tell of the disintegration of savagery by the entrance of the trader, the pathfinder of civilization; we read the annals of the pastoral stage in ranch life; the exploitation of the soil by the raising of unrotated crops of corn and wheat in sparsely settled farming communities; the intensive culture of the denser farm settlement; and finally the manufacturing organization with city and factory system. . . .

The effect of the Indian frontier as a consolidating agent in our history is important. From the close of the seventeenth century various intercolonial congresses have been called to treat with Indians and establish common measures of defense. Particularism was strongest in colonies with no Indian frontier. This frontier stretched along the western border like a cord of union. The Indian was a common danger, demanding united action. . . .

From the time the mountains rose between the pioneer and the sea-board, a new order of Americanism arose. The West and the East began to get out of touch of each other. The settlements from the sea to the mountains kept connection with the rear and had a certain solidarity. But the over-mountain men grew more and more independent. The East took a narrow view of American advance, and nearly lost these men. Kentucky and Tennessee history bears abundant witness to the truth of this statement. The East began to try to hedge and limit westward expansion. Through Webster could declare that there were no Alleghanies in his politics, yet in politics in general they were a very solid factor.

. . . Daniel Boone, the great backwoodsman, who combined the occupations of hunter, trader, cattle-raiser, farmer, and surveyor—learning, probably from the traders, of the fertility of the lands of the upper Yadkin, where the traders were wont to rest as they took their way to the Indians, left his Pennsylvania home with his father, and passed down the Great Valley road to that stream. Learning from a trader of the game and rich pastures of Kentucky, he pioneered the way for the farmers to that region. Thence he passed to the frontier of Missouri, where his settlement was long a landmark on the frontier. Here again he helped to open the way for civilization, finding salt licks, and trails, and land. His son was among the earliest trappers in the passes of the Rocky Mountains, and his party are said to have been the first to camp on the present site of Denver. His grandson, Col. A. J. Boone, of Colorado, was a power among the Indians of the Rocky Mountains, and was appointed an agent by the government. Kit Carson's mother was a Boone. Thus this family epitomizes the backwoodsman's advance across the continent.

. . . the frontier promoted the formation of a composite nationality for the American people. The coast was preponderantly English, but the later tides of continental immigration flowed across to the free lands. . . . In the crucible of the frontier the immigrants were Americanized, liberated, and fused into a mixed race, English in neither nationality nor characteristics. . . .

The legislation which most developed the powers of the national government, and played the largest part in its activity, was conditioned on the frontier. Writers have discussed the subjects of tariff, land, and internal improvement, as subsidiary to the slavery question. But when American history comes to be rightly viewed it will be seen that the slavery question is an incident. . . .

But the most important effect of the frontier has been in the promotion of democracy here and in Europe. As has been indicated, the frontier is productive of individualism. Complex society is precipitated by the wilderness into a kind of primitive organization based on the family. The tendency is anti-social. It produces antipathy to control, and particularly to any direct control. The tax-gatherer is viewed as a representative of oppression. Prof. Osgood, in an able article, has pointed out that the frontier conditions prevalent in the colonies are important factors in the explanation of the American Revolution, where individual liberty was sometimes confused with absence of all effective government. The same conditions aid in explaining the difficulty of instituting a strong government in the period of the confederacy. The frontier individualism has from the beginning promoted democracy. . . .

But the democracy born of free land, strong in selfishness and individualism, intolerant of administrative experience and education, and pressing individual liberty beyond its proper bounds, has its dangers as well as its benefits. Individualism in America has allowed a laxity in regard to governmental affairs which has rendered possible the spoils system and all the manifest evils that follow from the lack of a highly developed civic spirit. In this connection may be noted also the influence of frontier conditions in permitting lax business honor, inflated paper currency and wild-cat banking. The colonial and revolutionary frontier was the region whence emanated many of the worst forms of an evil currency. The West in the War of 1812 repeated the phenomenon on the frontier of that day, while the speculation and wild-cat banking of the period of the crisis of 1837 occurred on the new frontier belt of the next tier of States. Thus each one of the periods of lax financial integrity coincides with periods when a new set of frontier communities had arisen, and coincides in area with these successive frontiers, for the most part. The recent Populist* agitation is a case in point. Many a State that now declines any connection with the tenets of the Populists, itself adhered to such ideas in an earlier stage of the development of the State. A primitive society can hardly be expected to show the intelligent appreciation of the complexity of business interests in a developed society. The continual recurrence of these areas of paper-money agitation is another evidence that the frontier can be isolated and studied as a factor in American history of the highest importance. . . .

From the conditions of frontier life came intellectual traits of profound importance. The works of travelers along each frontier from colonial days onward describe certain common traits, and these traits have, while softening down, still persisted as survivals in the place of their origin, even when a higher social organization succeeded. The result is that to the frontier the American intellect owes its striking characteristics. That coarseness and strength combined with acuteness and inquisitiveness; that practical, inventive turn of mind, quick to find expedients; that masterful grasp of material things, lacking in the artistic but powerful to effect great ends; that restless, nervous energy; that dominant individualism, working for good and for evil, and withal that buoyancy and exuberance which comes with freedom—these are traits of the frontier, or traits called out elsewhere because of the existence of the frontier. Since the days when the fleet of Columbus sailed into the waters of the New World, America has been another name for opportunity, and the people of the United States have taken their tone from the incessant expansion which has not only been open but has even been forced upon them. He would be a rash prophet who should assert that the expansive character of American life has now entirely ceased. Movement has been its dominant fact, and, unless this training has no effect upon a people, the American energy will continually

---

* A political reform movement of farmers and working men, which reached its height in the first half of the 1890s.

demand a wider field for its exercise. But never again will such gifts of free
land offer themselves. For a moment, at the frontier, the bonds of custom
are broken and unrestraint is triumphant. There is no *tabula rasa*. The
stubborn American environment is there with its imperious summons to
accept its conditions; the inherited ways of doing things are also there;
and yet, in spite of environment, and in spite of custom, each frontier did
indeed furnish a new field of opportunity, a gate of escape from the bondage of the past; and freshness, and confidence, and scorn of older society,
impatience of its restraints and its ideas, and indifference to its lessons,
have accompanied the frontier. What the Mediterranean Sea was to the
Greeks, breaking the bond of custom, offering new experiences, calling out
new institutions and activities, that and more, the ever retreating frontier
has been to the United States directly, and to the nations of Europe more
remotely. And now, four centuries from the discovery of America, at the
end of a hundred years of life under the Constitution, the frontier has
gone, and with its going has closed the first period of American history.

The Middle West*

The ideals of the Middle West began in the log huts set in the midst
of the forest a century ago. While his horizon was still bounded by the
clearing that his ax had made, the pioneer dreamed of continental conquests. The vastness of the wilderness kindled his imagination. His vision
saw beyond the dank swamp at the edge of the great lake to the lofty
buildings and the jostling multitudes of a mighty city; beyond the rank,
grass-clad prairie to the seas of golden grain; beyond the harsh life of
the log hut and the sod house to the home of his children, where should
dwell comfort and the higher things of life, though they might not be for
him. The men and women who made the Middle West were idealists, and
they had the power of will to make their dreams come true. Here, also,
were the pioneer's traits—individual activity, inventiveness, and competition
for the prizes of the rich province that awaited exploitation under freedom
and equality of opportunity. He honored the man whose eye was the quickest
and whose grasp was the strongest in this contest: it was "every one for
himself."

The early society of the Middle West was not a complex, highly differ-

---

* From Frederick Jackson Turner, "The Middle West," *International Monthly*, IV
(December 1901), 818–819.

entiated and organized society. Almost every family was a self-sufficing unit, and liberty and equality flourished in the frontier periods of the Middle West as perhaps never before in history. American democracy came from the forest, and its destiny drove it to material conquests; but the materialism of the pioneer was not the dull contented materialism of an old and fixed society. Both native settler and European immigrant saw in this free and competitive movement of the frontier the chance to break the bondage of social rank, and to rise to a higher plane of existence. The pioneer was passionately desirous to secure for himself and for his family a favorable place in the midst of these large and free but vanishing opportunities. It took a century for this society to fit itself into the conditions of the whole province. Little by little, nature pressed into her mold the plastic pioneer life. The Middle West, yesterday a pioneer province, is to-day the field of industrial resources and systematization so vast that Europe, alarmed for her industries in competition with this new power, is discussing the policy of forming protective alliances among the nations of the continent. Into this region flowed the great forces of modern capitalism. Indeed, the region itself furnished favorable conditions for the creation of these forces, and trained many of the famous American industrial leaders. The Prairies, the Great Plains, and the Great Lakes furnished new standards of industrial measurement. From this society, seated amidst a wealth of material advantages, and breeding individualism, energetic competition, inventiveness, and spaciousness of design, came the triumph of the strongest.

The Problem of the West*

The problem of the West is nothing less than the problem of American development. A glance at the map of the United States reveals the truth. To write of a "Western sectionalism," bounded on the east by the Alleghenies, is, in itself, to proclaim the writer a provincial. What is the West? What has it been in American life? To have the answers to these questions, is to understand the most significant features of the United States of to-day.

The West, at bottom, is a form of society, rather than an area. It is the term applied to the region whose social conditions result from the application of older institutions and ideas to the transforming influences

---

* From Frederick Jackson Turner, "The Problem of the West," *Atlantic Monthly*, LXXVIII (September 1896), 289, 292–293.

of free land. By this application, a new environment is suddenly entered,
freedom of opportunity is opened, the cake of custom is broken, and new
activities, new lines of growth, new institutions and new ideals are brought
into existence. The wilderness disappears, the "West" proper passes on to
a new frontier, and in the former area, a new society has emerged from
its contact with the backwoods. Gradually this society loses its primitive
conditions, and assimilates itself to the type of the older social conditions
of the East; but it bears within it enduring and distinguishing survivals of
its frontier experience. Decade after decade, West after West, this rebirth
of American society has gone on, has left its traces behind it, and has
reacted on the East. The history of our political institutions, our democracy,
is not a history of imitation, of simple borrowing; it is a history of the
evolution and adaptation of organs in response to changed environment, a
history of the origin of new political species. In this sense, therefore, the
West has been a constructive force of the highest significance in our life. . . .

Western democracy included individual liberty, as well as equality. The
frontiersman was impatient of restraints. He knew how to preserve order,
even in the absence of legal authority. If there were cattle thieves, lynch
law was sudden and effective: the regulators of the Carolinas were the
predecessors of the claims associations of Iowa and the vigilance committees
of California. But the individual was not ready to submit to complex regulations. Population was sparse, there was no multitude of jostling interests,
as in older settlements, demanding an elaborate system of personal restraints. Society became atomic. There was a reproduction of the primitive
idea of the personality of the law, a crime was more an offense against the
victim than a violation of the law of the land. Substantial justice, secured
in the most direct way, was the ideal of the backwoodsman. He had little
patience with finely drawn distinctions or scruples of method. If the thing
was one proper to be done, then the most immediate, rough and ready,
effective way was the best way.

It followed from the lack of organized political life, from the atomic
conditions of the backwoods society, that the individual was exalted and
given free play. The West was another name for opportunity. Here were
mines to be seized, fertile valleys to be preëmpted, all the natural resources
open to the shrewdest and the boldest. The United States is unique in the
extent to which the individual has been given an open field, unchecked by
restraints of an old social order, or of scientific administration of government. The self-made man was the Western man's ideal, was the kind of
man that all men might become. Out of his wilderness experience, out of
the freedom of his opportunities, he fashioned a formula for social regeneration,—the freedom of the individual to seek his own. He did not
consider that his conditions were exceptional and temporary.

Contributions of the West
to American Democracy*

The last chapter in the development of Western democracy is the one that deals with its conquest over the vast spaces of the new West. . . . Men who had become accustomed to the narrow valleys and the little towns of the East found themselves out on the boundless spaces of the West dealing with units of such magnitude as dwarfed their former experience. The Great Lakes, the Prairies, the Great Plains, the Rocky Mountains, the Mississippi and the Missouri, furnished new standards of measurement for the achievement of this industrial democracy. Individualism began to give way to coöperation and to governmental activity. Even in the earlier days of the democratic conquest of the wilderness, demands had been made upon the government for support in internal improvements, but this new West showed a growing tendency to call to its assistance the powerful arm of national authority. In the period since the Civil War, the vast public domain has been donated to the individual farmer, to States for education, to railroads for the construction of transportation lines.

Moreover, with the advent of democracy in the last fifteen years upon the Great Plains, new physical conditions have presented themselves which have accelerated the social tendency of Western democracy. The pioneer farmer of the days of Lincoln could place his family on a flatboat, strike into the wilderness, cut out his clearing, and with little or no capital go on to the achievement of industrial independence. Even the homesteader on the Western prairies found it possible to work out a similar independent destiny, although the factor of transportation made a serious and increasing impediment to the free working-out of his individual career. But when the arid lands and the mineral resources of the Far West were reached, no conquest was possible by the old individual pioneer methods. Here expensive irrigation works must be constructed, coöperative activity was demanded in utilization of the water supply, capital beyond the reach of the small farmer was required. In a word, the physiographic province itself decreed that the destiny of this new frontier should be social rather than individual.

---

* From Frederick Jackson Turner, "Contributions of the West to American Democracy," *Atlantic Monthly*, XCI (January 1903), 89–90.

T. K. Whipple

T. K. Whipple (1890–1939), born in the border state of Missouri, took his doctorate at Princeton and then migrated to Berkeley and the University of California, where he taught in the department of English until his death. The move to the Far West combined with his midwestern origins to release him from enmeshment in certain rarefied topics of the seventeenth century that characterized his graduate career, and he turned to the twentieth century and American writers. In the essay reprinted here (written in 1929, nearly a generation before Henry Nash Smith published his perceptive study elaborating the same theme), Whipple calls attention to the role of myth and symbol in the American West. He accepts the romantic tradition of the American West and explains the lack of a Western epic as a failure of American writers rather than as a result of an environment inadequate to call forth genuine art.

The Myth of the Old West*

In all the talks about the West—or the frontier, for the terms are synonymous—and about how it has "formed our character as a nation" for better or for worse, one aspect of the subject has been neglected: its value as a national myth or symbol. To be sure, the sweep across the continent from Jamestown to Oregon has often been called—and quite rightly—the American epic, and our own heroic age. The story of the West is our Trojan War, our Volsunga Saga, our Arthurian Cycle or Song of Roland. But these parallels are less likely to illuminate than to mislead and confuse; and in any case, what of it?

Its value, I should say, is, or rather might be, symbolic and mythical. I do not mean in the least to imply falsity. A story, true or not, which exerts a strange power over us, which becomes a nucleus about which cluster many feelings and imaginings—such a story I should call a myth. It is also a symbol, replete with significance. Indeed, as soon as its import can be analyzed and made explicit and rational, it is likely to lose its power.

---

* From T. K. Whipple, "The Myth of the Old West," in *Study Out the Land* (Berkeley: University of California Press, 1943), pp. 59–68. Reprinted by permission.

Why nations and individuals profit from having their myths and symbols, it would be difficult to tell. Of course, the symbol gives form and body and vividness to much that would otherwise be formless and dim; it raises into consciousness what has been unconscious. Above all, it brings into actual manifest existence feelings, images, impulses, which before had existed only in potentiality, as music may be evoked from an instrument capable of music but hitherto silent. But why it is good for us to have these latent possibilities elicited is a perplexing question. I can only appeal to experience, and ask whether the kind of lift, of thrill, of quickening and invigoration, which comes when we are strongly affected by the power of a symbol, is not recognized as valuable.

Whether the West has any such power over Americans may well be doubted. One objection, sure to be raised, is that the old West was not actually heroic; to think of it so is to falsify and romanticize. There is undeniable truth in this objection; yet, for all that, it is based on a misconception. No age is in truth heroic, if "heroic" is taken to mean half-divine, superhumanly noble and magnanimous; King Arthur and Achilles were in reality barbarous chieftains, wild men, no doubt, sordid and grubby enough. But I am not sure that this is the meaning we of the present day ought to attach to "heroic."

Rather, I think, we should take it to mean strong in the primitive virtues —the animal virtues, if you like—physical vigor, physical courage, fortitude, sagacity, quickness, and the other qualities which enable a man to thrive in an uncivilized environment, to take care of himself amid primeval dangers and hardships. They are the individual, not the social virtues. To us who live in a highly differentiated society, these traits are bound to seem heroic, because they survive in us as unused but strong potentialities, undeveloped because inappropriate.

Although the fact that so much of the savage is latent in us may make civilization precarious, we ought nevertheless to be thankful, for certainly we cannot afford to lose the primitive virtues. The frontier myth retains them in consciousness and provides them with exercise and activity, and not only keeps them out of mischief but makes their value available. We get back from the myth or symbol the "virtue" or potency which we put into it. This I take to be the function which the myth of a heroic age has always performed: it has embodied and preserved for a complex culture the values of a simpler world.

To date, the western story has not done all it might for us, because it has never received adequate representation. And no symbol can exert much force unless it is somehow objectified and worthily embodied. The story of the West should be the Great American Epic—does not everyone agree? Yet does anyone doubt that the epic is still unsung? A strange situation, surely, when the United States is full of able writers, and when these writers are unanimous in their neglect of what is unanimously called the grandest of themes. Something is wrong, and since there is nothing the matter with the story of the West, it is easy to see that the trouble must be with the writers.

Nor is it very difficult to see what that trouble is: by and large, the better American writers are too highbrow. They find Henry James more interesting than Jesse. Following in the train of European leaders, they have spent their time hunting the exact word, like Flaubert, or they have been swamped by "a vast and desolating melancholy from Russia or a perverse and astringent misery from Scandinavia." Like Howells, they have fallen in love with the "foolish and insipid face" of "real life." They have abandoned themselves to trying to be subtle, minute, and accurate.

In a word these Howells and James young men find the West too strong meat for their stomachs. The western past is violence and melodrama; it is peril and excitement, blood and tears. To be sure, practically all the world's greatest literature is melodrama—danger, fighting, adultery, suicide, vengeance, infatuation, and murder. But such things have long been out of style, on the supposition—disproved by any daily paper—that they are not part of real life. The truth, I suspect, is that to write of the commonplace is easier, and that authors have avoided more powerful stuff because they had not the power to deal with it. However that may be, the West was set aside, along with the rest of human life that was not tame.

Furthermore, the West, after Bret Harte and Mark Twain, came into literature through the back door, under auspices that were undeniably lowbrow. The exploits of the James brothers and of Buffalo Bill were retailed, by Colonel Prentiss Ingraham and others, at ten cents a copy. The very success, commercially, of western stories has worked, by an odd twist, against their literary success. When Zane Grey and his compeers followed the dime novel and got rich, literary aspirants with serious purposes could not afford to soil their names by writing "best sellers." What would become of their reputations, if they wrote books anybody could enjoy? It must be said also that the public is partly to blame. It knew what it liked, and it knew that for the most part what it liked was not literature—especially the male half of the public, which above all liked tales of gunmen, scouts, and cowboys. The superstition, quite unwarranted—quite contrary to fact, indeed—grew up that western stuff was not the stuff of which literature is made.

Thus the "western" has suffered from a blight. A similar situation has existed in the movies. In spite of "The Covered Wagon" and a few other films, the "western" has been something that could not be taken seriously. Yet for the spectator it has been the most dependable kind of picture; during the dull seasons when Hollywood, in its magnificent isolation, has chosen to amuse itself by producing still-life studies of sex, one could always go see Tom Mix and Jack Holt galloping over the sagebrush. Thanks to "westerns," there have always been some movies in which something moved. And so it has been also with books. Zane Grey has always offered a refuge from the current studies in frustration and futility, in grease, drabness, and microscopic emotions. Yet even the most ardent partisan of Zane Grey can hardly maintain that he has sung the great American epic.

The West, then, has suffered from providing a story too good for modern literature; and it has also suffered from less obvious causes. One of these is the curse of analogy. Jesse James, for instance, is called the American Robin Hood; and no sooner is he so called than the writer of Jesse's tale goes looking for Maid Marian, and does well if he can leave out Friar Tuck and give up brown October ale for red-eye. Similarly, John G. Neihardt, who has written three long poems of the West, is reminded by his subject of the *Iliad;* and straightway rosy-fingered Aurora drives her chariot over the Bad Lands, with steeds in place of cayuses, and Tithonus sleeps in the Big Horn Mountains. Too few writers have been willing to tell the story of the West in its own terms. Even Zane Grey has looked through the eyes of a Sunday School superintendent; his moral fervor has prevented him from accepting his desperadoes and cowpunchers in their own spirit; they must be improved and improving.

To be sure, there have been numerous books purporting to deal with the historic West in its own temper. Thus Duncan Aikman has not felt that the story of Calamity Jane and her fellow wildcats could be either improved or improving. But the curse on these books is the curse of fact. They all strive, or pretend to strive, for accuracy. But who wants facts? They merely cramp the writer's style; he ought to busy himself with the glorified heroes of legend.

The blight which infects so many treatments of the West seems to extend even to a writer of such ability as W. R. Burnett, when he turns to western themes, as in *Saint Johnson.* That the author of *Little Caesar* and *Iron Man* could take the hardbitten, bloody feud of the Earps and the Clantons in the early days of Tombstone and make dry sawdust of it is incredible—but it has happened. No story—not that of Deadwood in its prime, nor of Abilene or Dodge City or Cheyenne, nor the life of Billy the Kid or Wild Bill Hickok—epitomizes so well the cold-blooded, wolfish ferocity bred by the frontier as the great feud of Tombstone; and the fact that it came so late—in the 1880's—serves to show that American lawlessness grew only the more deadly with the passage of time.

It is high time for the people of the United States to rebel against their recorders, and demand that some meaning be extracted from material so rich in significance as that concerning men or the children of men who left civilization and traveled the wilderness road. What really happened to these men? All America lies at the end of the wilderness road, and our past is not a dead past but still lives in us; thus the question is momentous. But it has not been answered. Our forebears had civilization inside themselves, the wild outside. We live in the civilization they created, but within us the wilderness still lingers. What they dreamed, we live; and what they lived, we dream. That is why our western story still holds us, however ineptly it is told.

It is an encouraging sign that one or two writers have attempted to answer that question, and to write of the West in its own terms. Harvey Fergusson's *Wolf Song* is almost what a "western" ought to be. His earlier novel of New Mexican life, *The Blood of the Conquerors,* portraying the defeat of the old Spanish order at the hands of the gringos, is an excellent novel but not a true "western." *Wolf Song,* however, has the proper ring; it is a good stiff story with plenty of excitement, and something of a legendary remoteness. Its mountain men are as salty as they ought to be, and the whole book is high in flavor—the flavor of the true "western." And it is admirably written, with a manifest delight which is itself delightful. A lyric yeast works strongly in both characters and author. Had it only, in addition, a certain magnitude it might be the great "western." ...

And there is James Boyd's *Long Hunt.* Mr. Boyd indulges only in truth, bitter truth; yet in and through this actuality he has managed perfectly to project a symbolic image. This extraordinary novel, this harsh and tragic story, full of poetic and unsentimental beauty, is replete with a significance which eludes formulation. Its hero, in his zeal for freedom entrapped by his very effort to escape from fettering ties, is a type of all frontiersmen, yet a sharp-cut individual; the best Western character since Cooper's Leatherstocking, he is conceived with an insight and a subtlety which were not in Natty Bumppo's creator. So far as *Long Hunt* goes, it is a worthy embodiment of the heroic frontier myth; but its scope is narrow, limited to a single theme in a single character.

Many living writers are abundantly supplied with many virtues—honesty, sympathy and insight, literary skill. But most of them would be all the better off if they had more of the dynamic vigor and spirit, the dry, quizzical humor, the pungent earthiness, and the sentiment, too, which are all in the western tradition. These are the qualities needed for an achievement which American literature sadly needs. That achievement is nothing less than the adequate rendering, in its own terms and spirit, of the heroic age which popular phantasy has already created. The man who can do that, who can bring first-class individual imagination and emotion into key with national, will heal the lasting breach in our literature between lowbrow and highbrow, between writer and public, and give American literature such a basis for greatness as it has never had.

For this split between the nation and its literature is needless and harmful. It results from that sinister precision with which American artists avoid anything likely to touch the people. As I have said, they would be none the worse off if their work had more of the gusto and vitality of the "western"; and if to the representation of the frontier myth they could bring their skill, their insight and sense of fact, their honesty and discernment, the combination might produce great work. We know what Melville contrived to do in *Moby-Dick* with whaling, and what Stephen Vincent Benét has done in *John Brown's Body* with the Civil War. The story of the West offers better opportunities than either of those, as it is more nearly a true national myth. What is needed is the interpretation of it by the mature feeling, thought, and imagination of gifted individuals. Certainly the artist would gain from this union of his individual spirit with the national spirit; and the nation would gain, because at last it would have a fitly embodied image and symbol from which it could derive those values that belong to the myth of the heroic age.

Henry Nash Smith

The selection below is taken from Virgin Land, *a brilliant interpretation of the American West by Henry Nash Smith, a scholar of American literature. These excerpts are from the chapter on Daniel Boone, wherein Smith traces the development of contradictory, though equally romantic, images of Boone: a child of nature unable to tolerate the fetters of society, or a self-conscious standard bearer of civilization. The theme is carried further in a subsequent chapter dealing with the mountain man. The fact that so many recent writers in American cultural history either explicitly or implicitly acknowledge indebtedness to Smith's book suggests that* Virgin Land *is the most original and influential work on the American West since the writings of Frederick Jackson Turner.*

Virgin Land*

During the summer of 1842, following his sophomore year at Harvard, Francis Parkman made a trip through northern New York and New England. After spending several days admiring the scenery along the shores of Lake George, he noted in his journal: "There would be no finer place of gentlemen's seats than this, but now, for the most part, it is occupied by a race of boors about as uncouth, mean, and stupid as the hogs they seem chiefly to delight in." The tone is even blunter than that of Timothy Dwight's famous description of backwoodsmen in this area a generation earlier, but it embodies a comparable aristocratic disdain. Observers from Eastern cities made similar comments about uncultivated farmers along every American frontier. The class bias underlying the judgment was one of the dominant forces shaping nineteenth-century attitudes toward the West.

When Parkman got away from farms and hogs, out into the forest, his tone changed completely. He wrote, for example, that a woodsman named James Abbot, although coarse and self-willed, was "a remarkably intelligent fellow; has astonishing information for one of his condition; is resolute and independent as the wind." The young Brahmin's delight in men of the wilderness comes out even more forcibly in the journal of his Far Western trip four years later. *The Oregon Trail* presents the guide Henry Chatillon, a French-Canadian squaw man, as a hero of romance—handsome, brave, true, skilled in the ways of the plains and mountains, and even possessed of "a natural refinement and delicacy of mind, such as is rare even in women."

Parkman's antithetical attitudes toward backwoods farmers and the hunters and trappers of the wilderness illustrate the fact that for Americans of that period there were two quite distinct Wests: the commonplace domesticated area within the agricultural frontier, and the Wild West beyond it. The agricultural West was tedious; its inhabitants belonged to a despised social class. The Wild West was by contrast an exhilarating region of adventure and comradeship in the open air. Its heroes bore none of the marks of degraded status. They were in reality not members of society at all, but noble anarchs owning no master, free denizens of a limitless wilderness.

Parkman's love of the Wild West implied a paradoxical rejection of

---

* From Henry Nash Smith, *Virgin Land: The American West as Symbol and Myth* (Cambridge, Mass.: Harvard University Press, 1950), pp. 51–57. Copyright, 1950, by The President and Fellows of Harvard College.

organized society. He himself was the product of a complex social order formed by two centuries of history, and his way of life was made possible by the fortune which his grandfather had built up as one of the great merchants of Boston. But a young gentleman of leisure could afford better than anyone else to indulge himself in the slightly decadent cult of wildness and savagery which the early nineteenth century took over from Byron. Historians call the mood "primitivism." Parkman had a severe case. In later life he said that from his early youth "His thoughts were always in the forest, whose features possessed his waking and sleeping dreams, filling him with vague cravings impossible to satisfy." And in a preface to *The Oregon Trail* written more than twenty years after the first publication of the book, he bewailed the advance of humdrum civilization over the wide empty plains of Colorado since the stirring days of 1846.

Such a mood of refined hostility to progress affected a surprising number of Parkman's contemporaries. Nevertheless, it could hardly strike very deep in a society committed to an expansive manifest destiny. A romantic love of the vanishing Wild West could be no more than a self-indulgent affectation beside the triumphant official cult of progress, which meant the conquest of the wilderness by farms and towns and cities. If there was a delicious melancholy for sophisticated and literary people in regretting the destruction of the primitive freedom of an untouched continent, the westward movement seemed to less imaginative observers a glorious victory of civilization over savagery and barbarism. For such people—and they were the vast majority—the Western hunter and guide was praiseworthy not because of his intrinsic wildness or half-savage glamor, but because he blazed trails that hard-working farmers could follow.

One of the most striking evidences of the currency of these two conflicting attitudes toward the westward movement is the popular image of Daniel Boone. The official view was set forth in a greatly admired piece of allegorical sculpture by Horatio Greenough in the National Capitol, which depicted the contest between civilization and barbarism as a fierce hand-to-hand struggle between Boone and an Indian warrior. George C. Bingham's painting "The Emigration of Daniel Boone" (1851) showed the celebrated Kentuckian leading a party of settlers with their wives and children and livestock out into a dreamily beautiful wilderness which they obviously meant to bring under the plow. . . .

By the side of Boone the empire builder and philanthropist, the anonymous popular mind had meanwhile created an entirely different hero, a fugitive from civilization who could not endure the encroachment of settlements upon his beloved wilderness. A dispatch from Fort Osage in the Indian territory, reprinted in *Niles' Register* in 1816, described an interview with Boone and added: "This singular man could not live in Kentucky when it became settled. . . . he might have accumulated riches as readily as any man in Kentucky, but he *prefers the woods,* where you see him in the dress of the roughest, poorest hunter."

Boone's flight westward before the advance of the agricultural frontier —actually dictated by a series of failures in his efforts to get and hold land—became a theme of newspaper jokes. The impulse that produced Western tall tales transformed him into the type of all frontiersmen who required unlimited elbow room. "As civilization advanced," wrote a reporter in the New York *American* in 1823, "so he, from time to time, retreated"—from Kentucky to Tennessee, from Tennessee to Missouri. But Missouri itself was filling up: Boone was said to have complained, "I had not been two years at the licks before a d——d Yankee came, and settled down *within an hundred miles of me!!*" He would soon be driven on out to the Rocky Mountains and would be crowded there in eight or ten years.

Seizing upon hints of Boone's flight before the advance of civilization, Byron paused in his description of the siege of Ismail in the eighth canto of *Don Juan* to insert an extended tribute to him. Although Byron's Boone shrank from men of his own nation when they built up unto his darling trees, he was happy, innocent, and benevolent; simple, not savage; and even in old age still a child of nature, whose virtues shamed the corruptions of civilization. Americans quoted these stanzas eagerly.

Which was the real Boone—the standard-bearer of civilization and refinement, or the child of nature who fled into the wilderness before the advance of settlement? An anonymous kinsman of Boone wrestled with the problem in a biographical sketch published a few years after the famous hunter's death in 1820. It would be natural to suppose, he wrote, that the Colonel took great pleasure in the magnificent growth of the commonwealth he had founded in the wilderness. But such was not the case. Passionately fond of hunting, "like the unrefined Savage," Boone saw only that incoming settlers frightened away all the game and spoiled the sport. He would "certainly prefer a state of nature to a state of Civilization, if he were obliged to be confined to one or the other."

Timothy Flint's biography, perhaps the most widely read book about a Western character published during the first half of the nineteenth century, embodies the prevalent confusion of attitudes. Flint says that Boone delighted in the thought that "the rich and boundless valleys of the great west—the garden of the earth—and the paradise of hunters, had been won from the dominion of the savage tribes, and opened as an asylum for the oppressed, the enterprising, and the free of every land." ... Yet we learn only a few pages later that he was driven out of Kentucky by "the restless spirit of immigration, and of civil and physical improvement." Even in Missouri, "the tide of emigration once more swept by the dwelling of Daniel Boone, driving off the game and monopolizing the rich hunting grounds." ... On yet other occasions Flint credits Boone with a sophisticated cult of pastoral simplicity greatly resembling his own, which he had imitated from Chateaubriand. When the frontiersman seeks to induce settlers to go with him into the new land, he is represented as promising them that the original pioneers, in their old age, will be surrounded by

consideration, and care, and tenderness from children, whose breasts were not steeled by ambition, nor hardened by avarice; in whom the beautiful influences of the indulgence of none but natural desires and pure affections would not be deadened by the selfishness, vanity, and fear of ridicule, that are the harvest of what is called *civilized and cultivated life*.

The debate over Boone's character and motives lasted into the next decade. The noted Western Baptist minister and gazetteer, John M. Peck, prepared a life of Boone for Jared Sparks's Library of American Biography in 1847 which repeatedly attacked the current conception of the hero as a fugitive from civilization. Peck says that Boone left North Carolina for the Kentucky wilderness because of the effeminacy and profligacy of wealthy slaveowners who scorned the industrious husbandman working his own fields. But by the time the biographer interviewed the aged hero in Missouri in 1818, Boone had become aware of an imposing historical mission. Although he had not consciously aimed to lay the foundations of a state or nation, he believed that he had been "a creature of Providence, ordained by Heaven as a pioneer in the wilderness, to advance the civilization and the extension of his country."

James H. Perkins of Cincinnati, writing in 1846 in the *North American Review,* was equally interested in the problem of Boone's motives, but inclined to a more modest interpretation. Boone, he said, was a white Indian. Although he and his companions were not at all like the boasting, swearing, drinking, gouging Mike Finks of the later West, they were led into the wilderness not by the hope of gain, nor by a desire to escape the evils of older communities, nor yet by dreams of founding a new commonwealth, but simply by "a love of nature, of perfect freedom, and of the adventurous life in the woods." Boone "would have pined and died as a nabob in the midst of civilization. He wanted a frontier, and the perils and pleasures of a frontier life, not wealth; and he was happier in his log-cabin, with a loin of venison and his ramrod for a spit, than he would have been amid the greatest profusion of modern luxuries."

If one detects a patronizing note in this account, it goes along with a greater respect for the simple, hearty virtues that are left to the frontiersman. Such a view seems to have become general in the 1840's. William H. Emory of the Army of the West which invaded New Mexico in 1846 invoked the figure of the Kentuckian to convey his impression of an American settler in the Mora Valley northeast of Santa Fé: "He is a perfect specimen of a generous open-hearted adventurer, and in appearance what, I have pictured to myself, Daniel Boone, of Kentucky, must have been in his day."

Bernard De Voto

Although Bernard De Voto (1897–1955) deserted Utah for Harvard Yard and Harper's "Easy Chair," his work as Mark Twain specialist, historian of the frontier in the tradition of Francis Parkman, and conservationist testifies to his lifelong commitment to the West. In an introduction to Wallace Stegner's biography of the government surveyor and geologist John Wesley Powell, De Voto defends the West and condemns American professional historians in characteristically stimulating and vigorous fashion. The bulk of that introduction is included here and serves as a provocative interpretation of the West "beyond the 100th meridian." In many respects De Voto's views are similar to those advanced by Walter Prescott Webb in The Great Plains *(1931). As for Turner's "frontier" thesis, De Voto insists that it fails, for the most part, to fit the arid West.*

*John Wesley Powell and the West**

. . . the reason historians [except for Walter Prescott Webb] have ignored Powell is that the *preconceptions* with which they have approached the area Powell figures in correspond exactly to the *misconceptions* with which the American people and their government approached the West.

Powell's importance is that seventy-five years ago he pierced through those misconceptions to the realities. His career was an indomitable effort

---

* From Bernard De Voto, Introduction to *Beyond the Hundredth Meridian: John Wesley Powell and the Second Opening of the West* by Wallace Stegner (Boston: Houghton Mifflin Company, 1954), pp. xvi–xxiii. Reprinted by permission.

to substitute knowledge for the misconceptions and to get it acted on. He tried to repair the damage they had done to the people and the land and to prevent them from doing further damage. He tried to shape legal and political and social institutions so that they would accord with the necessities of the West. He tried to conserve the West's natural wealth so that it could play to the full its potential part in the future of the United States. He tried to dissipate illusions about the West, to sweep mirage away. He was a great man and a prophet. Long ago he accomplished great things and now we are beginning to understand him . . . even out west.

That is the burden of Mr. Stegner's memorable book. My part here is to explain why writers of history have for so long failed to understand the massive figure of John Wesley Powell and therefore have failed, rather disastrously, to understand the fundamental meaning of the West in American history.

One of the reasons for that failure is beyond explanation: the tacit classification, the automatic dismissal, of Western history as merely sectional, not national, history. No such limitation has been placed on the experience of the American people in New England, the South, or the Middle West. These sections are taken to be organic in the United States and cannot safely be separated from their functional and reciprocal relationships. When you write Southern history in the round you must deal with such matters as, for instance, the cotton economy, the plantation system, slavery, States' rights, the tariff, secession, the Civil War, and Reconstruction. They are so clearly national as well as Southern in implication that it would be impossible to write about them without treating them in relation to the experience of the nation as a whole.

The experience of the West is just as inseparable from the central energies of American history. Any major Western topic, or any commonplace Western phenomenon, involves those energies the moment it is glanced at. Thus a favorite garment in the West (as in rural places throughout the United States) is a shirt whose trade name is Big Yank. It is a cotton shirt—made of a fiber once grown only in the South but now grown competitively in the West. It is a manufactured article—a product of industry located outside the West. So it cannot safely be dissected out from the national system. And the more you look at it, the more clearly you see that this involvement is complex. You encounter the mercantile-colonial status of the Western economy, the drainage of Western wealth eastward, the compensatory process of federal benefactions, preferential freight rates, and myriad concrete facts related to them—all national in implication. Make the shirt a woolen one and you bring in the tariff, absentee ownership of the West, Eastern control of Western finance, and the stockgrowing portion of Western agriculture. And if you will look at the woolen shirt just a little longer it will lead you straight to the basic conditions of the West.

The West was the latest and most adventurously romantic of our frontiers, and its history has been written, mostly, as frontier history. When the word "frontier" is used in history it has, to begin with, been raised to a tolerably high degree of abstraction. And its inherent abstractness has been almost immeasurably increased by a hypothesis which has dominated much writing about the West and has colored almost all of it, Frederick Jackson Turner's theory about the function of "the frontier" in American life. That theory has, I suppose, begotten more pages of American history than any other generalization. Till recently no one dreamed of writing about the West without its help. Indeed its postulate of a specific kind of "frontier" independence, which it derives from the public domain and which it calls the principal energy of American democracy, has heavily buttressed our illusions about the West. So our problem here exists in a medium of pure irony. For, to whatever degree the Turner hypothesis may be applicable to American experience east of the 100th meridian, it fails almost altogether when applied to the West. The study of a single water war, in fact of a single irrigation district, should reveal its irrelevance. Indeed as one who has written extensively of our sacred Western symbol, the covered wagon, I have frequently found myself wondering if the study of a single wagon train ought not to suffice.

But two other facts affect our problem more. In general, historians have been content to postulate that American institutions, orientations, and habits of thought which developed east of the 100th meridian maintained their form and retained their content after reaching the West, whereas in fact a good many important ones did not. In the second place, historians have generally been ignorant of or incurious about natural conditions that determine life in the West, differentiate it from other sections, and have given it different orientations.

Well, there isn't much rain out west. There is not enough rain to grow crops and so additional water has to be brought to them for irrigation. The additional water falls as snow on the mountains, it melts, and it flows down the brooks to the creeks and down them to the rivers. If you build dams, you can hold the runoff for use when and where it is needed. Then if you construct systems of canals—increasingly complex systems as you take the melted snow farther—you can bring the water to town mains and to the fields that won't grow crops without it. The historical process which we call the westward movement shattered against these facts. Neither hope nor illusion nor desire nor Act of Congress could change them in the least. But they were even harder for the American people to accept than they have been for historians to understand.

There is no need to describe how the "quarter-section" acquired mystical significance in American thinking—the idea that 160 acres were the ideal family-sized farm, the basis of a yeoman democracy, the buttress of our liberties, and the cornerstone of our economy. It was certainly true, however, that if you owned 160 acres of flat Iowa farmland or rolling Wisconsin prairie, you had, on the average, a farm which would support your family and would require all its exertions to work. So the quarter-section, thought of as the proper homestead unit, became the mystical one. But in the arid regions 160 acres were not a homestead. They were just a mathematical expression whose meanings in relation to agricultural settlement were disastrous.

To begin with, what kind of land? A hundred and sixty acres of redwood or Douglas fir or Western white pine never could be a homestead—but they were a small fortune. Hence the personal and corporate timber frauds which stand high in the record of our national corruption. A hundred and sixty acres of arid range land could not provide forage for enough stock to support a family. Hence two kinds of land fraud, on a large scale by wealthy or corporate stockgrowers to acquire big ranges, on a small scale by poor individuals trying to acquire the self-supporting homesteads that they could not get legally. What about 160 acres of valley farmland with the rich mineral soil of the West and capable of being irrigated? Two considerations: to irrigate so large a tract would usually cost more than an individual owner could afford, and the farming made possible by irrigation would mostly be so intensive that so big a farm could not be worked by a single family.

So the land in the arid country had better be classified, and the unit of ownership, the size of the homestead, had better be adjusted to the realities. Our system had always resisted land-classification for the public domain—the official ruling that standing timber was not farmland—in the interest of speculation and graft. But in the arid country not to classify land would on the one hand facilitate monopolization of land, and on the other hand would perpetuate and institutionalize the bankruptcy of Western homesteaders. And unless the unit of ownership was changed there would be no way of squaring either public or private interests with the immutable facts. But both changes would mean fundamental alteration of our legal and land system, and would produce further changes in many institutions related to them. The sum of change required was so great that the American mind did not take it in—and went on believing that there must be some way of licking climate or that climate would adapt itself to men's desires. Against this inherited set of mind, the tumultuous and tragic experience of the West could not prevail.

Again, not only what kind of land but whereabouts? A small holding that included a water source could prevent access to the basis of life and so would give its owner the usufructs of a much larger area which he could keep others from owning. Adjoining holdings along a stream could similarly dominate a much larger area. So at small expense (and by fraud) a corporation could keep individual stockgrowers from a really vast area it did not own but could thus make use of. Or a corporation could not only charge its own price for water, that is for life, but could control the terms of settlement with all that settlement implies. Here was another powerful force making for monopoly and speculation. Clearly, that is clearly to us now, the West could exist as a democratic society only if the law relating to the ownership and use of water were changed. The changes required were repugnant to our legal system and our set of mind, and again the experience of the West produced turbulence but not understanding.

Moreover, to bring water to land at any distance from the source was an undertaking expensive beyond the ability of an individual landowner to afford. As the distance increased it would become expensive beyond the ability first of co-operative groups, then of profit-making corporations, and finally of the individual states to afford. At the heyday of "individual enterprise" elsewhere in the United States, therefore, the natural conditions of the West demanded federal action in the procurement of water. And this was repugnant not only to our set of mind but, especially, to our mystical vision of the West, the very citadel, so we insisted on believing, of "rough individualism."

Furthermore, if in large parts of the West the individual landowner required a homestead of at least four square miles, then the traditional pattern of settlement would result in his living in fearful isolation from his kind. Loneliness, hardship, and social deterioration would inevitably follow. (Which is the history of the high plains down to the automobile and the coming of good roads.) What the Western realities demanded was not the ranch pattern of the Dakotas but the village pattern of the Spanish-American Southwest and of Mormon Utah. And in the arid region the traditional political organization within the states, by counties, would be cumbersome, illogical, and intolerably expensive. Far better to avoid such irrational units and to organize politically in accord with the Western realities, by river valley or watershed.

This does not state all the immutable conditions of the West against which institutions and eventually ideas shattered but it will do here. The history of the West derives from them—a history of experience failing to overcome in time our thinking, our illusions, our sentiments, and our expectations. The results were hardship, suffering, bankruptcy, tragedy, human waste—the overthrow of hope and belief to a degree almost incredible now, and only now beginning to be understood in the historical context.

ADDITIONAL READINGS

Most of Frederick Jackson Turner's essays are collected in *The Frontier in American History* (New York, 1920) and *The Significance of Sections in American History* (New York, 1932). In two other books Turner put his methods to work: *The Rise of the New West, 1819–1829* (New York, 1906), a book in the first "American Nation Series"; and *The United States, 1830–1850* (New York, 1935).

The so-called Turner thesis has attracted comment and criticism much as a magnet draws iron filings. Early attacks include Charles Beard, "Culture and Agriculture," *Saturday Review of Literature* (October 1928); Benjamin F. Wright, Jr., "American Democracy and the Frontier," *Yale Review* (December 1930); and Louis M. Hacker, "Sections—or Classes," *The Nation* (July 26, 1933). Later came Fred A. Shannon, "The Homestead Act and the Labor Surplus," *American Historical Review* (July 1936); George W. Pierson, "The Frontier and American Institutions," *New England Quarterly* (June 1942); and a host of other tilters against Turner. Turner also had his defenders—among them Frederic Logan Paxson, Joseph Schafer, and Stanley Elkins and Eric McKitrick. Ray Allen Billington's *The American Frontier* (Washington, D.C., 1958), pamphlet No. 8 in the American Historical Association's series of bibliographical essays for history teachers, is the most convenient bibliographical work on Turner, his critics, and his defenders.

Aside from Turner's work, perhaps the best-known interpretation of the West is Walter Prescott Webb's *The Great Plains* (Boston, 1931). Webb extended the frontier thesis to world history in *The Great Frontier* (Boston, 1952). Comparative studies of the frontier experience may be consulted in *The Frontier in Perspective,* edited by Walker D. Wyman and Clifton B. Kroeber (Madison, 1957). Two recent appraisals of the West are John Caughey's "Towards an Understanding of the West," *Utah Historical Quarterly* (January 1959); and Earl Pomeroy's "The Changing West," in *Reconstruction of American History,* edited by John Higham (New York, 1962).

2

THE EXPLORER
AND THE
GOVERNMENT

The explorers came first, in little bands, walking the untrodden ways. Like Hillary before Mt. Everest, they sometimes went simply because it was there. It was exciting: "the great attraction of mystery in going into unknown places," as Frémont said. Or A. B. Guthrie, Jr.: "It was as if everything was just made . . . laid out fresh and good and waiting for a man to come along and find it." This was the personal side of the exploring drive. There was a negative personal aspect, too, a desire to escape from civilization: "To one who has been long in city pent, 'Tis very sweet to look into the fair and open face of heaven." To quote Keats is to call up that whole romantic strain of nineteenth-century thought, that love of the exotic and mysterious, which was often deeply rooted in the explorer.

If the personal reasons for engaging in the exploring life were the sum total of the matter, we could call the explorer a spiritual individualist and close the question. But the explorer is not that easy to define, and he was likely to find himself on the trail for a wide variety of reasons. For example, some of the earliest information regarding the new land came from beaver hunters or French Jesuits or Spanish Franciscans; yet the trapper and the missionary are sometimes forgotten in the category of explorers.

What is usually meant by explorer is the man deliberately sent by a government to search out a particular area. When La Salle in 1682 stood at the mouth of the Mississippi and in a feeble voice claimed the whole of its immense watershed, the sovereign of Versailles stood figuratively beside him. (Or so we should feel, at any rate, in the magnificent prose of the Francis Parkman selection that follows.) And that sovereign, Louis XIV, subscribed to the theory known as mercantilism, in which the government had a duty to give direct encouragement to expansion. Thus in the early eighteenth century the French bureaucracy promised to Pierre de la Vérendrye a monopoly of the fur trade in the new regions if he found a Northwest passage; and Vérendrye, one of the more remarkable of the French explorers, not only searched almost to the foot of the Rockies but set up six forts running from Lake Superior northwestward. The same governmental impetus was behind Englishmen like Drake and Ralegh or Spaniards like Coronado and Cabrillo and Oñate—all reflecting the policies of expansion.

In nineteenth-century United States the matter of government support for exploration did not come from a mercantilist government; it came first from Thomas Jefferson, that great exponent of weak government and a philosopher of laissez faire. Jefferson—no more consistent than any of the practicing laissez-faire statesmen—held that the government could enter the field in strength if its purposes were to extend commerce or to free particular economies from unwanted competition (as in tariff policies) or to break down barriers. Thus, the United States was willing to support rather extensive naval expeditions into the far Pacific in order to extend commercial and whaling activities. Such naval expeditions were counterparts of the more familiar land explorations into the trans-Mississippi West.

Jefferson's deep-seated interest in Western discovery was motivated by his scientific as well as political and economic concerns. He had planned an exploring expedition long before the purchase of Louisiana; and thus what would be the Lewis and Clark expedition was originally conceived as an exploration across foreign soil. But when the journey materialized in 1804, Louisiana had legally become an appendage of the United States and, beyond Louisiana, the Oregon country remained an ostensible Yankee claim. England, however, held a considerably stronger pretension to Oregon; and the issue in that part of the continent was hardly an idle one, with the lucrative coastal fur trade of the Northwest involved.

By the Louisiana Purchase, ratified by Congress in October of 1803, the United States almost doubled its size. No one knew the exact boundaries of Louisiana, and Talleyrand was quite right when he told the Americans, "You have made a noble bargain for yourselves, and I suppose you will make the most of it." Many historians have proclaimed the Louisiana Purchase the most important event in American history, perhaps one of the most significant events in all modern history, for it turned the eyes of the nation irrevocably westward; made certain that the nation would not rest until the Pacific was reached; added immeasurable natural resources, paving the way for international power; and provided a ballast which would in time save the nation from internal disruption. In the selections that follow, Meriwether Lewis, William Clark, and Zebulon Pike illustrate America's intent to make the most of its "noble bargain."

With an explorer like John Charles Frémont, the motivations are again complex. Schooled in the French civil-engineering tradition, he was competent with the most recent instruments of surveying; he had wide scientific interests in botany, zoology, and geology; and, as we have seen, he was filled with a romantic love of the exotic and unknown. But he had also married into the family of Thomas Hart Benton, senator from Missouri and spokesman for the West. Benton, like Jefferson, was a strong proponent of laissez faire, but not when it came to the development of the West. In this area he was anxious for the government to explore and survey as a preliminary to expansion. His son-in-law, Frémont, was in full agreement and expressed these expansive sentiments through his work with the Army's Topographical Corps, which between 1838 and 1863 was particularly active in exploring and mapping the West.

It is hard for us to imagine so much of the land unknown and mysterious as was the American West a scant 150 years ago. On the maps of 1851, whole areas of the Great Basin between the Rockies and the Sierra Nevada were still marked "Unexplored." The explorer had a long task, and until almost the end of the frontier he was a persistent figure in the West. In his own right he was interesting. But he was also important as a comment on prevailing economic doctrines. Whether his sponsoring government in theory favored mercantilism or laissez faire—i.e., whatever its philosophy—in fact it found it desirable actively to support and extend that facet of political and economic development which we here call exploration.

Francis Parkman

No man wrote more eloquently of the West than Francis Parkman (1823–1893), Boston Brahmin, whose long shelf of exciting volumes related the epic conflict of France and England for North America. One of his books on French exploration, The Discovery of the Great West, *appeared in 1869 and was revised ten years later as* La Salle and the Discovery of the Great West. *Parkman as a romantic historian is very much a part of our nineteenth-century story, but La Salle is an anachronism. The selection is included here, however, because it is by Parkman; because it illustrates indirectly the support of a mercantilist government for exploration; and because it illuminates those individual qualities of self-reliance and independence that the explorer must exhibit while beyond the pale of his government. The selection begins in the late winter of 1680; the "Griffin" was a small ship built by La Salle to navigate the Great Lakes.*

La Salle and French Exploration*

It was the worst of all seasons for such a journey. The nights were cold, but the sun was warm at noon, and the half-thawed prairie was one vast tract of mud, water, and discolored, half-liquid snow. On the twenty-second, they crossed marshes and inundated meadows, wading to the knee, till at noon they were stopped by a river, perhaps the Calumet. They made a raft of hard-wood timber, for there was no other, and shoved themselves across. On the next day, they could see Lake Michigan dimly glimmering beyond the waste of woods; and, after crossing three swollen streams, they reached it at evening. On the twenty-fourth, they followed its shore, till, at nightfall, they arrived at the fort, which they had built in the autumn at the mouth of the St. Joseph. Here La Salle found Chapelle and Leblanc, the two men whom he had sent from hence to Michillimackinac, in search of the "Griffin." They reported that they had made the circuit of the lake, and had neither seen her nor heard tidings of her. Assured of her fate, he ordered them to rejoin Tonty at Fort Crèvecoeur; while he pushed onward with his party through the unknown wild of Southern Michigan.

---

*From Francis Parkman, *The Discovery of the Great West* (Boston: Little, Brown and Co., 1869), pp. 178–183 *passim,* 281–283, 364–366.

"The rain," says La Salle, "which lasted all day, and the raft we were obliged to make to cross the river, stopped us till noon of the twenty-fifth. when we continued our march through the woods, which was so interlaced with thorns and brambles that in two days and a half our clothes were all torn and our faces so covered with blood that we hardly knew each other. On the twenty-eighth, we found the woods more open, and began to fare better, meeting a good deal of game, which after this rarely failed us; so that we no longer carried provisions with us, but made a meal of roast meat wherever we happened to kill a deer, bear, or turkey. These are the choicest feasts on a journey like this; and till now we had generally gone without them, so that we had often walked all day without breakfast.

"The Indians do not hunt in this region, which is debatable ground between five or six nations who are at war, and, being afraid of each other, do not venture into these parts, except to surprise each other, and always with the greatest precaution and all possible secrecy. The reports of our guns and the carcasses of the animals we killed soon led some of them to find our trail. In fact, on the evening of the twenty-eighth, having made our fire by the edge of a prairie, we were surrounded by them; but as the man on guard waked us, and we posted ourselves behind trees with our guns, these savages, who are called Wapoos, took us for Iroquois, and thinking that there must be a great many of us, because we did not travel secretly, as they do when in small bands, they ran off without shooting their arrows, and gave the alarm to their comrades, so that we were two days without meeting anybody."

La Salle guessed the cause of their fright; and, in order to confirm their delusion, he drew with charcoal, on the trunks of trees from which he had stripped the bark, the usual marks of an Iroquois war-party, with signs for prisoners and for scalps, after the custom of those dreaded warriors. This ingenious artifice, as will soon appear, was near proving the destruction of the whole party. He also set fire to the dry grass of the prairies over which he and his men had just passed, thus destroying the traces of their passage. "We practised this device every night, and it answered very well so long as we were passing over an open country; but, on the thirtieth, we got into great marshes, flooded by the thaws, and were obliged to cross them in mud or water up to the waist; so that our tracks betrayed us to a band of Mascoutins, who were out after Iroquois. They followed us through these marshes during the three days we were crossing them; but we made no fire at night, contenting ourselves with taking off our wet clothes and wrapping ourselves in our blankets on some dry knoll, where we slept till morning. At last, on the night of the second of April, there came a hard frost, and our clothes, which were drenched when we took them off, froze stiff as sticks, so that we could not put them on in the morning without making a fire to thaw them. The fire betrayed us to the Indians, who were encamped across the marsh; and they ran towards us with loud cries, till they were stopped half way by a stream so deep that they could not get over, the ice which had formed in the night not being strong enough to bear them. We went to meet them, within gunshot; and whether our fire-arms frightened them, or whether they thought us more numerous than we were, or whether they really meant us no harm, they called out, in the Illinois language, that they had taken us for Iroquois, but now saw that we were friends and brothers; whereupon, they went off as they came, and we kept on our way till the fourth, when two of my men fell ill and could not walk."

In this emergency, La Salle went in search of some watercourse by which they might reach Lake Erie, and soon came upon a small river, which was probably the Huron. Here, while the sick men rested, their companions made a canoe. There were no birch-trees; and they were forced to use elm bark, which at that early season would not slip freely from the wood until they loosened it with hot water. Their canoe being made, they embarked in it, and for a time floated prosperously down the stream, when at length the way was barred by a matted barricade of trees fallen across the water. The sick men could now walk again, and, pushing eastward through the forest, the party soon reached the banks of the Detroit.

La Salle directed two of the men to make a canoe, and go to Michillimackinac, the nearest harborage. With the remaining two, he crossed the Detroit on a raft, and, striking a direct line across the country, reached Lake Erie, not far from Point Pelée. Snow, sleet, and rain pelted them with little intermission; and when, after a walk of about thirty miles, they gained the lake, the Mohegan and one of the Frenchmen were attacked with fever and spitting of blood. Only one man now remained in health. With his aid, La Salle made another canoe, and, embarking the invalids, pushed for Niagara. It was Easter Monday when they landed at a cabin of logs above the cataract, probably on the spot where the "Griffin" was built. Here several of La Salle's men had been left the year before, and here they still remained. They told him woeful news. Not only had he lost the "Griffin," and her lading of ten thousand crowns in value, but a ship from France, freighted with his goods, valued at more than twenty-two thousand livres, had been totally wrecked at the mouth of the St. Lawrence; and, of twenty hired men on their way from Europe to join him, some had been detained by his enemy, the Intendant Duchesneau, while all but four of the remainder, being told that he was dead, had found means to return home.

His three followers were all unfit for travel; he alone retained his strength and spirit. Taking with him three fresh men at Niagara, he resumed his journey, and on the sixth of May descried, looming through floods of rain, the familiar shores of his seigniory and the bastioned walls

of Fort Frontenac. During sixty-five days, he had toiled almost inces-
santly, travelling, by the course he took, about a thousand miles through
a country beset with every form of peril and obstruction; "the most arduous journey," says the chronicler, "ever made by Frenchmen in America."
Such was Cavelier de la Salle. In him, an unconquerable mind held at its
service a frame of iron, and tasked it to the utmost of its endurance. The
pioneer of western pioneers was no rude son of toil, but a man of thought,
trained amid arts and letters.

[*The following passage takes place in 1682 at the end of La Salle's
exploration of the length of the Mississippi River.*]

And now they neared their journey's end. On the sixth of April, the
river divided itself into three broad channels. La Salle followed that of the
West, and D'Autray that of the east; while Tonty took the middle passage. As he drifted down the turbid current, between the low and marshy
shores, the brackish water changed to brine, and the breeze grew fresh with
the salt breath of the sea. Then the broad bosom of the great Gulf opened
on his sight, tossing its restless billows, limitless, voiceless, lonely as when
born of chaos, without a sail, without a sign of life.

La Salle, in a canoe, coasted the marshy borders of the sea; and then
the reunited parties assembled on a spot of dry ground, a short distance
above the mouth of the river. Here a column was made ready, bearing the
arms of France, and inscribed with the words,

LOUIS LE GRAND, ROY DE FRANCE ET DE NAVARRE, RÈGNE;
LE NEUVIÈME AVRIL, 1682.

The Frenchmen were mustered under arms; and, while the New
England Indians and their squaws looked on in wondering silence, they
chanted the *Te Deum,* the *Exaudiat,* and the *Domine salvum fac Regem.*
Then, amid volleys of musketry and shouts of *Vive le Roi,* La Salle
planted the column in its place, and, standing near it, proclaimed in a loud
voice,

"In the name of the most high, mighty, invincible, and victorious Prince,
Louis the Great, by the grace of God King of France and of Navarre, Four-
teenth of that name, I, this ninth day of April, one thousand six hundred and
eighty-two, in virtue of the commission of his Majesty, which I hold in my
hand, and which may be seen by all whom it may concern, have taken, and do
now take, in the name of his Majesty and of his successors to the crown, possession of this country of Louisiana, the seas, harbors, ports, bays, adjacent
straits, and all the nations, peoples, provinces, cities, towns, villages, mines,
minerals, fisheries, streams, and rivers, within the extent of the said Louisiana.
from the mouth of the great river St. Louis, otherwise called the Ohio,... as
also along the river Colbert, or Mississippi, and the rivers which discharge
themselves thereinto, from its source beyond the country of the Nadouessioux

...as far as its mouth at the sea, or Gulf of Mexico, and also to the mouth of the River of Palms, upon the assurance we have had from the natives of these countries, that we are the first Europeans who have descended or ascended the said river Colbert; hereby protesting against all who may hereafter undertake to invade any or all of these aforesaid countries, peoples, or lands, to the prejudice of the rights of his Majesty, acquired by the consent of the nations dwelling herein. Of which, and of all else that is needful, I hereby take to witness those who hear me, and demand an act of the Notary here present."

Shouts of *Vive le Roi* and volleys of musketry responded to his words. Then a cross was planted beside the column, and a leaden plate buried near it, bearing the arms of France, with a Latin inscription, *Ludovicus Magnus regnat*. The weather-beaten voyagers joined their voices in the grand hymn of the *Vexilla Regis:*

"The banners of Heaven's King advance,
The mystery of the Cross shines forth";

and renewed shouts of *Vive le Roi* closed the ceremony.

On that day, the realm of France received on parchment a stupendous accession. The fertile plains of Texas; the vast basin of the Mississippi, from its frozen northern springs to the sultry borders of the Gulf; from the woody ridges of the Alleghanies to the bare peaks of the Rocky Mountains—a region of savannahs and forests, sun-cracked deserts, and grassy prairies, watered by a thousand rivers, ranged by a thousand warlike tribes, passed beneath the sceptre of the Sultan of Versailles; and all by virtue of a feeble human voice, inaudible at half a mile.

[*La Salle, at the behest of his government, later returned by sea to set up a post at the mouth of the Mississippi; but he missed the location and, in the process of trying to find it, was murdered in 1687 by his own men.*]

Thus in the vigor of his manhood, at the age of forty-three, died Robert Cavelier de la Salle, "one of the greatest men," writes Tonty, "of this age"; without question one of the most remarkable explorers whose names live in history. His faithful officer Joutel thus sketches his portrait: "His firmness, his courage, his great knowledge of the arts and sciences, which made him equal to every undertaking, and his untiring energy, which enabled him to surmount every obstacle, would have won at last a glorious success for his grand enterprise, had not all his fine qualities been counterbalanced by a haughtiness of manner which often made him insupportable, and by a harshness towards those under his command, which drew upon him an implacable hatred, and was at last the cause of his death."

The enthusiasm of the disinterested and chivalrous Champlain was not the enthusiasm of La Salle; nor had he any part in the self-devoted zeal of the early Jesuit explorers. He belonged not to the age of the knight-errant and the saint, but to the modern world of practical study and practical action. He was the hero, not of a principle nor of a faith, but simply of a fixed idea and a determined purpose. As often happens with concentred and energetic natures, his purpose was to him a passion and an inspiration; and he clung to it with a certain fanaticism of devotion. It was the offspring of an ambition vast and comprehensive, yet acting in the interest both of France and of civilization.

Serious in all things, incapable of the lighter pleasures, incapable of repose, finding no joy but in the pursuit of great designs, too shy for society and too reserved for popularity, often unsympathetic and always seeming so, smothering emotions which he could not utter, schooled to universal distrust, stern to his followers and pitiless to himself, bearing the brunt of every hardship and every danger, demanding of others an equal constancy joined to an implicit deference, heeding no counsel but his own, attempting the impossible and grasping at what was too vast to hold —he contained in his own complex and painful nature the chief springs of his triumphs, his failures, and his death.

It is easy to reckon up his defects, but it is not easy to hide from sight the Roman virtues that redeemed them. Beset by a throng of enemies, he stands, like the King of Israel, head and shoulders above them all. He was a tower of adamant, against whose impregnable front hardship and danger, the rage of man and of the elements, the southern sun, the northern blast, fatigue, famine, and disease, delay, disappointment, and deferred hope emptied their quivers in vain. That very pride which, Coriolanus-like, declared itself most sternly in the thickest press of foes, has in it something to challenge admiration. Never, under the impenetrable mail of paladin or crusader, beat a heart of more intrepid mettle than within the stoic panoply that armed the breast of La Salle. To estimate aright the marvels of his patient fortitude, one must follow on his track through the vast scene of his interminable journeyings, those thousands of weary miles of forest, marsh, and river, where, again and again, in the bitterness of baffled striving, the untiring pilgrim pushed onward towards the goal which he was never to attain. America owes him an enduring memory; for, in this masculine figure, she sees the pioneer who guided her to the possession of her richest heritage.

Thomas Jefferson

*On June 20, 1803, President Thomas Jefferson (1743–1826) sent
the following instructions to Meriwether Lewis. These directives, governing the Lewis and Clark expedition, are full of insights into the aims
of the government as well as Jefferson's own scientific interests. In this
selection, the larger political, economic, and expansionist ideas are present
behind each of the details.*

Instructions to Meriwether Lewis*

The object of your mission is to explore the Missouri river, & such
principal stream of it, as, by it's course & communication with the waters
of the Pacific Ocean, may offer the most direct & practicable water communication across this continent, for the purposes of commerce.

Beginning at the mouth of the Missouri, you will take observations
of latitude & longitude, at all remarkable points on the river, & especially
at the mouths of rivers, at rapids, at islands & other places & objects distinguished by such natural marks & characters of a durable kind, as that
they may with certainty be recognized hereafter. The courses of the river
between these points of observation may be supplied by the compass, the
log-line & by time, corrected by the observations themselves. The variations
of the compass too, in different places, should be noticed.

The interesting points of portage between the heads of the Missouri
& the water offering the best communication with the Pacific Ocean should
also be fixed by observation, & the course of that water to the ocean, in
the same manner as that of the Missouri.

Your observations are to be taken with great pains & accuracy, to be
entered distinctly, & intelligibly for others as well as yourself, to comprehend all the elements necessary, with the aid of the usual tables, to fix
the latitude and longitude of the places at which they were taken, & are
to be rendered to the war office, for the purpose of having the calculations
made concurrently by proper persons within the U. S. Several copies of

---

* From Paul Leicester Ford, ed., *The Writings of Thomas Jefferson* (New York:
G. P. Putnam's Sons, 1897), VIII, 194–199.

these, as well as your other notes, should be made at leisure times & put into the care of the most trustworthy of your attendants, to guard by multiplying them, against the accidental losses to which they will be exposed. A further guard would be that one of these copies be written on the paper of the birch, as less liable to injury from damp than common paper.

The commerce which may be carried on with the people inhabiting the line you will pursue, renders a knolege of these people important. You will therefore endeavor to make yourself acquainted, as far as a diligent pursuit of your journey shall admit, with

the names of the nations & their numbers;

the extent & limits of their possessions;

their relations with other tribes or nations;

their language, traditions, monuments;

their ordinary occupations in agriculture, fishing, hunting, war, arts, & the implements for these;

their food, clothing, & domestic accomodations;

the diseases prevalent among them, & the remedies they use;

moral & physical circumstances which distinguish them from the tribes we know;

peculiarities in their laws, customs & dispositions;

and articles of commerce they may need or furnish, & to what extent.

And considering the interest which every nation has in extending & strengthening the authority of reason & justice among the people around them, it will be useful to acquire what knolege you can of the state of morality, religion & information among them, as it may better enable those who endeavor to civilize & instruct them, to adapt their measures to the existing notions & practises of those on whom they are to operate.

Other object worthy of notice will be

the soil & face of the country, it's growth & vegetable productions; especially those not of the U. S.

the animals of the country generally, & especially those not known in the U. S.

the remains and accounts of any which may [be] deemed rare or extinct;

the mineral productions of every kind; but more particularly metals, limestone, pit coal & salpetre; salines & mineral waters, noting the temperature of the last, & such circumstances as may indicate their character.

Volcanic appearances.

climate as characterized by the thermometer, by the proportion of rainy, cloudy & clear days, by lightening, hail, snow, ice, by the access & recess of frost, by the winds prevailing at different seasons, the dates at which particular plants put forth or lose their flowers, or leaf, times of appearance of particular birds, reptiles or insects.

Altho' your route will be along the channel of the Missouri, yet you will endeavor to inform yourself, by inquiry, of the character & extent of the country watered by it's branches, & especially on it's southern side. The North river or Rio Bravo which runs into the gulph of Mexico, and the North river, or Rio colorado, which runs into the gulph of California, are understood to be the principal streams heading opposite to the waters of the Missouri, and running Southwardly. Whether the dividing grounds between the Missouri & them are mountains or flatlands, what are their distance from the Missouri, the character of the intermediate country, & the people inhabiting it, are worthy of particular enquiry. The Northern waters of the Missouri are less to be enquired after, because they have been ascertained to a considerable degree, and are still in a course of ascertainment by English traders & travellers. But if you can learn anything certain of the most Northern source of the Missisipi, & of it's position relative to the lake of the woods, it will be interesting to us. Some account too of the path of the Canadian traders from the Missisipi, at the mouth of the Ouisconsin river, to where it strikes the Missouri and of the soil & rivers in it's course, is desireable.

In all your intercourse with the natives treat them in the most friendly & conciliatory manner which their own conduct will admit[;] allay all jealousies as to the object of your journey, satisfy them of it's innocence, make them acquainted with the position, extent, character, peaceable & commercial dispositions of the U. S. of our wish to be neighborly, friendly & useful to them, & of our dispositions to a commercial intercourse with them; confer with them on the points most convenient as mutual emporiums, & the articles of most desireable interchange for them & us. If a few of their influential chiefs, within practicable distance, wish to visit us, arrange such a visit with them, and furnish them with authority to call on our officers, on their entering the U. S. to have them conveyed to this place at public expence. If any of them should wish to have some of their young people brought up with us, & taught such arts as may be useful to them, we will receive, instruct & take care of them. Such a mission, whether of influential chiefs, or of young people, would give some security to your own party. Carry with you some matter of the kine-pox, inform those of them with whom you may be of it'[s] efficacy as a preservative

from the small-pox; and instruct & incourage them in the use of it. This
may be especially done wherever you winter.

As it is impossible for us to foresee in what manner you will be re-
cieved by those people, whether with hospitality or hostility, so is it impossible to prescribe the exact degree of perseverance with which you are
to pursue your journey. We value too much the lives of citizens to offer
them to probably destruction. Your numbers will be sufficient to secure
you against the unauthorised opposition of individuals, or of small parties:
but if a superior force, authorised or not authorised, by a nation, should
be arrayed against your further passage, & inflexibly determined to arrest
it, you must decline it's further pursuit, and return. In the loss of yourselves, we should lose also the information you will have acquired. By returning safely with that, you may enable us to renew the essay with better
calculated means. To your own discretion therefore must be left the degree of danger you may risk, & the point at which you should decline,
only saying we wish you to err on the side of your safety, & bring back
your party safe, even if it be with less information.

As far up the Missouri as the white settlements extend, an intercourse
will probably be found to exist between them and the Spanish posts at St.
Louis, opposite Cahokia, or Ste. Genevieve opposite Kaskaskia. From still
farther up the river, the traders may furnish a conveyance for letters.
Beyond that you may perhaps be able to engage Indians to bring letters
for the government to Cahokia or Kaskaskia, on promising that they shall
there receive such special compensation as you shall have stipulated with
them. Avail yourself of these means to communicate to us, at seasonable
intervals, a copy of your journal, notes & observations of every kind,
putting into cypher whatever might do injury if betrayed.

Should you reach the Pacific ocean inform yourself of the circumstances which may decide whether the furs of those parts may not be collected as advantageously at the head of the Missouri (convenient as is supposed to the waters of the Colorado & Oregon or Columbia) as at Nootka
sound or any other point of that coast; & that trade be consequently conducted through the Missouri & U. S. more beneficially than by the cir-
cumnavigation now practised.

On your arrival on that coast endeavor to learn if there be any port
within your reach frequented by the sea-vessels of any nation, and to send
two of your trusty people back by sea, in such way as shall appear practicable, with a copy of your notes. And should you be of opinion that the
return of your party by the way they went will be eminently dangerous,
then ship the whole, & return by sea by way of Cape Horn or the Cape
of good Hope, as you shall be able. As you will be without money, clothes
or provisions, you must endeavor to use the credit of the U. S. to obtain
them; for which purpose open letters of credit shall be furnished you

authorising you to draw on the Executive of the U. S. or any of its officers in any part of the world, on which drafts can be disposed of, and to apply with our recommendations to the Consuls, agents, merchants, or citizens of any nation with which we have intercourse, assuring them in our name that any aids they may furnish you, shall [be] honorably repaid, and on demand. Our consuls Thomas Howes at Batavia in Java, William Buchanan on the isles of France and Bourbon, & John Elmslie at the Cape of good hope will be able to supply your necessities by draughts on us.

Should you find it safe to return by the way you go, after sending two of your party round by sea, or with your whole party, if no conveyance by sea can be found, do so; making such observations on your return as may serve to supply, correct or confirm those made on your outward journey.

In re-entering the U. S. and reaching a place of safety, discharge any of your attendants who may desire & deserve it, procuring for them immediate paiment of all arrears of pay & cloathing which may have incurred since their departure; & assure them that they shall be recommended to the liberality of the legislature for the grant of a soldier's portion of land each, as proposed in my message to Congress & repair yourself with your papers to the seat of government.

To provide, on the accident of your death, against anarchy, dispersion & the consequent danger to your party, and total failure of the enterprise, you are hereby authorised, by any instrument signed & written in your hand, to name the person among them who shall succeed to the command on your decease, & by like instruments to change the nomination from time to time, as further experience of the characters accompanying you shall point out superior fitness; and all the powers & authorities given to yourself are, in the event of your death, transferred to & vested in the successor so named, with further power to him, & his successors in like manner to name each his successor, who, on the death of his predecessor, shall be invested with all the powers & authorities given to yourself.

Given under my hand at the city of Washington, this 20th day of June 1803

Th. Jefferson
Pr. U S. of America

Edwin James

Not all government exploration was calculated to gladden the heart of expansionist and settler. Zebulon Pike in 1807 and Stephen H. Long in 1820, for example, both brought back reports which labeled the Great Plains practically unusable for farming, little more than a "Great American Desert." This kind of thinking on the Long expedition is seen in the following excerpts, written by Edwin James (1797–1861), a member of the expedition. The Plains, he suggests, would be valuable mainly as a kind of Sahara Desert buffer against foreign aggression.

The Expedition of Stephen H. Long*

It is not improbable, that a climate of a portion of country within the range of the immediate influence of the Rocky Mountains, may be more subject to hail-storms in summer, than any other parts of North America in the same latitude. The radiation of heat from so extensive a surface of naked sand, lying along the base of this vast range of snowy mountains, must produce great local inequalities of temperature. The diminished pressure of the atmosphere, and the consequent rapidity of evaporation, in these elevated regions, may also be supposed to have an important influence on the weather. We have not spent sufficient time in the country, near the eastern range of the Rocky Mountains, to enable us to speak with confidence of the character of its climate. It is, however, sufficiently manifest, that in summer it must be extremely variable, as we have found it; the thermometer often indicating an increase of near fifty degrees of temperature between sunrise and the middle of the day. These rapid alternations of heat and cold must be supposed to mark a climate little favourable to health, though we may safely assert that this portion of the country is exempt from the operation of those causes which produce so deleterious an atmosphere in the lower and more fertile portions of the Mississippi basin. If the wide plains of the Platte, the Upper Arkansa, and the Red river of

---

* From Edwin James, *Account of an Expedition from Pittsburgh to the Rocky Mountains, Performed in the Years 1819, 1820* (London: Longman, Hurst, Rees, Orme, and Brown, 1823), II, 313–314, 323–324; III, 6–7, 225–226, 237.

Louisiana should ever become the seat of a permanent civilized population, the diseases most incident to such a population will probably be fevers, attended with pulmonary and pleuritic inflammations, rheumatism, scrofula, and consumption. . . .

Looking back upon the broad valley of the river we had left, the eye rested upon insulated portions of the sandy bed disclosed by the inflections of its course or the opening of ravines, and resembling pools of blood, rather than wastes of sand. We had been so long accustomed to the red sands, that the intensity of the colouring ceased to excite any attention until a distant view afforded us the opportunity of contrasting it with the general aspect of the country.

The elevated plains we found covered with a plenteous but close-fed crop of grasses, and occupied by extensive marmot villages. The red soil is usually fine and little intermixed with gravel and pebbles, but too sandy to retain moisture enough for the purposes of agriculture. The luxuriance and fineness of the grasses, as well as the astonishing number and good condition of the herbivorous animals of this region, clearly indicate its value for the purposes of pasturage. There can be little doubt that more valuable and productive grasses than the native species can with little trouble be introduced. This may easily be effected by burning the prairies at a proper season of the year, and sowing the seeds of any of the more hardy cultivated gramina. Some of the perennial plants common in the prairies will undoubtedly be found difficult to exterminate, their strong roots penetrating to a great depth and enveloping the rudiments of new shoots placed beyond the reach of a fire on the surface. The soil of the more fertile plains is penetrated with such numbers of these as to present more resistance to the plough than the oldest cultivated pastures. . . .

We found, however, the annoyance of innumerable multitudes of minute, almost invisible, wood ticks, a sufficient counterpart to the advantages of our situation. These insects, unlike the mosquitoes, gnats, and sand flies, are not to be turned aside by a gust of wind or an atmosphere surcharged with smoke, nor does the closest dress of leather afford any protection from their persecutions. The traveller no sooner sets foot among them, than they commence in countless thousands their silent and unseen march; ascending along the feet and legs, they insinuate themselves into every article of dress, and fasten, unperceived, their fangs upon every part of the body. The bite is not felt until the insect has had time to bury the whole of his head, and in the case of the most minute and most troublesome species, nearly his whole body, under the skin, where he fastens himself with such tenacity, that he will sooner suffer his head and body to be dragged apart than relinquish his hold. It would perhaps be advisable, when they are once thoroughly planted, to suffer them to remain unmolested, as the head and claws left under the skin produce more irritation than the living animal; but they excite such intolerable itching, that the finger nails are sure very soon to do all finger nails can do for their destruction. The wound, which was at first almost imperceptible, swells and inflames gradually, and being enlarged by rubbing and scratching, at length discharges a serous fluid, and finally suppurates to such an extent as to carry off the offending substance. If the insect is suffered to remain unmolested, he protracts his feast for some weeks, when he is found to have grown of enormous size, and to have assumed nearly the colour of the skin on which he has been feeding; his limbs do not enlarge, but are almost buried in the mass accumulated on his back, which extending forward bears against the skin, and at last pushes the insect from his hold. Nothing is to be hoped from becoming accustomed to the bite of these wood ticks. On the contrary, by long exposure to their venomous influence, the skin acquires a morbid irritability, which increases in proportion to the frequency and continuance of the evil, until at length the bite of a single tick is sufficient to produce a large and painful phlegmon. This may not be the case with every one; it was so with us. . . .

Throughout this section of country the surface is occasionally characterized by water-worn pebbles, and gravel of granite, gneiss, and quartz, but the predominant characteristic is sand, which in many instances prevails almost to the entire exclusion of vegetable mould. Large tracts are often to be met with, exhibiting scarcely a trace of vegetation. The whole region, as before hinted, is almost entirely destitute of a timber-growth of any description. In some few instances, however, sandy knobs and ridges make their appearance, thickly covered with red cedars of a dwarfish growth. There are also some few tracts clad in a growth of pitch pine and scrubby oaks; but, in general, nothing of vegetation appears upon the uplands but withered grass of a stinted growth, no more than two or three inches high, prickly pears profusely covering extensive tracts, and weeds of a few varieties, which, like the prickly pear, seem to thrive best in the most arid and sterile soil.

In the vicinity of the Rocky Mountains, southwardly of the Arkansa river, the surface of the country, in many places, is profusely covered with loose fragments of volcanic rocks. On some occasions, stones of this description are so numerous as almost to exclude vegetation. . . . The whole of this region seems peculiarly adapted as a range for buffaloes, wild goats, and other wild game; incalculable multitudes of which find ample pasturage and subsistence upon it.

This region, however, viewed as a frontier, may prove of infinite importance to the United States, inasmuch as it is calculated to serve as a barrier to prevent too great an extension of our population westward, and secure us against the machinations or incursions of an enemy that might otherwise be disposed to annoy us in that part of our frontier.

John Charles Frémont

No single man did more to dispel the idea of the Great American Desert than John Charles Frémont (1813–1890). Between 1842 and 1853 he led five expeditions into the trans-Mississippi West; and after the first two he published glowing reports, lavishly and appealingly illustrated. Even the Great Basin appeared to Frémont suitable for settlement, and the Great Basin is far more inhospitable than the Great Plains. The following selections deal with his second and third expeditions. In them, observe the importance of his father-in-law, Senator Thomas Hart Benton, as a source of Frémont's enthusiasm. The last part of the selection reveals Frémont's role in the conquest of California. His third expedition, ostensibly scientific, was slowly leaving California when it was dramatically recalled to play a role in the acquisition of California during the Mexican War. The political implications of exploration were never so clearly realized.

*Reports on Expeditions**

The results of our journeys between the two great rivers had suggested to him [Benton] the same work for the broader field beyond the Missouri. His inquiries on this occasion were all of distinct pertinency. They were directed to know about our means and manner of traveling, the nature of the work required to be done, and the instruments employed. In the course of his inquiries he dwelt on the unoccupied country beyond the Missouri and the existing uncertain and incomplete knowledge concerning it. The interview left on me a profound impression and raised excited interest. The ideas suggested remained fixtures in my mind. The thought of penetrating into the recesses of that wilderness region filled me with enthusiasm—I saw visions. Formerly I had been entirely devoted to my intended profession of engineering. The lives of great engineers had been my treasured exem-

---

* From John Charles Frémont, *Memoirs of My Life* (Chicago: Belford, Clarke & Co., 1886), pp. 64–65, 418–419, 486–490. The excerpt on pages 47–49 is from Frémont's *Report of the Exploring Expedition to the Rocky Mountains in the Year 1842, and to Oregon and North California in the Years 1843–'44* (Washington, D.C.: Gales and Seaton, 1845), pp. 47–48, 276, 277.

plars. But strict engineering had lost its inspiration in the charm of the new field into which I had entered during the last few years.

In this interview with Mr. Benton my mind had been quick to see a larger field and differing and greater results. It would be travel over a part of the world which still remained the New—the opening up of unknown lands; the making unknown countries known; and the study without books —the learning at first hand from Nature herself; the drinking first at her unknown springs—became a source of never-ending delight to me. I felt that it was an unreasonable pleasure to expect that it might happen to me to be among the very few to whom the chance had fallen to work with Nature where in all her features there was still aboriginal freshness. . . .

If it is in contemplation to keep open the communications with Oregon territory, a show of military force in this country is absolutely necessary; and a combination of advantages renders the neighborhood of Fort Laramie the most suitable place, on the line of the Platte, for the establishment of a military post. It is connected with the mouth of the Platte and the Upper Missouri by excellent roads, which are in frequent use, and would not in any way interfere with the range of the buffalo, on which the neighboring Indians mainly depend for support. It would render any posts on the Lower Platte unnecessary; the ordinary communication between it and the Missouri being sufficient to control the intermediate Indians. It would operate effectually to prevent any such coalitions as are now formed among the Gros Ventre, Sioux, Cheyenne, and other Indians, and would keep the Oregon road through the valley of the Sweet Water and the South Pass of the mountains constantly open. . . . It lies at the foot of a broken and mountainous region, along which, by the establishment of small posts in the neighborhood of St. Vrain's Fort, on the South Fork of the Platte, and Bent's Fort, on the Arkansas, a line of communication would be formed, by good wagon roads, with our southern military posts, which would entirely command the mountain passes, hold some of the most troublesome tribes in check, and protect and facilitate our intercourse with the neighboring Spanish settlements. The valleys of the rivers on which they would be situated are fertile; the country, which supports immense herds of buffalo, is admirably adapted to grazing; and herds of cattle might be maintained by the posts, or obtained from the Spanish country, which already supplies a portion of their provisions to the trading posts mentioned above. . . .

We entered the basin at that point, and have traveled in it ever since, having its southeastern rim (the Wasatch Mountain) on the right, and crossing the streams which flow down into it. The existence of the basin is, therefore, an established fact in my mind; its extent and contents are yet to be better ascertained. It cannot be less than four or five hundred miles each way, and must lie principally in the Alta California; the demarcation latitude of 42° probably cutting a segment from the north part of the rim. Of its interior but little is known. It is called a desert, and from what I saw of it, sterility may be its prominent characteristic; but where there is so much water there must be some oases. The great river and the great lake, reported, may not be equal to the report; but where there is so much snow there must be streams; and where there is no outlet there must be lakes to hold the accumulated waters, or sands to swallow them up. In this eastern part of the basin, containing Sevier, Utah, and the Great Salt lakes, and the rivers and creeks falling into them, we know there is good soil and good grass adapted to civilized settlements. In the western part, on Salmon Trout River and some other streams, the same remark may be made. . . .

The whole idea of such a desert . . . is a novelty in our country, and excites Asiatic, not American, ideas. Interior basins, with their own systems of lakes and rivers, and often sterile, are common enough in Asia; people still in the elementary state of families, living in deserts, with no other occupation than the mere animal search for food, may still be seen in that ancient quarter of the globe; but in America such things are new and strange, unknown and unsuspected, and discredited when related. But I flatter myself that what is discovered, though not enough to satisfy curiosity, is sufficient to excite it, and that subsequent explorations will complete what has been commenced.

This account of the Great Basin, it will be remembered, belongs to the Alta California, and has no application to Oregon, whose capabilities may justify a separate remark. Referring to my journal for particular descriptions, and for sectional boundaries between good and bad districts, I can only say, in general and comparative terms, that in the branch of agriculture which implies the cultivation of grains and staple crops, it would be inferior to the Atlantic States, though many parts are superior for wheat, while in the rearing of flocks and herds it would claim a high place. Its grazing capabilities are great; and even in the indigenous grass now there, an element of individual and national wealth may be found. In fact, the valuable grasses begin within one hundred and fifty miles of the Missouri frontier, and extend to the Pacific Ocean. East of the Rocky Mountains it is the short curly grass on which the buffalo delight to feed, (whence its name of buffalo) and which is still good when dry and apparently dead.

West of those mountains it is a larger growth, in clusters, and hence called bunch grass, and which has a second or fall growth. Plains and mountains both exhibit them; and I have seen good pasturage at an elevation of ten thousand feet. In this spontaneous product, the trading or traveling caravans can find subsistence for their animals; and in military operations any number of cavalry may be moved and any number of cattle may be driven; and thus men and horses be supported on long expeditions, and even in winter in the sheltered situations.

Commercially, the value of the Oregon country must be great, washed as it is by the North Pacific Ocean; fronting Asia; producing many of the elements of commerce; mild and healthy in its climate; and becoming, as it naturally will, a thoroughfare for the East India and China trade. . . .

After the change of administration in March [1845] I accompanied Mr. Benton to visit the President, Mr. Polk. In speaking to him of the interesting facts in the geography of the West I mentioned that I had shortly before, at the Library of Congress, drawn out from the map stand one giving the United States and Territories, and found on it the Great Salt Lake represented as connected with the Pacific Ocean by three great rivers; one discharging into the Columbia River from the northwestern end; another from the southwestern end into the head of the Gulf of California; the third from the middle of the western side of the lake running westward, breaking through the Sierra Nevada and discharging into the Bay of San Francisco. Bearing in mind the account given me at Vancouver of the Buenaventura River, the known fact of the Great Colorado, and the existence of large streams flowing into the lake, it is easy to see how the reports of trappers scattered over that region, who had seen it only in widely separated parts, might be connected together in the compilation of maps so as to give the lake these outlets.

The President seemed for the moment skeptical about the exactness of my information and disposed to be conservative. He evidently "respected that ancient chaos" of the Western geography as it existed on the old maps. Like the Secretary, he found me "young," and said something of the "impulsiveness of young men," and was not at all satisfied in his own mind that those three rivers were not running there as laid down. . . .

My plans when I started on my journey into this region were to connect my present survey of the intervening country with my camp on the savannah, where I had met the Klamaths in that December; and I wished to penetrate among the mountains of the Cascade Range. As I have said, except for the few trappers who had searched the streams leading to the ocean for beaver, I felt sure that these mountains were absolutely unknown. No one had penetrated their recesses to know what they contained, and no one had climbed to their summits; and there remained the great attraction of mystery in going into unknown places—the unknown lands of which I had dreamed when I began this life of frontier travel. And possibly, I thought, when I should descend their western flanks, some safe harbor might yet be found by careful search along that coast, where harbors were so few; and perhaps good passages from the interior through these mountains to the sea. I thought that until the snow should go off the lower part of the mountains I might occupy what remained of the spring by a survey of the Klamath River to its heads, and make a good map of the country along the base of the mountains. And if we should not find game enough to live upon, we could employ the Indians to get supplies of salmon and other fish. But I felt sure that there was game in the woods of these mountains as well as in those more to the south. Traveling along the northern part of this range in December of '43, I had seen elk tracks in the snow, and at an old Cayuse village in the pine forest at the foot of the mountains, only about sixty miles farther north, there were many deer horns lying around. This showed that we should probably find both elk and deer, and bear, in the mountains, and certainly on the slope toward the sea, where every variety of climate would be found, and every variety of mast-bearing trees, as in the oak region of the Sierra Nevada. And I had not forgotten how fascinated I had been with the winter beauty of the snowy range farther north when at sunrise and at sunset their rose-colored peaks stood up out of the dark pine forests into the clear light of the sky. And my thoughts took the same color when I remembered that Mr. Kern, who had his colors with him, could hold these lovely views in all their delicate coloring.

How fate pursues a man! Thinking and ruminating over these things, I was standing alone by my campfire, enjoying its warmth, for the night air of early spring is chill under the shadows of the high mountains. Suddenly my ear caught the faint sound of horses' feet, and while I was watching and listening as the sounds, so strange hereabout, came nearer, there emerged from the darkness—into the circle of the firelight—two horsemen, riding slowly as though horse and man were fatigued by long traveling. In the foremost I recognized the familiar face of Neal, with a companion whom I also knew. They had ridden nearly a hundred miles in the last two days, having been sent forward by a United States officer who was on my trail with despatches for me; but Neal doubted if he would get through.

After their horses had been turned into the band and they were seated by my fire, refreshing themselves with good coffee while more solid food was being prepared, Neal told me his story. The officer who was trying to overtake me was named Gillespie. He had been sent to California by the Government and had letters for delivery to me. Neal knew the great danger from Indians in this country, and his party becoming alarmed and my trail being fresh, Mr. Gillespie had sent forward Neal and Sigler upon their best horses to overtake me and inform me of his situation. They had left him on the morning of the day before, and in the two days had ridden nearly a hundred miles, and this last day had severely tried the strength of their horses. When they parted from him they had not reached the lake, and for greater safety had not kept my trail quite to the outlet, but crossed to the right bank of the river, striking my trail again on the lake shore. They had discovered Indians on my trail after they had left Gillespie, and on the upper part of the lake the Indians had tried to cut them off, and they had escaped only by the speed and strength of their horses, which Neal had brought from his own rancho. He said that in his opinion I could not reach Gillespie in time to save him, as he had with him only three men and was traveling slow.

A quick eye and a good horse mean life to a man in an Indian country. Neal had both. He was a lover of horses and knew a good one, and those he had with him were the best on his rancho. He had been sent forward by the messenger to let me know that he was in danger of being cut off by the Indians.

The trail back along the shore at the foot of the mountains was so nearly impassable at night that nothing could be gained by attempting it, but everything was made ready for an early start in the morning. For the relief party, in view of contingencies, I selected ten of the best men, including Carson, Stepp, Dick Owens, Godey, Basil, and Lajeunesse, with four of the Delawares.

When the excitement of the evening was over I lay down, speculating far into the night on what could be the urgency of the message which had brought an officer of the Government to search so far after me into these mountains. At early dawn we took the backward trail. Snow and fallen timber made the ride hard and long to where I thought to meet the messenger. On the way no Indians were seen and no tracks later than those where they had struck Neal's trail. In the afternoon, having made about forty-five miles, we reached the spot where the forest made an opening to the lake, and where I intended to wait. This was a glade, or natural meadow, shut in by the forest, with a small stream and good grass, where I had already encamped. I knew that this was the first water to which my trail would bring the messenger, and that I was sure to meet him here if no harm befell him on the way. The sun was about going down when he was seen issuing from the wood, accompanied by three men.

He proved to be an officer of the Navy, Lieutenant Archibald Gillespie of the Marine Corps. We greeted him warmly. All were glad to see him, whites and Indians. It was long since any news had reached us, and everyone was as pleased to see him as if he had come freighted with letters from home, for all. It was now eleven months since any tidings had reached me.

Mr. Gillespie informed me that he had left Washington under orders from the President and the Secretary of the Navy, and was directed to reach California by the shortest route through Mexico to Mazatlan.

He was directed to find me wherever I might be, and was informed that I would probably be found on the Sacramento River. In pursuance of his instructions he had accordingly started from Monterey to look for me on the Sacramento. Learning upon his arrival at Sutter's Fort that I had gone up the valley, he made up a small party at Neal's rancho and, guided by him, followed my trail and had traveled six hundred miles to overtake me, the latter part of the way through great dangers.

The mission on which I had been originally sent to the West was a peaceful one, and Mr. Bancroft had sent Mr. Gillespie to give me warning of the new state of affairs and the designs of the President. Mr. Gillespie had been given charge of despatches from the Secretary of the Navy to Commodore Sloat, and had been purposely made acquainted with their import. Known to Mr. Bancroft as an able and thoroughly trustworthy officer, he had been well instructed in the designs of the Department and with the purposes of the Administration, so far as they related to California.

Through him I now became acquainted with the actual state of affairs and the purposes of the Government. The information through Gillespie had absolved me from my duty as an explorer, and I was left to my duty as an officer of the American Army, with the further authoritative knowledge that the Government intended to take California. I was warned by my Government of the new danger against which I was bound to defend myself; and it had been made known to me now on the authority of the Secretary of the Navy that to obtain possession of California was the chief object of the President.

He brought me also a letter of introduction from the Secretary of State, Mr. Buchanan, and letters and papers from Senator Benton and family. The letter from the Secretary was directed to me in my private or citizen capacity, and though importing nothing beyond the introduction, it accredited the bearer to me as coming from the Secretary of State, and in connection with the circumstances and place of delivery it indicated a purpose in sending it. From the letter itself I learned nothing, but it was intelligibly explained to me by the accompanying letter from Senator Benton and by communications from Lieutenant Gillespie.

This officer informed me that he had been directed by the Secretary of State to acquaint me with his instructions, which had for their principal objects to ascertain the disposition of the California people, to conciliate their feelings in favor of the United States; and to find out, with a view to counteracting, the designs of the British Government upon that country.

The letter from Senator Benton, while apparently of friendship and family details, contained passages and suggestions which, read by the light of many conversations and discussions with himself and others at Washington, clearly indicated to me that I was required by the Government to find out any foreign schemes in relation to California and, so far as might be in my power, to counteract them.

Neal had much to talk over with his old companions and pleasurable excitement kept us up late; but before eleven o'clock all were wrapped in their blankets and soundly asleep except myself. I sat by the fire in fancied security, going over again the home letters. These threw their own light upon the communication from Mr. Gillespie, and made the expected signal.

In substance, their effect was: The time has come. England must not get a foothold. We must be first. Act; discreetly, but positively.

Looking back over the contingencies which had been foreseen in the discussions at Washington, I saw that the important one which carried with it the hopes of Senator Benton and the wishes of the Government was in the act of occurring, and it was with thorough satisfaction I now found myself required to do what I could to promote this object of the President. Viewed by the light of these deliberations in Washington, I was prepared to comprehend fully the communications brought to me by Mr. Gillespie.

Now it was officially made known to me that my country was at war, and it was so made known expressly to guide my conduct. I had learned with certainty from the Secretary of the Navy that the President's plan of war included the taking possession of California, and under his confidential instructions I had my warrant. Mr. Gillespie was directed to act in concert with me. Great vigilance and activity were expected of us both, for it was desired that possession should be had of California before the presence in her ports of any foreign vessel of war might make it inconvenient. . . .

I saw the way opening clear before me. War with Mexico was inevitable; and a grand opportunity now presented itself to realize in their fullest extent the farsighted views of Senator Benton, and make the Pacific Ocean the western boundary of the United States. I resolved to move forward on the opportunity and return forthwith to the Sacramento Valley in order to bring to bear all the influences I could command.

Except myself, then and for nine months afterward, there was no other officer of the Army in California. The citizen party under my command was made up of picked men, and although small in number, constituted a formidable nucleus for frontier warfare, and many of its members commanded the confidence of the emigration.

This decision was the first step in the conquest of California.

ADDITIONAL READINGS

An enjoyable one-volume survey of Western exploration is John B. Brebner's *The Explorers of North America, 1492–1806* (New York, 1933). For a brief introduction to Francis Parkman, see Samuel Eliot Morison's introduction to *The Parkman Reader* (Boston, 1955). An equally helpful introduction, this time to the Lewis and Clark expedition, will be found in Bernard De Voto's edition of *The Journals of Lewis and Clark* (Boston, 1953). De Voto vividly re-creates the perils of exploration in *The Course of Empire* (Boston, 1952). *Frémont: Pathmarker of the West,* by Allan Nevins, remains the best biography of the so-called "Pathfinder." And a careful examination of the role of government in exploration is William H. Goetzmann's *Army Exploration in the American West, 1803–1863* (New Haven, 1959).

3

THE FAR WESTERN
FUR TRADE

At the cost of marring Frederick Jackson Turner's fine figure of speech, it may nonetheless be said that the cutting edge of the frontier in North America—particularly in the trans-Mississippi West—was frequently wrapped in fur. Trappers and traders, sometimes independent, sometimes serving corporate interests, opened the way for more stable migrations and served national purposes by penetrating virtually every corner of half a continent. A line drawn on a modern map connecting St. Louis, Santa Fe, San Diego, Astoria, Sitka, and Winnipeg suggests the sweep of their activities; and the short half century of their heyday (roughly 1787 to 1845) indicates how little time they wasted in their efforts. In a broad sense their achievement was a cooperative one—Frenchmen, Spaniards, Scots, English, Iroquois, and Americans engaged in a kind of unconscious collaboration in probing and exploiting a vast and unknown wilderness. Viewed more narrowly, the prosecution of the continental fur trade was viciously competitive; and only under conditions of monopoly, such as those of the Hudson's Bay Company and the American Fur Company, did the trade enjoy genuine stability.

With the elimination of France from North America in 1763, the way apparently was cleared (save for the fading force of Spain west of the Mississippi) for the British through the Hudson's Bay Company to engross the trade of a continent. However, in the next half century the "Honourable Company" faced challenges from two directions: from Canadians, operating out of Montreal; and from Americans, usually using St. Louis as their headquarters.

The Northwest Company, a competitor of the Hudson's Bay, grew out of a loose combination of Montreal traders—most of them Scotch, some of them colonial New Englanders—who learned the advantages of consolidation the hard way, through costly rivalry among themselves. After several starts they formed the Northwest Company, employing French Canadian and Iroquois *voyageurs* and pressing the search for furs ever farther to the west from their mid-continent warehouse at Fort William on Lake Superior. The Nor'westers were a colorful, aggressive breed who in their more romantic moods thought of themselves as "Lords of the Lakes and Forests." Challenging the Hudson's Bay Company's monopoly, the Nor'westers reached the interior through the southern waterways of the St. Lawrence and the Ottawa to the Great Lakes and thence over Rainy Lake passage to the Saskatchewan. Not content with contesting the Hudson's Bay Company on their own preserves, energetic Nor'westers like Alexander MacKenzie, David Thompson, and Simon Fraser surmounted the Continental Divide to reach the Pacific, discover the headwaters of the Columbia, and plant posts in the Oregon country; thereby they not only augmented their take in the Indian trade but reinforced British claims to the Pacific Northwest. After fifteen years of bitter trade war between the two companies—a war involving deceit, price slashing, irresponsible debauching of the Indians with liquor, and murder—parliamentary pressure forced a fusion of the rival concerns in 1821. Although the Northwest Company lost its identity in the merger, it gained from the older company the privilege and power of a long-standing monopoly and contributed in return new vigor, experienced personnel, and substantial physical holdings.

Meanwhile, the American threat to the British, incipient in the discovery of the mouth of the Columbia by Captain Robert Gray in 1792 and in the Lewis and Clark expedition of 1804–1806, became explicit when Manuel Lisa's Missouri Fur Company was launched from St. Louis in 1808 and when members of the Pacific Fur Company, an arm of Astor's American Fur Company, built the trading post of Astoria in 1811. Despite setbacks to both Lisa and Astor during the War of 1812, other American ventures in the fur trade sprang up in the 1820s to harass the British—notably, and in succession, the William H. Ashley–Andrew Henry partnership, the Smith-Jackson-Sublette trio, and the Rocky Mountain Fur Company. These outfits made fat profits and flourished between 1823 and 1833, the high-water mark of the fur trade in the Rockies. By 1835 the American Fur Company had won dominance in the trade; but for a variety of reasons —including depletion of fur-bearing animals; the shift in fashion from the beaver to the silk hat; and the defining of the Oregon Trail, which soon would permit the substitution of a farming for a fur frontier—the fur business was declining. The withdrawal of the Hudson's Bay Company from Fort Vancouver on the Columbia to Vancouver Island in 1845 simply marked in definitive fashion the end of an era.

The responses of the British and the Americans to the challenges on the fur frontier were different, but each embodied both the influence of tradition and the resort to innovation. Certainly the Hudson's Bay Company and to a lesser extent the Northwest Company were conservative concerns with a feudalistic flavor. They relied upon personal loyalty among employees and the Old World sense of class and caste to hold their agencies together in the wilderness. Three grades of tea issued according to status served as a simple but revealing reminder of class structure. On the other hand, under Sir George Simpson, the reorganized Hudson's Bay Company demonstrated genuine flexibility in developing the roving tactics of the former Northwest Company into the wide-ranging fur brigades under men like Donald McKenzie, Peter Skene Ogden, and John Work. Such brigades were effective both in swelling the take of peltries and in meeting the freer, more individualistic Americans on their own terms. The outstanding innovation contributed by the Americans to the fur trade was the system of the rendezvous, in which individuals or small parties stayed in the field most of the season and gathered once a year to exchange their catch for money, liquor, and supplies.

The Far Western fur trade produced a number of distinctive types. There were the reckless, gay, incredibly hardy *voyageurs,* who literally sang their way over rivers and lakes and agonizing portages. There were educated partners like Alexander MacKenzie, whose zest for exploration and advanced vision made him as much an instrument of British power and imperialism as a shrewd Scotch businessman. There was the devout, tough, conscientious Peter Skene Ogden, who could match the stamina and trail record of the best of the American trappers. There was the humane and fatherly despot John McLoughlin, maintaining a pocket of British culture and sophistication at Fort Vancouver. Finally, there was the free trapper or mountain man—in Paul Horgan's phrase, "an American original as hard as the hardest thing that could happen to him."

The story, then, of the Far Western fur trade is complex and colorful; it exhibits characteristics of tight control, shrewd management, and enlightened policy, as well as unrestrained individualism, cruel competition, rampage, and prodigious waste of resources, both human and natural. Out of the experience came profits, notable advances in understanding the physical dimensions of half a continent, and an heroic tradition.

Alexander Ross

Alexander Ross (1783–1856) entered the fur trade in 1810 as a clerk in John Jacob Astor's Pacific Fur Company and played a part in the founding of Astoria. In 1813, at the time of the forced sale of that post to the Northwest Company, Ross joined the Canadian concern and served as Chief Trader at Ft. Nez Percé (Walla Walla) until the amalgamation of the Northwest Company with the Hudson's Bay Company in 1821. In the fragment that follows, Ross comments authoritatively on the activities at an interior trading post. Further, his allusion to the company's over-all operations and his description of the privileged place of the bourgeois or partner underscore the influence of habit and tradition on the British fur frontier.

*Fur Hunters of the Far West**

A council sits annually at headquarters, which regulates all the important matters of the Company for the current year; but no person of less dignity than a bourgeois or proprietor is admitted to a seat, except by special invitation. The council of this year [1815] was strengthened by the arrival of three new functionaries from the east side of the mountains, yet nothing new transpired. The members sat for four days (nearly double the usual time), but no new channel was opened for extending the trade, nor was there the least deviation from the old and contemned system of their predecessors. The decision of the council was that there existed no new field that could be opened to advantage; consequently every one was again appointed to his old post, and I, of course, to mine.

During the sittings there is always a strong manifestation of anxiety out of doors, each one being desirous to know his appointment for the year; for it not unfrequently happens, that officers are changed without much ceremony, particularly if there be any individual who is not easily managed. And for an obnoxious individual to be removed to the most remote corner

---

* From Alexander Ross, *The Fur Hunters of the Far West: A Narrative of Adventures in the Oregon and Rocky Mountains* (London: Smith, Elder and Co., 1855), I, 55–304 *passim*.

of the country this year, and to some other equally remote next, by way of taming him is not at all uncommon.

But this part of their policy is not confined to the subordinates, it reaches even to the bourgeois, who is not infrequently admonished, by the example of others, that he stands on the brink of a precipice; for, if too refractory in the council, he is sure to get his appointment at such a distance, and under such circumstances, as to exclude most effectually his attending the meetings for some length of time. This is the course generally adopted to get rid of an importunate and troublesome member whether of high or low rank in the service; or to remove such as the Company are not disposed to, or cannot conveniently, provide for.

The council being over, the business of the year settled, and the annual ship arrived, the different parties destined for the interior and east side of the mountains took their departure from Fort George on the 25th of June. . . .

It is not easy to overcome the force of habit and no set of men could be more wedded to customs than the great nabobs of the fur trade. And I might here by way of confirming the remark, just point out one instance among many. The description of craft used on the Columbia by the Astor Company consisted of split or sawed cedarboats, strong, light, and durable, and in every possible way safer and better adapted to rough water than the birch-rind canoes in general use on the east side of the mountains. They carried a cargo or burden of about 3000 lbs. weight, and yet, nimbly handled, were easily carried across portages. A great partiality existed in favour of the good old bark canoes of northern reputation; they being of prettier form, and, withal, the kind of vessel of customary conveyance used by north-westers; and that itself was no small recommendation. Therefore, the country was ransacked for prime birch bark more frequently than for prime furs, and to guard against a failure in this fanciful article, a stock of it was shipped at Montreal for London, and from thence conveyed round Cape Horn for their establishment at Fort George, in case that none of equal quality could be found on the waters of the Pacific. . . .

. . . we shall [now] give an account of how trapping with a large party is generally carried on among Indians.

A safe and secure spot near wood and water is first selected for the camp. Here the chief of the party and property resides. It is often exposed to danger, or sudden attack in the absence of the trappers, and requires a vigilant eye to guard against the lurking savages. The camp is called head quarters. From hence all the trappers, some on foot, some on horseback according to the distance they have to go, start every morning in small parties in all directions, ranging the distance of some twenty miles around. Six traps is the allowance of each hunter, but to guard against wear and tear the complement is more frequently ten. These he sets every night and

visits again in the morning sometimes oftener; according to the distance
or other circumstances. The beaver taken in the traps are always conveyed
to the camp, skinned, stretched, dried, folded up with the hair inside, laid
by, and the flesh used for food. No sooner therefore has a hunter visited
his traps, set them again, and looked out for some other place than he
returns to the camp, to feast and enjoy the pleasures of an idle day.

There is however much anxiety and danger in going through the ordinary routine of a trapper's duty! For the enemy generally is lurking about
among the rocks and hiding places watching an opportunity, the hunter has
to keep a constant lookout. And the gun is often in one hand, while the
trap is in the other; but when several are together, which is often the case
in suspicious places, one half set the traps, and the other half keep guard
over them. Yet notwithstanding all the precautions some of them fall
victims to Indian treachery.

The camp remains stationary while two-thirds of the trappers find
beaver in the vicinity, but whenever the beaver gets scarce, the camp is
removed to some more favourable spot; in this manner the party keeps
moving from place to place during the whole season of hunting. Whenever
serious danger is apprehended, all the trappers make for the camp. Were
we however to calculate according to numbers, the prospects from such an
expedition would be truly dazzling, say twenty-five men with each six traps,
to be successfully employed during five months, that is, two in the spring,
and three in the fall, equal to 131 working days, the result would be 58,950
beaver! Practically however the case is very different. The apprehension of
danger at all times is so great that three-fourths of their time is lost in the
necessary steps taken for their own safety! There is also another serious
drawback unavoidably accompanying every large party. The beaver is a
timid animal, the least noise therefore made about its haunt will keep it
from coming out for nights together; and noise is unavoidable where the
party is large. But when the party is small, the hunter has a chance of being
more or less successful. Indeed were the nature of the ground such as to
admit of the trappers moving about in safety at all times, and alone, six
men with each six traps would, in the same space of time and at the same
rate, kill as many beavers, say 4716, as the whole twenty-five could be expected to do! and yet the evil is without a remedy. For no small party can
exist in these parts. Hence the reason why beaver are so numerous.

The fur trade has a mixture of the mercantile and the military. The
clerks have charge of trading posts, according to their merits and abilities,
some upon a very considerable scale. They are first taught to obey, afterwards they learn to command. At all times much is expected of them. It
sometimes happens to be long before they receive charge of a first-rate
establishment; but when the general posture of affairs is propitious to their
employers, it is not very often that their laudable prospects are disappointed.

They at length arrive at the long wished goal of partners, and are entitled to a vote in all weighty decisions, and are henceforth styled Esquires.

The Bourgeois lives in comfort. He rambles at his pleasure, enjoys the merry dance or the pastime of some pleasing game. His morning ride, his fishing rod. His gun and his dog, or a jaunt of pleasure to the environs in his gay canoe. In short, no desires remain unfulfilled. He is the greatest man in the land. The buildings belonging to the Company are both neat and commodious, each class is provided with separate abodes. The apartments are appropriately divided into bedrooms, ante-chambers and closets. Here is seen the counting room, the mess room, the kitchen and pantry, the cellars, and Indian Hall and there are handsome galleries. Nor can we pass over in silence one chief object of attraction. Even in this barbarous country, woman claims and enjoys her due share of attention and regard. Her presence brightens the gloom of the solitary post, her smiles add a new charm to the pleasures of the wilderness. Nor are the ladies deficient in the accomplishments that procure admiration. Although descended from aboriginal mothers, many of the females at the different establishments throughout the Indian countries are as fair as the generality of European ladies, the mixture of blood being so many degrees removed from the savage as hardly to leave any trace; while at the same time their delicacy of form, their light yet nimble movements, and the penetrating expression of the "bright black eye" combine to render them objects of no ordinary interest. They have also made considerable progress in refinement, and with their natural acuteness and singular talent for imitation, they soon acquire all the ease and gracefulness of polished life. On holidays the dresses are as gay as in polished countries and on these occasions the gentleman puts on the beaver hat and the ladies make fine show of silks and satins, and even jewelry is not wanting. It is not surprising therefore that the roving North-Wester, after so many rural enjoyments under residence of twenty years, should feel more real happiness in these scenes than he can in any other country.

Hudson's Bay Company

The Hudson's Bay Company, chartered by the English Crown in 1670, was at once a successful commercial enterprise and a powerful arm of British imperialism. The following extracts from the company's correspondence during the critical year of the merger with the Northwest Company indicate that policy decisions were the product of instructions from the Gover-

nor and Committee in London, as implemented and often modified by Governor George Simpson and the Council in Canada. Here is big business, under the direction of shrewd and sophisticated executives, manifesting the concern with broad, long-range policy and the meticulous attention to detail that made Hudson's Bay Company the most formidable and durable agency of the fur trade in North America.

Executive Planning*

Hudsons Bay House
London *27th February* 1822

George Simpson Esqr.
Sir

It is our intention to send next autumn a small ship with provisions for the Columbia for Winter 1823/24 and any articles of trading goods which ... upon a careful examination of the Inventories and Invoices may ... be necessary ; and to bring the returns of furs direct to this Market.

Should the result of all your enquiries be unfavourable to the plan of continuing the trade of Columbia it will be proper to consider, whether it will be better to continue the trading establishments there, until the goods are nearly all expended, or to transport those remaining after the business of the Winter 1823/24 is finished to New Caledonia.

The Russians are endeavouring to set up claims to the North West Coast of America as low as Latitude 51, and we think it desirable to extend our trading posts as far to the West and North from Frazer's River in Caledonia, as may be practicable, if there appears any reasonable prospect of doing so profitably. It is probable that the British Government would support us in the possession of the Country, which may be occupied by trading posts, and it is desirable to keep the Russians at a distance. . . .

In considering the general arrangements respecting wages it appears very desirable not to adopt the system of equipments either for the Clerks or Servants (with the exception of the Apprentices) which was pursued by the late North West Company but which was only very partially and occasionally adopted by the Company. We think it is a much better plan to fix a fair scale of wages and to allow every man to dispose of his money in the way most agreeable to himself ; fixing at the same time a moderate price

---

* From R. Harvey Fleming, ed., *Minutes of Council, Northern Department of Rupert Land, 1821–31* (Toronto: The Champlain Society, 1940), pp. 301–312, 342–357 *passim*. Published by permission of the Hudson's Bay Record Society.

on all articles except spirits which ought to be kept at rather a high price and only limited quantities to be sold to each individual.

We are confident, that it will be found cheaper and safer to use boats in preference to Canoes and that it will be practicable to do so in every part of the Country except to New Caledonia and McKenzies River. And as Orkney men are better adapted for the conducting of boats than Canadians and are generally more careful servants we recommend that all the Canadians, whose Contracts expire this year should be discharged, with the exception of such useful men as may be in debt to the Concern, or whom it may be desirable from some particular circumstance to retain in the service. A sufficient number of men to transport the articles to be sent to Montreal, and which we calculate will require 18 Canoes and 108 men ought to be sent down accordingly—of the remainder, such as desire it, or have families may be sent to Red River. And we recommend, that all the Orkney Men, who may be good useful servants and willing to renew their Contracts on the new scale of wages should be retained in the Service; those who are unfit or unwilling to engage on these terms may be discharged and either sent to Europe or to Red River as they may themselves be disposed.

Light Canoes from the interior to the Depots are a great expence and under the present circumstances have become almost entirely unnecessary. It is only from the most distant posts that it will be proper to incur this expence, vizt. one Canoe from the Columbia; and the accounts and intelligence from McKenzies River, and New Caledonia, being forwarded to Athabasca, one Canoe will bring the requisite information from these three Departments, and one Gentleman in each Canoe will be sufficient to take care of the Dispatches. In all other cases it ought to be considered part of the duty of the Chief Factors, Chief Traders and Clerks, to accompany their Brigades of Boats or Canoes both in coming out with the furs, and in going in with the goods, as their presence & attention will be the means of the people taking more care of the property and provisions and making more dispatch in the journey.

We think it will be proper to prevent the Indians from desponding, under the idea that they will suffer from the total absence of competition among the traders, to amend the standard of trade, & to make it more favorable to them by 20 or 25 per cent on the present rate. At the same time the system of presents to Indians should be abandoned, except under very special circumstances; this with the advantages to be gained by economical arrangements in regard to the number of men, and the almost entire saving of spirits will make the trade profitable, notwithstanding the increased price paid to the Indians. The best mode of encouraging the Indians to be industrious in hunting is to give them a liberal price for their furs and put an end to those presents and treats, which from opposition in the trade came to be given to them, whether they brought a good hunt and paid their debts or no. It will also be unnecessary, to give such large credits to Indians as hitherto ; but these changes must be made with discretion.

In the course of 2 or 3 years at farthest we think the use of spirits among the Indians of all the best fur countries may be entirely given up, and that the quantities given to them may safely be reduced immediately to 1/3d. In the provision Countries and among the Indians of the Plains more caution will be necessary on this Subject but even there we are confident the quantity may be reduced one half, and in the course of a few years still lower.

It is necessary also that the Councils furnish us with the most accurate Estimates that circumstances enable them to make, of the numbers of the Indians, stating families and number of individuals, and distinguishing tribes and districts of Country as far as may be practicable.

It will be proper for the Councils to take the necessary measures to discourage the Indians from hunting the Beaver & valuable fur animals, in summer and when out of Season, also to discourage the killing of cub beaver. The use of beaver traps should also be prevented.

Castorum produces a better price here than at Montreal, therefore the whole ought to be sent to this market.

We highly approve of the plan of sending a Hunting Expedition to the Head Waters of the Missouri—connected with the trade of the South branch of the Shaskatchuian, (or Bow River) which has been proposed ;— The state of the country at the present moment, when so many hands (of all classes,) will be unemployed appears peculiarly favorable for engaging in such an undertaking—and for carrying the object into full effect. The adoption of it therefore *for the ensuing Season* is recommended. We inclose a project for this object for the consideration of the Council and would recommend the number of hunters to be increased if it can be done con-veniently, as the more numerous the party is made, the safer and probably the more profitable the Expedition will prove.

We are your affectionate friends

J. B[erens]
J. H. P[elly]
T. L[angley]
B. H[arrison]
A. C[olvile]
T. P[itt]
N. G[arry]

George Simpson

Sir George Simpson (1792–1860) was the administrator of Hudson's Bay Company's territory from 1821 to 1856. These excerpts from his account of a tour of inspection from Hudson's Bay to the Pacific hint at the scope of the company's holdings in the Far West. More important for purposes of this section are Simpson's contemptuous comments on American methods in the fur trade and his caustic appraisal of the American trapper.

Letters to Hudson's Bay Company, London*

Fort Vancouver, *1st March,* 1829

Honble. Sirs

... I shall now take the liberty of requesting your Honors attention, to the business of the Snake Country, which for a length of time has attracted the jealous Eye of the United States Government, and called forth the loud complaints of many of the Citizens against us. The boundaries of this Country, are by us considered, the Rocky Mountains on the East, and a chain of mountains running nearly parallel with the Coast on the West: on the North, the 46th parallel of Latitude from the Rocky Mountains 'till it strikes the South branch of the Columbia near its junction with the Main Stream, and on the South, the Waters of the Rio Colorado. And the operations of its Expeditions, may be considered as extending as far in a Southerly & Westerly direction as Beaver can be found. The Southern part of that Country, is occupied by several Tribes of little note; and in regard to the Territorial rights of the Mexican Republic, we follow the example of the Spanish functionaries on the Coast, and our opponents from the United States, by making no enquiries about them altho' the License of the latter, authorises them to hunt down to

---

* From E. E. Rich, ed., *Part of Dispatch from George Simpson Esq., Governor of Rupert's Land, to the Governor and Committee of the Hudson's Bay Company, London, March 1, 1829. Continued and Completed March 24 and June 5, 1829* (Toronto: The Champlain Society, 1947), pp. 3–67 *passim.*

Latitude 38. Until the last three or four Years, we have merely been hunting on the Eastern and Northern borders of this Country, but of late we have pushed as far South as Latitude 42, and we have now an Expedition on its way to hunting Grounds in the neighbourhood of St. Francisco, in about Lat. 38. Our largest Expedition was that of 1824, consisting of 58 men, of whom, 38 deserted to the Americans or otherwise left us; its profits amounted to £3700; In 1825 an other Expedition of 38 men was fitted out, the profits of which amounted to £3000. In 1826 a party of 30 men was outfitted, whose hunts yielded a profit of about £2000. In 1827 another party of 30 was outfitted, the profits on whose hunts amounted to £2500, and in 1828 two parties were fitted out, the one, of 32 Men, proceeding by the Nez Percés Country to hunt in the heart of the Snake Country; and the other, of 30 men, proceeding by the coast, to hunt on the banks of the Buona Ventura, or wherever they can find Beaver on the West of the Rocky Mountains.

It may now be proper, to draw your Honors attention to the operations of our opponents in that quarter. There was an American party in the Snake Country as long ago as 1809 or 1810, who established themselves at a place called (after their Leader) Henrys Forks; but who only remained one Season, finding themselves in danger of being cut off by War parties. Their next visit, was in 1824, when Genl. (a Militia Genl.) Ashley of St. Louis, (who notwithstanding his dignified title has had a number of ups and down in life having been a Farmer, a Shopkeeper, a Miner and latterly an Indian Trader) fitted out a large party of Trappers & Servants. [Jedediah] Smith the conductor of one of his parties, joined our Expedition in the Autumn of 1824, and passed part of the following Winter at the Flat Head Post, taking the benefit of Mr. Ogden's protection from thence to the Snake country where they parted, and immediately afterwards in return for our hospitality and protection, Gardner the leader of an other of Ashleys detachments, on falling in with Mr. Ogden, laid his plans to decoy our Trappers and break up our Expedition, in which he succeeded. Ashley's returns that year amounted to between 5 & 6000 Beaver, a great part of which however was taken out of what is called the "Blackfeet Country," about the head Waters of the Missouri. In 1824/26 Ashleys part was made up by our Deserters, and a reenforcement from St. Louis, to about 100 Men, who hunted in small parties all over the Snake Country, and about the Eastern skirts of the Mountains, and collected about the same quantity of Beaver; when he retired from the business with a fortune, which in Dollers sounded large in the United States, and resumed his Shopkeeping concerns in St. Louis: but the fortune in question, was entirely nominal as the profits arising from the two prosperous years on the West side barely covered the losses sustained during the two preceding years on the East side the Mountains; the fact therefore is, that Ashley gained merely a little eclat by his trapping speculations, notwithstanding all the bombast that appeared in the American News papers of 1824, 1825 & 1826 in regard to their "enterprizing Countryman." The Trapping business was then taken up, by three of "the Genl." late conducters; men who had formerly been practical Trappers, but who all at once promoted themselves to the Travelling title of Captains, while their mercantile operations were conducted under the firm of Smith Jackson & Siblit.* Their first year was prosperous having collected from 5 to 6000 Beaver; but since then, they have been very unfortunate. With regard to Jackson & Siblit, we learn that they had several parties scattered about the Snake Country some of whom Mr. Ogden saw, but they complained of the poverty of the Country, had lost the greater part of their Horses without which they could do little good, and one of their parties consisting of Tullock and Eleven Men we last Autumn understood had been cut off by the Blackfeet. Jackson, accompanied by a Clerk Fitzpatrick, and a Major Pilcher with a Clerk Gardner & 40 Trappers, was the band alluded to as having visited the Flat head Post last Winter; they had very few Skins, and of those few, about half fell into our hands in exchange for some necessary supplies. Pilcher, who made his first appearance on this side the Mountains last Summer, is the head of a Trading association called the "Missouri Fur Coy." of St. Louis, which failed in the year 1825 and 'tis probable the same fate awaits his present concern as it must have been in a desperate state indeed, when the head thereof, could not find better employment for himself and followers than watching the Flat Head Camp. "The Major," and Smith Jackson & Siblit, are in hot opposition to each other, and both court our protection and countenance, while we contrive to profit by their strife....

The American Trapping Expeditions are never sufficiently well organised to hold together for any length of time: the heads of the concern or Outfitters, are merely adventurers who have nothing to lose, and are ever on the watch to take some petty advantage of their followers, who being aware of this, have no respect for, and are always ready to cheat them in their turn. The conductors or Leaders of parties, are men who have been common Trappers, and therefore possess no influence: and the Trappers themselves are generally speaking, people of the worst character, runaways from Jails, and outcasts from Society, who take all their bad qualities along with them: this "motley crew" acknowledge no master, will conform to no rules or regulations, and are never on their guard, so that they are frequently cut off and their camps plundered. When

---

* Jedediah Smith, David Jackson, and William Sublette, American mountain men and founders of the Rocky Mountain Fur Company.

they fall in with Friendly Indians, their conduct is so indiscreet that they scarcely ever fail to make Enemies of them, and it is a well known fact, that War parties frequently pass our Camps without offering the least annoyance; yet will haunt and watch an American Camp, for Days and Weeks, until a favorable opportunity occurs to make an attack. We might repeatedly have broken up their parties, but the spirit of insubordination which characterises those fellows, is particularly infectious in the plains, we therefore allow as little intercourse as possible between them and our people, and in order to guard against the baneful influence of bad example, do not encourage desertion and have not at present above 10 or 12 of their people in our Service.

We learn from our American visitant Smith, that the flattering reports which reached St. Louis of the Wilhamot Country, as a field for Agricultural speculation, had induced many people in the States to direct their attention to that quarter; but he has on his present journey, discovered difficulties which never occurred to their minds, and which are likely to deter his Countrymen from attempting that enterprize. In the American Charts this River, (the Wilhamot or Moltnomah) is laid down, as taking its rise in the Rocky Mountains, (indeed Mr. Rush in his official correspondence with President Adams on the subject of a boundary line distinctly says so) and the opinion was, that it would merely be necessary for Settlers with their Horses, Cattle, Agricultural implements &c. &c. to get (by the main communication from St. Louis to Sta. Fee) to the height of Land in about Lat. 38, there to embark on large Rafts & Batteaux and glide down current about 800 or 1000 Miles at their ease to this "land of Promise." But it now turns out, that the Sources of the Wilhamot are not 150 Miles distant from Fort Vancouver, in Mountains which even Hunters cannot attempt to pass, beyond which, is a Sandy desert of about 200 miles, likewise impassable, and from thence a rugged barren country of great extent, without Animals, where Smith and his party were nearly starved to Death. And the other route by Louis's River, Settlers could never think of attempting. So that I am of opinion, we have little to apprehend from Settlers in this quarter, and from Indian Traders nothing; as none, except large capitalists could attempt it, and the attempt would cost a heavy Sum of Money, of which they could never recover much. This they are well aware of, therefore as regards formidable opposition, I feel perfectly at ease unless the all grasping policy of the American Government, should induce it, to embark some of its National Wealth, in furtherence of the object.

Kenneth Wiggins Porter

The American counterpart to the Hudson's Bay Company was John Jacob Astor's American Fur Company. The following selection, from Kenneth W. Porter's definitive biography of Astor, provides some understanding of the scope, methods, and achievements of this early example of big business in the American West.

*The American Fur Company**

The West was now, as it had been almost from the first establishment of the Western Department [of the American Fur Company], by far the most active front. In the Northern Department, the region of the Great Lakes and Upper Mississippi, the American Fur Company already possessed a practical monopoly. According to George Boyd, the Indian agent at Mackinac, the headquarters of the Northern Department, "the Amount of furs & peltries brought yearly to this Island, are supposed to be worth from 250 to 300,000 dollars—nineteen twentieths of the same being for and on account of the American Fur Co.—" . . .

The situation in the Western Department, however, was altogether different. In 1822, the very year in which the American Fur Company established western headquarters at St. Louis, the Rocky Mountain Fur Company was founded by William H. Ashley and Andrew Henry for the purpose of exploiting the virgin beaver-territory of that great area. This company was so successful that within five years Ashley, its founder, was able to sell out to his ablest lieutenants and retire on a fortune to take up politics. The American Fur Company, through its new partners, Bernard Pratte & Co., had been concerned in the proportion of one-half in Ashley's expedition of 1827, which brought in net profits of seventy per cent. It was, then, the very formidable opposition of the new Rocky Mountain Fur Company partners, Jedediah S. Smith, David E. Jackson, and William L. Sublette, that the Western Department and especially McKenzie's Upper Missouri Outfit, would be forced to meet.

McKenzie, remembering the profits of the last Ashley expedition, was

* From Kenneth Wiggins Porter, *John Jacob Astor, Business Man* (2 vols.; Cambridge, Mass.: Harvard University Press, 1931), II, 765–770. Copyright, 1931, by The President and Fellows of Harvard College. Renewal 1959 by Kenneth Wiggins Porter.

quite ready to inaugurate an immediate campaign against his rivals of the Rocky Mountains, but Pierre Chouteau persuaded him to postpone such a move until more thorough preparations had been made. Accordingly, 1828 was spent in establishing "a permanent post at the mouth of the Yellowstone, which would afford a safe and convenient base for the operations of the upper country." In the fall of that year McKenzie sent Etienne Provost, a former member of the Rocky Mountain Fur Company, to look up the free trappers and bring them to the new post, Fort Floyd, and in the next spring dispatched Henry Vanderburgh with goods to a *rendezvous* with these trappers after the spring hunt of 1829.

The history of the Western Department's Upper Missouri Outfit during its second term, and especially of that side of its business which pertains to the Rocky Mountain fur trade, is by no means pleasant reading. True, McKenzie distinguished himself by the utmost daring and efficiency in forming a connection in 1831 with the hitherto hostile Blackfeet, bringing about a treaty in the same year between them and the Assiniboines, and also establishing a post in the Blackfeet country at the junction of the Marias River with the Yellowstone. In 1832 he established a post among the Crows on the Yellowstone near the mouth of the Bighorn, which was appropriately christened Fort Cass, after the Company's most consistent ally in governmental circles, then occupying the influential position of secretary of War. McKenzie was also responsible in 1831 for putting a steamboat, the *Yellowstone,* on the Missouri, to make the journey between St. Louis and Fort Union (the successor of Fort Floyd) at the mouth of the Yellowstone. The voyage was first completed in June, 1832, and did much to turn the Indians along the Canadian border from the Hudson's Bay Company to its great American rival. Another ingenious contrivance to win over the Indians on the border from British influence was the striking off of medals . . . bearing the likeness of John Jacob Astor, for distribution to the chiefs, in imitation of the British custom of distributing medals with the image of the reigning monarch! This was done with the consent of the always complaisant Lewis Cass, then, as we have noted, secretary of War.

There was, of course, nothing objectionable in these broad strokes of the American Fur Company, but both the Company's agents and their rivals, when once in the Indian country, were guilty of activities some of which would doubtless have horrified the Astors, in the comparatively civilized surroundings of New York or of France, whither John Jacob had returned in the summer of 1832. The Rocky Mountain fur trade was carried on much more by parties of white trappers who brought their returns to an annual *rendezvous,* where they were met by representatives of the various companies with supplies of goods, than by outfits of traders, clerks, and *voyageurs* who bartered for furs secured by the Indians. Consequently, it was the policy of the American Fur Company's employees, among whom Vanderburgh, Drips, and Fontenelle were the most conspicuous, to follow the Rocky Mountain Company partners, who now, since August 4, 1830, were Thomas Fitzpatrick, Milton G. Sublette, Henry Fraeb, Jean Baptiste Gervais, and James Bridger, into the Rocky Mountain region in an attempt to learn where the best beaver country was. Finally, in 1832, Fitzpatrick and Bridger deliberately led Vanderburgh and Drips into the heart of the Blackfeet country until Vanderburgh was attacked and killed, while Bridger himself was wounded before he could escape from the dangerous region into which he had lured his rivals. In the next year the American Fur Company retaliated by stirring up the Crows to rob Fitzpatrick, later buying his peltries, marked plainly with the initials of his Company, from the guilty parties. In 1834 the Rocky Mountain Fur Company was dissolved. But their rivals in the American Fur Company had not profited by the mountain trade, having always been late at the annual *rendezvous,* and the trade in the mountains had been continued largely to maintain the Company's prestige among the Indians and the free trappers. Then, too, as Chouteau wrote Astor in the spring of 1833, "I am convinced that these expeditions have been an annual loss. But we have hoped for improvement from year to year. *Generally the loss falls upon the traders."* The italics are mine.

Meanwhile upon the Upper Missouri, McKenzie, who, owing to his distance from the legal code of civilization, was always the most unscrupulous of the Company's agents, had been throttling opposition in his usual ruthless style. Among his exploits was the arrest by his agents of an ex-employee of the Company, one Narcisse Leclerc, for taking liquor into the Indian country, as absolutely forbidden by an act of July 9, 1832. As Leclerc had received permission from the superintendent of Indian Affairs at St. Louis to take the liquor with him up the Missouri, owing to the fact that the act of July 9, 1832, had not yet been officially promulgated, this arrest was utterly without legal sanction. Leclerc promptly instituted criminal proceedings against the responsible agent, J. P. Cabanné, and likewise sued the Company, recovering $9,200, but the Upper Missouri Outfit probably profited much more than this amount by being freed from competition with a trader possessing liquor.

A much more formidable opposition was offered by the firm of Sublette & Campbell, formed on December 20, 1832, and backed by General Ashley, then a member of Congress. This company intended to oppose the American Fur Company at all points on the Upper Missouri. But by dint of paying four times the usual price for furs McKenzie soon weakened the opposition, and would probably have extinguished it entirely had not his superiors at St. Louis become frightened and bought out their rivals early in 1834, on condition that Sublette & Campbell should retire for one year from the Upper Missouri, while the American Fur Company should similarly withdraw from the mountain trade. It may be that the St. Louis house was partly influenced by the fact that the Company was just then in very bad odor at Washington, owing to Fitzpatrick's robbery, Leclerc's illegal arrest, and finally, in 1833, McKenzie's scheme of dodging the liquor law by *distilling whiskey in the Indian country,* thus, as he professed to believe, avoiding the penalty attached to "bringing" liquor into the Indian country. This device was, of course, discovered, and it was only by some strenuous pleading with the friendly secretary of War, Lewis Cass, that the Company avoided being barred from the trade. But had such a result actually taken place, it would not have greatly affected Astor, for in 1833 he had definitely decided to withdraw from the fur trade, and took the final step in the following year.

Osborne Russell

Far-ranging forays under Hudson's Bay Company fur brigades were fundamental to the British way of conducting the trapping business in the Far West. These roving bands returned with their "take" to established company outposts in the Pacific Northwest. The Americans devised the rendezvous system, whereby trading goods were brought to the mountains and a kind of open-air warehouse was temporarily established. Here free trappers, "company men," Mexicans from Taos, French-Canadian fugitives from the Hudson's Bay Company, and Indians converged, usually in late June or early July, to meet the caravan of trading goods from St. Louis. These "Rocky Mountain fairs" made entrepreneurs like William Henry Ashley wealthy, with gross profits mounting as high as 2,000 per cent; at the same time, they separated the trapper from his total catch in furs, since what might be left him after he had bought supplies from the trader (powder, traps, food, tobacco, and "foofaraw") was commonly squandered in an extended debauch of gambling, drinking, and sexual excess with compliant Indian women. Although the mountain man was absolutely dependent on the rendezvous as a market for his furs, the fact that the supplies came to him in a sense preserved his independence by making it unnecessary for him to return to civilized society. Curiously, even though the rendezvous was the dominant institution of the mountain trade, extended and detailed first-hand accounts of the event are hard to find. Most of them—as in this selection by Osborne Russell (1814–1892), one of the more literate mountain men—make a start at description but are diverted by a dramatic incident that prevents the narrator from dealing fully with the more routine features of the wilderness fair.

Rendezvous at Green River*

Here [in the valley of the Green River, near the mouth of Horse Creek] we found the hunting parties all assembled waiting for the arrival of supplies from the States. Here presented what might be termed a mixed multitude. The whites were chiefly Americans and Canadian French, with some Dutch, Scotch, Irish, English, half-breed and fullblood Indians of nearly every tribe in the Rocky Mountains. Some were gambling at cards, some playing the Indian game of "hand" and others horse racing, while here and there could be seen small groups collected under shady trees relating the events of the past year, all in good spirits and health, for sickness is a stranger seldom met with in these regions. Sheep, elk, deer, buffalo and bear skins mostly supply the mountaineers with clothing, lodges and bedding, while the meat of the same animals supply them with food. They have not the misfortune to get any of the luxuries from the civilized world but once a year, and then in such small quantities that they last but a few days.

We had not remained in this quiet manner long before something new arose for our amusement. The Bannock Indians had for several years lived with the whites on terms partly hostile, frequently stealing horses and traps, and in one instance killed two white trappers. They had taken some horses and traps from a party of French trappers who were hunting Bear River in April previous, and they were now impudent enough to come with the village of sixty lodges and encamp within three miles of us in order to trade with the whites as usual, still having the stolen property in their possession and refusing to give it up. On the 15th of June [1837] four or five whites and two Nez Percé Indians went to their village and took the stolen horses (whilst the men were out hunting buffalo) and returned with them to our camp. About three o'clock p.m. of the same day thirty Bannocks came riding at full gallop up to the camp, armed with their war weapons. They rode into the midst and demanded the horses

---

* From Osborne Russell, *Journal of a Trapper or Nine Years in the Rocky Mountains, 1834–1843* (Boise, Idaho: Syms-York Company, Inc., 1921), pp. 62–64.

which the Nez Percés had taken saying they did not wish to fight with the whites. But the Nez Percés, who were only six in number, gave the horses to the whites for protection, which we were bound to give, as they were numbered among our trappers and far from their own tribe. Some of the Bannocks, on seeing this, started to leave the camp. One of them as he passed me observed that he did not come to fight the whites; but another, a fierce looking savage, who still stopped behind, called out to the others, saying, "We came to get our horses or blood and let us do it." I was standing near the speaker and understood what he said. I immediately gave the whites warning to be in readiness for an attack. Nearly all the men in camp were under arms. Mr. Bridger was holding one of the stolen horses by the bridle when one of the Bannocks rushed through the crowd, seized the bridle and attempted to drag it from Mr. Bridger by force, without heeding the cocked rifles that surrounded him any more than if they had been so many reeds in the hands of children. He was a brave Indian, but his bravery proved fatal to himself, for the moment he seized the bridle two rifle balls whistled through his body. The others wheeled to run, but twelve of them were shot from their horses before they were out of reach of rifle. We then mounted horses and pursued them, destroyed and plundered their village, and followed and fought them three days, when they begged us to let them go and promised to be good Indians in future. We granted their request and returned to our camp, satisfied that the best way to negotiate and settle disputes with hostile Indians is with the rifle, for that is the only pen that can write a treaty which they will not forget. Two days after we left them three white trappers, ignorant of what had taken place, went into their village and were treated in the most friendly manner. The Indians said, however, they had been fighting with the Blackfeet.

July 5th a party arrived from the States with supplies. The cavalcade consisted of forty-five men and twenty carts drawn by mules, under the direction of Mr. Thomas Fitzpatrick, accompanied by Capt. William Stewart on another tour of the Rocky Mountains.

Joy now beamed in every countenance. Some received letters from their friends and relations; some received the public papers and news of the day; others consoled themselves with the idea of getting a blanket, a cotton shirt or a few pints of coffee and sugar to sweeten it just by way of a treat, gratis, that is to say, by paying 2,000 per cent on the first cost by way of accommodation. For instance, sugar $2 per pint, coffee the same, blankets $20 each, tobacco $2 per pound, alcohol $4 per pint, and common cotton shirts $5 each, etc. And in return paid $4 or $5 per pound for beaver. In a few days the bustle began to subside. The furs were done up in packs ready for transportation to the States and parties were formed for the hunting the ensuing year. One party, consisting of 110 men, was destined for the Blackfeet country, under the direction of L. B. Fontanelle as commander and James Bridger as pilot. I started, with five others to hunt the headwaters of the Yellowstone, Missouri and Big Horn Rivers, a portion of the country I was particularly fond of hunting.

Paul Horgan

Clearly, the mountain man was a more uncouth and less benevolent symbol than the figure of the pioneer settler epitomized by Daniel Boone. The fur trapper lived in harmony with the wilderness, it is true; but the ennoblement lent by nature was largely gone, and the man of the plains and the mountains took on much of the indifference and savagery of his surroundings. At least that is the way Paul Horgan—in a passage from the second volume of his Pulitzer Prize book, Great River—*sees the trapper. In a few pages Horgan sketches vividly the trapper of the Southwest, comments on his ingenuity, and captures the raw exuberance of his periodic sprees at trail's end in Taos.*

The Mountain Man*

For by then [1810] the beaver's fur was in great demand for the making of men's hats. The hatters of London and Paris, New York, Boston and Philadelphia consumed great cargoes of beaver pelt, and the fur trade moved westward out of St. Louis over the American continent to Astoria and the northern Rockies. While Stephen Austin was completing his organized arrangements with the new government of Mexico to bring new settlers from the east nearer to the lower Rio Grande, the river's upper reaches knew another sort of growing infiltration by men who whether they came alone, or with a few companions, or many, still came without formal approval by the Mexican government, and with no resounding program of colonial loyalty or pious hope.

---

* From Paul Horgan, *Great River: The Rio Grande in North American History* (New York: Holt, Rinehart and Winston, 1954), II, 461–462, 464–469. Copyright 1954 by Paul Horgan. Reprinted by permission of Holt, Rinehart and Winston, Inc.

They came to take beaver in the mountain waters, in spring and autumn up north, or all through the winter in New Mexico if the season was mild. Many of them were French Canadians; the rest were from anywhere in the United States, though mostly from the frontier settlements. They outfitted themselves at St. Louis, and remembering what was commonly known out of Pike's reports, crossed the plains and entered the mountains by the hundreds in the 1820s. Among their number were men who made the first trails beyond the prairies, that led overland so early as 1826, to the Pacific. Jedediah Smith, Charles Beaubien, the Roubidoux brothers, Ceran St. Vrain, Bill Williams, the youthful runaway Kit Carson for whose return a reward of one cent was posted by the employer to whom he was apprenticed—such men went to the mountains after beaver skins to sell for a few dollars a pound, and all unwitting showed the way across the continent.

The mountain man was almost Indian-colored from exposure to the weather. His hair hung upon his shoulders. He was bearded. Next to his skin he wore a red flannel loincloth. His outer clothes were of buckskin, fringed at all the seams. The jacket sometimes reached to the knee over tight, wrinkled leggings. His feet were covered by moccasins made of deer or buffalo leather. Around his waist was a leather belt into which he thrust his flintlock pistols, his knife for skinning or scalping, and his shingling hatchet. Over one shoulder hung his bullet pouch, and over the other his powder horn. To their baldrics were attached his bullet mould, ball screw, wiper and an awl for working leather. When he moved he shimmered with fringe and rang and clacked with accoutrements of metal and wood. The most important of these were his traps, of which he carried five or six, and his firearm with its slender separate crutch of hardwood. It was always a rifle—never a shotgun, which he scorned as an effete fowling piece. Made in the gun works of the brothers Jacob and Samuel Hawken, of St. Louis, the rifle had two locks for which he kept about him a hundred flints, twenty-five pounds of powder and several pounds of lead. The barrel, thirty-six inches long, was made by hand of soft iron. The recoil of its blast shocked into a hardwood stock beautifully turned and slender. Peering vividly out from under his low-crowned hat of rough wool, he was an American original, as hard as the hardest thing that could happen to him.

Alone, or with a companion or a small party, he packed his supplies on two horses and, riding a third, left Taos for the mountains in the autumn. He was wary of roaming Indians, dangerous animals—and other trapper parties. For nobody could stake a claim on hunting country, and every trapper party competed against every other. He did his best to keep his movement and direction secret, to throw others off the trail, and find the wildest country where he would be most free from rivalry. Following the groins of the foothills, the mountain men came among high slopes and rocky screens. If two worked as a pair, they sought for a concealed place where they could make camp and tether their horses, near beaver water. There they built a shelter, and if their goal was a mountain lake, or a slow passage of stream, they set to work hacking out a cottonwood canoe. In natural forest paths they looked for the little musky mounds that marked beaver trails. They searched currents for the drift of gnawed beaver sticks. Every such sign took them closer to their prey. When they were sure they had found its little world, at evening under the pure suspended light of mountain skies they silently coasted along the shores of quiet water to set their traps.

They laid each trap two or three inches underwater on the slope of the shore, and, a little removed, they fixed a pole in deep mud and chained the trap to it. They stripped a twig of its bark and dipped one end into a supply of castorum, the beaver's own secretion that would be his bait. They fastened the twig between the open jaws of the trap leaving the musky end four inches above water. The beaver in the nighttime was drawn to it by scent. He raised his muzzle to inhale, his hind quarters went lower in the water, and the trap seized him. He threw himself into deeper water; but the trap held him, and the pole held the trap, and presently he sank to drown. In the high, still daybreak, the trappers coasted by their traps again in the canoe, and took up their catch.

Working a rocky stream from the bank the trappers lodged the trap and its chained pole in the current, where the beaver found the scent. In his struggles he might drag the trap and pole to the shore, where his burden became entangled in "thickets of brook willows," and held him till found. Sometimes he struggled to deeper midstream water, where the pole floated as a marker; and then the trappers putting off their buckskins that if saturated would dry slowly and then be hard as wood, went naked and shivering into the cold mountain stream to swim for their take. And some parties rafted down the whole length of the river in New Mexico, all the way to El Paso. Their method astonished the New Mexicans, to whom it seemed suspect because it was new. Was it proper to use a new kind of trap, and float noiselessly to a beaver site taking their catch by surprise, and spend the night in midstream with the raft moored to trees on each bank to be out of reach of wild animals? And at the end of the journey, to sell the timbers of the raft for a good price at El Paso where wood was so scarce, take up the catch and vanish overland eastward without reporting to the government? The New Mexicans frowned at such ingenuity, energy and novelty.

When in the mountains they had exhausted a beaver site the trappers moved on to another. With their traps over their shoulders they forded streams amidst floating ice; or with their traps hanging down their backs, they scaled and descended the hard ridges between water-courses where the harder the country the better the chance that no others had come there before them. The trap weighed about five pounds, and its chain was about five feet long. A full-grown beaver weighed between thirty and forty pounds. The catch was an awkward burden to carry back to camp for skinning. Removing the pelt from the animal, the trappers stretched it on a frame of sprung willow withes to dry. The flesh they cooked by hanging it before a fire from a thong. The carcass turned by its own weight, roasting evenly. The broad, flat tail they liked best of all. They cut it off, skinned it, toasted it at the end of a stick, and ate it with relish, as a relief from the usual hunter's diet of deer, elk, antelope, bear, lynx, or buffalo meat, or buffalo marrowbones, or buffalo blood drunk spurting and warm from the throat of a newly killed specimen.

All through the winter-fast months the mountain men worked, obedient to animal laws and themselves almost animal in their isolation, freedom and harmony with the wilderness. Their peltries were cached and the piles grew, in the end to be baled with rawhide thongs. A trapper took in a good season about four hundred pounds of beaver skins. Sometimes his cache was invaded and destroyed by prowling animals, or stolen by mountain Indians; and then his months of hardship went for nothing. But if he kept his pile, he was ready to come out of the boxed mountains whose cool winds brushing all day over high-tilted meadows carried the scent of wild flowers down the open slopes where he descended with his haul. At five dollars a pound it would bring him two thousand dollars in the market.

In any case, after his mountain months, he was ready to burst his bonds of solitude, and he did so with raw delight. All his general passion and violence that his mountain work required him to suppress while moving lithe and crafty after watchful creatures he now broke free in the clay village where he returned among men and women. He had a frosty look of filth over him. His hair was knotted and his beard was a catch-all for the refuse of months. His clothes reeked like his body. His mouth was dry with one kind of thirst and his flesh on fire with another. If the one tavern in the town was full, he went to a house and asked for a corner of the packed mud floor where he could throw his gear, and was granted it. The family knew what he came to seek with his comrades. The women took kettles out of doors and built fires around them to heat water. When it was hot they brought it in, and found him waiting in his crusted skin sitting in a wooden tub. The women poured the water over him. He thrashed. He was as hairy as an animal and as unmindedly lustful. The water hit him and he gave the recognized cry of the mountain man— "Wagh!"—a grunt, a warning, and a boast. Bathing as violently as he did all other acts, he began again to know forgotten satisfactions. As he emerged with wet light running on his skin, white everywhere but on face and hands whose weather would not wash off, he was a new man.

The whiskey of Taos—they called it "lightning"—now warmed him within. He drank until he had fire under his scowl. The women did what they could to improve his clothes. He rattled his money and they made him a supper that burned him inside with chilis and spices. Early in the evening he stamped his way to the tavern in the plaza where a fandango was about to start. All benches and tables were pushed back against the walls of the large room. Tin lanterns pierced with little nail holes in a design hung from the raw beams of the ceiling. Two fiddlers, a guitarist and a flutist began to make up the music together. They played popular ballads—the same ones that at slower tempos also served for accompaniments to the Mass and to processions. As the crowd grew the room was hazed with blue cigarette smoke from the mouths of men and women alike. The women were powdered till their faces looked pale lavender. They clustered together at one side of the room. From the other the men came and took them somewhat as cocks took hens—a dusty pounce met by a bridling glare, and then an impassive harmony between the sexes suggesting absent-minded enjoyment. Lacking milled lumber the floor was a hard and polished cake of earth. The couples moved with expressionless faces—all but the mountain man. In his face there glared a starved animation. His heels made muffled thunder on the ground. The Mexican dances were set pieces, with evolutions and patterns. He did not heed them. He threw himself in baleful joy through whatever movements occurred to him, "Wagh!" The lightning jug went around. The music scratched and squealed. The windows of the tavern hall were like lanterns in the pure darkness below Taos Mountain. When the fandango was over, all went home. The mountain man took a woman from the ball to her house. At rut like a big, fanged mountain cat—"Wa-a-a-g-h!"—he spent the night with her to nobody's surprise or censure; and, as one such man said, he had no reason afterward to bring "charges of severity" against her.

Presently he travelled to a trading post on the prairies, or to St. Louis, to sell his catch. In the frontier cities of the United States he was a prodigal spender, uneasy in their relatively ordered society, loose as it was compared to life in older and more easterly places. When the season rolled around again, he was off again to his lost lakes and rivers where obscurely content he felt more like the self he imagined until it came true.

For over three decades the trapping trade flourished. At its height the annual shipment of beaver skins from Abiquiu on the Chama and Taos on the Rio Grande was worth two hundred thousand dollars. But in the 1830s the market for beaver began to break, for the China trade out of England and New England was growing, and the clipper ships were bringing silk in great quantities to the manufacturing cities of the world.

Fashion changed. Silk was offered for hats instead of fur; and the change brought the decline and finally the almost virtual abolishment of the Rocky Mountain fur trade. The trapper was cast adrift to find new work. He could abide it only in the land of his hardy prowess, and there he found it, whether he joined the overland commercial caravans as a wagon hand, or the American Army's later surveying expeditions as a guide, or amazingly settled on river land as a farmer. He knew the craft of the wilderness and he made its first trails for the westering white man. Some of the earliest venturers in the Mexico trade were trappers; and as the trade continued to grow and establish its bases ever farther west, the trappers met it with their wares; and what had been a memorized path became a visible road; and along it moved another of the unofficial invasions of the Mexican Rio Grande that could only end by changing nations. The first sustained effort toward that end was made by the individual trapper. His greatest power to achieve it lay in his individualism.

James Ohio Pattie

James Ohio Pattie (1804–c. 1850) was one of the more perceptive and articulate of the trapping fraternity, although he was not above garnishing fact with fancy. In this passage lifted out of his Narrative, *Pattie provides a convincing explanation of the free trapper's rugged independence and relates the expedient resorted to by his father in the effort to maintain discipline, encourage cooperation, and hold a trapping expedition together.*

A Trapping Expedition*

On the 23d, my father was chosen captain or commander of the company, and we started on our expedition. We retraced our steps down the del Norte, and by the mines to the river Helay [Gila], on which we arrived on

---

* From James Ohio Pattie, *Personal Narrative,* in Reuben Gold Thwaites, ed., *Early Western Travels, 1748–1846* (Cleveland: The Arthur H. Clark Company, 1905), XVIII, 181–187.

the 6th of October, and began to descend it, setting our traps as we went, near our camp, whenever we saw signs of beavers. But our stay on this stream was short, for it had been trapped so often, that there were but few beavers remaining, and those few were exceedingly shy. We therefore pushed on to some place where they might be more abundant, and less shy. We left this river on the 12th, and on the 15th reached Beaver river. Here we found them in considerable numbers, and we concluded to proceed in a south course, and trap the river in its downward course. But to prevent the disagreement and insubordination which are apt to spring up in these associations, my father drew articles of agreement, purporting that we should trap in partnership, and that the first one who should show an open purpose to separate from the company, or desert it, should be shot dead; and that if any one should disobey orders, he should be tried by a jury of our number, and if found guilty should be fined fifty dollars, to be paid in fur. To this instrument we all agreed, and signed our names.

The necessity of some such compact had been abundantly discovered in the course of our experience. Men bound only by their own will and sense of right, to the duties of such a sort of partnership are certain to grow restless, and to form smaller clans, disposed to dislike and separate from each other, in parties of one by one to three by three. They thus expose themselves to be cut up in detail by the savages, who comprehend all their movements, and are ever watchful for an opportunity to show their hatred of the whites to be fixed and inextinguishable. The following are some of the more common causes of separation: Men of incompatible tempers and habits are brought together; and such expeditions call out innumerable occasions to try this disagreement of character. Men, hungry, naked, fatigued, and in constant jeopardy, are apt to be ill-tempered, especially when they arrive at camp, and instead of being allowed to throw themselves on the ground, and sleep, have hard duties of cooking, and keeping guard, and making breast-works assigned them. But the grand difficulty is the following. In a considerable company, half its numbers can catch as many beavers as all. But the half that keep guard, and cook, perform duties as necessary and important to the whole concern, as the others. It always happens too, in these expeditions, that there are some infinitely more dextrous and skilful in trapping and hunting than others. These capabilities are soon brought to light. The expert know each other, and feel a certain superiority over the inexpert. They know that three or four such, by themselves, will take as many beavers as a promiscuous company of thirty, and in fact, all that a stream affords. A perception of their own comparative importance, a keen sense of self interest, which sharpens in the desert, the mere love of roving in the wild license of the forest, and a capacity to become hardened by these scenes to a perfect callousness to all fear and sense of danger, until it actually comes; such passions are sufficient to thicken causes of separation among such companions in the events of every day.

Sad experience has made me acquainted with all these causes of disunion and dissolution of such companies. I have learned them by wounds and sufferings, by toil and danger of every sort, by wandering about in the wild and desolate mountains, alone and half starved, merely because two or three bad men had divided our company, strong and sufficient to themselves in union, but miserable, and exposed to almost certain ruin in separation. Made painfully acquainted with all these facts by experience, my father adopted this expedient in the hope that it would be something like a remedy for them.

But notwithstanding this, and the prudence and energy of my father's character, disunion soon began to spring up in our small party. Almost on the outset of our expedition, we began to suffer greatly for want of provisions. We were first compelled to kill and eat our dogs, and then six of our horses. This to me was the most cruel task of all. To think of waiting for the night to kill and eat the poor horse that had borne us over deserts and mountains, as hungry as ourselves, and strongly and faithfully attached to us, was no easy task to the heart of a Kentucky hunter. One evening, after a hard day's travel, my saddle horse was selected by lot to be killed. The poor animal stood saddled and bridled before us, and it fell to my lot to kill it. I loved this horse, and he seemed to have an equal attachment for me. He was remarkably kind to travel, and easy to ride, and spirited too. When he stood tied in camp among the rest, if I came any where near him, he would fall neighing for me. When I held up the bridle towards him, I could see consent and good will in his eye. As I raised my gun to my face, all these recollections rushed to my thoughts. My pulses throbbed, and my eyes grew dim. The animal was gazing me, with a look of steady kindness, in the face. My head whirled, and was dizzy, and my gun fell. After a moment for recovery, I offered a beaver skin to any one who would shoot him down. One was soon found at this price, and my horse fell! It so happened that this was the last horse we killed. Well was it for us that we had these surplus horses. Had it been otherwise, we should all have perished with hunger.

It was now the 15th of November, and while the horse flesh lasted, we built a canoe, so that we could trap on both sides of the river; for it is here too broad and deep to be fordable on horseback. One of our number had already been drowned, man and horse, in attempting to swim the river. A canoe is a great advantage, where the beavers are wild; as the trapper can thus set his traps along the shore without leaving his scent upon the ground about it.

On the 17th, our canoe was finished, and another person and myself took some traps in it, and floated down the river by water, while the rest of the company followed along the banks by land. In this way, what with the additional supply which the canoe enabled our traps to furnish, and a chance deer or wolf that Providence sometimes threw in our way, with caution and economy we were tolerably supplied with provisions; and the company travelled on with a good degree of union and prosperity, until the 26th.

Here the greater part of the company expressed disinclination to following our contemplated route any longer. That is, they conceived the route to the mouth of the Helay, and up Red river of California too long and tedious, and too much exposed to numerous and hostile Indians. They, therefore, determined to quit the Helay, and strike over to Red river by a direct route across the country. My father reminded them of their article. They assured him they did not consider themselves bound by it, and that they were a majority, against which nothing could be said. My father and myself still persevered in following the original plan. Two of the men had been hired on my father's account. He told them he was ready to pay them up to that time, and dismiss them, to go where they chose. They observed, that now that the company had commenced separating, they believed that in a short time, there would be no stronger party together than ours; that they had as good a disposition to risk their lives with us, as with any division of our number, and that they would stay by us to the death. After this speech four others of the company volunteered to remain with us, and we took them in as partners.

George Frederick Ruxton

The American mountain man displayed considerable inventiveness in the use—or abuse—of his native tongue, evolving in the process a distinctive patois that served his need for pungent expression and also unequivocally identified legitimate members of the trapper fraternity, setting them apart from tyros to the trade. No one has captured the flavor and cadence of the fur-trade idiom more convincingly than George Frederick Ruxton (1820–1848), an English adventurer in the Far West in the 1840s.

*Trapper Talk**

They were a trapping party from the north fork of Platte, on their way to wintering-ground in the more southern valley of the Arkansa; ... The elder of the company was a tall gaunt man, with a face browned by twenty years' exposure to the extreme climate of the mountains; his long black hair, as yet scarcely tinged with grey, hanging almost to his shoulders, but his cheeks and chin clean shaven, after the fashion of the mountain men. ... Whilst his companions puffed their pipes in silence, he narrated a few of his former experiences of western life; and whilst the buffalo "hump-ribs" and "tender loin" are singing away in the pot, preparing for the hunters' supper, we will note down the yarn as it spins from his lips, giving it in the language spoken in the "far west:—

" 'Twas about 'calf-time,' maybe a little later, and not a hundred year ago, by a long chalk, that the biggest kind of rendezvous was held 'to' Independence, a mighty handsome little location away up on old Missoura. A pretty smart lot of boys was camp'd thar, about a quarter from the town, and the way the whisky flowed that time was 'some' now, *I* can tell you. Thar was old Sam Owins—him as got 'rubbed out' by the Spaniards at Sacramenty, or Chihuahuy, this hos doesn't know which, but he 'went under' any how.† Well, Sam had his train along, ready to hitch up for the Mexican country—twenty thunderin big Pittsburg waggons; and the way *his* Santa Fe boys took in the liquor beat all—eh, Bill?"

"Well, it did."

"Bill Bent—his boys camped the other side the trail, and they was all mountain men, wagh!—and Bill Williams, and Bill Tharpe (the Pawnees took his hair on Pawnee Fork last spring) : three Bills, and them three's all 'gone under.' Surely Hatcher went out that time; and wasn't Bill Garey along, too? Didn't him and Chabonard sit in camp for twenty hours at a deck of Euker? Them was Bent's Indian traders up on Arkansa. Poor Bill Bent! them Spaniards made meat of him. He lost his topknot to Taos. A 'clever' man was Bill Bent as *I* ever know'd trade a robe or 'throw' a bufler in his tracks. Old St. Vrain could knock the hind-sight off him though, when it came to shootin', and old silver heels spoke true, she did: 'plum-center' she was, eh?"

---

* From George Frederick Ruxton, *Life in the Far West* (Edinburgh and London: William Blackwood and Sons, 1849), pp. 2–8.

† "Rubbed out" (killed) and "went under" (died) are terms adapted from the Indian figurative language.

"*Well,* she wasn't nothing else."

"The Greasers* payed for Bent's scalp, they tell me. Old St. Vrain went out of Santa Fe with a company of mountain men, and the way they made 'em sing out was 'slick as shootin'.' He 'counted a coup,' did St. Vrain. He throwed a Pueblo as had on poor Bent's shirt. I guess he tickled that nigger's hump-ribs. Fort William† aint the lodge it was, an' never will be agin, now he's gone under; but St. Vrain's 'pretty much of a gentleman,' too; if he aint, I'll be dog-gone, eh, Bill?"

"He is *so-o.*"

"Chavez had his waggons along. He was only a Spaniard any how, and some of his teamsters put a ball into him his next trip, and made a raise of *his* dollars, wagh! Uncle Sam hung 'em for it, I heard, but can't b'lieve it, nohow. If them Spaniards wasn't born for shootin', why was beaver made? You was with us that spree, Jemmy?"

"No *sirre-e;* I went out when Spiers lost his animals on Cimmaron: a hundred and forty mules and oxen was froze that night, wagh!"

"Surely Black Harris was thar; and the darndest liar was Black Harris —for lies tumbled out of his mouth like boudins out of a bufler's stomach. He was the child as saw the putrefied forest in the Black Hills. Black Harris come in from Laramie; he'd been trapping three year an' more on Platte and the 'other side;' and, when he got into Liberty, he fixed himself right off like a Saint Louiy dandy. Well, he sat to dinner one day in the tavern, and a lady says to him :—

" 'Well, Mister Harris, I hear you're a great travler.'

" 'Travler, marm,' says Black Harris, 'this niggur's no travler; I ar' a trapper, marm, a mountain-man, wagh!'

" 'Well, Mister Harris, trappers are great travlers, and you goes over a sight of ground in your perishinations, I'll be bound to say.'

" 'A sight, marm, this coon's gone over, if that's the way your 'stick floats.'‡ I've trapped beaver on Platte and Arkansa, and away up on Missoura and Yaller Stone; I've trapped on Columbia, on Lewis Fork, and Green River; I've trapped, marm, on Grand River and the Heely (Gila). I've fout the 'Blackfoot' (and d____d bad Injuns they ar); I've 'raised the hair'§ of more *than one* Apach, and made a Rapaho 'come' afore now; I've

---

* The Mexicans are called "Spaniards" or "Greasers" (from their greasy appearance) by the Western people.

† Bent's Indian trading fort on the Arkansa.

‡ Meaning—if that's what you mean. The "stick" is tied to the beaver trap by a string; and floating on the water, points out its position, should a beaver have carried it away.

§ Scalped.

trapped in heav'n, in airth, and h＿＿: and scalp my old head, marm, but I've seen a putrefied forest.'

" 'La, Mister Harris, a what?'

" 'A putrefied forest, marm, as sure as my rifle's got hind-sights, and *she* shoots center. I was out on the Black Hills, Bill Sublette knows the time—the year it rained fire—and every body knows when that was. If thar wasn't cold doins about that time, this child wouldn't say so. The snow was about fifty foot deep, and the bufler lay dead on the ground like bees after a beein'; not whar we was tho', for *thar* was no bufler, and no meat. and me and my band had been livin' on our mocassins (leastwise the parflesh*), for six weeks; and poor doins that feedin' is, marm, as you'll never know. One day we crossed a 'canon' and over a 'divide,' and got into a peraira, whar was green grass, and green trees, and green leaves on the trees, and birds singing in the green leaves, and this in February, wagh! Our animals was like to die when they see the green grass, and we all sung out, 'hurraw for summer doins.'

" 'Hyar goes for meat,' says I, and I jest ups old Ginger at one of them singing birds, and down come the crittur elegant; its darned head spinning away from the body, but never stops singing, and when I takes up the meat, I finds it stone, wagh! 'Hyar's damp powder and no fire to dry it,' I says, quite skeared.

" 'Fire be dogged,' says old Rube. 'Hyar's a hos as 'll make fire come; and with that he takes his axe and lets drive at a cotton wood. Schr-u-k— goes the axe agin the tree, and out comes a bit of the blade as big as my hand. We looks at the animals, and thar they stood shaking over the grass, which I'm dog-gone if it wasn't stone, too. Young Sublette comes up, and he'd been clerking down to the fort on Platte, so he know'd something. He looks and looks, and scrapes the trees with his butcher knife, and snaps the grass like pipe stems, and breaks the leaves a-snappin' like Californy shells.'

" 'What's all this boy?' I asks.

" 'Putrefactions,' says he, looking smart, 'putrefactions, or I'm a niggur.'

" 'La, Mister Harris,' says the lady, 'putrefactions! why, did the leaves, and the trees, and the grass smell badly?'

" 'Smell badly, marm!' says Black Harris, 'would a skunk stink if he was froze to stone? No, marm, this child didn't know what putrefaction was, and young Sublette's varsion wouldn't 'shine' nohow, so I chips a piece out of a tree and puts it in my trap-sack, and carries it in safe to Laramie. Well, old Captain Stewart, (a clever man was that, though he was an Englishman), he comes along next spring, and a Dutch doctor chap was

---

* Soles made of buffalo hide.

along too. I shows him the piece I chipped out of the tree, and he called it a putrefaction too; and so, marm, if that wasn't a putrefied peraira, what was it? For this hos doesn't know, and *he* knows 'fat cow' from 'poor bull,' anyhow.

"Well, old Black Harris is gone under too, I believe. He went to the 'Parks' trapping with a Vide Poche Frenchman, they're no account any way you lays your sight. (Any bacca in your bag, Bill? this beaver feels like chawing.)"

ADDITIONAL READINGS

The standard general treatment of the fur trade is Hiram M. Chittenden's *The American Fur Trade of the Far West* (3 vols., New York, 1902). Alongside it must be placed a recent and even broader work: Paul C. Phillips, *The Fur Trade* (Norman, Oklahoma, 1961). For business aspects of American enterprise in furs and a definitive biography of the American master in the trade, see Kenneth W. Porter, *John Jacob Astor, Business Man* (2 vols., Cambridge, 1931). A more romantic if less comprehensive and reliable narrative is Washington Irving's *Astoria* (New York, 1846). John Galbraith's *The Hudson's Bay Company as an Imperial Factor, 1821–1869* (Berkeley, 1957) is a balanced and impressive interpretation of the company's expansion west. Frederick Merk combines an accurate account of Hudson's Bay Company operations with competent editing of Governor Simpson's journal in *Fur Trade and Empire, George Simpson's Journal* (Cambridge, 1931). The best biography of an American mountain man is Dale L. Morgan's *Jedediah Smith and the Opening of the West* (Indianapolis, 1953). More popular but still reliable treatments of the American trade are Bernard De Voto's *Across the Wide Missouri* (Boston, 1947) and Robert G. Cleland's *This Reckless Breed of Men: The Trappers and Fur Traders of the Southwest* (New York, 1950).

4

OREGON:
FROM TRAIL
TO TERRITORY

To the sober citizen the Oregon Trail more than any other overland route epitomizes the continental crossing. This was pre-eminently the road of the home seeker, the churchgoer, the town builder; a way West uncontaminated by the lust for gold and to a degree dedicated to tipping the scales against the British in the contest for the Oregon country. It was the longest of the overland trails and, during the decisive decade of the 1840s, the most heavily traveled. Natural difficulties abounded: long stretches with little fuel or water, rivers to ford, mountains to get over, dust that caked and choked, rain that chilled and blinded, monotony that dulled senses and frayed tempers. Yet, by and large, the main trail was the easiest way across the land, and there were those who put on pounds during the long journey. The main segments of the trace were worn clear by 1832, nearly a decade before the first emigrant train moved out for the Pacific. This was the work of trappers and overland explorers: Wilson Price Hunt's party meandering along the Snake River, returning Astorians finding their way from the mouth of the Walla Walla to the future site of Fort Hall, the Snake River brigades of Peter Skene Ogden, the effective discovery of South Pass by Jedediah Smith, Captain B. L. E. Bonneville taking the first wagons through that pass—these men and others like them, known and unknown, shaped what became the road to Oregon.

The original Oregon Trail lay like a great rope flung carelessly from the Missouri north and west across the country, with its terminal tip lying in the Columbia where the Walla Walla enters from the east. In time and with use the rope frayed at each end, with "jumping-off places" opening at Westport, Leavenworth, St. Joseph, and Independence, and a short cut branching northwest from the Grande Ronde Valley along the Umatilla to Fort Walla Walla. Strands worked loose along the rope's middle too, in the form of cutoffs such as the Lander and Sublette. However, the way west for the bulk of the emigrants was along the main trail leading from Independence to Fort Walla Walla.

With the start of grass in early spring, the wagons began to converge on one of the "jumping-off places" along the Missouri. Here families got acquainted; equipment was checked; last-minute purchases were made; and then the various companies or caravans moved on to a rendezvous point, where officers were elected and regulations drafted. More often than not, the rigors of transcontinental travel revealed errors in judgment in the initial selection of officers; and it was a rare wagon train that reached its destination with the political organization effected at the outset still intact.

The wagons followed the Santa Fe Trail to what is now Gardner, Kansas, and then slanted northwest until they reached the Platte in the vicinity of Grand Island. They followed the Platte until it forked; they took the south branch for a short distance and then crossed to the North Platte, along which there rose successively the reassuring landmarks of Court House Rock, Chimney Rock, and Scott's Bluffs. At Fort Laramie, 667 miles from the settlements, a halt of several days was generally called. Leaving Fort Laramie, the caravans roughly paralleled the arc of the Platte; they crossed it to the north near present-day Caspar, then dipped south to Independence Rock. Up the Sweetwater ran the trail and around the deep rift in a granite ridge called Devil's Gate to South Pass—the wide, nearly imperceptible crossing of the Continental Divide—which marked the halfway point in the journey (947 miles) and was regarded as the gateway to Oregon. From South Pass the Lander cutoff led due west to Fort Hall on the Snake, while the main trail dropped south to Fort Bridger and, tending north and west again past Soda Springs, reached Fort Hall (1,288 miles). This fort, raised in 1834 by Nathaniel Wyeth and sold to Hudson's Bay Company in 1837, was a general rest and refitting station, where some emigrants finally decided whether to go to Oregon or California.

From Fort Hall the Oregon Trail paralleled the Snake, crossing it to the north up to the Boise River and then along that stream back to its junction with the Snake near Fort Boise. Moving north and west, the wagons ascended the Powder River to the site of Baker City and then wound through the rough-hewn country of eastern Oregon to the dramatic descent into the green Grande Ronde Valley, convincing proof to emigrants that the kind of "Promised Land" featured in guidebooks and promotional literature was at last at hand. From here the trail led north to the Whitmans' mission near present Walla Walla, downstream to the fort, and later to The Dalles. The last leg and often the most dangerous part of the journey was by boat down the Columbia to Fort Vancouver. At trail's end the emigrants usually found they had come about 2,000 miles in from 100 to 120 days.

Why thousands of Americans in the 1840s and 50s should strike out across a sprawling continent sprinkled with unpredictable native peoples is not easy to explain. There was a restlessness in the land then, particularly in the Mississippi Valley, which was filling up with settlers in whom the habit of moving west was already firmly fixed and whose roots were shallow enough to be easily pulled loose. The impulse to be on the move was largely a matter of the same appetite for land that had propelled the Atlantic migration of the seventeenth century and had been operating ever since. This land hunger was whetted by the knowledge that Senator Lewis F. Linn had a bill before Congress calling for a grant of 640 acres in Oregon to every adult male plus 160 acres for every child. Linn's bill was never enacted, although it did pass the Senate in 1843; nevertheless, the expectation of its passage was an effective lure to migration west. Moreover, free land was forthcoming through the Donation Land Act of 1850, which antedated the national Homestead Act by a dozen years. The Donation Land Act awarded 640 acres to settlers already in Oregon and promised 320 acres to those who would migrate without delay—thereby increasing traffic on the Oregon Trail. Then, too, the shadow of the Panic of 1837 lay across the land, leaving farmers disconsolate over depressed price levels and vulnerable to the propaganda that stressed better markets in the Far West, as well as double, sometimes triple, productive seasons in a single year. Some there were who left for Oregon to get away from slave-holding neighbors; others, malaria-ridden, hoped to lose "the shakes" in the allegedly healthier climate of the Pacific Northwest. Poised on the edge of the treeless, semi-arid Great Plains were thousands willing to travel 2,000 miles to duplicate and perhaps improve upon the kind of environment that was so much a part of their pioneering experience—a garden land of lush valleys, forested slopes, and rushing water. Nor was the migration as sudden as it seemed. For at least two decades enthusiasts for the Oregon country had been at work—men like John Floyd, Congressman; Hall Jackson Kelley, pure prophet and pamphleteer; Washington Irving, romantic historian; and the Lees and Whitmans, missionaries. Finally, the presidential campaign of 1844 turned on expansionism, intensifying the notion already abroad that mass migration could terminate joint occupation in the Oregon country by dislodging the British. Considerations like the foregoing, in varying degrees and combinations—along with such psychological imponderables as man's zest for adventure and new experience and the general human tendency to participate in a popular movement—made the "Oregon Fever" an uncommonly virulent contagion.

Untrue to the stereotype of the frontier experience, in the Willamette Valley the Oregon pioneers found no howling wilderness. In the 1840s there was already a nucleus of settlers made up of former Astorians, mountain men, and French-Canadians; many of these last were members, active or retired, of the Hudson's Bay Company. The Indian threat was negligible, in part because the Valley Indians were less formidable than the peoples east of the Cascades or to the south along the Rogue River, and in part because the Hudson's Bay Company, with headquarters at Ft. Vancouver and a warehouse on the Willamette, represented an authority that the Indians respected. American emigrants arriving destitute of provisions were spared the "starving time" of other frontiers not only because the Willamette Valley soil was fecund, and fish and game were plentiful, but because the benign and foresighted Dr. John McLoughlin (Chief Factor of the Hudson's Bay Company—who became an American citizen after he parted ways with the company) extended credit to incoming settlers and purchased their surplus products. Moreover, when the first emigrant trains reached the Oregon country, they found Protestant and Catholic missions and a school for their children at the Oregon Institute in present-day Salem. In short, rather than moving into a primitive and hostile environment, the Oregon pioneers found a modest but genuine community with churches, a school, and a friendly and effective system of authority in the Hudson's Bay Company.

The major lack was an American government and a written organic law. Although the land was peaceful, Americans were restive under joint occupation. The presence of the British and uncertainty as to how much of Oregon would ultimately be American led to the formation of tentative political groupings. Doubtless, too, some were concerned with the absence of legal sanction for land holdings and property rights. Others were convinced that before long the Oregon boundary dispute with Great Britain would be settled and the mantle of United States authority would be thrown over the Oregon settlements. Meanwhile, Oregonians took steps toward strengthening their community.

In 1837 the Willamette Valley Cattle Company was organized. Led by Ewing Young, former fur trapper in the Southwest, the company made a successful expedition to California to purchase cattle and drive them back to Oregon. This was the first significant example of cooperation among the Willamette Valley settlers; and, although the Hudson's Bay Company purchased some shares in the company, it was clearly an American venture.

The next year the first of several memorials, praying that the United States recognize the "infant colony" and extend it protection, was dispatched to Congress.

In 1841 Ewing Young died intestate, and leaders in the community established sufficient informal civil authority to probate Young's estate. In 1842 the Oregon Lyceum debated the question of forming a provisional government; and at a "wolf meeting" early in 1843, convened ostensibly to discuss the control of predators, a resolution was passed calling for consideration of the propriety of forming a civil government. The decision to organize a provisional government was made in May 1843 at Champoeg. On July 5, 1843, an organic act—providing, among other things, for a plural executive, a legislative committee, and a supreme court—was passed. Oregon operated under a provisional government until territorial status was vouchsafed her in 1848. These gropings toward self-government suggest the innovative impulse on this Far Western frontier; the form that government took demonstrates the force of imitation and tradition.

Hall Jackson Kelley

There was no more insistent or persistent voice urging migration to Oregon than that of the Massachusetts schoolteacher Hall Jackson Kelley (1790–1874), pedantic schemer and dreamer. For twenty years, between 1824 and 1844, through pamphlets, letters, memorials, speeches, and articles, Kelley urged American colonization on the Columbia. Although no precise measure of his influence is possible, he contributed substantially to the generation of an "Oregon Fever" in the 1840s. This fragment from a General Circular *(originally published in 1829) is a fair sample of the burden of his argument and is faithful to the fervor and flavor of his promotional prose.*

National Advantages of Acquiring Oregon*

To the Honorable, the Senate and House of Representatives, in Congress assembled.

The American Society, for encouraging the Settlement of the Oregon Territory, instituted in A.D. 1829, and incorporated by the Commonwealth of Massachusetts, actuated by a faithful regard to duty, have cheerfully engaged in the work of opening to a civilized and virtuous population, that part of Western America, called OREGON.

They are convinced, that if that country should be settled under the auspices of the Government of the United States of America, from such of her worthy sons, who have drank of the spirit of those civil and religious institutions which constitute the living fountain, and the very perennial source of her national prosperity, great benefits must result to mankind. They believe, that there, the skilful and persevering hand of industry might be employed with unparalleled advantage; that there, Science and the Arts, the invaluable privileges of a free and liberal government, and the refinements and ordinances of Christianity, diffusing each its blessing, would harmoniously unite in meliorating the moral condition of the Indians, in promoting the comfort and happiness of the settlers, and in augmenting the wealth and power of the Republic.

The uniform testimony of an intelligent multitude have established the fact, that the country in question, is the most valuable of all the unoccupied parts of the earth. Its peculiar location and facilities, and physical resources for trade and commerce; its contiguous markets; its salubrity of climate; its fertility of soil; its rich and abundant productions; its extensive forests of valuable timber; and its great water Channel diversifying, by its numerous branches the whole country, and spreading canals through every part of it, are sure indications that Providence has designed this last reach of enlightened emigration to be the residence of a people, whose singular advantages will give them unexampled power and prosperity. . . .

The Society view with alarm the progress, which the subjects of that nation [Great Britain] have made, in the colonization of the Oregon Territory. Already, have they, flourishing towns, strong fortifications, and cultivated farms. The domicile is made the abode of domestic comforts—the

---

* From Fred Wilbur Powell, ed., *Hall J. Kelley on Oregon* (Princeton: Princeton University Press, 1932), pp. 75-77. Copyright 1932 Princeton University Press.

social circle is enlivened by the busy wife and the prattle and sport of children. In the convention of 1818, England secured for her subjects, the privilege of a free trade, that of buying furs of the Indians; but, at first, they practiced trapping and hunting; now, they practice buying and improving lands, and assiduously pursue the business of the farmer and mechanic. Their largest town is Vancouver, which is situated on a beautiful plain, in the region of tide water, on the northern bank of the Columbia. At this place, saw and grist mills are in operation. Three vessels have been built, one of about 300 tons, and are employed in the lumber trade. Numerous herds and flocks of horses, horned cattle, and sheep, of the best European breeds, are seen grazing in their ever verdant fields. Grain of all kinds, in abundant crops, are the productions of the soil.

Everything, either in the organization of the government, or in the busy and various operations of the settlements, at this place, at Wallawalla, at Fort Colville, and at De Fuca, indicate the intentions of the English to colonize the country.—Now, therefore, your memorialists, in behalf of a large number of the citizens of the United States, would respectfully ask Congress to aid them in carrying into operation the great purposes of their institution—to grant them troops, artillery, military arms, and munitions of war, for the defence and security of the contemplated settlement—to incorporate their Society with power to extinguish the Indian title, to such tracts and extent of territory, at the mouth of the Columbia, and at the junction of the Multnomah with the Columbia, as may be adequate to the laudable objects and pursuits of the settlers, and with such other powers, rights and immunities, as may be, at least, equal and concurrent to those given by Parliament to the Hudson's Bay Company; and such as are not repugnant to the stipulations of the Convention, made between Great Britain and the United States, wherein it was agreed, that any country on the Northwest Coast of America, to the westward of the Rocky Mountains, should be free and open to the citizens and subjects of the two powers, for a term of years; and to grant them such other rights and privileges, as may contribute to the means of establishing a respectable and prosperous community.

Your memorialists are pledged to one another, to their children, to their friends, and to mankind, to sustain by all just and possible means, the interests of their country; and to co-operate in advancing its prosperity. They love their native land, and will ever continue its devoted friends; and most grateful and gladdening would it be, to receive for the settlement, the protection and fostering care of Congress.

Peter H. Burnett

Peter H. Burnett (1807–1895) was a reliable and literate member of the "Great Migration" to Oregon in 1843. Here he writes to a friend in the East, summarizing (from a journal that he kept en route) the experiences of the continental crossing. Despite his optimism and enthusiasm over the Oregon country, he left the Willamette Valley for California, where in 1850 he became the first governor of that first state on the Pacific slope.

*The Continental Crossing**

LINNTON, Oregon Territory, January 18, 1844.

James G. Bennett, Esq.—

DEAR SIR: Having arrived safely in this beautiful country, and having seen, at least, its main features, I propose to give you some concise description of the same, as well as a short history of our trip. I reached the rendezvous, twenty miles from Independence, on the seventeenth of May, and found a large body of emigrants there, waiting for the company to start. On the 18th we held a meeting, and appointed a committee to see Doctor Whitman, for the purpose of obtaining information in regard to the practicability of the trip. Other committees were also appointed, and the meeting adjourned to meet again, at the Big Spring, on the 20th. On the 20th, all the emigrants, with few exceptions, were there, as well as several from the western part of Missouri. The object of the meeting was to organize, by adopting some rules for our government. The emigrants were from various places, unacquainted with each other, and there were among them many persons emulous of distinction, and anxious to wear the honors of the company. A great difference of opinion existed as to the proper mode of organization, and many strange propositions were made. I was much amused at some of them. A fat, robust, old gentleman, who had, as he said, a great deal of "beatherlusian," whose name was McHealy, proposed that the company, by contribution, should purchase two wagons and teams for the purpose of hauling two large boats, to be taken all the way with us, that we might be able to cross the streams. A red-faced old gentleman from east

---

* From "Letters of Peter H. Burnett," *Oregon Historical Quarterly*, III (December 1902), 405–407.

Tennessee state, high up on Big Pidgeon, near Kit Bullard's Mill, whose name was Dulany, generally styled "Captain," most seriously proposed that the meeting should adopt the criminal laws of Missouri or Tennessee, for the government of the company. This proposition he supported by an able speech, and several speeches were made in reply. Some one privately suggested that we should also take along a penitentiary, if Captain Dulany's proposition should pass. These two propositions were voted for by the movers alone. A set of rules were adopted, a copy of which I send you. Capt. John Grant [Gant?] was employed as our pilot, and a general understanding that we should start on the 22d. . . .

The following are the rules and regulations for the government of the Oregon Emigrating Company:

Resolved, Whereas we deem it necessary for the government of all societies, either civil or military, to adopt certain rules and regulations for their government, for the purpose of keeping good order and promoting civil and military discipline. In order to insure union and safety, we deem it necessary to adopt the following rules and regulations for the government of the said company:—

Rule 1. Every male person of the age of sixteen, or upward, shall be considered a legal voter in all affairs relating to the company.

Rule 2. There shall be nine men elected by a majority of the company, who shall form a council, whose duty it shall be to settle all disputes arising between individuals, and to try and pass sentence on all persons for any act for which they may be guilty, which is subversive of good order and military discipline. They shall take especial cognizance of all sentinels and members of the guard, who may be guilty of neglect of duty, or sleeping on post. Such persons shall be tried, and sentence passed upon them at the discretion of the council. A majority of two thirds of the council shall decide all questions that may come before them, subject to the approval or disapproval of the captain. If the captain disapprove of the decision of the council, he shall state to them his reasons, when they shall again pass upon the question, and if the same decision is again made by the same majority, it shall be final.

Rule 3. There shall be a captain elected who shall have supreme military command of the company. It shall be the duty of the captain to maintain good order and strict discipline, and as far as practicable, to enforce all rules and regulations adopted by the company. Any man who shall be guilty of disobedience of orders shall be tried and sentenced at the discretion of the council, which may extend to expulsion from the company. The captain shall appoint the necessary number of duty sergeants, one of whom shall take charge of every guard, and who shall hold their offices at the pleasure of the captain.

Rule 4. There shall be an orderly sergeant elected by the company, whose duty it shall be to keep a regular roll, arranged in alphabetical order, of every person subject to guard duty in the company; and shall make out his guard details by commencing at the top of the roll and proceeding to the bottom, thus giving every man an equal tour of guard duty. He shall also give the member of every guard notice when he is detailed for duty. He shall also parade every guard, call the roll, and inspect the same at the time of mounting. He shall also visit the guard at least once every night, and see that the guard are doing strict military duty, and may at any time give them the necessary instructions respecting their duty, and shall regularly make report to the captain every morning, and be considered second in command.

Rule 5. The captain, orderly sergeant, and members of the council shall hold their offices at the pleasure of the company, and it shall be the duty of the council, upon the application of one third or more of the company, to order a new election for either captain, orderly sergeant, or new member or members of the council, or for all or any of them, as the case may be.

Rule 6. The election of officers shall not take place until the company meet at Kansas River.

Rule 7. No family shall be allowed to take more than three loose cattle to every male member of the family of the age of sixteen and upward.

Jesse Applegate

The following selection, delivered first as an address before the Oregon Pioneer Association in 1876, re-creates a typical day with the "cow column" in the westward crossing of 1843. The address, by Jesse Applegate (1811–1888), has come to epitomize the pioneer spirit and experience in the trans-Mississippi West. Applegate made his home in the Oregon country; he settled in southwestern Oregon. Over the years he built up an impressive library and became an articulate and influential farmer, dispensing a combination of homily and hospitality that earned him the title "Sage of Yoncalla."

A Day with the Cow Column*

The migration of a large body of men, women and children across the continent to Oregon was, in the year 1843, strictly an experiment; not only in respect to the members, but to the outfit of the migrating party. Before

---

*From Jesse Applegate, "A Day with the Cow Column," *Oregon Historical Quarterly,* I (December 1900), 371–383.

that date, two or three missionaries had performed the journey on horse-back, driving a few cows with them. Three or four wagons drawn by oxen had reached Fort Hall, on Snake River, but it was the honest opinion of most of those who had traveled the route down Snake River, that no large number of cattle could be subsisted on its scanty pasturage, or wagons taken over a country so rugged and mountainous.

The emigrants were also assured that the Sioux would be much op-posed to the passage of so large a body through their country, and would probably resist it on account of the emigrants' destroying and frightening away the buffaloes, which were then diminishing in numbers.

The migrating body numbered over one thousand souls, with about one hundred and twenty wagons, drawn by six-ox teams, averaging about six yokes to the team, and several thousand loose horses and cattle.

The emigrants first organized and attempted to travel in one body, but it was soon found that no progress could be made with a body so cumbrous, and as yet so averse to all discipline. And at the crossing of the "Big Blue" it divided into two columns, which traveled in supporting distance of each other as far as Independence Rock on the Sweetwater.

From this point, all danger from Indians being over, the emigrants separated into small parties better suited to the narrow mountain paths and small pastures in their front.

Before the division on the Blue River there was some just cause for discontent in respect to loose cattle. Some of the emigrants had only their teams, while others had large herds in addition, which must share the pas-ture and be guarded and driven by the whole body. This discontent had its effect in the division on the Blue. Those not encumbered with or having but few loose cattle attached themselves to the light column; those having more than four or five cows had of necessity to join the heavy or cow column. Hence the cow column, being much larger than the other and much encumbered with its large herds, had to use greater exertion and observe a more rigid discipline to keep pace with the more agile consort. It is with the cow column that I propose to journey with the reader for a single day.

It is four o'clock A.M.; the sentinels on duty have discharged their rifles—the signal that the hours of sleep are over—and every wagon and tent is pouring forth its night tenants, and slow-kindling smokes begin largely to rise and float away in the morning air. Sixty men start from the corral, spreading as they make through the vast herd of cattle and horses that make a semicircle around the encampment, the most distant perhaps two miles away.

The herders pass to the extreme verge and carefully examine for trails beyond, to see that none of the animals have strayed or been stolen during the night. This morning no trails led beyond the outside animals in sight, and by 5 o'clock the herders begin to contract the great, moving circle, and the well-trained animals move slowly towards camp, clipping here and there a thistle or a tempting bunch of grass on the way. In about an hour five thousand animals are close up to the encampment, and the teamsters are busy selecting their teams and driving them inside the corral to be yoked. The corral is a circle one hundred yards deep, formed with wagons connected strongly with each other; the wagon in the rear being connected with the wagon in front by its tongue and ox chains. It is a strong barrier that the most vicious ox cannot break, and in case of an attack of the Sioux would be no contemptible intrenchment.

From 6 to 7 o'clock is a busy time; breakfast is to be eaten, the tents struck, the wagons loaded and the teams yoked and brought up in readiness to be attached to their respective wagons. All know when, at 7 o'clock, the signal to march sounds, that those not ready to take their proper places in the line of march must fall into the dusty rear for the day.

There are sixty wagons. They have been divided into fifteen divisions or platoons of four wagons each, and each platoon is entitled to lead in its turn. The leading platoon today will be the rear one tomorrow, and will bring up the rear unless some teamster, through indolence or negligence, has lost his place in the line, and is condemned to that uncomfortable post. It is within ten minutes of seven; the corral but now a strong barricade is everywhere broken, the teams being attached to the wagons. The women and children have taken their places in them. The pilot (a borderer who has passed his life on the verge of civilization and has been chosen to the post of leader from his knowledge of the savage and his experience in travel through roadless wastes) stands ready, in the midst of his pioneers and aids, to mount and lead the way. Ten or fifteen young men, not today on duty, form another cluster. They are ready to start on a buffalo hunt, are well mounted and well armed, as they need be, for the unfriendly Sioux have driven the buffalo out of the Platte, and the hunters must ride fifteen or twenty miles to reach them. The cow drivers are hastening, as they get ready, to the rear of their charge, to collect and prepare them for the day's march.

It is on the stroke of seven; the rush to and fro, the cracking of whips, the loud command to oxen, and what seemed to be the inextricable confusion of the last ten minutes has ceased. Fortunately every one has been found and every teamster is at his post. The clear notes of a trumpet sound in the front; the pilot and his guards mount their horses; the leading divisions of the wagons move out of the encampment, and take up the line of march; the rest fall into their places with the precision of clock work, until the spot so lately full of life sinks back into that solitude that seems to reign over the broad plain and rushing river as the caravan draws its lazy length towards the distant El Dorado. . . .

. . . the picture in its grandeur, its wonderful mingling of colors and distinctness of detail, is forgotten in contemplation of the singular people who give it life and animation. No other race of men with the means at their command would undertake so great a journey, none save these could successfully perform it, with no previous preparation, relying only on the fertility of their own invention to devise the means to overcome each danger and difficulty as it arose. They have undertaken to perform with slow-moving oxen a journey of two thousand miles. The way lies over trackless wastes, wide and deep rivers, ragged and lofty mountains, and is beset with hostile savages. Yet, whether it were a deep river with no tree upon its banks, a rugged defile where even a loose horse could not pass, a hill too steep for him to climb, or a threatened attack of an enemy, they are always found ready and equal to the occasion, and always conquerors. May we not call them men of destiny? They are people changed in no essential particulars from their ancestors, who have followed closely on the footsteps of the receding savage, from the Atlantic seaboard to the great Valley of the Mississippi. . . .

The pilot, by measuring the ground and timing the speed of the wagons and the walk of his horses, has determined the rate of each, so as to enable him to select the nooning place, as nearly as the requisite grass and water can be had at the end of five hours' travel of the wagons. Today, the ground being favorable, little time has been lost in preparing the road, so that he and his pioneers are at the nooning place an hour in advance of the wagons, which time is spent in preparing convenient watering places for the animals, and digging little wells near the bank of the Platte, as the teams are not unyoked, but simply turned loose from the wagons, a corral is not formed at noon, but the wagons are drawn up in columns, four abreast, the leading wagon of each platoon on the left, the platoons being formed with that in view. This brings friends together at noon as well as at night.

Today an extra session of the council is being held, to settle a dispute that does not admit of delay, between a proprietor and a young man who has undertaken to do a man's service on the journey for bed and board. Many such engagements exist, and much interest is taken in the manner in which this high court, from which there is no appeal, will define the rights of each party in such engagements. The council was a high court in the most exalted sense. It was a senate composed of the ablest and most respected fathers of the emigration. It exercised both legislative and judicial powers, and its laws and decisions proved it equal and worthy of the high trust reposed in it. Its sessions were usually held on days when the caravan was not moving. It first took the state of the little commonwealth into consideration; revised or repealed rules defective or obsolete, and enacted such others as the exigencies seemed to require. The common weal being cared for, it next resolved itself into a court to hear and settle private disputes and grievances. The offender and the aggrieved appeared before it; witnesses were examined, and the parties were heard by themselves and sometimes by counsel. The judges being thus made fully acquainted with the case, and being in no way influenced or cramped by technicalities, decided all cases according to their merits. There was but little use for lawyers before this court, for no plea was entertained which was calculated to hinder or defeat the ends of justice. Many of these judges have since won honors in higher spheres. They have aided to establish on the broad basis of right and universal liberty two pillars of our great Republic in the Occident. Some of the young men who appeared before them as advocates have themselves sat upon the highest judicial tribunals, commanded armies, been governors of states and taken high position in the senate of the nation.

It is now one o'clock; the bugle has sounded and the caravan has resumed its westward journey. It is in the same order, but the evening is far less animated than the morning march; a drowsiness has fallen apparently on man and beast; teamsters drop asleep on their perches and even when walking by their teams, and the words of command are now addressed to the slowly creeping oxen in the soft tenor of women or the piping treble of children, while the snores of the teamsters make a droning accompaniment. But a little incident breaks the monotony of the march. An emigrant's wife, whose state of health has caused Doctor Whitman to travel near the wagon for the day, is now taken with violent illness. The Doctor has had the wagon driven out of the line, a tent pitched and a fire kindled. Many conjectures are hazarded in regard to this mysterious proceeding, and as to why this lone wagon is to be left behind. And we too must leave it, hasten to the front and note the proceedings, for the sun is now getting low in the west and at length the painstaking pilot is standing ready to conduct the train in the circle which he has previously measured and marked out, which is to form the invariable fortification for the night. The leading wagons follow him so nearly around the circle that but a wagon length separates them. Each wagon follows in its track, the rear closing on the front, until its tongue and ox-chains will perfectly reach from one to the other, and so accurate the measure and perfect the practices, that the hindmost wagon of the train always precisely closes the gateway, as each wagon is brought into position. It is dropped from its team (the teams being inside the circle), the team unyoked and the yokes and chains are used to connect the wagon strongly with that in its front. Within ten minutes from the time the leading wagon halted, the barricade is formed, the teams unyoked and driven out to pasture. Every one is busy preparing fires of buffalo chips to cook the evening meal, pitching tents and otherwise preparing for the night. There are anxious watchers for the absent wagon, for there are many matrons who may be afflicted like its inmate before the journey is over; and they fear the strange and startling practice of this Oregon doctor will be dangerous. But as the sun goes down the absent wagon rolls into camp[;]

the bright, speaking face and cheery look of the doctor, who rides in advance, declare without words that all is well, and both mother and child are comfortable. I would fain now and here pay a passing tribute to that noble and devoted man, Doctor Whitman. I will obtrude no other name upon the reader, nor would I his were he of our party or even living, but his stay with us was transient, though the good he did was permanent, and he has long since died at his post.

From the time he joined us on the Platte until he left us at Fort Hall, his great experience and indomitable energy were of priceless value to the migrating column. His constant advice, which we knew was based upon a knowledge of the road before us, was, "Travel, *travel,* TRAVEL; nothing else will take you to the end of your journey; nothing is wise that does not help you along; nothing is good for you that causes a moment's delay." His great authority as a physician and complete success in the case above referred to, saved us many prolonged and perhaps ruinous delays from similar causes, and it is no disparagement to others to say that to no other individual are the emigrants of 1843 so much indebted for the successful conclusion of their journey as to Dr. Marcus Whitman.

All able to bear arms in the party have been formed into three companies, and each of these into four watches; every third night it is the duty of one of these companies to keep watch and ward over the camp, and it is so arranged that each watch takes its turn of guard duty through the different watches of the night. Those forming the first watch tonight will be second on duty, then third and fourth, which brings them through all the watches of the night. They begin at 8 o'clock P.M., and end at 4 o'clock A.M.

It is not yet 8 o'clock when the first watch is to be set; the evening meal is just over, and the corral now free from the intrusion of cattle or horses, groups of children are scattered over it. The larger are taking a game of romps; "the wee toddling things" are being taught that great achievement that distinguishes man from the lower animals. Before a tent near the river a violin makes lively music, and some youths and maidens have improvised a dance upon the green; in another quarter a flute gives its mellow and melancholy notes to the still night air, which, as they float away over the quiet river, seem a lament for the past rather than a hope for the future. It has been a prosperous day; more than twenty miles have been accomplished of the great journey. The encampment is a good one; one of the causes that threatened much future delay has just been removed by the skill and energy of that "good angel" of the emigrants, Doctor Whitman, and it has lifted a load from the hearts of the elders. Many of these are assembled around the good doctor at the tent of the pilot (which is his home for the time being), and are giving grave attention to his wise and energetic counsel. The care-worn pilot sits aloof, quietly smoking his pipe, for he knows the brave doctor is "strengthening his hands."

The Oregon Archives

The Oregon Archives *is a compilation of documents relating to the evolution of provisional government in the Oregon country. The best-known episode of this period is the public meeting held at Champoeg on May 2, 1843. The minutes of that meeting (the fifth document reproduced below) constitute the official record of the event, but they are sparing in detail and do not agree with subsequent and more colorful accounts by participants. Moreover, regional chauvinists have so embellished and dramatized the story that the possibility of even a reasonably precise account of the Champoeg meeting seems remote. More important is the report of the legislative committee of July 5, 1843, in which the main outlines of the new government are defined. In 1844 the original scheme of government was altered to meet the community's needs more adequately. The most important changes and additions were the provision for a single rather than a plural executive, the substitution of taxation for individual subscriptions, and the elimination from the land law of the clause favoring missions and threatening John McLoughlin's land claim at Oregon City. The most casual examination of the documents to follow reveals the extent to which the committee leaned on the experience of established states and territories. Two features reminiscent of the confederation period—the plural executive and the reliance upon requisitions to defray the costs of government—were repudiated after a brief trial.*

Public Meetings*

February 17, 1841

At a meeting of some of the inhabitants of the Willamette Valley, for consultation concerning the steps necessary to be taken for the formation of laws, and the election of officers, to execute the same, for the better preservation of peace and good order, the following business was transacted:—

---

* From La Fayette Grover, ed., *The Oregon Archives, Including the Journals, Governors' Messages and Public Papers of Oregon* (Salem, Oregon: Asahel Bush, Public Printer, 1853), pp. 5–6, 8–11, 14–15.

Rev. Jason Lee was chosen chairman, and Rev. Gustavus Hines was chosen secretary.

On motion,

Resolved—That an addition of one be made to the committee of arrangement, chosen at a previous meeting.

On motion,

Resolved—That the chairman nominate this committee-man.

Geo. Le Breton, was nominated and elected.

Resolved—That it be recommended that there be a committee of seven, elected for the purpose of drafting a constitution and code of laws, for the government of the settlements, south of the Columbia River.

It was then

Resolved—That all settlers, north of the Columbia River, not connected with the Hudson Bay Company, be admitted to the protection of our laws, on making application to that effect.

The meeting then proceeded to advise the committee of arrangements, to propose the making of certain officers, to wit :—

A Governor; a Supreme Judge, with probate powers; three Justices of the Peace; three constables; three Road Commissioners; an Attorney-General; a Clerk of the Courts, and Public Recorder; one Treasurer; two Overseers of the Poor.

It was recommended to nominate persons to fill the several offices, and that they be chosen *viva voce*.

The meeting then resolved itself into committee of the whole, for the purpose of choosing candidates for the several offices, and after having nominated persons to fill the various offices, it was

Resolved—That the doings of the committee of the whole be deposited in the hands of the chairman, to be presented to the meeting to-morrow.

On motion, the meeting then adjourned, to meet at eight o'clock, to-morrow.

FEBRUARY 18, 1841

At a full meeting of the inhabitants of Willamette Valley, at the American Mission House,

David Leslie was elected chairman, and Sidney Smith, and Gustavus Hines, were chosen secretaries.

The doings of the previous meeting were presented to the assembly, and were accepted, in part; viz. :—

That a committee be chosen for framing a constitution, and drafting a code of laws; and that the following persons compose the committee; to wit :—

Rev. F. N. Blanchet, Rev. Jason Lee, David Donpierre, Gustavus

Hines, Mr. Charlevon, Robt. Moore, J. L. Parrish, Etienne Lucier, and Wm. Johnson.

I. L. Babcock, was appointed to fill the office of supreme judge, with probate powers.

Geo. Le Breton, was chosen to fill the office of clerk of courts, and public recorder.

Wm. Johnson, was chosen to fill the office of high sheriff.

Havier Laderant, Pierre Billique, and Wm. M'Carty, were chosen constables.

Resolved—That, until a code of laws be adopted by this community, Dr. Babcock be instructed to act, according to the laws of the state of New York.

Resolved—That this meeting now adjourn, to meet on the first Tuesday of June, at the New Building, near the Catholic church.

February 2, 1843

A public meeting, of a number of the citizens of this colony, was called, in order to take into consideration the propriety of adopting some measures, for the protection of our herds, &c., in this country.

On motion,

Dr. I. L. Babcock was called to the chair, who proceeded to state the objects of the meeting, and the necessity of acting.

Mr. W. H. Gray moved, and Mr. Torn seconded the motion,—That a committee of six be appointed to notify a general meeting, and report business, &c., which motion was carried, and Messrs. Gray, Beers, Gervais, Willson, Barnaby, and Lucier, were appointed said committee.

Mr. Beers moved, that a general meeting be called, at the house of Mr. Jos. Gervais, on the first Monday in March next, at ten o'clock, A.M., which motion was carried.

W. H. Willson   I. L. Babcock
Secretary   *Chairman*

1st Monday in March, 1843

In pursuance of a resolution of a previous meeting, the citizens of Willamette Valley met, and the meeting being called to order,

Mr. James O'Neil was chosen chairman.

Mr. Monture was chosen as secretary, but declining to serve,

Mr. Le Breton was chosen.

The doings of the former meeting were read.

The committee, appointed to notify a general meeting, and report business, made the following report, to wit:—

Your committee beg leave to report as follows:—

It being admitted by all, that bears, wolves, panthers, &c., &c., are destructive to the useful animals, owned by the settlers of this colony, your committee would respectfully submit the following resolutions, as the sense of this meeting, by which the community may be governed in carrying on a *defensive* and *destructive* WAR against all such animals :—

Resolved—That we deem it expedient for this community, to take immediate measures for the destruction of all wolves, bears, and panthers, and such other animals as are known to be destructive to cattle, horses, sheep, and hogs. . . .

That a bounty of fifty cents be paid for the destruction of a small wolf; $3 00, for a large wolf; $1 50, for the lynx; $2 00, for the bear; and $5 00, for the panther.

That no bounty be paid, unless the individual claiming said bounty give satisfactory evidence, or by presenting the skin of the head with the ears, of all animals for which he claims a bounty. . . .

That the bounties, specified in the 4th resolution, be limited to whites and their descendants. . . .

Resolved—That no one receive a bounty, (except Indians,) unless he pay a subscription of $5 00. . . .

It was moved and seconded, that the Indians receive one-half as much as the whites.

It was moved and seconded, that, all claims, for bounties, be presented within ten days from the time of becoming entitled to said bounties, and, if there should be any doubts, the individual claiming a bounty shall give his oath to the various circumstances, which was carried. . . .

Resolved—That no money be paid to any white, or his descendants, previous to the time of his subscription.

Resolved—That the bounty of a minor child be paid to a parent or guardian. . . .

Resolved—That a committee be appointed to take into consideration the propriety of taking measures for the civil and military protection of this colony.

Resolved—That said committee consist of twelve persons.

Messrs. Dr. Babcock, Dr. White, O'Neil, Shortess, Newell, Lucier, Gervais, Hubbard, M'Kay, Gray, Smith, and Gay, were appointed said committee.

On motion, the meeting adjourned.

G. W. Le Breton   James O'Neil
Secretary   *President*

May 2, 1843

At a public meeting of the inhabitants of the Willamette settlements, held in accordance with the call of the committee, chosen at a former meeting, for the purpose of taking steps to organize themselves into a civil community, and provide themselves with the protection, secured by the enforcement of law and order,

Dr. I. L. Babcock was chosen chairman, and Messrs. Gray, Le Breton, and Willson, secretaries.

The committee made their report, which was read, and

A motion was made, that it be accepted, which was lost.

Considerable confusion existing in consequence,

It was moved by Mr. Le Breton, and seconded by Mr. Gray, that the meeting divide, preparatory to being counted; those in favour of the objects of this meeting taking the right, and those of a contrary mind taking the left, which being carried by acclamation, and a great majority being found in favour of organization, the greater part of the dissenters withdrew.*

It was then moved and carried, that the report of the committee be taken up, and disposed of article by article.

A motion was made and carried, that a supreme judge, with probate powers, be chosen to officiate in this community.

Moved and carried, that a clerk of the court, or recorder, be chosen.

Moved and carried, that a sheriff be chosen.

Moved and carried, that three magistrates be chosen.

Moved and carried, that three constables be chosen.

Moved and carried, that a committee of nine persons be chosen, for the purpose of drafting a code of laws, for the government of this community, to be presented to a public meeting to be hereafter called by them, on the fifth day of July next, for their acceptance.

A motion was made and carried, that a treasurer be chosen.

Moved and carried, that a major, and three captains, be chosen.

Moved and carried, that we now proceed to choose the persons to fill the various offices, by ballot.

W. E. Willson was chosen to act as supreme judge, with probate powers.

G. W. Le Breton was chosen to act as clerk of court, or recorder.

J. L. Meek was chosen to fill the office of sheriff.

W. H. Willson was chosen treasurer.

Moved and carried, that the remainder of the officers be chosen by hand ballot, and nomination from the floor.

Messrs. Hill, Shortess, Newell, Beers, Hubbard, Gray, O'Neil, Moore, and Dougherty, were chosen to act as the legislative committee.

---

* Testimony of participants varies on the vote. Only Le Breton claims that a great majority favored organization. The most popular version has it that there was a simple majority of two.

Messrs. Burns, Judson, and A. T. Smith, were chosen to act as magistrates.

Messrs. Elbert, Bridges, and Lewis, were chosen to act as constables.

Mr. John Howard was chosen mayor.

Messrs. Wm. M'Carty, C. M'Kay, and S. Smith, were chosen captains.

Moved and carried, that the legislative committee make their report on the 5th day of July next, at Champooick.

Moved and carried, that the services of the legislative committee be paid for, at $1 25, per day, and that the money be raised by subscription.

Moved and carried, that the mayor and captains be instructed to enlist men to form companies of mounted riflemen.

Moved and carried, that an additional magistrate and constable be chosen.

Mr. Campo was chosen as an additional magistrate.

Mr. Matthew was chosen as an additional constable.

Moved and carried, that the legislative committee shall not sit over six days.

The meeting was then adjourned.

The question having arisen, with regard to what time the newly-appointed officers shall commence their duties, the meeting was again called to order, when

It was moved and carried, that the old officers remain in office till the laws are made and accepted, or until the next public meeting.

Attest.

G. W. Le Breton

Report of Legislative Committee*

The legislative committee recommend that the following laws (upon judiciary) be adopted.

SEC. 1. We, the people of Oregon Territory, for purposes of mutual protection, and to secure peace and prosperity among ourselves, agree to adopt the following laws and regulations, until such time as the United States of America extend their jurisdiction over us.

Be it therefore enacted, by the free citizens of Oregon Territory, that

---

* From *Oregon Archives,* pp. 28–32. This report (headed "Report of Legislative Committee, upon the Judiciary") was dated July 5, 1843.

the said territory, for purposes of temporary government, be divided into not less than three, nor more than five, districts; subject to be extended to a greater number, when an increase of population shall require it.

For the purpose of fixing the principles of civil and religious liberty, as the basis of all laws and constitutions of government that may hereafter be adopted,

Be it enacted, that the following articles be considered as articles of compact, among the free citizens of this territory :—

ART. 1.   No person, demeaning himself in a peaceable and orderly manner, shall ever be molested, on account of his mode of worship, or religious sentiments.

ART. 2.   The inhabitants of said territory shall always be entitled to the benefits of the writ of *habeas corpus,* and trial by jury; of a proportionate representation of the people in the legislature,—and of judicial proceedings, according to the course of common law. All persons shall be bailable, unless for capital offences, where the proof shall be evident, or the presumption great. All fines shall be moderate, and no cruel or unusual punishments inflicted. No man shall be deprived of his liberty, but by the judgment of his peers, or the law of the land; and, should the public exigencies make it necessary, for the common preservation, to take any person's property, or to demand his particular services, full compensation shall be made for the same. And, in the just preservation of rights and property, it is understood and declared that no law ought ever to be made, or have force, in said territory, that shall in any manner whatever interfere with, or affect private contracts, or engagements, *bona fide,* and without fraud, previously formed.

ART. 3.   Religion, morality, and knowledge, being necessary to good government, and the happiness of mankind, schools, and the means of education shall forever be encouraged.

The utmost good faith shall always be observed towards the Indians. Their lands and property shall never be taken from them without their consent; and, in their property, rights, and liberty, they shall never be invaded or disturbed, unless in just and lawful wars, authorized by the representatives of the people; but laws, founded in justice and humanity, shall, from time to time, be made, for preventing injustice being done to them, and for preserving peace and friendship with them.

ART. 4.   There shall be neither slavery nor involuntary servitude in said territory, otherwise than for the punishment of crimes whereof the party shall have been duly convicted.

SEC. 2.   ART. 1.   *Be it enacted, by the authority aforesaid,* that the officers, elected on the 2nd of May, inst., shall continue in office, until the second Tuesday in May, 1844, and until others are elected and qualified.

ART. 2.   *Be it further enacted,* that an election of civil and military officers shall be held annually, on the second Tuesday in May, in the several districts of such places as shall be designated by law.

ART. 3. Each officer heretofore elected, or hereafter to be elected, shall, before entering upon the duties of his office, take an oath or affirmation, to support the laws of the territory, and faithfully to discharge the duties of his office.

ART. 4. Every free male descendent of a white man, an inhabitant of this territory, of the age of twenty-one years and upwards, who shall have been an inhabitant of this territory at the time of its organization, shall be entitled to vote at the election of officers, civil and military, and be eligible to any office in the territory—*Provided,* that all persons of the description entitled to vote by the provisions of this section, who shall have emigrated to this territory after organization, shall be entitled to the rights of citizens after having resided six months in the territory.

ART. 5. The executive power shall be vested in a committee of three persons, elected by the qualified voters at the annual election, who shall have power to grant pardons and reprieves for offences against the laws of the territory, to call out the military force of the territory to repel invasion, or suppress insurrection, to take care that the laws are faithfully executed, and to recommend such laws as they may consider necessary, to the representatives of the people, for their action. Two members of the committee shall constitute a quorum to transact business.

ART. 6. The legislative power shall be vested in a committee of nine persons, who shall be elected by the qualified electors at the annual election, giving to each district a representation in ratio of its population, excluding Indians; and the said members of the committee shall reside in the district for which they shall be chosen.

ART. 7. The judicial power shall be vested in a supreme court, consisting of a supreme judge and two justices of the peace, a probate court, and in justices of the peace. The jurisdiction of the supreme court shall be both appellate and original. That of the probate court and justices of the peace, as limited by law—*Provided,* that individual justices of the peace shall not have jurisdiction of any matter of controversy, when the title or boundary of land may be in dispute, or where the sum claimed exceed fifty dollars.

ART. 8. There shall be a recorder elected by the qualified electors, at the annual election, who shall keep a faithful record of the proceedings in the legislative committee, supreme, and probate courts; also, record all boundaries of land presented for that purpose; and all marks and brands used for marking live stock; procure and keep the standard weights and measures required by law, seal weights and measures, and keep a record of the same; and also record wills and deeds, and other instruments of writing, required by law to be recorded. . . .

ART. 9. There shall be a treasurer elected by the qualified electors of the territory, who shall, before entering upon the duties of his office, give bond to the executive committee, in the sum of fifteen hundred dollars, with two or more sufficient securities, to be approved by the executive committee, conditioned for the faithful discharge of the duties of his office. The treasurer shall receive all moneys belonging to the territory, that may be raised by contribution, or otherwise, and shall procure suitable books, in which he shall enter an account of his receipts and disbursements.

ART. 10. The treasurer shall in no case pay money out of the treasury, but according to law, and shall annually report to the legislative committee, a true account of his receipts and disbursements, with necessary vouchers for the same, and shall deliver to his successor in office, all books, money, accounts, or other property, belonging to the territory, so soon as his successor shall become qualified.

ART. 11. The treasurer shall receive, for his services, the sum of five per cent. of all moneys received and paid out, according to law, and three per cent. of all moneys in the treasury when he goes out of office, and two per cent. upon the disbursement of money in the treasury when he comes into office.

ART. 12. The laws of Iowa territory shall be the law of this territory, in civil, military, and criminal cases; where not otherwise provided for, and where no statute of Iowa territory applies, the principles of common law and equity shall govern.

ART. 13. The law of Iowa territory, regulating weights and measures, shall be the law of this territory—*Provided,* that the supreme court shall perform the duties of the county commissioners, and the recorder shall perform the duties of the clerk of the county commissioners, as prescribed in said laws of Iowa—*And provided,* that 60 lbs., avordupois weight, shall be the standard weight of a bushel of wheat, whether the same be more or less than 2150 2-5 cubic inches.

ART. 14. The laws of Iowa territory, respecting wills and administrations, shall be the law of this territory, in all cases not otherwise provided for.

ART. 15. The law of Iowa, respecting vagrants, is hereby adopted, as far as adapted to the circumstances of the citizens of Oregon.

ART. 16. The supreme court shall hold two sessions annually, upon the third Tuesdays in April and September; the first session to be held at Champooick, on the third Tuesday of September, 1843, and the second session at Twality Plains, on the third Tuesday of April, 1844. At the sessions of the supreme court, the supreme judge shall preside, assisted by two justices—*Provided,* that no justice shall assist in trying any case that has been brought before the court, by appeal from his judgment. The supreme court shall have original jurisdiction, in cases of treason, felony, or breaches of the peace, and in civil cases, where the sum claimed exceed fifty dollars.

ART. 17. All male persons, of the age of sixteen years and upwards, and all females of the age of fourteen and upwards, shall have right in engaging in marriage—*Provided,* that where either of the parties shall be under the age of twenty-one, the consent of the parents or guardians of such minors shall be necessary to the validity of such matrimonial engagement. Every ordained minister of the gospel of any religious denomination, the supreme judge, and all justices of the peace, are hereby authorized to solemnize marriages according to law, to have the same recorded, and pay the recorder's fee. All marriages shall be recorded by the territorial recorder, within one month from the time of such marriage taking place and being made known to him officially. The legal fee for marriage shall be one dollar, and for recording the same, fifty cents.

ART. 18. All offices subsequently made shall be filled by election and ballot in the several districts, in the most central and convenient place in each district, upon the day appointed by law, and under such regulations as the laws of Iowa provide.

ART. 19. *Resolved*—That a committee of three be appointed to draw up a digest of the doings of the people of this territory, with regard to an organization, and transmit the same to the United States Government, for their information.

Law of Land Claims*

ART. 1. Any person now holding, or hereafter wishing to establish, a claim to land in this territory, shall designate the extent of his claim by natural boundaries, or by marks at the corners, and on the lines of such claim, and have the extent and boundaries of said claim recorded in the office of the territorial recorder, in a book to be kept by him for that purpose, within twenty days from the time of making said claim—*Provided,* that those who shall already be in possession of land, shall be allowed one year from the passage of this act, to file a description of his claim in the recorder's office.

ART. 2. All claimants shall, within six months of the time of recording their claims, make permanent improvements upon the same by build-

---

* From *Oregon Archives,* p. 35.

ing or enclosing, and also become an occupant upon said claim within one year from the date of such record.

ART. 3. No individual shall be allowed to hold a claim of more than one square mile, or 640 acres in a square or oblong form, according to the natural situation of the premises; nor shall any individual be allowed to hold more than one claim at the same time. Any person complying with the provisions of these ordinances, shall be entitled to the same recourse against trespass as in other cases by law provided.

ART. 4. No person shall be entitled to hold such a claim upon city or town sites, extensive water privileges, or other situations necessary for the transaction of mercantile or manufacturing operations, and to the detriment of the community—*Provided,* that nothing in these laws shall be so construed as to affect any claim of any mission of a religious character, made previous to this time, of an extent not more than six miles square.

Approved by the people, July 5th, 1843.

Peter H. Burnett

Peter H. Burnett (1807–1895) spent nearly six years in the Willamette Valley before he moved to California. During that time, he was a prominent and active participant in the political and civil affairs of the community. As a member of the Legislative Committee of 1844, Burnett had a hand in revising the original government of 1843. His comments, taken from his published reminiscences, illumine and enliven the official record.

Recollections of an Old Pioneer*

Soon after my arrival at Linnton, I was consulted as to the right of the people of Oregon to organize a Provisional Government. At first I gave my opinion against it, thinking we had no such right; but a few weeks' reflection satisfied me that we had such a right, and that necessity

---

* From Peter H. Burnett, *Recollections and Opinions of an Old Pioneer* (New York: D. Appleton and Co., 1880), pp. 168–174.

required us to exercise it. Communities, as well as individuals, have the natural right of self-defense; and it is upon this ground that the right to institute governments among men must ultimately rest. This right of self-preservation is bestowed upon man by his Creator.

We found ourselves placed in a new and very embarrassing position. The right of sovereignty over the country was in dispute between the United States and Great Britain, and neither country could establish any government over us. Our community was composed of American citizens and British subjects, occupying the same country as neighbors, with all their respective natural prejudices and attachments, and so distant from the mother countries as to be to a great extent beyond the reach of home influences. We had, therefore, a difficult population to govern; but this fact only rendered government the more necessary.

We also found, by actual experiment, that some political government was a necessity. Though political government be imperfect, it is still a blessing, and necessary for the preservation of the race. Without it, the strongest and most reckless characters in the community would be tyrants over the others. The theory of the wandering savage, to leave the kindred of the murdered victim to revenge his death, would not answer for a civilized race of men. The weak and timid, the peaceful and conscientious, and those who had no kindred, could not be protected under such a theory. Without any law but that of individual self-defense, we found it impossible to get along in peace. When a person died, the worst characters could seize upon his estate under some pretense or other, and defeat the just rights of defenseless heirs. So long as these violent, bad men had only to overcome and defeat single individuals, they had no fears. It is only when the combined force of a whole community is brought to bear upon these desperadoes that they can be effectually kept in order.

As we could not, with any exact certainty, anticipate the time when the conflicting claims of the two contending governments would be settled, we determined to organize a Provisional Government for ourselves. In this undertaking our British neighbors ultimately joined us with good will, and did their part most faithfully, as did our American citizens.

I was a member of "the Legislative Committee of Oregon" of 1844. It was composed of nine members elected by the people, and consisted of only one house. The year before, the people of Oregon had substantially organized a Provisional Government; but the organization was imperfect, as is necessarily the case in the beginning of all human institutions. We improved upon their labors, and our successors improved upon ours.

Our legislative committee held two sessions, one in June, and the other in December of that year, each session lasting only a few days. In our then condition, we had but little time to devote to public business. Our personal needs were too urgent, and our time too much occupied in making a support for our families. Our legislation, however, was ample for the time. There was then no printing establishment in Oregon. We passed an act in relation to land claims, the first section of which provided that "all persons who have heretofore made, or shall hereafter make permanent improvements upon a place, with a *bona fide* intention of occupying and holding the same for himself, and shall continue to occupy and cultivate the same, shall be entitled to hold 640 acres, and shall hold only one claim at the same time; *provided,* a man may hold town lots in addition to his claim." The seventh and last section gave all persons complying with the provisions of the act "the remedy of forcible entry and detainer against intruders, and the action of trespass against trespassers." This act was passed June 25, 1844. It will be seen that the remedy against intruders was simple, cheap, quick, and efficient, and well adapted to existing circumstances.

By an act passed June 27, 1844, the executive power was vested in a single person, to be elected at the then next annual election by the people, and at the annual election to be held every two years thereafter, to hold his office for the term of two years, and receive an annual salary of $300. By the same act the judicial power was vested in the circuit courts, and in the justices of the peace; and the act provided that one judge should be elected by the qualified voters at the annual election, who should hold his office for one year, and whose duty it was to hold two terms of the circuit court in each county every year; and for his services he should receive an annual salary of $500, and also legal fees for probate business. By the same act the legislative power was vested in a house of representatives, composed of members elected annually by the people.

The first section of the third article of the same act was as follows:

Section 1. All the statute laws of Iowa Territory passed at the first session of the legislative assembly of said Territory, and not of a local character, and not incompatible with the condition and circumstances of this country, shall be the law of this government, unless otherwise modified; and the common law of England and principles of equity, not modified by the statutes of Iowa or of this government, and not incompatible with its principles, shall constitute a part of the law of this land.

Article V was in these words:

Section 1. All officers shall be elected by the people once a year, unless otherwise provided, at a general election to be held in each county on the first Tuesday in June in each year, at such places as shall be designated by the judge of the circuit court.

Sec. 2. As many justices of the peace and constables shall be elected from time to time as shall be deemed necessary by the circuit court of each county.

The seventh article fixed the time of holding the terms of the circuit courts in the several counties, and gave the judge the power to designate the several places of holding said terms by giving one month's notice thereof.

We also passed on June 24th an act consisting of eight sections, prohibiting the importation, distillation, sale, and barter of ardent spirits. For every sale or barter the offender was to pay a fine of $20; and for establishing and carrying on a distillery, the offender was subject to be indicted before the circuit court as for a nuisance, and, if convicted, to a fine of $100; and it was made the duty of the court to issue an order directing the sheriff to seize and destroy the distilling apparatus, which order the sheriff was bound to execute.

On June 22d an act containing 26 sections was passed concerning roads and highways. On December 24th an act was passed allowing the voters of Oregon at the annual election of 1845 to give their votes for or against the call of a convention.

The following act in relation to Indians was passed December 23d:

Whereas, The Indians inhabiting this country are rapidly diminishing, being now mere remnants of once powerful tribes, now disorganized, without government, and so situated that no treaty can be regularly made with them;

And Whereas, By an act passed in July 1843, this government has shown its humane policy to protect the Indians in their rights;

And Whereas, The Indians are not engaged in agriculture, and have no use for or right to any tracts, portions, or parcels of land, not actually occupied or used by them; therefore,

Be it enacted by the legislative committee of Oregon, as follows:

Section 1. That the Indians shall be protected in the free use of such pieces of vacant land as they occupy with their villages or other improvements, and such fisheries as they have heretofore used.

Sec. 2. That the executive power be required to see that the laws in regard to Indians be faithfully executed; and that whenever the laws shall be violated, the said Executive shall be empowered to bring suit in the name of Oregon against such wrong-doer in the courts of the country.

An act was passed on June 27th fixing the number of members of the next House of Representatives at 13, and apportioning the representation among the then five counties of Oregon.

All necessary local bills were passed, and our little government was put into practical and successful operation. Having adopted the general statutes of Iowa and the common law, we had a provision for every case likely to arise in so small a community.

At first the great difficulty was to make our little government efficient. Our people honestly differed very much in their views as to our right to institute government. In 1843 there were 52 affirmative and 50 negative votes. There were so many of our people who were conscientiously opposed to the organization of any government that we found it a delicate matter to use force against men whose motives we were sure were good. Still, government had to be practically enforced.

Joseph L. Meek was selected in May or July, 1843, for sheriff. He was the very man for the position. He was both as brave and as magnanimous as the lion. Do his duty he would, peacefully if possible, but forcibly if he must. If we had selected a rash or timid man for sheriff, we must have failed for a time. To be a government at all, the laws must be enforced.

Meek soon had his courage fully tested. A stout carpenter named Dawson was engaged in a fight in the winter of 1843–44, and a warrant was at once issued for his arrest, and placed in Meek's hands to be executed. Dawson was no doubt of opinion that we had no right to organize and enforce our government. Meek went to Dawson's shop, where he was at work at his bench with his jack-plane. Meek walked in, and said laughingly, "Dawson, I came for you." Dawson replied that Meek had come for the wrong man. Meek, still laughing, said again, "I came for you," and was about to lay his hands on Dawson, when the latter drew back with his jack-plane raised to strike. But Meek was not only stout, but active and brave; and, seizing the plane, he wrested it by force from Dawson. Dawson at once turned around and picked up his broad-axe; but at the moment he faced Meek he found a cocked pistol at his breast. Meek, still laughing, said: "Dawson, I came for you. Surrender or die!" Very few men will persist under such circumstances; and Dawson, though as brave as most men, began to cry, threw down his broad-axe, and went with Meek without further objection. Dawson declared that, as *he* had to submit, every other man must; and he was no longer an enemy of our government.

This intrepid performance of his official duty so established Meek's character for true courage in the exercise of his office that he had little or no trouble in the future; and the authority of our little government was thus thoroughly established.

ADDITIONAL READINGS

There is no comprehensive account of the migrations to Oregon, although W. J. Ghent's *The Road to Oregon* (New York, 1929) approaches what is needed. The best-known title on the Oregon Trail is Francis Parkman's famous book by that name; but of course the young historian never reached Oregon, going no farther than the eastern slope of the Rockies. Representative collections of documents dealing with the western migrations include two books by Archer B. and Dorothy P. Hulbert—*Where Rolls the Oregon: Prophet and Pessimist Look Northwest* (Denver, 1933) and *The Call of the Columbia: Iron Men and Saints Take the Oregon Trail* (Denver, 1934); and the volume *Hall J. Kelley on Oregon,* edited by Fred W. Powell (Princeton, 1932). Broader than simply the Oregon Trail is Jay Monaghan's *The Overland Trail* (Indianapolis, 1937). The best treatment of the Oregon migration in fiction is A. B. Guthrie's *The Way West* (New York, 1950).

For detailed consideration of the provisional-government episode, see R. C. Clark, *History of the Willamette Valley* (3 vols., Chicago, 1927); and J. R. Robertson, "Genesis of Political Authority and of a Commonwealth Government in Oregon," *Oregon Historical Quarterly* (March 1900).

For more recent summaries of early Oregon settlement, consult Oscar O. Winther, *The Great Northwest* (New York, 1956); and Dorothy Johansen and Charles Gates, *Empire on the Columbia* (New York, 1958).

5

NEW SPAIN
AND THE
SANTA FE TRAIL

Spanish expansion in the New World began, of course, with Columbus, who represented one segment in the fanning out of Europe. The fan, in fact, provides a symbolic approximation of the way the Spaniards moved in the Western Hemisphere. Their bases in the Caribbean were both spots on the perimeter of their fan from Spain and foci for new fans along the Gulf of Mexico. Again, from Mexico City they radiated northward into what became the American Southwest.

This latter push continued sporadically from the sixteenth to the nineteenth centuries. It was often sparked by energetic officials, like Hernando Cortez or Antonio de Mendoza in the sixteenth century or José de Gálvez in the eighteenth. These men were responsible for dispatching an uneven but sometimes glittering line of explorers and conquistadores—the Coronados, the Cabrillos, and the Oñates of New Spain.

There were various reasons behind the energy. A mining frontier to the north of Mexico City, including the old silver centers of Zacatecas and San Luis Potosí, had early lured the Spaniards. But their minds were spinning with stories of Peruvian treasure, and their hope for something richer than Zacatecas drove them across difficult ranges and into forbidding deserts, which were supposed to conceal the seven golden cities of Cibolá.

Sometimes the energy was dictated not so much by gold as by imperial power and political position. When Sir Francis Drake nettled the Spaniards in 1578–79 by penetrating the Straits of Magellan and sailing his *Golden Hind* into the restricted Spanish ports on the Pacific, his activities catalyzed renewed efforts by Spain, just as in later centuries Russian rumblings in the North would set imperial wheels to turning.

But of all the causes of Spanish expansion, none bulked larger than religion. The padre was often the first man on the scene, and the soldier followed. Sometimes the two came together, but never was the padre missing as a prime factor in colonization.

By 1700 the far northern frontier of New Spain consisted of a fringe borderland in Texas—sometimes infiltrated by French traders from Louisiana but contained on the north by the fierceness of Apache and Comanche —and New Mexico, a full-fledged province of priests, settlers, and soldiers, centering in Santa Fe, a city roughly as old as Jamestown, Virginia. Santa Fe was to become a crucial contact between the emerging United States and Mexico. Spain, in good mercantilistic style, did not wish its trade to be shared with others, and many an American trader after 1806 followed Lieutenant Zebulon Pike into the jails of New Spain. But Santa Fe was 1,500 miles from Mexico City, and it needed the manufactured goods that St. Louis could supply. After Mexican independence and particularly after William Becknell opened the routes in 1821, the Santa Fe Trail became a thriving commercial artery, over which silver, furs, mules, textiles, knives, and guns were vigorously traded. The trail incidentally provides us with some insight into frontier individualism. The trappers, traders, and soldiers who traveled this early road were often men with an independent spirit as vast as the plains' horizon; but at the same time their very survival frequently depended on a complicated network of cooperative activity.

But to return to Spanish settlement. In the eighteenth century—for all the reasons mentioned above and also because of a particular imperial threat posed by Russian penetration southward from Alaska—Alta California was settled. Baja California, the peninsula to the south, had long held a chain of missions; and in 1769 and 1770 Don Gaspar de Portolá and Father Junipero Serra established similar settlements at San Diego and Monterey. Initially these Alta California missions and presidios were woefully weak, struggling outposts, dependent on the sea for their supplies. In order for them to survive and exert any kind of military or political strength, a reasonable number of settlers were required, and consequently an overland route across Sonora was highly desirable. The job fell to Juan Bautista de Anza, who in 1774 broke the trail and in 1775 brought a group of families to settle San Francisco the following year.

In the drama of the De Anza story—one man of magnificent heroism plus long preparation by many men—we feel again the balance required on any frontier between individual initiative and carefully organized group action. When we learn that to obtain the necessary number of colonists the government and De Anza had to provide complete outfits of clothing and promise daily rations of food for five years, the unadulterated individualism of this particular frontier comes into question.

Indeed, the three characteristic institutions of the Spanish frontier—mission, presidio, and pueblo—all illustrate this individual-group alliance. The individual heroism of the Jesuit Father Kino or the Franciscan Father Serra stands always against the ideal of the cooperative, communitarian mission settlement, with groups of Indian neophytes learning the brotherhood of man under the fatherhood of God. Likewise, the soldier of the presidio and the alcalde of the pueblo have their own particular functions in the larger scheme—to the glory of God and his regent, the King. And these institutions are a part of the American frontier, even in a certain sense the result of that frontier.

Juan Bautista de Anza

In September 1775, under orders from the viceroy, Juan Bautista de Anza (1735–1788) left the frontier post of Horcasitas in Sonora to follow the trail that he had reconnoitered the previous year overland to Alta California. Instead of the small military detail that he had taken with him on the previous trip, this time he shepherded 240 persons (men, women, and a large number of children), 165 pack mules, 340 saddle animals, and 302 beef cattle. It was a major undertaking. Only one person died en route, and that one in childbirth. His colonists and cattle were to provide an enduring base for the province, even as far north as San Francisco (named for the protecting saint of the expedition). Fortunately, De Anza kept a detailed journal. The brief portions here quoted should give some hint of the magnitude of his accomplishment.

Journal of California Expeditions*

Well notorious, and accredited by original documents which I have sent to his Excellency the Viceroy, are the efforts which I have made in order that this expedition might begin the march for its destination at the end of the month just past from the presidio in my charge, whence it sets forth today. But, as I have informed his Excellency, the event which took place here on the 7th of September cited, resulting in the theft of all its horse herd by the common enemy, the Apaches, together with other occurrences, prevented the arrival early in the same month of September of the ten soldiers who were to go from this presidio as escort and protection of the expedition. And without them it was not possible to make the march from the presidio of San Miguel, to which they were ordered, to the presidio of Tubac, because the whole distance is greatly exposed to danger, and frequent misfortunes are being experienced in traveling over it.

As soon as I got the news of that occurrence I made arrangements to send from San Miguel to Tubac saddle animals to carry the ten soldiers mentioned; nevertheless, the best that could be done, since the month was well under way, was that these ten soldiers should arrive at San Miguel and we set out from that presidio for Tubac on the 29th of the month named. Before our departure I made efforts to increase the escort, in order to make the journey with some security, but because of the impoverished condition to which the citizens and the militia of the province are reduced my efforts had no more effect than the addition of five men. But, in spite of having seen enemies on the march when only three days' travel from San Miguel, and of having made the march through one of the regions reputed to be most dangerous, divine providence was pleased to bring the expedition in safety as far as Tubac, where it arrived, by regular marches and with three days of rest, on the 16th of October.

Monday, October 23, 1775.—All the foregoing having been arranged and noted; Mass having been chanted with all the solemnity possible on the Sunday preceding for the purpose of invoking the divine aid in this expedition, all its members being present; and the Most Holy Virgin of Guadalupe, under the advocation of her Immaculate Conception, the Prince Señor San Miguel, and San Francisco de Assís having been named as its

---

* From Herbert Eugene Bolton, ed., *Anza's California Expeditions* (Berkeley: University of California Press, 1930), III, 3–60 *passim*. Reprinted by permission of University of California Press.

protectors, at eleven today the march was begun toward the north. Making some minor turns to the northeast, and having traveled four hours and as many leagues, we halted at the place which they call La Canoa, situated on the River of Tubac. Here during most of the year water is found, although it is not running, but by a little digging in the sand enough can be had for whatever may be required.

At the end of the afternoon today the wife of one of the soldiers of the expedition began to feel the first pains of childbirth. We aided her immediately with the shelter of a field tent and other things useful in the case and obtainable on the road, and she successfully gave birth to a very lusty boy at nine o'clock at night, the rest of which was passed without any other happening. . . .

October 24.—At three o'clock in the morning, it not having been possible by means of the medicines which had been applied in the previous hours, to remove the afterbirth from our mother, other various troubles befell her. As a result she was taken with paroxysms of death, and after the sacraments of penance and extreme unction had been administered to her, with the aid of the fathers who accompany us she rendered up her spirit at a quarter to four.

Sunday, October 29 . . . At nine o'clock on the same morning, after having celebrated the holy sacrifice of the Mass, all the members of the expedition attending, I issued a proclamation making known the penalties imposed by the Ordinance on any one who should violate women, especially heathen, or steal their goods. Under the same penalties I forbade any one to raise arms against the heathen in the country through which we pass, except in a case of necessity for the defense of life, or at my orders, and likewise against any one who should spread any report which might withdraw these heathen from the true religion and the dominion of his Majesty. For this purpose and in order that such important aims may be achieved, I likewise urged them to accord these people good treatment, and exhorted them to set the example which we ought to show them by our customs, and by our attendance upon all the acts of devotion which may offer themselves in our expedition. . . .

Sunday, November 19.—At two o'clock in the morning a soldier reported that his wife, Dolores, had been taken with violent parturition pains. I got up immediately to arrange that she be given assistance, wherewith she successfully gave birth to a boy, for which reason I suspended the march for today. At a suitable hour the child was baptized.

Monday, November 20.—The mother not being in a fit condition to travel, it was necessary to remain here today.

Tuesday, November 21.—The patient being taken with severe pains and other troubles following upon the childbirth, it was not possible to march today. In the days just past, especially yesterday and today, the cold has been so severe that as a result of it and of the ice, six of our saddle animals have died during the last four days. . . .

Thursday, December 7.—At this place we are to leave the river, and have to make three marches without any pasturage and with very little water, for lack of which and especially of the latter it is necessary to make the march in divisions on different days, in order to get enough water for all. I have therefore decided to rest the animals here for two days and give time for our invalids to recuperate somewhat, so that they may be able to stand the three marches which are necessary. The cattle, likewise, will have to make two marches without water, for in their wild condition it is not possible to water them with vessels as is done with the horses.

[*The divided expedition now was to reassemble on the western side of the desert.*]

Friday, December 15.—At daybreak it was very windy, and the snow which had fallen the day and the night before was very hard from the freezing weather which had preceded, as a result of which six of our cattle and one mule died. At a quarter past twelve the second division began to arrive, in charge of the sergeant. The people were crippled by the storm, which overtook them midway between Santa Rosa and here. In spite of all their efforts to reach here yesterday they were unable to do so, and on the way several persons were frozen, one of them so badly that in order to save his life it was necessary to bundle him up for two hours between four fires. As a result of these inclemencies five saddle animals died in their division. But aside from these there were no disasters on their march, and, indeed, because the division was slower than the first and came by a made road, with wells open, it was more conveniently supplied with water than the former division.

Saturday, December 16.—I remained in this place awaiting the third division. This morning four of our cattle died from injuries and cold because of the severe freezing weather. At eleven o'clock they informed me that when they were looking for some saddle animals which had disappeared from sight, they found that they were being driven off by four of the heathen who had come to see us. I therefore ordered the sergeant and four soldiers to go and follow them, with orders that if they should overtake the thieves in the open or in their villages they should three times require them to deliver the stolen animals, giving them to understand that if they did this again they would feel the force of our arms, but that they were not to punish them with weapons except in case the Indians by force of their own arms should attempt to retain the saddle animals or refuse to deliver them. At seven o'clock the sergeant returned with the report that he found the mounts in two different villages, distant about four leagues, where not a single man was to be seen, but he gave the women who were there to understand what his orders were, so that they might report them to their men.

Sunday, December 17.—Since the third division did not appear yesterday, at seven o'clock in the morning I sent two soldiers to meet it with twenty saddle animals, in order that they may have new mounts to replace those which may be tired out or made useless because of the cold.

At half past three in the afternoon the third division arrived at this place in command of Alférez Don Joseph Moraga. His forces were in worse condition than the two earlier divisions because the storm of snow and cold had caught them in a more exposed position, and as a result several persons were frozen to the point of being in danger of death. From the same cause six saddle animals were left by the wayside and four others died. In attending to his division, providing fire for them, and in other services for their relief, this officer so exposed himself that he contracted very severe pains in his ears, and although these have been cured, the weather is so bad that he has been left totally deaf in both ears. Today two more of our cattle have died as a result of injury and cold.

In the midst of these misfortunes which have been caused us by the snowstorms, with the loss of the animals which have died, it almost seems to have been designed for the benefit of the health of our people, for whereas nine days ago we counted more than fifteen invalids, three of them dangerously ill, today there are less than five of the first class and none of the second. Their sudden recovery, which we have not hitherto experienced since we began the march, is attributed partly to the many watermelons which were eaten at the lake of Santa Olaya.

Josiah Gregg

As has been noted, the crucial spark-gap between the young United States and New Spain, later Mexico, was at Santa Fe; and the trail from Missouri to that capital provided a fascinating contact between the two cultures. One of the classics of the frontier is Commerce of the Prairies *(1844), the epic of the Santa Fe Trail, by Josiah Gregg (1806–c. 1850). Gregg knew of what he spoke, for he was himself a trader and, from 1831 to 1840, had crossed the Plains with caravans no fewer than four times. He was driven to the West partly by a dislike of cities. In the words of Max Moorhead, "he was an escapist, forever fleeing to his beloved prairies. There and only there he breathed as a free, happy, and well man."*

The Santa Fe Trade*

The early traders having but seldom experienced any molestations from the Indians, generally crossed the plains in detached bands, each individual rarely carrying more than two or three hundred dollars' worth of stock. This peaceful season, however, did not last very long; and it is greatly to be feared that the traders were not always innocent of having instigated the savage hostilities that ensued in after years. Many seemed to forget the wholesome precept, that they should not be savages themselves because they dealt with savages. Instead of cultivating friendly feelings with those few who remained peaceful and honest, there was an occasional one always disposed to kill, even in cold blood, every Indian that fell into their power, merely because some of the tribe had committed some outrage either against themselves or their friends.

Since the commencement of this trade, returning parties have performed the homeward journey across the plains with the proceeds of their enterprise, partly in specie, and partly in furs, buffalo rugs and animals. Occasionally, these straggling bands would be set upon by marauding Indians, but if well armed and of resolute spirit, they found very little difficulty in persuading the savages to let them pass unmolested; for ... the Indians are always willing to compromise when they find that they cannot rob "without losing the lives of their warriors, which they hardly ever risk, unless for revenge or in open warfare."

The case was very different with those who through carelessness or recklessness ventured upon the wild prairies without a sufficient supply of arms. A story is told of a small band of twelve men, who, while encamped on the Cimarron river, in 1828, with but four serviceable guns between them, were visited by a party of Indians (believed to be Arrapahoes), who made at first strong demonstrations of friendship and good will. Observing the defenceless condition of the traders, they went away, but soon returned about thirty strong, each provided with a lazo, and all on foot. The chief then began by informing the Americans that his men were tired of walking, and must have horses. Thinking it folly to offer any resistance, the terrified traders told them if one animal apiece would satisfy them, to go and catch them. This they soon did; but finding their requests so easily complied with, the Indians held a little parley together, which resulted in a new demand for more—they must now have two apiece. "Well, catch

---

* From Josiah Gregg, *Commerce of the Prairies* (New York: H. G. Langley, 1844), I, 25–83 *passim;* II, 156–158.

them!" was the acquiescent reply of the unfortunate band—upon which the savages mounted those they had already secured, and swinging their lazos over their heads, plunged among the stock with a furious yell, and drove off the entire *caballada* of near five hundred head of horses, mules and asses. . . .

Such repeated and daring outrages induced the traders to petition the Federal Government for an escort of United States troops. The request having been granted, Major Riley, with three companies of infantry and one of riflemen, was ordered to accompany the caravan which left in the spring of 1829. The escort stopped at Chouteau's Island, on the Arkansas river, and the traders thence pursued their journey through the sand-hills beyond. . . .

The position of Major Riley on the Arkansas was one of serious and continual danger. Scarce a day passed without his being subjected to some new annoyance from predatory Indians. The latter appeared, indeed, resolved to check all further concourse of the whites upon the Prairies; and fearful of the terrible extremes to which their excesses might be carried, the traders continued to unite in single caravans during many years afterwards, for the sake of mutual protection. This escort under Major Riley, and one composed of about sixty dragoons, commanded by Captain Wharton, in 1834, constituted the only government protection ever afforded to the Santa Fe trade, until 1843, when large escorts under Captain Cook accompanied two different caravans as far as the Arkansas river. . . .

The designation of 'Council Grove,' after all, is perhaps the most appropriate that could be given to this place; for we there held a 'grand council,' at which the respective claims of the different 'aspirants to office' were considered, leaders selected, and a system of government agreed upon, —as is the standing custom of these promiscuous caravans. One would have supposed that electioneering and 'party spirit' would hardly have penetrated so far into the wilderness: but so it was. Even in our little community we had our 'office-seekers' and their 'political adherents,' as earnest and as devoted as any of the modern school of politicians in the midst of civilization. After a great deal of bickering and wordy warfare, however, all the 'candidates' found it expedient to decline, and a gentleman by the name of Stanley, without seeking, or even desiring the 'office,' was unanimously proclaimed 'Captain of the Caravan.' The powers of this officer were undefined by any 'constitutional provision,' and consequently vague and uncertain: orders being only viewed as mere requests, they are often obeyed or neglected at the caprice of the subordinates. It is necessary to observe, however, that the captain is expected to direct the order of travel during the day, and to designate the camping-ground at night; with many other functions of a general character, in the exercise of which the company finds it convenient to acquiesce. But the little attention that is paid to his commands in cases of emergency, I will leave the reader to become acquainted with, as I did, by observing their manifestations during the progress of the expedition.

But after this comes the principal task of organizing. The proprietors are first notified by 'proclamation' to furnish a list of their men and wagons. The latter are generally apportioned into four 'divisions,' particularly when the company is large—and ours consisted of nearly a hundred wagons, besides a dozen of dearborns and other small vehicles, and two small cannons (a four and six pounder), each mounted upon a carriage. To each of these divisions, a 'lieutenant' was appointed, whose duty it was to inspect every ravine and creek on the route, select the best crossings, and superintend what is called in prairie parlance, the 'forming' of each encampment.

Upon the calling of the roll, we were found to muster an efficient force of nearly two hundred men without counting invalids or other disabled bodies, who, as a matter of course, are exempt from duty. There is nothing so much dreaded by inexperienced travellers as the ordeal of guard duty. But no matter what the condition or employment of the individual may be, no one has the smallest chance of evading the 'common law of the prairies.' The amateur tourist and the listless loafer are precisely in the same wholesome predicament—they must all take their regular turn at the watch. There is usually a set of genteel idlers attached to every caravan, whose wits are forever at work in devising schemes for whiling away their irksome hours at the expense of others. By embarking in these 'trips of pleasure,' they are enabled to live without expense; for the hospitable traders seldom refuse to accommodate even a loafing companion with a berth at their mess without charge. But then these lounging *attachés* are expected at least to do good service by way of guard duty. None are even permitted to furnish a substitute, as is frequently done in military expeditions, for he that would undertake to stand the tour of another besides his own, would scarcely be watchful enough for the dangers of the Prairies. Even the invalid must be able to produce unequivocal proofs of his inability, or it is a chance if the plea is admitted. For my own part, although I started on the 'sick list,' and though the prairie sentinel must stand fast and brook the severest storm (for then it is that the strictest watch is necessary), I do not remember ever having missed my post but once during the whole journey.

The usual number of watches is eight, each standing a fourth of every alternate night. When the party is small the number is generally reduced; while in the case of very small bands, they are sometimes compelled for safety's sake to keep one watch on duty half the night. With large caravans the captain usually appoints eight 'sergeants of the guard,' each of whom takes an equal portion of men under his command. . . .

The guards were often very careless. This was emphatically the case with us, notwithstanding our knowledge of the proximity of a horde of savages. In fact, the caravan was subject to so little control that the patience of Capt. Stanley underwent some very severe trials; so much so that he threatened more than once to resign. Truly, there is not a better school for testing a man's temper, than the command of a promiscuous caravan of independent traders. The rank of captain is, of course, but little more than nominal. Every proprietor of a two-horse wagon is apt to assume as much authority as the commander himself, and to issue his orders without the least consultation at head-quarters. It is easy then to conceive that the captain has anything but an enviable berth. He is expected to keep order while few are disposed to obey—loaded with execrations for every mishap, whether accidental or otherwise; and when he attempts to remonstrate he only renders himself ridiculous, being entirely without power to enforce his commands. It is to be regretted that some system of 'maritime law' has not been introduced among these traders to secure subordination, which can never be attained while the commander is invested with no legal authority. For my own part, I can see no reason why the captain of a prairie caravan should not have as much power to call his men to account for disobedience or mutiny, as the captain of a ship upon the high seas. . . .

Since that time [his final trip across the Plains] I have striven in vain to reconcile myself to the even tenor of civilized life in the United States; and have sought in its amusements and its society a substitute for those high excitements which have attached me so strongly to Prairie life. Yet I am almost ashamed to confess that scarcely a day passes without my experiencing a pang of regret that I am not now roving at large upon those western plains. Nor do I find my taste peculiar; for I have hardly known a man, who has ever become familiar with the kind of life which I have led for so many years, that has not relinquished it with regret.

There is more than one way of explaining this apparent incongruity. In the first place—the wild, unsettled and independent life of the Prairie trader, makes perfect freedom from nearly every kind of social dependence an absolute necessity of his being. He is in daily, nay, hourly exposure of his life and property, and in the habit of relying upon his own arm and his own gun both for protection and support. Is he wronged? No court or jury is called to adjudicate upon his disputes or his abuses, save his own conscience; and no powers are invoked to redress them, save those with which the God of Nature has endowed him. He knows no government—no laws, save those of his own creation and adoption. He lives in no society which he must look up to or propitiate. The exchange of this untrammelled condition—this sovereign independence, for a life in civilization, where both his physical and moral freedom are invaded at every turn, by the complicated machinery of social institutions, is certainly likely to commend itself to but few,—not even to all those who have been educated to find their enjoyments in the arts and elegancies peculiar to civilized society;—as is evinced by the frequent instances of men of letters, of refinement and of wealth, voluntarily abandoning society for a life upon the Prairies, or in the still more savage mountain wilds.

A 'tour on the Prairies' is certainly a *dangerous* experiment for him who would live a quiet contented life at home among his friends and relatives: not so dangerous to life or health, as prejudicial to his domestic habits. Those who have lived pent up in our large cities, know but little of the broad, unembarrassed freedom of the Great Western Prairies. Viewing them from a snug fireside, they seem crowded with dangers, with labors and with sufferings; but once upon them, and these appear to vanish—they are soon forgotten.

There is another consideration, which, with most men of the Prairies, operates seriously against their reconciliation to the habits of civilized life. Though they be endowed naturally with the organs of taste and refinement, and though once familiar with the ways and practices of civilized communities, yet a long absence from such society generally obliterates from their minds most of those common laws of social intercourse, which are so necessary to the man of the world. The awkwardness and the *gaucheries* which ignorance of their details so often involves, are very trying to all men of sensitive temperaments. Consequently, multitudes rush back to the Prairies, merely to escape those criticisms and that ridicule, which they know not how to disarm.

It will hardly be a matter of surprise then, when I add, that this passion for Prairie life, how paradoxical soever it may seem, will be very apt to lead me upon the plains again, to spread my bed with the mustang and the buffalo, under the broad canopy of heaven,—there to seek to maintain undisturbed my confidence in men, by fraternizing with the little prairie dogs and wild colts, and the still wilder Indians—the *unconquered Sabaeans* of the Great American Deserts.

Lewis Garrard

Young Lewis Garrard (1829–1887) celebrated his eighteenth birthday in a tiny fort along the Arkansas River, which was drenched in rain and surrounded by yelling Comanches. "Well," he wrote, "there is something refreshing in variety." He was young—and confident. "Oh! our hearts are big," he said, "and we are all center shots." Footloose, in 1846 he had joined a caravan for Bent's Fort and the following year wandered south to Taos and back to Leavenworth. He set down his experiences from notes and published them in 1850 as Wah-to-yah (the Indian name for the Spanish Peaks, "the breasts of the world"). His story of the frontiersman's admonition to mind his own business (individualism at its zenith) is reminiscent of that South African folk song " 'T isn't my affair; 't isn't your affair;/ It's the other fellow's trouble, so we needn't care."

The Taos Trail*

Not being able to catch my horse this morning, I hung my saddle on a wagon and walked, talking to the loquacious Canadians, whose songs and stories were most acceptable. They are a queer mixture anyhow, these Canadians; rain or shine, hungry or satisfied, they are the same garrulous, careless fellows; generally carolling in honor of some brunette Vide Poche or St. Louis Creole beauty, or lauding, in the words of their ancestry, the soft skies and grateful wine of La Belle France; occasionally uttering a "sacré," or "enfant de garce," but suffering no cloud of ill humor to overshadow them but for a moment. While walking with a languid step, cheering up their slow oxen, a song would burst out from one end of the train to the other, producing a most charming effect. . . .

Good humor reigned triumphant throughout camp. Canadian songs of mirth filled the air; and, at every mess fire, pieces of meat were cooking *en appolas;* that is, on a stick sharpened, with alternate fat and lean meat, making a delicious roast. Among others, *boudins* [intestines] were roasting without any previous culinary operation but the tying of both ends, to prevent the fat, as it was liquefied, from wasting; and when pronounced "good" by the hungry, impatient judges, it was taken off the hot coals, puffed up with the heat and fat, the steam escaping from little punctures, and coiled on the ground or a not particularly clean saddle blanket, looking for all the world like a dead snake.

The fortunate owner shouts, "Hyar's the doins, and hyar's the coon as *savys* 'poor bull' from 'fat cow;' freeze into it, boys!" And all fall to with ready knives, cutting off savory pieces of this exquisitely appetizing prairie production.

---

* From Lewis H. Garrard, *Wah-to-yah and the Taos Trail: or Prairie Travel and Scalp Dances, with a Look at Los Rancheros from Muleback and the Rocky Mountain Campfire* (Cincinnati: H. W. Derby & Co., 1850), pp. 11–286 *passim.*

At our mess fire there was a whole side of ribs roasted. When browned thoroughly, we handled the long bones, and as the generous fat dripped on our clothes, we heeded it not, our minds wrapped up with the one absorbing thought of satisfying our relentless appetites; progressing in the work of demolition, our eyes closed with ineffable bliss. Talk of an emperor's table —why they could imagine nothing half so good! The meal ended, the pipe lent its aid to complete our happiness; and, at night, we retired to the comfortable blankets, wanting nothing, caring for nothing. One remarkable peculiarity is there about buffalo meat—one can eat beyond plenitude without experiencing any ill effects. . . .

At night, the rain fell and the wind blew, driving the smoke in our faces: all went to bed early, leaving me sitting by the fire. It was my favorite pastime to take a blanket and lie on the ground with it wrapped around me, with back to the wind, apart from the noisy camp, to read, or scrawl a few words in a blank book of the events of the day, or think of friends far away; or, perchance, nodding, and, in a dreamy state, with the warm sun beaming on me, build castles in the air. Many object to this idle run of thought, as it exerts, say they, a pernicious influence on the mind; that it drives away rational, sober thought, and distracts the mind from business; but what satisfaction it is, especially on the prairie, where there is no mental occupation, to think of things not in our power to possess; for, during the brief moments we indulge in this train, we are as much gratified and happy as if in actual possession; and why deprive one of this *poor* luxury? With myself it was like the two-mile heats in races—"once around and repeat;" for, on every opportunity, I endeavored to resume the thread of the last reverie, and dream away, sometimes in a conflict with the Indians, or rescuing a fair maiden from the hands of ruthless savages; or, again, chasing buffalo and feasting off the fat of the land. Anyone, in the Far West, is romantically inclined.

We awoke in the morning, again drenched, cold, and uncomfortable, with saturated clothes hanging on us. A kettle of beans was on the fire cooking when the men went to bed; and, while I was punching the savages in imagination, I had punched the fire too much. The consequence was a mess of burnt beans; some tough, stringy, old steer meat, emitting such an unpleasant smell, which to eat seemed almost a sin. Maybe the fellows didn't swear at me! Tell it not in Gath! but I laughed until their woe-begone faces relaxed into good-humored smiles.

The pelting rain enlivened the scene; and Drinker, General Lee, and I started for the fort, nearly forty miles distant. The sorry breakfast sat uneasily on our craving stomachs, and we spurred our animals over the ground for miles without speaking, with rain falling just enough to penetrate our clothing and cause suicidal feeling. Our ideas of the beautiful had fled . . .

Though the wind was piercingly cold, Hatcher was up early, making a fire, "for," said he, "this hos is no b'ar to stick his nose under cover all the robe season, an' lay round camp, like a darned Ned; but," he added in an undertone, as he looked to see if the government men were awake, "that's two or three in this crowd—wagh!—howsomever, the *green* is 'rubbed out' a little. This child hates an American what hasn't seen Injuns skulped, or doesn't know a Yute from a Khian mok'sin. Sometimes he thinks of makin' tracks for white settlement, but when he gits to Bent's big lodge, on the Arkansa, and sees the bugheways, an' the fellers from the States, how they roll thar eyes at an Injun yell, worse nor if a village of Camanches was on 'em, an' pick up a beaver trap, to ask what it is—just shows whar the niggurs had thar brungin' up—this child says—'a little bacca, if its a plew [pelt], a plug, an' Dupont an' G'lena [powder and lead], a Green River [knife] or so,' and he leaves for the Bayou Salade. Darn the white diggins, while thar's buffler in the mountains. Whoo-pee!" shouted he to us, "are you for Touse? This hos is thar in one sun, wagh! Louy, the cavyard's out picking grass—half froze to travel."

We dispatched a cup of coffee, and, driving our shivering mules to camp, saddled and packed them—the Captain and companions fixing their American saddles with a frail buckle and girth; while Hatcher and Louy first laid on their mules the half of a robe, and on that a bare Mexican tree, without pad, cover, or other appendage, save a few long buckskin thongs tied to the back part of the cantle, and a pair of huge wooden stirrups dangling directly *under*—not forward—the seat. With an *adios* to the Mexican, who, returning the salute, started for the rancho, we mounted. . . .

The sighing of the wind, zephyr-like, bland, and refreshing—mournful yet pleasing—the pine-clad hills above, around, and below—the mystery in which the customs of the present and the past inhabitants of this region have been kept through paucity of knowledge or descriptive powers of visitors—the thoughts engendered by the perusal of Prescott's "Conquest," and Stephens's Central American researches, and the fact of traversing the same road along which the munitions of grim-visaged war were, but a few days before, transported, rendered strange my fancy, and gave my wandering imagination many a theme for instant, yet lengthy, discussion. . . . Reaching the suburbs of Fernandez [Taos], I recognized a ranchero, driving before him a mule laden with shucks.

He exclaimed, as he doffed his hat—"*Comme la va Senors, esta buen —ah, Bonita!*" "How are you, Sirs—ah, Bonita"—(to my mule). "*Senors una fandango grandote, esta noche,*" his eye brightening as he spoke, "*muy Senoritas bonita.*" "There's a big fandango tonight; a great many pretty ladies there, too—wish to go?"

"Certainly we do," replied Louy, " 'specially if thar's liquor on hand."

Passing some low, flat-roofed mud structures, several American sol-

diers on guard near, we met at every step gracefully moving women and
sarape-enveloped men, the shuck cigarillo between the lips of many; and
turning to one side of the plaza, drew rein in front of a house, where were
numbers of Americans talking and smoking. Fisher came forward, with his
hand outstretched before reaching us, with a hearty, "How are ye? I swar'
you look tired; come in and take a 'horn'—a little of the *arwerdenty*—come
—good for your stomach!"

Mr. St. Vrain, at this juncture, approaching, took me kindly by the
hand, coupled with an invitation to his own house. Leading my mule by the
bridle, we crossed the south side of the plaza and entered a courtyard enclosed by high walls. A Mexican took Bonita, and, pulling off the saddle,
led him to a pile of shucks and corn.

I was ushered into an oblong, handsomely furnished room, with a fireplace in one corner and the walls hung with portraits of holy characters,
crosses, etc., showing the prevailing religion; and to furnish additional evidence, a *padre* (priest) was taking his *congé* as we opened the door. An
introduction to Senora St. Vrain—a dark-eyed, languidly handsome woman
—followed my appearance. The Mexican mode of salutation is to meet, and
one arm of the gentleman or lady is thrown around the other's shoulder;
then stepping back one pace, they shake hands, accompanied with the usual
comme la va. But I did not understand this most cordial mode of greeting,
and when the Senora sidled alongside, in expectation of the usual embrace,
I thought how strangely she acted, and only extended my hand, saying in
American, "How do you do?" Most assuredly, such a fashion with our
ladies would meet with enthusiastic followers.

At supper, I sat at table and ate potatoes for the first time in several
months. A fandango was to be held that night, but declining an invitation to
attend, a mattress was unrolled from the wall, where, in daytime, it served
as a seat, and I turned in between sheets. Yes! sheets! For months I had
enveloped myself with blankets in the open air, pulling off no clothing but
the blue blanket topcoat, which, with my saddle, served as pillow—but now
a change came over the spirit of my dream. A house, table, vegetables, and
sheets—to say nothing of the charming smiles of women and the Taos
aguardiente.

Shortly after lying down, the room filled with gay ladies, revelling in
the excess of paint and flaunting dress, and partaking of the favorite aguardiente by way of support against the fatigues of the fandango. I looked at
them through my partially closed eyes, to notice more closely without an
imputation of rudely staring. The musical tone of their voices, uttering
their sweet language, fell gently on my ear, and, as perception gradually
failed, amid a delicious reverie, I sank to sleep. . . .

I must say that there is much romance to a superficial observer in having a Mexican wife; but, were we to come down to sober reality, the affair

would show forth in a different light. From the depraved moral education of the New Mexicans, there can be no intellectual enjoyment. The only attractions are of the baser sort. From youth accustomed to a life of servitude and vitiated habits, we look in vain for true woman's attraction—modesty—that attribute which encircles as a halo the intelligent, virtuous, and educated woman. Surely 'twas pardonable pride in me to notice, by contrast, the superiority of those of my own country. . . .

[*Later, on the trail home*:] The sun was setting as we turned from the trail and unsaddled in a horseshoe bend of El Rio Canadiano, near a grove of cottonwoods. The oxen were unyoked, the droves directed to water, and the cows milked. When night overshadowed the scene, we sat on outspread blankets close to the fire, with "a heap" inside and pipe in mouth, enjoying our ease with dignity.

This section of country I have often heard spoken of as uninteresting; but to me there were many attractions. Here, with mule and gun and a few faithful friends, one experiences such a grand sensation of liberty and a total absence of fear; no one to say what he shall do; costumed as fancy, or comfort, dictates; his blanket his house, the prairie his home. Money he needs not, except to buy coffee, ammunition, and "Touse." No conventional rules of society restrict him to any particular form of dress, manner, or speech—he can swear a blue streak or pray; it is his own affair entirely. Here, too, one soon learns to say nothing, and do less, but for himself; and the greenhorn is often reminded, amid showers of maledictions, to confine his philanthropic deeds and conversations to his own dear self. I was quite amused by the kindly-intentioned remarks of an old mountaineer to me, shortly after my appearance in the country. "If you see a man's mule running off, don't stop it—let it go to the devil; it isn't yourn. If his possible sack falls off, don't tell him of it; he'll find it out. At camp, help cook—get wood an' water—make yourself active—get your pipe, an' smoke it—don't ask too many questions, an' you'll pass!" . . .

A mile beyond, we came upon a group of three men cooking, the leader of whom was a man known from the Yellowstone to El Rio Bravo, from Salt Lake to Sangre Cristo, from Santa Fe to Missouri—the shrewd, independent Jim Beckwith [Beckwourth]. He claimed parentage on the maternal side from one who, in childhood, played 'neath the palm trees in the golden sands displaced by "Afric's sunny fountains"—and, on the paternal, from a slip reared among the vine-clad hills of La Belle France and transplanted in reluctant haste on the western shore of the great Mississippi.

While yet a boy, Beckwith ran from St. Louis with a trapping party, who, with dollars and beaver galore, stalked the thoroughfares of the then frontier town in pardonable pride and consequence. After much buffeting to the headwaters of the Yellowstone, he took a wife with the Crow Indians, and to that nation attached himself—joining their war parties with alacrity, dancing around the scalp trophies, and making trades of his squaw's well-dressed robes to the fur companies.

But what whiteman was ever long constant to his Indian nymph, or Mexican muchacha? And Jim Beckwith, ere many moons, found himself traversing the prairie-skirted Black, Sweetwater, Wet, and other noted mountains; now trapping beaver on Bijou; now "fetching" the "goats" from Pike's toppling crags; and now again at Greenhorn settlement, "raking" the "plews" from the less fortunate "euker" and "poker" players, who after solitary sojourns of months in their favorite haunts emerge and "make" for rendezvous, to revel in the pleasures of intoxicating forgetfulness, and to dance, in a rude but genuine way, with the laughing squaws and thoughtless senoritas.

In Santa Fe last winter, Beckwith kept the best-furnished saloon in the place—the grand resort for liquor-imbibing, monte-playing, and fandango-disposed American officers and men.

He was a large, good-humored fellow; and, while listening to the characteristic colloquy, I almost forgot that he was of a race who, in the much-boasted land of liberty, are an inferior, degraded people. . . .

While in motion, the next morning, a party of men was descried coming. It proved to be Captain Jackson, and his company of mounted men, en route for Santa Fé. Volunteer-like, they were in the rear, at the side, and in advance of their commander; they disregarding military deference, he military control. For a mile and a half, others were strung along the trace, in irregular squads, riding, sauntering carelessly, some without arms, and a few with muskets, beating the sage bushes for hares. . . .

Judging from all appearances, discipline had been drummed out of the service some time previous to our meeting with the company; for they seemed to have no knowledge of anything relative to their position, except that they were entitled every day to three-fourths of a pound of mess pork or "Ned," a pound of super-fine flour, and as much coffee as could conveniently be stowed away 'neath their dingy blue jacket. Despite their seeming want of the attributes of soldiers, they astonish the braggadocio New Mexicans in battle or fandango amazingly.

It is an irresistible inference to draw from the premises our volunteer service affords that Americans born were never intended to fight under the strict discipline of the regular service. Deference and subordination they learn neither as children nor as men—and an army of invasion is a poor school to remedy the defect in education.

ADDITIONAL READINGS

Herbert E. Bolton condensed a good deal of his vast scholarship on the Spanish Southwest into his *Spanish Borderlands* (New Haven, 1921). Bolton's biography of De Anza appears as the first volume of his five-volume *Anza's California Expeditions;* the book also appeared separately as *Outpost of Empire* (Berkeley, 1930). George P. Hammond's *Don Juan de Oñate and the Founding of New Mexico* (Santa Fe, 1926) provides good insight into the founding of that territory. The standard work on the Santa Fe Trail is by R. L. Duffus: *The Santa Fe Trail* (New York, 1930); and Kate L. Gregg has edited a collection, *The Road to Santa Fe* (Albuquerque, 1952), which fills in the role of the government in protecting the trade.

ADDITIONAL READINGS

6

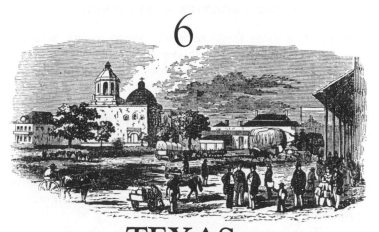

TEXAS:
FROM SETTLEMENT
TO REVOLUTION

A Texan is proud and independent, seemingly the most individualistic of Americans. The reasons for the growth of this feeling lie deep in Texas history; but the more we examine the founding of this sub-nation within the nation, the more evidence we find of group action, corporate development, land companies (often with Eastern capital), and the protection of borders by cooperative action, as with the Texas Rangers.

The dream of Texas settlement began with Moses Austin, a Connecticut merchant who roamed West, became a Spanish citizen, received a land grant for a colonization scheme in the Spanish provinces, and died in 1821 on a return trip from Texas, the area he had chosen. That same year Stephen F. Austin, his son, carried on his father's work, leading the first group of settlers to the Brazos River, near the future city of Austin. By 1825 there were 1,800 persons in the colony, 443 of them slaves.

Stephen Austin had had some political experience as a territorial judge and legislator; and, as his letters indicate, he needed all of it to govern the frontiersmen. He ruled singlehandedly until 1828, when a municipal government (*ayuntamiento*) was established under the new state constitution of 1827. In effect, Austin was the buffer between the settlers and the Mexican government—on the one hand, trying to keep the Americans happy under political and religious forms to which they were little accustomed; on the other, attempting to keep clear the legal titles of his lands in the face of a dizzying succession of Mexican revolutions.

These were years of turmoil for Mexico, beginning with Hidalgo's "Cry of Dolores" in 1810 and progressing through Iturbide's dictatorship of 1821–23. In 1824 Mexico adopted its first republican constitution; partly because it was modeled after that of the United States, the Texas settlers were willing to pledge it their allegiance. But for Mexico at large, the period continued to be one of political confusion—with a long series of *coups d'état* and the figure of Santa Anna moving in and out of the intrigues. There were times following 1835 when effectual central government was suspended entirely.

Meanwhile the settlement of Texas-Coahuila (the official name of the state) continued. The Austin colony was not alone. *Empresarios* like David Burnet, Joseph Vehlein, and Lorenzo de Zavala—land speculators whose purpose was profit and whose political ideas were motivated by their investments—were granted large tracts of land for settlement. In 1830 these three men pooled their resources and, with the addition of Eastern capital, formed the Galveston Bay and Texas Land Company, an illustration of the corporate background for much of the Texas settlement.

There were three key problems facing all American settlers in Mexican Texas. First was the problem of religion. Most of the Americans had been Protestants, and they came from a frontier heavily immersed in evangelical revivalism—the emotional, camp-meeting kind of religiosity typified by Peter Cartwright and Alexander Campbell. The latter had once declared, "The Roman Catholic religion . . . is essentially anti-American, being opposed to the genius of all free institutions, and positively subversive of them." Such a prejudice was widely held by frontier Protestants. In Texas, however, before he could receive land, a settler was required by law to become a Roman Catholic. In theory the matter could have been serious; in practice it proved otherwise, since the individual was not required to attend Mass or openly observe Catholic customs. His Catholicism thus tended to be a paper fiction. Nevertheless, because the system did effectively prohibit the growth of Protestant churches in the area, some colonists resented it.

Second, there was the question of slavery. A large proportion of the settlers were Southern; but during the period of settlement the Texans, as Mexican citizens, could not own slaves. Fortunately for the cause of colonization, the practice—as in the matter of religion—softened the system. After 1828 in Texas-Coahuila it was possible officially to free slaves and then turn around and make them lifetime indentured servants.

The third problem, the political one, was probably the most significant factor. Not that the early settlers were disloyal to their new government; far from it. In 1826 in the little settlement of Fredonia an unsavory *empre-*

sario, Haden Edwards, led an uprising against the Mexican government; but the majority of the Anglo-Americans remained loyal to Mexico, and the Austin colony even sent troops to help quell the revolt. It was not, then, a question of disloyalty; but, as the years went by, it did become a question of local versus central government. The Texans demanded statehood for Texas (i.e., separation from Coahuila); and Santa Anna, for one, in his plans for a more centralized Mexico, never understood these demands. To him, as to many a Mexican, the Texans represented the ambitious dreams of a grasping United States. In the words of the Mexican Secretary of War:

Too late have we come to know the restless and enterprising neighbor who set himself up as our mentor, holding up his institutions for us to copy them, institutions which when transplanted to our soil could not but produce constant anarchy, and which, by draining of our resources, perverting our character, and weakening our vigor, have left us powerless against the attacks and the invasions of this modern Rome.*

So by 1836 the Texans and the Mexicans parted company in a revolution which established a Texas Republic. At the Alamo, Texans created for themselves a symbol of identity; and in that revolution Sam Houston, a tough frontiersman, became their political leader. By then it was hard to remember that the first Texans apparently intended to become loyal Mexican citizens. In 1845 the Republic became a State of the Union, bringing with it boundary problems that helped to cause the Mexican War. Stephen Austin, once ostensibly happy to belong to Mexico, was long since dead.

Stephen Austin

Stephen Austin (1793–1836) was a bachelor, and a psychologist might say he transferred potential familial affections to his colonists. At least, in his circular letters to the settlers, he frequently pointed out that he considered them all one family and that his job as "father" was difficult. The same concern for his colony may be sensed in his letters to his own mother

---

* Jose Maria Tornel y Mendivil, "Tejas y Los Estados Unidos de America en sus Relaciones con la República Mexicana," in C. E. Castaneda, trans., *Mexican Side of the Texan Revolution* (Dallas: P. L. Turner Co., 1928), p. 288.

and sister before they came to Texas. It is perhaps symbolic that Austin died in 1836, the revolutionary year, for his life had stood for colonization and conciliation. It was Sam Houston who came to symbolize independence for Texas. In the following selections, the location is generally the present city of Austin, and the Colorado River should not be confused with the larger river of that name further west. In his personal correspondence, Austin, like so many frontiersmen, was anything but a careful speller.

Letters to Texas Colonists*

Colarado River House of Mr. Castlemans
August 6   1823

Fellow Citizens,

I have once more the pleasure of addressing you a few lines from the Colorado— My absence has been protracted greatly beyond my calculations and has been in the highest degree unpleasant to me, as it has retarded the progress of the most favourite enterprise I ever engaged in in my life; but I now flatter myself with the hope of receiving a full compensation for the difficulties I have encountered by witnessing the happiness of those who compose this Colony. I assure you that if my own private and personal interest had been the only incentive to induce me to persevere I should probably have abandoned the enterprise rather than surmounted the difficulties produced by the constant state of revolution in which the country has been, since my arrival in the city of Mexico. But I was animated by the gratifying hope of providing a home for a number of meritorious citizens and of placing them and their families in a situation to make themselves happy the balance of their lives. One of the greatest pleasures a virtuous mind can receive in this world is the consciousness of having benefited others, this pleasure I now have in prospect. . . .

All that depends on me, towards the advancement of the Colony will be executed in good faith, so far as my abilities extend, and with all the promptness in my power; but to enable me to benefit them to the full extent that I wish, it is necessary that the settlers should have confidence in me, and be directed by me. I have a better opportunity of knowing what will be advantageous to them as regards their conduct and intercourse with the Government than any of them could have had, and I feel almost the same

*From Stephen F. Austin, *Papers,* in American Historical Association, *Annual Report, 1919* (Washington, D.C.: American Historical Association, 1924), II, part 1, 679–681, 784–787. Reprinted by permission.

interest for their prosperity that I do for my own family—in fact I look upon them as one great family who are under my care. I wish the settlers to remember that the Roman Catholic is the religion of this nation, I have taken measures to have *Father Miness* [Maynes] formerly of Nachitoches, appointed our Curate, he is a good man and acquainted with the Americans —we must all be particular on this subject and respect the Catholic religion with all that attention due to its sacredness and to the laws of the land. . . .

I shall proceed immediately to the mouth of this River, and on my return go to the Brazos. The settlers have now nothing to fear, there is no longer any cause for uneasiness. They must not be discouraged at any little depradations of Indians, they must remember that *American blood* flows in their veins, and that they must not dishonor that noble blood by yielding to trifling difficulties. I shall adopt every possible means for their security and defence, I have brought some powder from Bexar, a part of which will be sent to Capt. Robison for the use of the militia when needed—*Let every man do his duty, and we have nothing to fear—Let us be united as one man —discord must be banished from amongst us, or those who cause it will meet with most severe treatment.*

Hoping to meet you soon in peace and happiness, I am Resptlly your friend and fellow citizen

Stephen F. Austin

St. Felipe de Austin
May 4   1824

Dr. Mother and Sister—

. . . You must not bring much of anything except beds and bedding and Castings and crockery ware for House use—as to furniture we must do without untill we get able to buy from Orleans, I like this plan better than any—if you come in a steam boat it will be uncertain whether you can get up Red River, as it will depend on the rise of that River in the fall, tho you must be governed in some measure by circumstances . . .

We have all had a good Schooling in the best School in the World, that of Adversity and I hope have profited by it—Our prospects now are beginning to look up, but we must still remember our past troubles and not forget that wealth is hard to acquire and easily lost—let our motto therefore be *economy* and *plain* living. It is my wish that nothing should be worn in the family but homespun, at least for several years. It is the cheapest but what is of much more importance it will set an example to the rest of the Settlers that will have a very good effect—also I wish everything about the house to be plain and pritty much like the rest of my neighbors—we are all poor in this country and therefore all on an equality and so long as this continues we shall all go on well and harmoniously as regards good neighborship, and our industry will soon remidy our poverty if we have the proper econemy with it—The situation I am placed in here will cause all the acts of any of my family to be observed and it will require a uniform affible deportment to all, without regarding their appearance or poverty to prevent giving offences, the only distinction that must be shown here is between the *good* and the *bad* and that must be very marked and decisive—I make these observations that you may have a better idea of the course that will be necessary to adopt here from the beginning—for you know how easy it is to give offence to a certain class of mankind. . . .

It is my wish that Aunt Austin and family should move with you if possible, all I can say is that if she comes I will provide well for her family in land and Settle her as near you as I can[.] the land Shall cost her nothing, and I will lend her as much corn as She wants for her family the first year and do any thing else in my power to aid her—with George and her Sons She can Soon live well here and have a League of good land to divide amongst her children[;] in fact I have picked out a league for her and Shall keep it reserved untill I hear from her, brother can discribe it to her —it is next to what I call my Spring tract on the East side of the Colorado River next above Jacksons. It has the river on one side and a running creek and a large Prairie on the other and has about 30 acres that was well tended last year and will also be well tended in corn this year, but has no fence—my own opinion is that if she were to give away every thing she has in the world except her negros and by so doing could get here, that She would be worth more than double as much the day she arrived here as She was before in her life—but Still I do not advise her to move, what I have promised to do I will do if she comes. . . .

Bring all your books and beds and beding. The furniture and other heavy articles except castings, sell for pork flour Beans etc to use on the road for you must Start with provisions enough to last the whole journey, also try and bring a pair or two of Geese and tame ducks—also all kind of Gardin Seeds particularly Cabbage Lettice, beats, Sage—Summer Savory, horse reddish etc, etc, and at Nachez or lower down try and get some orange fig and grape roots—and be particular to make brother get some Nectarine and peach stones from E. Bates and a dozen young Pears, or the seeds of his best Pears and apples, also some crab apple seeds, I want them to try and make a hedge[;] also the cypress vine or any other vine for an arbor and some roots of the double Rose, all these can be brought in a small box and watered . . .

Be particular to inform any who move with you that the Roman Catholic is the established Religion here to the absolute exclusion of all others. . . .

Bring all the books you can, we shall want them to pass away the time —Your Piano have carfully put up and sent to New Orleans to the Care of Nathaniel Cox, that is if you wish to Keep it, and if not, sell it in Mis-

souri and I will buy another in Orleans for you next year—If you can sell
your furniture and Castings for any thing that would be of use here, do so
for those things are very cheap in New Orleans—The family of negros you
must bring with you at all hazards and I will settle with Bryan for them—
All these arrangements you must make the best way you can, and be very
particular to be as saving of every cent as possible—probably you can sell
off many things for homeade Linsey or Cotton cloth or tow or flax linin,
all those things sell high here—at Alexandria or Natchez lay in a good
Supply of sugar and Coffee and tea and spices and Rice and bring with you
from Missouri several barrels of beans or peas and hominy etc etc for the
journey also dryed apples and peaches—they will sell at Nackitosh. Have
some good Bacon and Pickeld Pork, and Beef dried and pickeled, put up
—if you have a large pair of good Steel yards bring them as I have none
large—also get a good Steel Mill at Natchez. You will want it on the road
and it will always be usefull here, if Aunt comes She ought also to bring a
Steel Mill—they cost about 12 doll^s. She ought also to bring the best of her
farming and other tools.

Pray do not forget to bring Me a Copy of the Laws of Missouri,
Gyers digest, or if there is a later one bring it, also the Constitutions of
Missouri and Illinois do not forget this— You must have a good large
tent for camping out and be particular to have every thing well arranged
and so as to occupy as little bulk as possible. May the great disposer of all
things take you under his protection and bring us all together once more
in this world. Kiss your Sweet little ones for their uncle. I will have a little
poney for William to ride about with me on—

Your affectione

S. F. Austin

Address to the Colonists*

As the late regulation relative to the expences to be paid On Lands in
this Colony has as I am informed caused some Animadversions in a few
persons I deem it a duty due to myself as well as to my friends to enter
into a full exposition of this subject and to give an explanation of the Steps
which I have taken since the first Commencement of this Settlement. To do
this I must necessarily give a short history of this establish^t from its Origin up to the present time. This will probably be satisfactory to all as it

---

* From Stephen F. Austin, *Papers*, II, part 1, 811–817, 823–824. Austin gave this
address in 1824.

will more clearly shew the efforts that I have made to secure to the settlers the Titles to their lands, and that I have spared neither labor or expense to complete those Titles in a way which will render them safe for ever unless forfeited by a noncompliance on the part of the settlers with the conditions required as to the Occupancy and improvement of the land. I ask your candid attention to this Statement—Look at the difficulties I have had to surmount, the risks of property, of Life, of all, which I have exposed myself to—Consider the advantages which you will receive from my labours, And then let your unbiassed Judgment decide upon my Motives, and say whether I have been right or wrong in the measures which I have adopted. It is well known to you all that this Settlement was commenced under a permission granted to my Father Moses Austin by the Competent Authorities of the Spanish Government Anterior to the Mexican Revolution. . . . On the death of my Father I proceeded to Nachitoches And met the said Commissioner who was The Honble Don Erasmo Seguin the present Deputy in Congress from this Province And Accompanied him to San Antonio de Bexar where we Arrived in August 1821.

On as full an investigation of the nature of the Grant to my Father as the interpretations I received would enable me to make I found that the permission to introduce And settle the 300 families in this Province was complete And that the Governor had authority from the Commandant Genl to designate the quantity of Land for each family. After much Conversation with the said Governor as to the quantity of Land and as to the place for the settlement he by an official answer to a Letter of mine dated the 19th day of August 1821 authorised me to promise the quantity of Land stated in my first publication relative to this settlement which was 640 acres for the head of a family, 320 for his wife and 160 for each child etc. And also gave me written Authority to explore the Province and select the place for the Colony. With this object I explored the Guadalupe from the Tuscoset road to its mouth and thence along the Coast untill the Labacca Compelled us to bear up to the road which we followed to the Colorado and explored some distance down it and the Brasos. The result of this Trip was a determination to settle on the Brasos and Colorado, and accordingly on my arrival at Nachitoches in October I informed the Governor thereof and also informed him that as the land which I was to receive for myself would be no compensation for my labors and expences in an enterprize of such magnitude I must receive something from the Settlers or I could not proceed with the Business. Accordingly on my arrival in New Orleans sometime in November I published the terms of settling in this Colony and explicitly Stated that those who settled under the said permission to my Father must pay me 12½ cts per Acre which would be in full for all expences of Surveying and every thing else. I was particular to make these terms as public as possible that no one might come without knowing distinctly the Conditions of his reception. They were republished in most of the Western papers and I considered it from that moment in the nature of an absolute contract between me and the settlers.

I Bound myself on the one hand to procure for them a complete Title for a certain specific quantity of Land according to the size of their family for which they were to pay me a certain specific sum which was to be in full for all expences of Surveying and All others whatever they might be, and all this was done with the knowledge of the then Governor of the Province and besides if I had believed that I had no authority to make any such Contract with the settlers, would I have laid myself liable to detection by the open frank and public manner in which I avowed the terms of settlement; Would I have published them in the Newspapers when I very well knew that those papers were sent to Mexico, to Monterrey, to San Antonio and to an-hundred other places where the Government would see or hear of them? Or would I myself have sent the paper which contained the terms to the Governor of this Province which I did in Nov^r· 1821 immediately after it was issued? Let me ask you as candid men does this look like an intention on my part to deceive or to do an act which I thought [I] was not Authorised to? Put yourselves in my situation and look at the vast burthen of responsibility which has Oppressed me like a deadly weight ever since I engaged in this enterprize, An enterprize which originated in the active mind and indefatigable perseverance of my much honored and lamented father who sacrificed his life by the too ardent pursuit of an object which it was always evident would result more to the credit of the projectors enterprize and perseverance than to his profit and in which the advantages secured to the settler and the benefits accruing to this Province and Government would bear no just proportion to the Compensation which was expected or asked. For let it be remembered that at that time this Province with the exception of San Antonio and La Bahia was a desart, that it was interdicted to the American Settler who but a short time before had been driven from it with fire and Sword; And until this permission was obtained by my Father, those who emigrated here did so as it were by stealth and without any other security for their property or lives than the Caprice of the Commandants who Governed, for their Emigration was not sanctioned by the Superior Government. Consider the difficulties which my Father must have had to surmount, to obtain a permission which could never before be got by any person. Consider that on his death I assumed upon myself the responsibility not only of Securing to the Settlers Complete titles to their lands, but Also of being personally responsible to the Government for their good conduct, and look at the labors and probable expences which such an enterprize was calculated to cost, and ask yourselves whether any of you would in 1821 have taken upon you the weight of responsibility which I then did? Whether you would have jeopardized your property, hazarded your health, your lives, your all to make the fortunes of others and been content to do so without the hope of any greater compensation than you could give to an individual who joined you as a settler and who would have no responsibility, labour, or expence to encounter more than the care of his own family. Would you have been content I ask to do it; or would it have been just that you should have done so? If not can you blame me for making the public declaration in the beginning of this Settlement that the Settlers must aid me by paying a specific sum for the benefits I secured to them; And was there then any thing unjust or improper in such an arrangement in its Origin? . . .

I will now make a few observations relative to the Civil Government of this Colony and then close this Statement. The responsibility of the public Order and Administration of justice in this Colony was imposed upon me by the Superior Government as you see by the Decree of the Emperor. This charge is however only provisional as I have always informed you untill the Colony is filled up and you have the members to appoint your Ayuntamientos . . . These divisions are called partidos or prescincts and also elect their Alcaldes. A number of these prescincts forms a district, and the Ayuntamiento of the Capital of the District has in some respects a kind of superintendance in a few things over the others, and there is Also appointed a Judge for each of said Districts called in Spanish a *Juez de letras* or Judge of Learning. In this way this Colony will be organized as soon as it can be done. I wished the Governor to do it when here, but he thought it too soon and promised to do it in the fall. I am particularly Anxious to see this arrangement completed for it will release me from the disagreeable task now imposed upon me and will probably be much more satisfactory to the people as then they will be governed by Men elected by themselves, for these Ayuntamientos are a species of Select Men or Council elected Annually by the people of the prescinct, and the Alcaldes are also elected in the same way.

The office I now hold was never sought for by me from choice or inclination but it must have been filled by some one untill the Colony was organized and I thought it would promote the general interests of us all much more to take it myself than to run the risk of having an officer sent here who knew nothing of our language customs or dispositions. I have never sought after appointments and never shall, but I deem it the duty of every one to serve his Country when called on to do it so far as his capacity will admit.

June 5: 1824.

Your fellow Citizen

Stephen F. Austin

The Trials of Governing*

One great difficulty under which I have labor^d is that the Settlers are unacquainted with the language and nature of this Gov^t—There are no interpreters but myself and my secretary and consequently no way for them to know the orders of the Gov^t but through one of us—this places me in a truly unpleasant situation for you know that it is innate in an American to suspect and abuse a public officer whether he deserves it or not—I have had a mixed multitude to deal with collected from all quarters strangers to each other, to me, and to the laws and language of the country, they come here with all the ideas of Americans and expect to see and understand the laws they are governed by, and many very many of them have all the licentiousness and wild turbulence of frontiersmen added to this[;] when they arrive here the worst of the human passions avarice is excited to the highest extent and it directs the vanguard in their attacks on me, jealousy and envy direct the flanks and maliciousness lurks in the rear to operate as occasion may require. Could I have opposed them by showing a law defining positively the quantity of land they were to get and no more and a code of written laws by which they were to be governed I should have had no difficulty—but they saw at once that my powers were discretionary, and that a very great augmentation to their grants could be made, and thus the colonization law itself and the authority vested in me under that law holds me up as a public Mark to be shot at by every one. If a person gets a League he knows that more could have been granted and he is therefore dissatisfied and instead of thanking me for what he gets, abuses me for treating him unjustly because he does not get more. . . . Another difficulty that I have had to contend with is that my temper is naturally rather hasty and impetuous—the good of the Settlement required that I should control it and disregard the iddle slander of those who abused me from malice, from misconception, or from interested views—for one rash act in a moment of passion in my cituation might have jeopardised the welfare of many—also my disposition as I have when too late discovered is confidential[,] unsuspicious and accomodating to a fault and therefore open to impositions—it is said by philosophers that he is a wise man who knows himself and he who governs himself is certainly still wiser—few such men appear in this world. I am not one of those and never expect to be—my temper has met many tryals and knowing it as I think I do I give myself some credit for governing it

---

* Letter from Austin to B. W. Edwards (dated San Felipe, September 15, 1825). In Stephen F. Austin, *Papers*, II, part 2, 1203–1204.

as well as I have, tho my friends have blamed me for being too mild. I may have err^d on that extreme for fear of falling on the opposite one, but I deem^d it the safe side to err on and I still think so considering the temper and dispositions of the people with whom I had to deal for among the ignorant part of the Americans indipendence means resistance and obstinacy right or wrong—this is particularly the case with frontiersmen—a violent course with such dispositions might have kindled a flame that would have destroyed them and the settlement entirely.

W. B. DeWees

W. B. DeWees, an early member of the Austin colony, wrote extensively to his friends in the States. In the following letters, note the feeling of satisfaction with the Mexican constitution, the ties that bound the settlers together, but also the intimations of those deeper problems, like religion, which were to estrange Texans from Mexicans. Note, too, how the tone of the letters changes between 1824 and 1832.

Letters from a Colonist*

Colorado River, Coahuila and Texas,
November 5, 1824.

Dear Friend:—I can only excuse myself for not writing you some time ago, by informing you that the Land Office has opened, for the purpose of giving grants to the three hundred settlers of Austin's colony. What time I have not been occupied in Indian warfare, or hunting, to obtain the means of subsistence, I have been engaged in looking out, and locating lands. . . .

San Antonio de Bexar, Texas,
March 6, 1828.

Dear friend:—It seems to me that the Republic of Mexico is destined to be forever revolutionizing. The Mexicans are never long at peace with

---

*From W. B. DeWees, *Letters from an Early Settler of Texas* (Louisville: Morton & Griswold, 1852), pp. 49–142 *passim.*

each other; ignorant and degraded as many of them are, they are not capable of ruling nor yet of being ruled. Texas, being so far removed from the interior, is but little affected by these constant revolutions in Mexico; but I dwelling among them as I now am, am forced to feel in some degree the deplorable effect of the civil wars which threaten to deluge the whole of that beautiful and lovely land in blood.

[*He here relates for his friend the entire contents of the Mexican con-*
·stitution.]

I hope that we shall long enjoy the blessings of that liberty which this Constitution promises us, and think we have no reason to doubt but we shall.

Affectionately yours,

W. B. D.

Colorado River, Texas,
November 6, 1831.

Dear Friend :—You mentioned in your last that you wished me to give you a description of the manners and customs of the people of this country. We have all sorts of manners and customs drawn from all nations! Here is a receptacle for people from all parts of the earth! Every one who is driven from all other places flies to this country as a city of refuge. We are here all united together. There is no jar or contention in politics, as all of us are obliged to take the oath of allegiance to help the Constitution of the country. We, the old settlers, are bound together by an indissoluble tie; we have fought and bled together, we have suffered together for want of food and clothing, and now we begin to enjoy the blessings of peace, and to see happiness smiling upon us.

It would amuse you very much could you hear the manner in which the people of this new country address each other. It is nothing uncommon for us to inquire of a man why he ran away from the States! but few persons feel insulted by such a question. They generally answer for some crime or other which they have committed; if they deny having committed any crime, and say they did not run away, they are generally looked upon rather suspiciously. . . .

The people of this country seem to have forgotten that there is such a commandment as "Remember the Sabbath day and keep it holy." This day is generally spent in visiting, driving stock, and breaking mustangs. There is no such thing as attending church, since no religion except the Roman Catholic is tolerated, and we have no priests among us. Indeed, I have not heard a sermon since I left Kentucky, except at a camp-meeting in Arkansas. . . .

Colorado River, Texas,
December 1st, 1832.

Dear Friend:—You have, perhaps, heard before this of the danger of war which at this time threatens our beloved land. But I do not suppose that you know the true cause and circumstances connected with this melancholy event. Mexico has been for a long time slightly encroaching upon us, in a manner which we, as native Americans, could scarcely endure. All of the Mexican States, save Texas, are in a sort of a state of servility. Mexico, perhaps being moved partly by jealousy and partly by fear of our increasing strength, has made an attempt to bring us more fully under subjection. Step by step she has slowly and stealthily taken, striving at the same time, to draw the cap over our eyes that we might not be aware of her intentions while she riveted the chains of slavery about us. Her movements, although guarded, have yet been apparent to us, and we have watched them with an interest which nothing but an ardent love of liberty could create. Still we would gladly believe her motives kind, her professions sincere, did we not too plainly see the chain with which she is ready to bind us, if she can succeed in lulling our fears and blinding our eyes.

The crisis, I fear, has already arrived! The goal is passed and we can never look upon Mexico again as we have heretofore done! Her last act was one which we cannot forget; the attempt to oppress us was too evident for the sons of a boasted land of liberty to endure. . . .

Affectionately, your friend,

W. B. D.

Walter Prescott Webb

The late Walter Prescott Webb (1888–1963), a dean of modern writing on the West, felt that whatever was unique in the Texas character was shaped in part by the interaction of three cultures, symbolized by the Indian warrior, the Mexican vaquero, and the Texas Ranger. This triangular conflict, plus the geography, produced the high level of group cohesiveness and cooperative action that characterized the Rangers. Such cooperation should be kept in mind later, when we examine methods of establishing law and order elsewhere in the West, such as on the mining frontier.

The Texas Rangers*

By the opening of the Revolution the three races that were to struggle for supremacy were all present in Texas. The Indians held undisputed possession of the Plains; the Mexicans held the southwest with their line of occupation resting on the Rio Grande; and the Anglo-Americans, henceforth called Texans, had virtual possession of the timbered portion of the then Mexican province. Since the three races were to wage constant war one with another, it was necessary for each to produce its representative fighting man. The Comanche had his warrior brave and the Mexican his *caballero, ranchero,* or *vaquero.* To meet these the Texans created the Ranger, who, since he was the latest comer, found it necessary to adapt his weapons, tactics, and strategy to the conditions imposed by his enemies. In spite of the fact that each of these fighters influenced the others, each remained the true representative of the customs and ideals of his respective race, a symbol of the fighting genius of his group. . . .

The Texan, who composed the third side of this cultural triangle, was a transplanted American, an outrunner of the American frontier. His qualities are too well known to warrant description. The mountains of Tennessee, the turbulent society of Missouri, the aristocracy of Virginia contributed their adventurous elements to his composition. These outriding frontiersmen were farmers primarily, woodsmen, riflemen, and fighters. They were Protestant in religion, democratic in politics and social life, individualists in all things, following only such leaders as could stay out in front. These early Texans knew nothing of Mexican character, had never seen the Plains, and had no knowledge of fighting Indians on horseback. They had used horses for transportation, but they were not habitual horsemen, and their weapons were unsuited to mounted warfare. They were intelligent, cool, calculating, and capable of sustained endurance and suffering. For weapons they carried the long rifle, which they used with unerring precision; the horse pistol and the knife constituted their side arms. Finding none of these weapons suitable for use on horseback, they later adopted and improved the revolver which became their own sweet weapon.

The Texas Rangers represented the Texans in their conflict with Plains warriors and Mexican *vaqueros* and *caballeros* and in the fighting that followed they learned much from their enemies. In order to win, or even to survive, they combined the fighting qualities of three races. In the words of

---

* From Walter Prescott Webb, *The Texas Rangers: A Century of Frontier Defense* (Boston: Houghton Mifflin Co., 1935), pp. 11–15, 19–20. By permission.

an observer a Texas Ranger could ride like a Mexican, trail like an Indian, shoot like a Tennessean, and fight like a devil. . . .

When the Anglo-American society was first established in Texas, institutions were as yet unformed and needs but vaguely felt. These Americans of Texas had been on the frontier long enough to know that neither fine theories of government nor nicely adjusted institutions would endure unless they were suited to conditions. These men were 'practical' in a narrow sense to the uncompromising necessities of wilderness life, alert to every event, ready to adapt themselves to the immediate situation and to the solution of the immediate problem.

If the Indians gave trouble, the Texans banded together under a local leader and went forth to war. When the expedition was over, the organization broke up and the men returned to their homes and farms. These early experiences taught the Texans how to act in emergencies, gave them training, developed their fighting technique, and brought forth by degrees leaders who were qualified to meet the foe, Mexican or Indian. These early fighters were not Rangers in the sense that they bore that name or that they constituted a permanent organization or a profession. With this explanation, a few of these early episodes may be related to show why and how some of them became Rangers.

Stephen F. Austin was the first Texan to be captured by the Comanche Indians. Austin had brought a few settlers to Texas in 1821. In order to adjust a misunderstanding with the Mexican government about the location of the colonists, Austin found it necessary early in the following year to go to Mexico City. He left San Antonio in March, going by way of Laredo and Monterey. Near the Nueces River he and his two companions were captured by the Comanches who seized all their belongings. While these Indians were very hostile towards all Mexicans, they had as yet but little experience with the Americans, and were friendly towards them. This fact probably saved Austin's life. The Comanches released him and his companions and restored all their property save four blankets, a bridle, and a Spanish grammar.

While Austin was absent, the Indians caused the few settlers some trouble. The Karankawas of the coast were accustomed to preying on the shipping that came into Texas harbors. Because of these hostilities, the settlers became discouraged, and Baron de Bastrop, who had charge in Austin's absence, appealed to the Spanish governor, Trespalacios, who ordered the enlistment of a sergeant and fourteen men to be stationed near the mouth of the Colorado. These men entered the service in May, 1823; they were poorly equipped and unpaid, but evidently accomplished some good as Austin asked that they be continued in the service. These men were similar to the later Rangers in that they were irregular, wore no uniforms, and were neither militia nor regular. There is no record, however, that they were called Rangers, and we do not know whether they were composed of Mexicans or Americans.

The use of the word 'Ranger' occurs in 1823, when Austin employed on his own account and at his own expense ten men to serve as Rangers. We know nothing further of this organization. A little later, however, when the Tonkawas persisted in stealing, and finally made a raid on the Colorado settlements, Austin raised thirty men and followed them. He compelled the chief to give up the horses and to whip the braves that stole them. The Texans insisted on helping with the whipping, and, according to the account, proved much more thorough than did the Indian chief in applying the lash. Austin ordered the chief to leave the settlements alone, and threatened to shoot instead of whip in the future.

David G. Burnet

When the revolution against Mexico finally erupted, it was not all the heroism and united action of the Alamo. In the following proclamation, David G. Burnet (1788–1870), first president of the Texas Republic, expresses his concern over rumors and dissatisfactions.

Proclamation to the Citizens of Texas*

Executive Department of the Republic of Texas
Washington [Texas] 18th March 1836
To the People in Eastern Texas.

Gen. Houston is at his post on the frontier with eight hundred men and reinforcements constantly arriving. Our army is in high spirits and full confidence. Yet in the midst of the security which this state of things should inspire[,] the officers of Government are surprised and grieved to learn, that a portion of the people of Eastern Texas under the influence of idle and groundless rumours are leaving their homes and by the circulation of

---

* From William C. Binkley, ed., *Official Correspondence of Texan Revolution* (New York: Appleton-Century-Crofts, 1936), I, 515–516. Copyright, 1936, The American Historical Association. Reprinted by permission.

false news may prevent others of their countrymen from repairing to the standard of their country where alone their homes and families are to be defended. Under these circumstances, I have thought proper to issue this my proclamation to the people of Texas, calling upon them to organise themselves under the laws of their country. I conjure you my countrymen to repair to the field forthwith to deafen your ears against all rumours from whatever quarter they may come. The officers of your Government will take special care to obtain true information of the movements of the enemy and our own army, and keep their fellow citizens regularly informed on all matters, which may affect their safety. To the field then my countrymen, to the standard of liberty, and defend your rights in a manner worthy of your sires and yourselves.

PROCLAMATION

Citizens of Texas,

But recently called to discharge the executive duties of your government, it is with inexpressible regret that I observe the slightest indication of alarm among us. To provide for and protect our wives and children is a sacred duty, prompted by nature and sanctioned by every manly feeling. But in the manner of discharging that duty we may commit many and fatal errors. The best security for families is to be found in a gallant bearing before the enemy. Our army is in the field and preparing to meet, and, as it ever has done, to repel that enemy. General Houston calls for reinforcements; a small accession to his noble band will enable him to advance and speedily chastise the presumption of the invader. Rally, then, fellow-citizens, to the standard of freedom. Let not every idle rumour, circulated perhaps by the artifices of the enemy, paralyse your hands or divide your thoughts from one grand purpose, the *Independence of Texas*. By an unbroken unanimity of voices, you have declared that Texas shall be "free, sovereign and independent." Let us with equal unanimity resolve to sustain that declaration; to ratify it with our blood. Our fathers achieved their emancipation, and were abundantly rewarded for their toils. But they persevered through many reverses, surmounted many disasters, and gloriously triumphed. We have sustained *no* reverse. The fall of the Alamo is the surest guarantee of our ultimate success. The Spartan band who so nobly perished there, have bequeathed to us an example, which ought and will be imitated; and have inflicted on the enemy a terror and a loss that are equivalent to a defeat.

Rally, then, fellow-citizens, to the standard of your country. While the army is between your families and the enemy, they are safe. Reinforce and sustain that army, and our wives and children are secure from pollution.

The government will remove to Harrisburgh, but that removal is not the result of any apprehension that the enemy are near us. It was resolved

upon as a measure conducive to the common good, before any such report
was in circulation, and it has not been expedited by such report.

Again I conjure you, fellow-citizens, listen not to every rumor that
runs, trumpet-tongued, through the country. The government is perfecting
arrangements, as rapidly as possible, to insure the transmission of official
intelligence, on which they and you may rely with confidence.

Let us acquit ourselves like men; gird up the loins of our minds, and
by one united, prompt and energetic exertion, turn back this impotent invader; and, planting our standard on the banks of the Rio Grande, dictate
to him the terms of mutual recognition.

David G. Burnet
Washington, March 18, 1836   President of the Republic.

James Gaines

*The following letter from James Gaines, written about the same time
as President Burnet's proclamation, reflects the confusions and "absquat-
tulations" (a graphic frontier word meaning to decamp or make off), which
so often accompany revolutions.*

*Letter on the Texan Revolution**

March 20th 1836

Messrs Secretaries Rusk Potter and Hardeman

Gentlemen   I wrote his Excellency the President last night after
which arrive at this place (Suq Robins) a number of our members which
have been absquattulated to the Southerd and Eastward to evade the responsibility of the main road. Among them is John W. Hall and company
reported on government business. It appears curious that at this important
crisis so many men should continue be sent to the Eastward on government
business. I thought that the Great Chief [Austin] had gone ahead with such

---

* From William C. Binkley, ed., *Official Correspondence of Texan Revolution*
(New York: Appleton-Century-Crofts, 1936), I, 522. Copyright, 1936, The American
Historical Association. Reprinted by permission.

powers. He [Hall] stated that no doubt Goliad had shard the same fate of the Alamo before this, the people are breaking to the Eastward and the Upper Country, and was at the point of leaving every where. I stopd at every house with a view to pacify them and hope I have succeeded.

I am told Houston has sent another Express and that the Alamo had actually fallen. I repeat to you the necessity of keeping a company of spies on the Western Frontier bound to report daily so as to prevent the circulation of so many falsehoods. If we suffer them to continue Texas is ruined. I fear we are viscously infested with land pirates who circulate these desperate reports.

I beg you to authorise all authorities to stop the arms and ammunition from going out of the country.

Do send a man to Washington City that will not absquattulate from the road or his duty. Excuse my pen please, I have no table.

Respectfully yours
Jas. Gaines

William Hogan

In a study of the Texas Republic, William Hogan, historian and archivist, has eloquently summarized the individualism of the Texan.

The Texan Character*

The Republic of Texas gave exuberant expression to the spirit described by Walt Whitman as "the American contempt for statutes and ceremonies, the boundless impatience of restraint." This temper characterized many American frontiers, yet for more than a century pronounced individualism has marked Texas as a region apart, even in the West. Phrases such as "those traditional and genuine individualists, the Texans" constantly recur in the writings of respected moderns.

---

* From William Hogan, *The Texas Republic* (Norman: University of Oklahoma Press, 1946), pp. 267–270. Copyright 1946 University of Oklahoma Press. Reprinted by permission of the publisher.

The exact beginnings of a trait attributed to a region must remain among the insolvable problems of history. Perhaps this one germinated in the uniqueness of the establishment of the Republic and the maintenance of its independence. Certainly the frontier commonwealth attracted a group of unconformable leaders, headed by coruscating Sam Houston, and the whole country reflected—and still reflects—their characteristics. If a key to the nature of William Barret Travis, who led his men to patriotic suicide at the Alamo, is to be found anywhere, it appears in his diary at the entry for March 9, 1834; "Started to Mill Creek waters all swimming & prairie so boggy—could not go—*The first time I ever turned back in my life.*" It is also true that the Texas reputation for toughness in the eighteen thirties and forties, whether deserved or not, repelled timid prospective immigrants, and many were rejected in the usual process of frontier selectivity. As one man wrote shortly after his arrival in 1839: "This country is full of enterprising and persevering people. The timid and the lazy generaly return to the States." In 1846 a visitor found an economic basis for Texas independence, and concluded that "the Texans are the most independant people under the whole canopy of heaven the wealthey of the old states not excepted."

Individualism manifested itself among all classes, in all types of activity. In religion it was reflected in a report on the prospects of the Disciples of Christ in Texas which was made to Alexander Campbell: "There is a kind of manly independence among them here (all denominations) that you do not see in the United States." That it existed among the doctors as late as 1850 was the belief of Dr. Ashbel Smith, who wrote: "We have, so far as I am aware, no medical organization in our State; nor is there such prospect of any change. Each member of the faculty [the medical profession] is a separate independancy, and sometimes adopts a sort of armed neutrality system." In law the common man was made a king in his own domain by the homestead acts of 1829 and 1839. Among other manifestations of individualism were resentment of encroachments on personal "rights" and a concomitant readiness by some persons who were "a law unto themselves" to settle disputes without adjudication; a democratic willingness to accept any person regardless of his past record; and a state of affairs wherein tough-fibered women like Mrs. Pamelia Mann could come to the forefront, economically and otherwise. The whole pattern of "freedom" and unrestricted individual profits made inevitable the beginnings of irrevocable sacrifices of grasslands, forests, and wildlife, but destruction of these resources occurring in the pioneer period was not serious.

Cultural individualism in the raw was present in the realm of imaginative, exaggerative humor. Texans made striking contributions to the tall tales of the period. From yarns about the unprecedented size and ferocity of crawfish and turkey buzzards, those "hereditary proprietors of the prairies of Texas," it was but a step to the assertion of the superiority of all things Texan. "An Old Kentuckian" claimed that he could raise ten calves in Texas with less trouble than one in Kentucky. Then came the "Munchhausen-like idea of Texan prowess" which a Virginia lawyer observed was possessed by most Texans. And by 1846 it even was reported that Texas children "can make more noise with impunity than any other children on the face of God's earth."

Swearing was another widely practiced "art," which required highly individualized creative imaginations in its most sublime demonstrations. Charles Hooton, the English author whose Texas experiences left him misanthropic, wrote that Texas oaths were "of a character so entirely new and diabolical, that one would be apt to imagine the genius of Depravity herself had tasked her utmost powers to produce them for the especial use of this rising State." One candidate for the title of most talented practitioner of this "art" was Dr. Branch T. Archer ("The Old Roman")—secretary of war and holder of other important offices—who justified himself by asserting that he meant to honor God by his lack of verbal inhibitions. Another candidate was Watt Moorman, leader of the Regulators in the East Texas "Regulator-Moderator War" of the early eighteen forties, who claimed to have "invented more oaths than any other man in the world." Such wordmongering was one indication of a widespread passion for freedom of speech, which the motto of the Matagorda *Colorado Herald* further exemplified: "Give me liberty to know, to utter, and to argue freely, above all liberties." But most liberties have attendant penalties. Unbridled talk contributed to the frequency of fights and, to a lesser extent, of duels.

Chief among those who fought with sheer gusto was James B. ("Brit") Bailey of Brazoria, one of the hardy group that settled in Texas before Stephen F. Austin began to lead other Anglo-Americans across the Sabine in the early eighteen twenties. Though lame and hoarse, he had salt in his soul and was by no means a weakling. He had a quaint habit (according to family tradition) of joining in fist fights, whether personally concerned or not, yelling "Free fight, boys" as he began throwing punches. Countless tales—true and untrue—have been told about this eccentric individualist. In the early eighteen thirties his frame house near Brazoria was painted red, presenting "a very novel appearance for Texas." It is legally recorded that his will particularly enjoined his friends and executors "to have my remains inter'd erect with my face fronting the west—." Legend tells that Brit requested that his coffin be further ornamented by his rifle, powder horn, bullets, and whisky jug. Though Bailey's past record and his early movements in Texas were subject to suspicion, he lived to acquire the appreciation of his fellow colonists as well as a respectable estate, including one of the first brick houses erected in Austin's Colony. It is a reflection on machine-age progress that few of his kind walk the earth today, even in Texas.

ADDITIONAL READINGS

The best one-volume summary of Texas history is Rupert N. Richardson's *Texas: The Lone Star State* (New York, 1958). Eugene C. Barker's *Life of Stephen F. Austin* (Nashville, 1925) is broadly conceived and will probably be the definitive biography for a long time to come. *The Raven: A Biography of Sam Houston,* by Marquis James (Indianapolis, 1929), is somewhat journalistic in style and tone, but it is entertaining. A short book, but high in its level of interpretation, is William C. Binkley's *The Texas Revolution* (Baton Rouge, 1952).

7

MANIFEST DESTINY
AND THE
MEXICAN WAR

If ever a term was born out of the frontier experience, that term is "Manifest Destiny." The phrase (expressing the belief in a "general law which is rolling our population westward") was coined about the middle of the nineteenth century, but the impulse to follow the arc of the sun sprang from a much earlier period, beginning with the first Europeans in North America. Sometimes it was a vision and poetically expressed—as in 1771, when the young Princetonian Philip Freneau, in "The Rising Glory of America," sang of the day ". . . when Britain's sons shall spread/ Dominion to the north and south and west/ Far from th' Atlantic to Pacific shores." More prosaically, but no less optimistically, the New England geographer Jedediah Morse, writing in the year the Constitution was ratified, anticipated an era ". . . not far distant, when the AMERICAN EMPIRE will comprehend millions of souls, west of the Mississippi." The same mood is reflected in the resigned tone of Governor Dunmore of Virginia, when he complained to the Colonial Secretary that England's attempt at containment through the Proclamation of 1763 could not check the restless advance of colonial frontiersmen. Whether advanced as a form of geopolitics, as with President Jefferson, or simply reflecting an unarticulated response to land hunger, as with the migration into east Texas, the westering urge was firmly fixed in the American tradition well before 1840. Soon or late, that urge must stretch the limits of the United States to continent's end. It is perhaps appropriate that a shibboleth should at last be found to dramatize and rationalize western expansion at this time—just as the nation was about to acquire its most extensive piece of territory, by force of arms.

The presidential order that sent General Zachary Taylor and his troops to the Rio Grande in January of 1846, thereby precipitating the Mexican War, is generally and correctly viewed as part of a pattern largely imposed by the spread-eagle spirit of the times. The Democratic victory in 1844, on a platform that linked the Texas and Oregon questions, put an avowed expansionist in the executive chair. There followed fast the annexation of Texas by joint resolution of Congress in the last, lame-duck days of President Tyler's administration. Such an act, if the Mexicans were to be taken at their word, might be expected to bring on war between the two countries. With Texas in tow, her boundary dispute with Mexico over the strip between the Nueces and the Rio Grande became ours. Moreover, Mexico was vulnerable along the Pacific slope. Her restless and weakly held province of California, with its incomparable San Francisco Bay, had tempted an earlier Democratic President, Andrew Jackson, to offer the Mexicans half a million dollars for the bay and the northern part of the province. The bid was premature; but another tack was taken in 1842, when Secretary of State Webster's interest in California was kindled by the enthusiasm of Tyler's minister to Mexico, Waddy Thompson. Webster tried to set up cession of both Texas and California through a tripartite arrangement with Mexico and Great Britain, whereby the United States would accept a northern border along the Columbia River if the British would urge Mexico to part with upper California. This scheme, already in the stages of internal collapse, was given the *coup de grâce* when the overeager Commodore Thomas Ap Catesby Jones seized Monterey on the false rumor of war between the United States and Mexico.

On yet another front, the rising tide of immigration along the Oregon Trail (epitomized by the "Great Migration" of nearly a thousand settlers into the Willamette Valley in 1843), coupled with the withdrawal of the Hudson's Bay Company headquarters from north of the Columbia to Vancouver Island in 1845, suggested that a favorable time had come for the United States to move toward a decision in Oregon. The resolution citing intention to terminate joint occupation passed Congress on April 23, 1846. Clearly, the currents of expansion were running strong. James Polk, although not an extremist, was intent upon pushing through a program of territorial spread, which would include the settlement of the boundary disputes with Britain over the Oregon country and with Mexico over Texas, as well as the acquisition of California.

In one sense Manifest Destiny in the 1840s seems to have operated as a virtually irrepressible force, with individuals caught up in the general contagion of the "Oregon Fever" or, in the West and Southwest at least, responding enthusiastically and often heedlessly to the call for volunteers to fight in Mexico. On the other hand, there was substantial anti-expansionist and anti-war sentiment in the land. The hard-core opposition came from New England abolitionists, who viewed the war as a sinister plot designed to further the extension of slavery. There was also considerable heel-dragging by influential Whigs, and their discontent mounted and coalesced as the war became increasingly a political as well as a military affair. Most intransigent of all was Henry David Thoreau, who—in perhaps the most uncompromising statement of individualism in our history—carried the transcendental doctrine of self-reliance to the point of defiance of the state. Nevertheless, most Americans blew with the winds of Manifest Destiny doctrine. In fact, some expansionists of 1845 viewed individualism in quite another context than Thoreau—insisting that territorial extension was essential to the fullest liberty of the individual and finding personal freedom to be incompatible with a crowded population.

The farthest reach of the Manifest Destiny spirit developed in the closing stages of the war with the movement simply to take by conquest and incorporate "all of Mexico." The plan was inspired in part by the desire to regenerate the Mexicans through absorption by a democratic republic and, more important, by considerations of national self-interest. The repudiation of both these ideas, through the acceptance of the relatively undemanding treaty of Guadalupe Hidalgo, indicates Polk's surrender to expediency and suggests that the nation was not yet ready to take in territory thickly populated with an alien people.

The war itself may be viewed from several angles. It was, first of all, a war of conquest. The theaters of action were defined by American expansionist hankering after California and New Mexico, and by the need to occupy Mexico and, ultimately, to take the war to the capital itself. This meant extended operations involving arduous marches dangerously distant from bases of supply, so that frequently the forces of nature—drought, rain, disease, and punishing terrain—were more formidable than the foe. There were also hidden struggles embedded in the over-all campaign: notably, the antagonism and mutual contempt between the regulars and the volunteers; and the play of politics and temperament that set the Whig generals Taylor and Scott sniping at one another as well as at their Democrat commander-in-chief, who was no mean sniper himself. Then too, the Mexican War provided a baptism in battle for young officers who were to be antagonists within a decade and a half—Meade and Beauregard, Jackson and McClellan, Grant and Lee—giving them valuable experience in managing the American citizen-soldier who would make up the bulk of their commands in that longer, tougher, more painful struggle. The war had its ludicrous aspects: the clumsy and cruel Bear Flag revolt in California; Mexican cannon balls that drew near the enemy at bowling-ball pace; and the precipitous flight of Governor Armijo, talked out of his stronghold at Santa Fe by a persuasive Kentucky Irishman, James Magoffin. Offsetting any *opéra bouffe* cast, however, was the desperate fighting at Buena Vista and Churubusco and the ravages of dysentery and fever in the camps and on the march. To cap a far-flung and victorious campaign, there was the confusion of a peace, negotiated by a repudiated commissioner, in which an absolutely defeated Mexico received five sixths of what had been offered for the same general area before hostilities began. Nevertheless, United States authority now stretched to the southern sea. Aside from the Gadsden nibble in 1853, and the unpopular purchase of Alaska in 1867, the maw of American expansionism was filled, for a time at least. When next American destiny became as manifest as in the 1840s, it would carry the country beyond its continental limits.

John L. O'Sullivan

The cry "manifest destiny" was first raised by John L. O'Sullivan, the fighting Irish editor of the Democratic Review. *O'Sullivan, an attorney-journalist, was a Jacksonian Democrat who dedicated his magazine to the party during the administrations of Van Buren and Polk. The following excerpts are from his essay justifying the annexation of Texas and forecasting the acquisition of California; the essay appeared in the* Review *in the summer of 1845. O'Sullivan used the term again the following December, in an editorial in the New York* Morning News; *and soon the phrase rang in the halls of Congress and ricocheted across the land.*

The Annexation of Texas*

It is time now for opposition to the Annexation of Texas to cease, all further agitation of the waters of bitterness and strife, at least in connexion with this question,—even though it may perhaps be required of us as a

---

*From John L. O'Sullivan, "Annexation," *United States Magazine and Democratic Review,* New Series, XVII (July–August 1845), 5–10.

necessary condition of the freedom of our institutions, that we must live on for ever in a state of unpausing struggle and excitement upon some subject of party division or other. But, in regard to Texas, enough has now been given to Party. It is time for the common duty of Patriotism to the Country to succeed;—or if this claim will not be recognized, it is at least time for common sense to acquiesce with decent grace in the inevitable and the irrevocable.

Why, were other reasoning wanting, in favor of now elevating this question of the reception of Texas into the Union, out of the lower region of our past party dissensions, up to its proper level of a high and broad nationality, it surely is to be found, found abundantly, in the manner in which other nations have undertaken to intrude themselves into it, between us and the proper parties to the case, in a spirit of hostile interference against us, for the avowed object of thwarting our policy and hampering our power, limiting our greatness and checking the fulfilment of our manifest destiny to overspread the continent allotted by Providence for the free development of our yearly multiplying millions. This we have seen done by England, our old rival and enemy; and by France, strangely coupled with her against us, under the influence of the Anglicism strongly tinging the policy of her present prime minister, Guizot. The zealous activity with which this effort to defeat us was pushed by the representatives of those governments, together with the character of intrigue accompanying it, fully constituted that case of foreign interference, which Mr. Clay himself declared should, and would unite us all in maintaining the common cause of our country against the foreigner and the foe. We are only astonished that this effect has not been more fully and strongly produced, and that the burst of indignation against this unauthorized, insolent and hostile interference against us, has not been more general even among the party before opposed to Annexation, and has not rallied the national spirit and national pride unanimously upon that policy. . . .

It is wholly untrue, and unjust to ourselves, the pretence that the Annexation has been a measure of spoliation, unrightful and unrighteous —of military conquest under forms of peace and law—of territorial aggrandizement at the expense of justice, and justice due by a double sanctity to the weak. This view of the question is wholly unfounded, and has been before so amply refuted in these pages, as well as in a thousand other modes, that we shall not again dwell upon it. The independence of Texas was complete and absolute. It was an independence, not only in fact but of right. No obligation of duty towards Mexico tended in the least degree to restrain our right to effect the desired recovery of the fair province once our own—whatever motives of policy might have prompted a more deferential consideration of her feelings and her pride, as involved in the question. If Texas became peopled with an American population, it was by no contrivance of our government, but on the express invitation of that of Mexico herself; accompanied with such guaranties of State independence, and the maintenance of a federal system analogous to our own, as constituted a compact fully justifying the strongest measures of redress on the part of those afterwards deceived in this guaranty, and sought to be enslaved under the yoke imposed by its violation. She was released, rightfully and absolutely released, from all Mexican allegiance, or duty of cohesion to the Mexican political body, by the acts and fault of Mexico herself, and Mexico alone. There never was a clearer case. It was not revolution; it was resistance to revolution; and resistance under such circumstances as left independence the necessary resulting state, caused by the abandonment of those with whom her former federal association had existed. What then can be more preposterous than all this clamor by Mexico and the Mexican interest, against Annexation, as a violation of any rights of hers, any duties of ours?

... The country which was the subject of Annexation in this case, from its geographical position and relations, happens to be—or rather the portion of it now actually settled, happens to be—a slave country. But a similar process might have taken place in proximity to a different section of our Union; and indeed there is a great deal of Annexation yet to take place, within the life of the present generation, along the whole line of our northern border. Texas has been absorbed into the Union in the inevitable fulfilment of the general law which is rolling our population westward; the connexion of which with that ratio of growth in population which is destined within a hundred years to swell our numbers to the enormous population of *two hundred and fifty millions* (if not more), is too evident to leave us in doubt of the manifest design of Providence in regard to the occupation of this continent. It was disintegrated from Mexico in the natural course of events, by a process perfectly legitimate on its own part, blameless on ours; and in which all the censures due to wrong, perfidy and folly, rest on Mexico alone. And possessed as it was by a population which was in truth but a colonial detachment from our own, and which was still bound by myriad ties of the very heartstrings to its old relations, domestic and political, their incorporation into the Union was not only inevitable, but the most natural, right and proper thing in the world—and it is only astonishing that there should be any among ourselves to say it nay.

California will, probably, next fall away from the loose adhesion which, in such a country as Mexico, holds a remote province in a slight equivocal kind of dependence on the metropolis. Imbecile and distracted, Mexico never can exert any real governmental authority over such a country. The impotence of the one and the distance of the other, must make the relation one of virtual independence; unless, by stunting the province of all natural growth, and forbidding that immigration which can alone develop its capabilities and fulfil the purposes of its creation, tyranny may retain a military dominion which is no government in the legitimate sense of the term. In the case of California this is now impossible. The Anglo-Saxon foot is already on its borders. Already the advance guard of the irresistible army of Anglo-Saxon emigration has begun to pour down upon it, armed with the plough and the rifle, and marking its trail with schools and colleges, courts and representative halls, mills and meeting-houses. A population will soon be in actual occupation of California, over which it will be idle for Mexico to dream of dominion. . . .

Away, then, with all idle French talk of *balances of power* on the American Continent. There is no growth in Spanish America! Whatever progress of population there may be in the British Canadas, is only for their own early severance of their present colonial relation to the little island three thousand miles across the Atlantic; soon to be followed by Annexation, and destined to swell the still accumulating momentum of our progress. And whatsoever may hold the balance, though they should cast into the opposite scale all the bayonets and cannon, not only of France and England, but of Europe entire, how would it kick the beam against the simple solid weight of two hundred and fifty or three hundred millions —and American millions—destined to gather beneath the flutter of the stripes and stars, in the fast hastening year of the Lord 1845?

Congressional Globe

Well before O'Sullivan's famous piece on the annexation of Texas, expansionists in Congress were expounding the substance of manifest destiny without hitting on the precise label. The following excerpts—from the recapitulation of a speech by Representative Belser of Alabama, delivered before the House early in January 1845—capture the admixture of complacency, cupidity, presumption, and optimism that characterized so much of the expansionist oratory of the times, and suggest as well the protean nature of the argument.

On Annexation*

... He [Representative Belser] meant to vote for Texas, if he could. And if gentlemen are in doubt, he would say to them, with Hoyle in his treatise on whist, "When you are in doubt, take the trick." [Great laughter.]

But [said Mr. B.] we are told by the opponent of annexation, that our citizens settled in Texas; that the United States encouraged them in it; and that it is through their influence that the country has been wrested from Mexico, and consequently, it would subject us to improper suspicions, if we annex the republic at this time. Here arises a home view of this question. How was it that this government had removed the Indians west of the Mississippi? When the first navigators from the Old World discovered this continent, it was in the possession of independent nations or tribes. European powers were anxious to annex it to their own dominions, and nautical adventurers were found sailing along the coast, claiming for their rulers certain countries between the Atlantic and the Pacific oceans. Since then, in the arrangements of Providence, Indian possession had gradually given way before the advances of civilization. And so it must ever be. Gentlemen might talk as they pleased about their devotion to the thirteen original States—about prescribing limits to the American people. There were none—there could be none! They would go, and go, and still continue to go, until they reached the ultimate boundary which the God of nature had set to the progress of the human race. He, for one, hoped that the day was not far distant when they would go a little farther. [A laugh.] He meant farther than the point at which his friend from Pennsylvania had fixed their ultimate boundary, when he had so eloquently described it as being marked "in the configuration of this continent by an Almighty hand:" he was not, he hoped, so impious as to throw out the idea that they could transcend a point fixed for them by the decrees of God.

After this continent had been discovered, we succeeded to the rights of Great Britain. We inherited the soil by the sword. The country was still ours. We could almost trace, in the neighborhoods of Jamestown and of Plymouth, the ancient track of the postboy; as we could in the great West the footsteps of the Catholic missionary and of the French soldier. The land was ours; but where were the people? Where was that brave aboriginal race which once chased the deer and conquered the bear in its

---

* From the *Congressional Globe,* 28th Cong., 2d Sess. (January 3, 1845), App., pp. 42–43.

mountains and valleys? They were gone, and we were in their places. And how had we obtained their country? Talk of cessions and Indian treaties: it was a farce! We had got their possessions by the strong arm of power. We removed these tribes from their hunting-grounds, who did not cultivate the land, in order that we might accomplish the greatest amount of good to the human race. And has Texas done anything more than we did before her? No, sir!—no, sir!...

And does the history of the past furnish no insight into the future? What is to become of our population in a half century or a century hence? According to a calculation derived from the best of sources, in fifty years it will number one hundred million; and in double that period, three hundred millions. Talk to him about confining the area of liberty!— it could not be done. Freedom's pure and heavenly light was here, and it would continue to burn, with increasing brightness, till it had illumined this entire continent.

Why, what did gentlemen suppose was to become of the rising generation in the West? Did they think it was to stay there, to vegetate like a plant and die on the spot where it grew? No, you had as well attempt to arrest Niagara. It would go onward and onward; it would fill Oregon; it would fill Texas; it would pour like a cataract over the Rocky mountains, and, passing to the great lakes of the West, it would open the forests of that far distant wilderness to the light of the rising sun. And whoever should live and visit this continent at that day might hear the voice of the American reaper on the far shores of the Pacific. The idea thrown out by President Houston, in one of his messages, that the lone star of Texas would yet one day float in triumph over the ancient palace of the Montezumas had been much ridiculed; but, in his apprehension, it was likely to be converted into sober fact.

Mr. B. then did not believe in limiting the spread of liberty, or in checking the migration of our people. Extension, in his opinion, was the antagonistical principle of centralization. Our duration as a nation consists in our inestimable institutions, in our expansive territory, in the virtue of the people; and, combined with these, were our noble rivers, our internal communications, the abundance which we raise, and the certainty of bringing into requisition in the hour of need our physical force....

The inhabitants of the new States had entered Texas in large numbers, with the hope of bettering their condition, and with an honest ambition to occupy elevated stations in the new republic. This was the genius and spirit of the popular system which distinguished our country. And are we prepared to reject Texas again? In the language of one of her sons, *"What! reject a proffered territory as extensive as four or five of our largest States, equal in fertility to the most favored, superior to most of them in natural advantages; with a thousand miles of sea coast; from*

*its position constituting an unseemly interference with our territory? What!
reject a compact which secures to Texas no advantages—save the solitary
isolated one of nestling in the folds of the star spangled banner."*

In conclusion, Mr. B. observed that he had recently been reading a historical legend which afforded an exemplification of what he thought ought to be our national condition and character. When the city of Corinth was taken, sacked, and burnt by the Roman consul, Mummius, in the fusion of metals produced by the intensity of the heat, a mixed and compounded one was produced of far greater brilliancy and beauty than any of the materials of which it was composed. It was called Corinthian brass, and was held more precious than gold. He desired to see the day speedily come when our country will, so far as a spirit of brotherhood can exist, resemble just such a metal as was formed at Corinth. And that that government whose independence was first proclaimed by the Henrys, the Thompsons, the Adamses, the Middletons. the Rutledges, and the Lees, will survive the ghastly glare of an unbridled fanaticism; and that some interceding spirit will yet rise up to check the now widespread flames. Long may our country prove itself the asylum of the oppressed. Let its institutions and its people be extended far and wide, and when the waters of despotism shall have inundated other portions of the globe, and the votary of liberty be compelled to betake himself to his ark, let this government be the Ararat on which it shall rest.

Congressional Globe

*As the course of the Mexican War advanced and American victories
mounted, the Manifest Destinarian spirit grew more expansive, more
benevolent, more coated with altruism, until some of its advocates came to
believe that America had a duty—a mandate from civilization—to absorb
all of Mexico. Such was the notion of Senator Breese of Illinois, speaking
before the Senate in mid-February 1848. His views demonstrate a shift
from the concept of regeneration of territory to the regeneration of an entire people and their culture. Although the movement he represented
aborted, it attests to the viability of the "Manifest Destiny" tradition.*

On the Mexican War*

Mr. President, at the outset of this war, and in its first year, it was distinctly avowed by the Executive, and reiterated by his friends, that as it was brought upon us by Mexico, he had no other desire in waging it, than an honorable peace, including indemnity for the past injuries we had sustained at her hands, and such security against future aggressions, as Mexico might be enabled to give. And is it unreasonable, sir, that as the war is protracted by Mexico, she refusing all offers of accommodation, that our demands should rise in proportion? In my own opinion, in the view I have taken of this matter, we would not be doing justice to our own country, by a show of too much lenity to Mexico, and that sheer justice would demand from her full indemnity also for the expenses of this war; and in her peculiar position—she not being able to provide any other indemnity—that the cession of the sovereignty and jurisdiction over a part of her territory, should be insisted upon as a *sine qua non;* for I believe with the President, that the doctrine of no territory, which was broached here at the last session, and found so many advocates, is the doctrine of no indemnity. In territory only can Mexico make reparation for the past, and afford security for her future good behavior; and although we are strong as a nation, yet, like the strong man who desires security against the attack of a lurking, cowardly assassin, so should we insist on it in such a line of boundary between us as will secure us against future aggressions. . . . Our policy, sir, is, emphatically, peace with all nations, but with none at the sacrifice of our national honor, the dearest possession of a nation. We have never, sir, since the birth of our nation, given occasion for war, not even with the barbarous tribes upon our borders. It is our pride to be able to say, that our whole history may be explored, and no single act of national injustice can be found upon its page—no blot of that kind upon our national escutcheon. We, sir, would have never disturbed our peaceful relations with Mexico, by any act of our own; she has brought the war upon herself, under a delusion that one of our sister States belonged to her; and resolving to possess it by force of arms, and refusing to hear our minister upon the matters in dispute, sought to end them by the sword; and as she has appealed to that dread arbiter, she must abide its fortune. . . . It is true, sir, war is an evil—a great evil, but it has also its advantages, and though the land may be, for a time,

---

* From the *Congressional Globe,* 30th Cong., 1st Sess. (February 14, 1848), pp. 344–350.

crushed by its armed heel, it is but preparing it for the reception of that seed whose fruit is commerce, science, the arts, and the highest and purest forms of civilization.... The roads traced by the soldiery are soon followed by the merchant, greatly facilitating the commerce of ideas—favoring the sympathies of nations, and in the end will fraternize the whole human race. It is one of the great instruments of God's providence, by which to accomplish such grand results; and can any Senator doubt that this most remarkable war will not greatly redound to the advantage of Mexico, securing to her, in the end, every blessing we so abundantly enjoy?

It has been a war waged thus far, not against the people of Mexico, but emphatically against the army alone, with a view only to its destruction, and upon principles of the most enlightened humanity. Not one single act of oppression or injustice has been committed by us—our path, as we have strode from victory to victory, has not been lighted by the flames of their dwellings, their defenceless women and children given to the sword, nor their cities sacked, nor churches defiled, nor fields laid waste. Though we have been terrible to the combatant, we have been generous to him when vanquished—never forgetting, in the midst of the excitement, that the fairest chaplet victory wears is that which mercy twines. These, sir, are what make it a most extraordinary war; and the faithful historian, as he writes its varied and stirring events, will dwell with peculiar pleasure and pride on this, its bright and most distinguishing feature. So humane and generous has been our conduct, that the people of Mexico, those who have suffered by the oppression of the military tyrants, regard our armies rather as benefactors than as enemies; and if accounts can be relied on, are utterly opposed to their withdrawal....

The avowed objects of the war which we declared to exist by the act of Mexico [were] to obtain redress of wrongs, a permanent and honorable peace, and indemnity for the past and security for the future; and if they cannot be obtained in any other way than by the conquest of Mexico, and incorporating it into the Union, or holding it as a province, such a result would be in harmony with those objects. Nor would it be contrary to the spirit and genius of our Government, nor against its settled policy, to conquer, in a defensive war, any country, and annex it, which might be thought, from its contiguity, to be necessary to our own safety.... How the annexation of Mexico to our Union would tend to subvert our free institutions, I cannot discover.... I see in [the Mexican people] attributes and elements quite susceptible, by proper appliances, of high improvement. Could they be brought under the happy influences of such a Government as our own, having all their rights, civil and religious, protected, what might we not hope from them? The Indian population, numbering about four millions, are reputed to be very gentle and quiet in their dispositions, apt to learn, and willing to improve, and, if not possessed of all the manlier virtues, have at least those which fully ensure their cheerful acquiescence to our control and rapid advancement under it. . . . I do not suppose, sir, the Mexicans are at this time fitted for an equal union with us; and much is to be done before they will be. By the infusion of our own population among them, (and they are now there in great numbers, according to the Senator of Delaware, Mr. Clayton,) together with emigrants from Europe, who will not be slow to avail themselves of the unsurpassed advantages such a country enjoys, a gradual change in their manners, customs, and language, will ensue. Education will be diffused among the masses; speech, the press, and religion will be free, and high opinions of themselves speedily generated; and considering the rapidity of past events, the aids to knowledge, and for its rapid spread, which the world now possesses, the period of their pupilage will be of short duration. Sir, it has been alike our pride and boast, that our institutions were better calculated to elevate the masses than any others which have yet existed, and we feel it to be true; and it cannot be that it is the decree of Heaven that none but the white race shall enjoy them. It has been the abiding hope of the philanthropist, that in God's good time all nations should enjoy them, and the down-trodden millions of both hemispheres be exalted by their agency. There is nothing, sir, in the history of that beautiful country, or in the character of its people, to discourage the belief that they can, in a very short time, be brought to a condition qualifying them for admission into this great American family, adorning and strengthening it by a commingling and full development of all those grand and mighty elements they possess, and thus fulfill her own and our happy destiny. And, sir, it is the fervent wish and hope of her most eminent citizens and patriots, that this war may accelerate it; and, if "coming events cast their shadows before," may it not be regarded as its certain precursor? In my musings upon this subject, Mr. President, I have been cheered by the hope, that if I did not, my children would live to see that day when our institutions shall extend over the whole of this portion of our continent, all to be bound by one common ligament, and all to run one common career of honor, happiness, and renown. . . . Sir, our liberty can be preserved only by progress. Being stationary it stagnates, and in that condition the flame will expire. It is by action alone—by ceaseless, constant action—we can preserve it. Let us expand to our true and proper dimensions, and our liberty will be eternal; for, in the process, it will increase in strength, and the flame grow brighter, whilst it lights a more extensive field. Does any Senator believe our attachment to liberty would have been any stronger than it is now, or that we would have been more powerful and happy, had our Confederacy been confined within the Atlantic coast and the range of the Alleganies? Would any one of them willingly restore to their former owners Louisiana, Florida, and Texas, or surrender either without a deathly struggle? I apprehend not. Our history shows, thus far, that there is no danger in our extension. Our form of government is peculiarly fitted for this—it has a peculiar aptitude for expansion, a principle which no other Government ever did possess, and it is one of its greatest excellencies. Will any Senator deny that the new States have contributed new vigor to our system, and increased strength to our circle? Have any symptoms of disaffection to the Union been observed in any of them? Has any spirit of insubordination or of restlessness under the ties which bind them, ever been manifested by any of them? No, sir, it is not in them where man enjoys the largest liberty, only restrained by laws he makes himself that *émeutes,* riots, and rebellions occur, but it is among a crowded population, in pent up masses, easily excited by collision, with no extended field of action to arouse their energies, and no attainable objects before them to guide them aright. . . .

As I believe, sir, there are but two alternatives—either to flee the country, or to hold on to our acquisitions, the result of which may be the final absorption of Mexico, I have not hesitated to declare for the latter, being well satisfied that great ultimate good to us, to her, and to humanity is to flow from it.

James K. Polk

One Mexican War specialist insists that the real hero of the piece was none other than James K. Polk (1795–1849). Certainly, most would agree that no more fascinating document emerged from the times than the President's diary. Even the few fragments it is possible to present here reveal a man who, despite his irascibility and pettiness, was the most clear-eyed and dogged Manifest Destinarian of them all. Moreover, as a product of the southwestern border, he seems to conform to the popularly accepted frontier code of courage and independence. Worn out by his labors and broken in health, Polk died little more than a year out of office—as much a casualty of the war as any who succumbed in the field.

Diary*

Saturday, 9th May, 1846.—The Cabinet held a regular meeting to-day; all the members present. I brought up the Mexican question, and the question of what was the duty of the administration in the present state of our relations with that country. The subject was very fully discussed. All agreed that if the Mexican forces at Matamoras committed any act of hostility on Gen'l Taylor's forces I should immediately send a message to Congress recommending an immediate declaration of War. I stated to the Cabinet that up to this time, as they knew, we had heard of no open act of aggression by the Mexican army, but that the danger was imminent that such acts would be committed. I said that in my opinion we had ample cause of war, and that it was impossible that we could stand in *statu quo,* or that I could remain silent much longer; that I thought it was my duty to send a message to Congress very soon & recommend definitive measures. I told them that I thought I ought to make such a message by tuesday next, that the country was excited and impatient on the subject, and if I failed to do so I would not be doing my duty. I then propounded the distinct question to the Cabinet and took their opinions individually, whether I should make a message to Congress on tuesday, and whether in that message I should recommend a declaration of War against Mexico. All except the Secretary of the Navy gave their advice in the affirmative. Mr. Bancroft dissented but said if any act of hostility should be committed by the Mexican forces he was then in favour of immediate war. Mr. Buchanan said he would feel better satisfied in his course if the Mexican forces had or should commit any act of hostility, but that as matters stood we had ample cause of war against Mexico, & he gave his assent to the measure. It was agreed that the message should be prepared and submitted to the Cabinet in their meeting on tuesday.

About 6 o'clock P.M. Gen'l R. Jones, the Adjutant General of the army, called and handed to me despatches received from Gen'l Taylor by the Southern mail which had just arrived, giving information that a part of [the] Mexican army had crossed to the Del Norte [crossed the Rio Grande Del Norte], and attacked and killed and captured two companies of dragoons of Gen'l Taylor's army consisting of 63 officers & men. The despatch also stated that he had on that day (26th April) made a requisition on the Governors of Texas & Louisiana for four Regiments each,

---

* From Milo M. Quaife, ed., *The Diary of James K. Polk* (4 vols., Chicago: A. C. McClurg and Co., 1910), I, 384–401 *passim;* II, 347–348.

to be sent to his relief at the earliest practicable period. Before I had finished reading the despatch, the Secretary of War called. I immediately summoned the Cabinet to meet at 7 ½ O'Clock this evening. The Cabinet accordingly assembled at that hour; all the members present. The subject of the despatch received this evening from Gen'l Taylor, as well as the state of our relations with Mexico, were fully considered. The Cabinet were unanimously of opinion, and it was so agreed, that a message should be sent to Congress on Monday laying all the information in my possession before them and recommending vigorous & prompt measure[s] to enable the Executive to prosecute the War. The Secretary of War & Secretary of State agreed to put their clerks to work to copy the correspondence between Mr. Slidell & the Mexican Government & Secretary of State and the correspondence between the War Department & Gen'l Taylor, to the end that these documents should be transmitted to Congress with my message on Monday.

Wednesday, 13th May, 1846.—A very large number of visitors called on me this morning, consisting of Senators, Representatives, citizens, & strangers. All took a deep interest and many were excited at the declaration of war which passed Congress on yesterday, and now only awaited my approval to become a law. All approved the acts. Many members of Congress especially from the Western States desired that volunteers under the law should be accepted from their respective States.

About 1 O'Clock P.M. a committee of Congress waited on me and presented the act declaring War against Mexico for my approval. I read it in their presence & approved and signed it.

Gen'l Scott, commander in chief of the U.S. Army, called in company with the Secretary of War. I had requested the Secretary to invite Gen'l Scott to call. I held a conference with them in relation to the execution of [the] act declaring War against Mexico. Gen'l Scott presented a project of the number and distribution among the State[s] of the number of troops required. It was incomplete and after giving him my views [I] requested him to make a more formal report to me during the day. I tendered to Gen'l Scott the command of the army to be raised. He accepted and retired. Though I did not consider him in all respects suited to such an important command, yet being commander in chief of the army, his position entitled him to it if he desired it.

Mr. Buchanan read the draft of a despatch which he had prepared to our Ministers at London, Paris, & other Foreign Courts, announcing the declaration of War against Mexico, with a statement of the causes and objects of the War, with a view that they should communicate its substance to the respective Governments to which they are accredited. Among other things Mr. Buchanan had stated that our object was not to dismember Mexico or to make conquests, and that the Del Norte was the boundary to which we claimed; or rather that in going to war we did not do so with a view to acquire either California or New Mexico or any other portion of the Mexican territory. I told Mr. Buchanan that I thought such a declaration to Foreign Governments unnecessary and improper; that the causes of the war as set forth in my message to Congress and the accompanying documents were altogether satisfactory. I told him that though we had not gone to war for conquest, yet it was clear that in making peace we would if practicable obtain California and such other portion of the Mexican territory as would be sufficient to indemnify our claimants on Mexico, and to defray the expenses of the war which that power by her long continued wrongs and injuries had forced us to wage. I told him it was well known that the Mexican Government had no other means of indemnifying us. Mr. Buchanan said if when Mr. McLane announced to Lord Aberdeen the existence of the War with Mexico the latter should demand of Mr. McLane to know if we intended to acquire California or any other part of the Mexican territory and no satisfactory answer was given, he thought it almost certain that both England and France would join with Mexico in the war against us. I told him that the war with Mexico was an affair with which neither England, France, or any other power had any concern; that such an inquiry would be insulting to our Government, and if made I would not answer it, even if the consequence should be a war with all of them. I told him I would not tie up my hands or make any pledge to any Foreign power as to the terms on which I would ultimately make peace with Mexico. I told him no Foreign [power] had any right to demand any such assurance, and that I would make none such let the consequences be what they might. Then, said Mr. Buchanan, you will have war with England as well as Mexico, and probably with France also, for neither of these powers will ever stand by and [see] California annexed to the U.S. I told him that before I would make the pledge which he proposed, I would meet the war which either England or France or all the Powers of Christendom might wage, and that I would stand and fight until the last man among us fell in the conflict. I told him that neither as a citizen nor as President would I permit or tolerate any intermeddling of any European Power on this Continent. Mr. Buchanan said if my views were carried out, we would not settle the Oregon question & we would have war with England. I told him there was no connection between the Oregon & Mexican question[s], and that sooner than give the pledge he proposed[,] that we would not if we could fairly and honourably acquire California or any other part of the Mexican Territory which we desired, I would let the war which he apprehended with England come & would take the whole responsibility. The Secretary of the Treasury engaged warmly & even in an excited manner against the proposition of Mr. Buchanan in his draft of his despatch. The Secretary of the Navy, the Atto. Gen'l, & the P. M. Gen'l in succession expressed similar opinions. Mr. Buchanan stood alone in the Cabinet, but was very earnest in expressing his views and enforcing them. Towards the close of the discussion, which lasted for more than two hours, I stepped to my table and wrote a paragraph to be substituted for all that part of Mr. B's proposed despatch which spoke of dismembering Mexico, of acquiring California, or of the Del Norte as the ultimate boundary beyond which we would not claim or desire to go. I strongly expressed to Mr. Buchanan that these paragraphs in his despatch must be struck out. Mr. Buchanan made no reply, but before he left took up his own draft and the paragraph which I had written and took them away with [him]. I was much astonished at the views expressed by Mr. Buchanan on the subject. The discussion to-night was one of the most earnest & interesting which has ever occurred in my Cabinet.

The Cabinet adjourned about 11 O'Clock P.M. and I retired to rest much exhausted after a day of incessant application, anxiety, and labour.

Thursday, 14th May, 1846.—At 8 O'Clock P.M. the Secretary of War and Gen'l Scott of the U.S. Army called. I had a long conference with them concerning the plan of conducting the war with Mexico. I gave it as my opinion that the first movement should be to march a competent force into the Northern Provinces and seize and hold them until peace was made. In this they concurred. The whole field of operations was examined with all the information before us, but it would be tedious to detail all the views and the reasons for them which were expressed.

It was agreed to call out immediately for service 20,000 volunteers, and we proceeded to apportion this force among the State[s] of Texas, Arkansas, Illinois, Missouri, Ohio, Indiana, Kentucky, Tennessee, Alabama, Mississippi, & Georgia. After very full examination of the subject the Secretary of War & Gen'l Scott retired between 11 & 12 O'Clock P.M. Gen'l Scott did not impress me favourably as a military man. He has had experience in his profession, but I thought was rather scientific and visionary in his views. I did not think that so many as 20,000 volunteers besides the regular army was necessary, but I did not express this opinion, not being willing to take the responsibility of any failure of the campaign by refusing to grant to Gen'l Scott all he asked.

Monday, 21st February, 1848.—I saw no company this morning. At 12 O'Clock the Cabinet met; all the members present. I made known my decision upon the Mexican Treaty, which was that under all the circumstances of the case, I would submit it [to] the Senate for ratification, with a recommendation to strike out the 10th article. I assigned my reasons for my decision. They were, briefly, that the treaty conformed on the main question of limits & boundary to the instructions given to Mr. Trist in

April last; and that though, if the treaty was now to be made, I should
demand more territory, perhaps to make the Sierra Madra the line, yet
it was doubtful whether this could be ever obtained by the consent of
Mexico. I looked, too, to the consequences of its rejection. A majority of
one branch of Congress is opposed to my administration; they have
falsely charged that the war was brought on and is continued by me with
a view to the conquest of Mexico; and if I were now to reject a Treaty
made upon my own terms, as authorized in April last, with the unanimous
approbation of the Cabinet, the probability is that Congress would not
grant either men or money to prosecute the war. Should this be the result,
the army now in Mexico would be constantly wasting and diminishing in
numbers, and I might at last be compelled to withdraw them, and thus
lose the two Provinces of New Mexico & Upper California, which were
ceded to the U.S. by this Treaty. Should the opponents of my administration succeed in carrying the next Presidential election, the great probability
is that the country would lose all the advantages secured by this Treaty. I
adverted to the immense value of Upper California; and concluded by
saying that if I were now to reject my own terms, as offered in April last,
I did not see how it was possible for my administration to be sustained.

George B. McClellan

*A rather dubious individualism found explosive expression among
the volunteers who constituted the bulk of American fighting forces in
the West and in Mexico. The typical* voluntario *hailed from the Southern
or border states and was inclined to be unruly, incompetent in camp,
rapacious, and insubordinate. In the following selection, Lieutenant George
B. McClellan (1826–1885) is severely critical of the volunteer. However,
for all his faults, the volunteer fought savagely and well when the battle
was joined. The victory at Buena Vista by troops made up almost entirely
of volunteers is but the most conspicuous example of the citizen soldier's
effectiveness in combat.*

Mexican War Diary*

[December 5th, 1846. Mouth of the Rio Grande.] . . . I have seen more suffering since I came out there than I could have imagined to exist. It is really awful. I allude to the sufferings of the Volunteers. They literally die like dogs. Were it all known in the States, there would be no more hue and cry against the Army, all would be willing to have so large a regular army that we could dispense entirely with the volunteer system. The suffering among the Regulars is comparatively trifling, for their officers know their duty and take good care of the men. . . .

On . . . (December 24th) we marched to Santa Teresa [en route to Tampico], a distance of 27 miles. It was on this march that we made the "raise" on General Patterson's birds. He sent us four for supper. We ate as many as we could and had five left for breakfast—fully equal to the loaves and fishes this. We stopped for nearly an hour at Salina—a pond of rather bad water about half way to Santa Teresa—what a rush the Voluntarios made for the water! When we arrived we found the mustang crowd taking their lunch.† As Songo [a Mexican servant] had just then made one of his periodical disappearances we were left without any thing to eat for some time, but at last we descried him caracoling across the prairie on his graceful charger. The mustangs did not have the politeness to ask us to partake of their lunch, but when Songo *did come our* brandy was better than theirs anyhow. At Santa Teresa the water was very bad—being obtained from a tancho. I bluffed off a volunteer regiment some 100 yards from our camp. As the Lieutenant Colonel of this same regiment (3rd Illinois) was marching them along by the flank he gave the command "by file left march!"—to bring it on the color line. The leading file turned at about an angle of 30 degrees. "Holloa there" says the Colonel "you man there, you dont know how to file." "The h____l I dont" yells the man "d____n you, I've been marching all day, and I guess I'm tired. . . ."

January 1st, 1847. Woke up and found the ridge pole *off* at one end.

---

* From William Starr Myers, ed., *The Mexican War Diary of George B. Mc-Clellan* (Princeton: Princeton University Press, 1917), 18–43. *passim*. Copyright 1917 Princeton University Press. Reprinted by permission.

† "Mustang cavalry" was a term reserved for volunteer infantrymen who bought or appropriated Mexican horses or *burros* and thereby immediately entered the mustang cavalry. Mustang, it seems, soon became a label of contempt employed by regular army personnel to describe volunteers from privates on up to generals.

I rather suspect that G. W. [Smith] must have done it by endeavoring to see the old year out—perhaps the new one came in via our tent, and did the damage in its passage. We began the new year by starting on the wrong road. After invading about two miles of the enemies' country we were overtaken by an officer at full gallop, who informed us that the column had taken another road and that we must make our way to the front as we best could. Smith had been informed the preceding day by Winship (General Pillow's Adjutant General) that the road we took was the right one to Victoria. We quickly discovered the magnitude of our mistake, for we got amongst the Volunteers, and the lord deliver us from ever getting into such a scrape again. Falstaff's company were regulars in comparison with these fellows—most of them without coats; some would have looked much better without *any pants* than with the parts of pants they wore; all had torn and dirty shirts—uncombed heads—unwashed faces—they were dirt and filth from top to toe. Such marching! They were marching by the flank, yet the road was not wide enough to hold them and it was with the greatest difficulty that you could get by—all hollowing, cursing, yelling like so many incarnate fiends—no attention or respect paid to the commands of their officers, whom they would curse as quickly as they would look at them. They literally straggled along for miles.

January 4th. Very early we started for Victoria—and had to work our way through the camp of the Illinois regiments which was placed along the road. At last we cleared them and found ourselves marching by moonlight through a beautiful grove of pecan trees. I know nothing more pleasant than this moonlight marching, everything is so beautiful and quiet. Every few moments a breath of warm air would strike our faces—reminding us that we were almost beneath the Tropic. After we had marched for about four hours we heard a little more yelling than usual among the Volunteers. Smith turned his horse to go and have it stopped when who should we see but the General and his staff in the midst of the yelling. We concluded that *they* must be yelling too, so we let them alone. This is but one instance of the many that occurred when these Mustang Generals were actually *afraid* to exert their authority upon the Volunteers—*Their popularity would be endangered.* I have seen enough on this march to convince me that Volunteers and Volunteer Generals wont do. I have repeatedly seen a Second Lieutenant of the regular army exercise more authority over the Volunteers—*officers and privates*—than a Mustang General.

George Gordon Meade

George Gordon Meade (1815–1872) was a graduate of West Point and a veteran of the Seminole War in Florida. In 1845 at the age of thirty he was sent to Texas with General Zachary Taylor's army of occupation. During the Mexican War he fought at Palo Alto and Resaca de la Palma and participated in the siege of Vera Cruz. His comments below, directed against the volunteers, particularly the Kentuckians, point to the independence and unruliness of the citizen soldier from the border state and suggest the problems of controlling an army of invasion. General Meade won later fame as commander of the forces that defeated Robert E. Lee at Gettysburg.

Mexican War Correspondence*

To Mrs. George G. Meade:

Point Isabel, July 24, 1846

Indeed, so irregular and undisciplined is the force sent here that I shall be surprised if I ever find myself at Monterey; for I really do not see how General Taylor can carry on operations with a force which he cannot depend upon for doing the slightest thing for itself. A regiment cannot move its camp eight or ten miles, without incurring the risk of starving; for though furnished with wagons and ample means of transportation, they will overload their wagons with baggage and sutler's goods, and leave their provisions, thinking this a clever trick by which they will force the Government officers to send on their provisions by extra transportation. The consequence is they arrive at their new position, and the next day they have nothing to eat, and then complain of the regular officers. Everything, in consequence, connected with these people is one mass of confusion, and I do not believe they ever will be taught to take care of themselves, and of course our operations will be proportionately impeded.

---

* From George Meade, *The Life and Letters of George Gordon Meade* (2 vols., New York: Charles Scribner's Sons, 1913), I, 115–116, 121, 161–162.

In Camp near Camargo, Mexico, August 13, 1846

. . . Already have they in almost every volunteer regiment reported one-third their number sick, and in many cases half the whole regiment, and I fear the mortality will be terrible among them, from their utter ignorance of the proper mode of taking care of themselves. This large number of sick is a dead weight upon us, taking away so many men as hospital attendants, requiring quarters, etc.; and if taken sick on the march, requiring transportation in wagons or on litters; all these things tell in the long run . . .

Monterey, December 2, 1846

The volunteers have been creating disturbances, which have at last aroused the old General so much that he has ordered one regiment, the First Kentucky foot, to march to the rear, as they have disgraced themselves and their State.

The amount of the story is this: Some few days ago, a party of volunteers, to what regiment attached unknown, went into a house in the suburbs of the town, and after forcibly driving out the husband, committed outrages on the wife. A day or two afterwards, a Kentucky volunteer was found in the morning with his throat cut, supposed to have been done by the outraged husband as an act of retaliation. The same day two Mexicans were shot while working in a corn-field, said to have been done by Kentucky volunteers, in revenge. The next day another Kentuckian was brought into camp with his throat cut, and several more Mexicans were shot. The General in the meantime had brought the thing to the notice of all the volunteer regiments, giving strict orders that no man should be allowed to go out with arms, and impressed upon the officers the necessity of controlling the men and putting a stop to these outrages, which would inevitably end in the massacre of many innocent persons.

It came to his notice, however, that the Kentucky regiment, notwithstanding his orders, had left its camp, in squads of twenty and thirty, all armed, and avowing their intention of killing Mexicans, to revenge their murdered comrades, and the same day one man, a Mexican, was shot within a hundred yards of the camp, and a little boy of twelve years of age, who was cutting cornstalks to bring to the camp for sale, was shot in the field and his leg broken. This poor little fellow, all bleeding and crying, was brought by his relatives and laid down in front of the General's tent, and he called out to look at him. Of course, the General was much excited, and as he could only ascertain that armed parties of Kentuckians had gone out, he told the colonel of the regiment that he held him and his officers responsible, and ordered them to the rear in disgrace. Afterwards, however, intercession was made, and on their making promises to endeavor to find out the guilty individuals, and promising to prevent such things in future, the old man countermanded the order.

The volunteers have in this war, on the whole, behaved better than I had believed they would, and infinitely better than they did in the Florida war, under my own eye. Still, without a modification of the manner in which they are officered, they are almost useless in an offensive war. They are sufficiently well-drilled for practical purposes, and are, I believe, brave, and will fight as gallantly as any men, but they are a set of Goths and Vandals, without discipline, laying waste the country wherever we go, making us a terror to innocent people, and if there is any spirit or energy in the Mexicans, will finally rouse the people against us, who now are perfectly neutral. In addition to which they add immensely to the expenses of the war. They cannot take any care of themselves; the hospitals are crowded with them, they die like sheep; they waste their provisions, requiring twice as much to supply them as regulars do. They plunder the poor inhabitants of everything they can lay their hands on, and shoot them when they remonstrate, and if one of their number happens to get into a drunken brawl and is killed, they run over the country, killing all the poor innocent people they find in their way, to avenge, as they say, the murder of their brother.

Josiah Royce

A generation after the war with Mexico, Josiah Royce (1855–1916), a young Californian on his way to a distinguished career in philosophy, wrote a history of his native state. In the passage reproduced below, Royce—an impressive critic of expansion in the 1840s—peels off layers of sanctimony and sham to lay bare the conscience of the conqueror and to point up the mid-nineteenth-century American's capacity for self-deception. His evaluation to some extent reflects the passions and prejudices of an idealist who detested injustice and hypocrisy, but Royce was also a thorough scholar with a sound historical sense.

The American as Conqueror*

The American as conqueror is unwilling to appear in public as a pure aggressor; he dare not seize a California as Russia has seized so much land in Asia or as Napoleon, with full French approval, seized whatever he wanted. The American wants to persuade not only the world but himself that he is doing God service in a peaceable spirit, even when he violently takes what he has determined to get. His conscience is sensitive, and hostile aggression, practiced against any but Indians, shocks this conscience, unused as it is to such scenes. Therefore Semple and Ide, and the cautious Secretary of State, and the gallant captain, and the venerable Senator, all alike, not only as individuals, but also as men appealing for approval to their fellow countrymen at large, must present this sinful undertaking in private and in public as a sad, but strictly moral, humane, patriotic, enlightened, and glorious undertaking. Other peoples, more used to shedding civilized blood, would have swallowed the interests of the people of twenty such Californias as that of 1846 without a gasp. The agents of such nations would have played at filibustering without scruple if they had been instructed to adopt that plan as the most simple for getting the land desired; or they would have intrigued readily, fearlessly, and again without scruple if that plan had seemed to their superiors best for the purpose. But our national plans had to be formed so as to offend our squeamish natures as little as possible. Our national conscience, however, was not only squeamish, but also, in those days, not a little hypocritical. It disliked, moreover, to have the left hand know what the right hand was doing when both were doing mischief. And so, because of its very virtues, it involved itself in disastrously complex plots.

All the actors concerned worked, namely, in the fear of this strictly virtuous, of this almost sanctimonious public opinion—a public opinion that was at the same time, both in the North and in the South, very sensitive to flattery, very ambitious to see our territory grow bigger, and very anxious to contemplate a glorious national destiny. Moreover, all these our agents not only feared the public, but participated themselves in the common sentiments. Hence we find the Polk cabinet elaborately considering, not merely how to prosecute successfully their intended aggressive war,

---

* From Josiah Royce, *California from the Conquest in 1846 to the Second Vigilance Committee in San Franciso: A Study of American Character* (Boston and New York: Houghton Mifflin & Company, 1886), pp. 151–156.

just as the leaders of any other rapacious nation would have considered such a matter, but also how to put their war into harmony with the enlightened American spirit. And, in the autumn of 1845, their pious plans were apparently well formed. To Mexico the Slidell mission should be sent, with its offer to purchase California. This would be a liberal offer and, if it ever became public, would set us right as a powerful and generous nation in the eyes of the world, while it would give us in the meantime a chance to get California for nothing, by the completion of our intrigue in that territory and by the act of its own people. The beautiful and business-like compromise must be carefully expressed by the honorable Secretary of State in such language as would not offend the sensitive American spirit in case, by some accident, the whole scheme should some day come plainly to light. Larkin must be instructed that we had "no ambitious aspirations to gratify," and that we only desired to arouse in the Californian breast "that love of liberty and independence so natural to the American continent." It was all very kindly, this desire, and poor Mexico ought to have been thankful for such a neighbor, so devoted to the cause of freedom, and so generous to the weak!

But this combination of the Slidell mission with the Larkin dispatch, a combination whose genuine character has not hitherto been properly understood by the historians of the Mexican War, was not more characteristic of our nation than was the combination by which the pious plan was defeated. One active and not over-cautious young agent [Frémont] who had good reason to know the importance of the crisis and who was not altogether unwilling to turn it to account for various private ends was in California just then and received certain advices in a confidential "family cipher"; and these advices somehow, whether wholly by his own fault or also by the fault of his father-in-law, led him to thwart the carefully prepared plans of the government. In acting as he did, he not only became for the moment a filibuster, pure and simple, but endangered our whole scheme by, perhaps unwittingly, doing his best to drive California directly into the arms of England. Either because England really was not anxious for California just then, or because her agents in the Pacific were not sufficiently on the alert, this result was averted, yet not in consequence of the gallant captain's undertaking, but only through Sloat's arrival with the news of those hostilities on the Rio Grande which superseded all previous plots and pretenses, and which, "by the act of Mexico," as our veracious President declared, forced us, unwilling, conscientious, and humane as we were, into an unequal contest with a physically puny foe.

Meanwhile, the gallant captain's undertaking, although a plain violation of his orders, was itself not un-American in its forms and methods, at least in so far as they were reported to the public. He felt himself, after all, to be a peaceful and scientific gentleman, who shunned war and loved the study of nature. He was a type of our energy and of our mild civilization, in the presence of crafty and wily Spaniards, who, as he somehow persuaded either himself or his followers, had incited the Indians of the unknown Klamath wilderness against him, had threatened the ripening wheat-fields of his countrymen, and at last had begun marching against his own party with an armed force. This armed force marching against him was indeed not at the moment to be seen in the whole territory by any human eye; but its asserted existence nevertheless thenceforth justified him in the clearer eyes of heaven and his absent fellow countrymen. So at least he himself and the venerable Senator would seem in all sincerity to have felt; and the public, by the nomination of the young hero to the presidency in 1856, and by the large vote then polled in his favor, set their seal of approval also upon the verdict of his conscience. And both he himself and the public, as we have seen, ever afterwards considered his methods of procedure to have been as noble and unaggressive as they were fearless and decisive; while all concerned thought our national energy and kindliness finely represented by the acts of this party of armed surveyors and trappers, who disturbed the peace of a quiet land and practiced violence against inoffensive and helpless rancheros.

But when hostilities had once begun, the men who were not in the state secrets were as American and as moral as those who were initiated. To them the whole thing appeared partly as a glorious revolution, a destined joy for the eyes of history-reading posterity, a high and holy business; and partly as a missionary enterprise, destined to teach our beloved and erring Spanish American brethren the blessings of true liberty. The Bear Flag heroes interpreted the affair, in their way also, to a large and representative American public; and these heroes, like their betters, show us what it is to have a national conscience sensitive enough to call loudly for elaborate and eloquent comfort in moments of doubt, and just stupid enough to be readily deluded by mock-eloquent cant. The result of the whole thing is that although, in later years, the nation at large has indeed come to regard the Mexican War with something of the shame and contempt that *The Biglow Papers** and other expressions of enlightened contemporary opinion heaped upon the unworthy business, still, in writing California history, few have even yet chosen to treat the acts of the conquest with the deserved plainness of speech, while, in those days, the public both in the South and in the whole of the West, together with a considerable portion of the public elsewhere, was hoodwinked by such

---

* Two series of satirical verses in Yankee dialect by James Russell Lowell (1819–1891), the first attacking the Mexican War and the second in support of the North in the Civil War.

methods as were used, and so actually supposed our acquisition of the new territory to be a God-fearing act, the result of the aggression and of the sinful impotence of our Spanish neighbors, together with our own justifiable energy and our devotion to the cause of freedom. It is to be hoped that this lesson, showing us as it does how much of conscience and even of personal sincerity can coexist with a minimum of effective morality in international undertakings, will some day be once more remembered; so that when our nation is another time about to serve the devil, it will do so with more frankness and will deceive itself less by half-unconscious cant. For the rest, our mission in the cause of liberty is to be accomplished through a steadfast devotion to the cultivation of our own inner life, and not by going abroad as missionaries, as conquerors, or as marauders, among weaker peoples.

ADDITIONAL READINGS

The most thorough and in many respects the best history of the Mexican War is still Justin H. Smith's *The War with Mexico* (2 vols., New York, 1919). *Rehearsal for Conflict,* by A. Hoyt Bill (New York, 1947), is a readable single volume on the war, as is Otis Singletary's *The Mexican War* (Chicago, 1960). Relations between the United States and Mexico before war began are thoroughly covered by George L. Rives in *The United States and Mexico, 1821–1848* (2 vols., New York, 1913). A useful biography of Polk is Eugene I. McCormac's *James K. Polk: A Political Biography* (Berkeley, 1922); however, it may well be superseded by a biography in progress by Charles G. Sellers, Jr., whose first volume, *James K. Polk, Jacksonian, 1795–1843* (Princeton, 1957), is impressive. Bernard De Voto ingeniously develops expansionist themes in *The Year of Decision: 1846* (Boston, 1943). For the acquisition of California, see John A. Hawgood, "The Pattern of Yankee Infiltration in Mexican Alta California, 1821–1846," *Pacific Historical Review* (February 1958). An intriguing modification of the Manifest Destiny theme is in Norman Graebner's *Empire on the Pacific* (New York, 1955).

8

THE MORMONS

The settlement of the valleys of Oregon and the savannahs of Texas was the result of the imagination and ambition of a few men, coupled with the desire of many men for cheap, fertile land. Two decades later, the peopling of the caked flats and arid stretches of the Great Salt Lake Valley presented a decided variation on that theme. A vigorous voice there was— perhaps the strongest leader ever to walk the West in the nineteenth century; but the reasons this particular population trekked west were less economic than religious. Out of their new belief, transplanted in the 1840s to a hostile physical environment, grew a highly dramatic and successful cooperative experiment.

The Church of Jesus Christ of Latter-Day Saints, better known as the Mormons, began when in 1820 a young farmer by the name of Joseph Smith stood atop Mt. Cumorah near Palmyra in up-state New York and talked with angels. Moroni, the son of the angel Mormon, directed Smith to a cache of golden plates inscribed with mysterious figures and gave him two stones that would help him miraculously to translate the cryptic message into English. When Joseph Smith finished the long task of transcription, the plates were recalled to Heaven, but the manuscript was left on earth as the *Book of Mormon* (1830).

No man should properly laugh at another's faith, but from the beginning the Mormon cosmology was subject to ridicule and its believers to persecution. Admittedly, it was an unusual set of doctrines—an explanation of the North American Indians as descendants of the Lost Tribes of Israel, peculiar temple rites, an uncommon version of Heaven and its inhabitants, and the later revelation sanctioning polygamy. But these doctrines did not make the Mormons particularly remarkable. Persecution came rather because the believers formed a cohesive group whose religious solidarity became so genuine that it transformed their economic and political lives. As economic cooperators and as a political bloc, the Mormons could not be tolerated by the individualistic Americans among whom they first tried to live.

After 1830, when the church was constituted, Smith received revelations that took the growing band of converts on a series of moves. They left New York and settled first at Kirtland, Ohio. Here the strongly cooperative Mormon economy prospered until the Depression of 1837 caused an hegira to the town of Far West, Missouri. They had already come to feel persecution, and even in this frontier town, anti-Mormon mobs forced them out within a year. This time they protected themselves by establishing their own community at Nauvoo, Illinois, wringing from the state the right to pass certain of their own laws, establish their own courts, and maintain a militia.

Within four years, by 1844, the Mormon population of Nauvoo was nearly 15,000. Smith assumed more and more power and in 1844 announced himself a candidate for the presidency of the United States. The Mormons voted as a man, and they were becoming powerful. Their economic prosperity was undeniable and certainly caused envy. Anti-Mormon feeling outside the community began to rumble. Joseph Smith's 1843 revelation sanctioning polygamy did not help. Dissent arose within the community to augment the hatred from without. Mass meetings were held; mobs began to roam; and Smith and his brother were lodged, mostly for protection, in the jail of Carthage, a non-Mormon village nearby. But on June 27, 1844, the mobs found them, murdering the two; and Joseph Smith, the Prophet, became a Mormon martyr.

At this black moment, although the succession was disputed, Brigham Young in a masterful display of bluff and brilliance assumed leadership of the Saints. It was clear that they could no longer stay where they were, even clear that the United States and particularly its frontier areas would not tolerate their differences. So Brigham Young presided over the exodus of the Saints to another promised land, this time beyond the borders of the United States, far to the west.

The trek, which began early in 1846, took place by groups and in many stages. The vanguard arrived at the Great Salt Lake in the summer of 1847. Young had planned the locale in conversations with mountain men and had identified the final spot as he looked out from the Wasatch passes: "This is the place!" By the fall there were 4,000 Mormons in the wilderness valley.

They suffered, they worked, and they prayed together. The next year

4,500 more arrived. By 1856, there were 22,000 Saints living in the Great Basin. The Kingdom had been established.

The Mormons lived a highly communal life. That their communities bore a resemblance to the New England Puritan commonwealths, in which every man was his brother's keeper, has been frequently pointed out. The communal feeling grew out of Mormon religion—much of it directly from Smith's revelations. In the selections that follow, a good deal of attention is given to the early Mormon law and the ways in which Brigham Young understood and applied it. Chief among these communal teachings were the doctrines of stewardship and consecration—that a man's possessions belonged not to himself but to God, that God had entrusted men as only stewards of worldly goods, that unneeded surpluses should be freely given to the church.

In the West the Mormons had abundant opportunities to test such teachings and to work together. Year after year thousands of converts from the East and from Europe continued to cross the Plains. Most of them were poor, their chief asset a boundless hope for the new Zion. The Utah community, as a steward of God, did everything in its power to aid them; and they themselves banded together and even, during the years between 1856 and 1861, resorted to pulling and pushing their belongings across the Plains and Rockies in handcarts.

But no part of the Mormon story in Utah so well illustrates the cooperative strain as their regulations governing the use of water. Brigham Young was aware from the beginning that conditions in the arid valley would dictate careful planning. No new community was established, therefore, without the approval of committees to determine the flow of the streams. Together the new settlers dug the ditches, and together they planned the distribution of their water.

The Mormons were never complete socialists, i.e., allowing the state to own all means of production. As Howard Stansbury, a government topographer who visited Utah in 1849, said: they were orderly and industrious, "having the rights of personal property as perfectly defined and as religiously respected as with ourselves; nothing being farther from their faith or practice than the spirit of *communism*, which has been most erroneously supposed to prevail among them." But short of their contemporary communistic utopian colonies in the East, such as the Fourieristic experiments, the Saints in Utah achieved what may well be the most cooperative society yet known in the United States.

Leonard Arrington

In a thorough, recent study of Mormonism, Professor Leonard Arring-ton of Utah State University summarizes the early Mormon economic ideals. The seven basic doctrines enumerated by Arrington reveal both the ideas that the Mormons brought to the West and the way in which the ideas were "adapted to the conditions required for colonizing the Great Basin."

*Seven Basic Mormon Principles**

Out of the experiences of Jackson County, Kirtland, Far West, Nau-voo, and the exodus emerged the common economic ideals of the Mormons. These beliefs and practices—a unique coalescence of Jacksonian communi-tarianism—are of special importance because they were the foundation stones upon which the Kingdom was built in the Great Basin, and because they became the basis for conflict with businessmen and politicians whose views would become more and more hostile to such communitarian princi-ples and institutions. Above all, the ideals which came out of the laboratory of early experience were incorporated into Mormon dogma as a permanent aspect of religious belief. That is, they were established and supported by revelations which were believed to be proclamations of the Deity, and their constant reiteration in sermons and their frequent publication in church books and periodicals established them officially as an inherent part of Mor-mon theology and church government. The problems faced by the early Mormons dictated certain expedients; these expedients were an integral part of the early revelations; and the content of the revelations came to be accepted, officially and otherwise, as Mormon belief and practice.

These ideals—that is, the content of these revelations—can be sum-marized in terms of the following seven basic principles.

1. *The Gathering.* The earliest principle, as developed in New York, Kirtland, and Jackson County, counseled the "pure in heart" to "gather" out of "Babylon" (the sinful world) to a place called "Zion," where "God's people" would build the Kingdom, dwell together in righteousness, and pre-

---

*From Leonard J. Arrington, *Great Basin Kindom: An Economic History of the Latter-day Saints, 1830–1900* (Cambridge, Mass.: Harvard University Press, 1958), pp. 22–28. Copyright, 1958, by The President and Fellows of Harvard College. Reprinted by permission of the publishers.

pare for the Millennium. "Ye are called to bring to pass the gathering of mine elect," ran the revelation; "the decree hath gone forth from the Father that they shall be gathered in unto one place, upon the face of this land." Eventually, the concept of gathering was included in the Articles of Faith of the church: "We believe in the literal gathering of Israel ... [to] this (the American) continent." The promulgation of this doctrine led to the development in the 1830's of a large and highly effective missionary system, an overseas emigration service, and the establishment of a series of "Zions" or gathering places.

2. *The Mormon Village.* Once gathered, the Latter-day Saints were to be settled, as suggested in the Plat of the City of Zion, in a network of villages consisting of a cluster of homes on lots laid out "four square with the world," and with wide streets intersecting at right angles. The uniform home lots were to be large enough to permit the production of fruits and vegetables, poultry, and livestock. Farmers were to live in the town and drive out to their fields every day for work. The village would not necessarily be an agricultural village—usually it would include mining and manufacturing enterprises as well—but it would be a self-sufficient village.

The Mormon village concept, which in some respects resembled the New England village, was used as a guide in the settlement of Far West, Nauvoo, Salt Lake City, and almost every other Mormon community in the West; indeed, it proved peculiarly adapted to the conditions required for colonizing the Great Basin. It provided security against Indians; facilitated cooperative efficiency by placing the members of the community in ready touch with directing officers of the group; made possible the maintenance of religious, educational, and other social institutions; permitted effective irrigation culture; and assured, in general, a highly organized community life. By separating the residence area from the arable lands, it also made possible a more advantageous utilization of the lands, especially common pasturing of the fields after harvest.

3. *Property as a Stewardship.* The property rights and holdings of Mormon villagers were to be allocated and regulated by the church in accordance with the principle of "stewardship." "The earth is the Lord's," and man must consider his rights to land as derived and subject to church disposition. This principle assured primacy of group interest over individual interest, and every man was to consider his property as consecrated to the Lord for the building of the Kingdom.

The "true principle," as Brigham Young summarized it later, was "to hold emphatically everything we possessed upon the altar for the use and benefit of the Kingdom of God, and men shall be as stewards over that which they possess, not that everything shall be common or that all men shall be made equal in all things, for to one is given one talent, to another two, and to another five, according to their capacity."

4. *Redeeming the Earth.*   After the settlement of villages and the determination of property rights, the Saints were to proceed with the orderly development of local resources. This was a sacred assignment and was to be regarded as a religious as well as a secular function. One of the Articles of Faith of the church read: "We believe . . . that the earth will be renewed and receive its paradisiacal glory." As explained by a leading apostle in an authoritative work, Latter-day Saints believed that the earth was under a curse and that it was to be regenerated and purified, after which war and social conflict generally would be eliminated and the earth would "yield bounteously to the husbandman." The City of God would then be realized at last.

This purification was not to be accomplished by any mechanistic process nor by any instantaneous cleansing by fire and/or water. It was to be performed by God's chosen; it involved subduing the earth and making it teem with living plants and animals. Man must assist God in this process of regeneration and make the earth a more fitting abode for himself and for the Redeemer of Man. The earth must be turned into a Garden of Eden where God's people would never again know want and suffering. The Kingdom of God, in other words, was to be realized by a thoroughly pragmatic mastery of the forces of nature. An important early admonition to be industrious, and not idle, was supplementary to this belief.

Making the waste places blossom as the rose, and the earth to yield abundantly of its diverse fruits, was more than an economic necessity; it was a form of religious worship. As one early leader later wrote, the construction of water ditches was as much a part of the Mormon religion as water baptism. The redemption of man's home (the earth) was considered to be as important as the redemption of his soul. The earth, as the future abiding place of God's people, had to be made productive and fruitful. This would be accomplished "by the blessing and power of God, and . . . by the labors and sacrifices of its inhabitants, under the light of the Gospel and the direction of the authorized servants of God."

When the Mormons reached the Great Basin this concept stimulated tremendous exertion. "The Lord has done his share of the work," Brigham Young told them; "he has surrounded us with the elements containing wheat, meat, flax, wool, silk, fruit, and everything with which to build up, beautify and glorify the Zion of the last days." "It is [now] our business," he concluded, "to mould these elements to our wants and necessities, according to the knowledge we now have and the wisdom we can obtain from the Heavens through our faithfulness. In this way will the Lord bring again Zion upon the earth, and in no other."

The acceptance of the principle of resource development explains the passionate and devoted efforts of the Mormon people to develop the resources of the Great Basin to the full extent of their potentiality. While it

was a sacred duty of Latter-day Saints to purify their hearts, it was an
equally sacred duty for them to devote labor and talent to the task of "removing the curse from the earth," and making it yield an abundance of
things needed by man. Devices for converting arid wastes into green fields
thus assumed an almost sacramental character; they served to promote an
important spiritual end.

5. *Frugality and Economic Independence.*   The goal of colonization,
of the settled village, and of resource development was complete regional
economic independence. The Latter-day Saint commonwealth was to be financially and economically self-sufficient. A "law" of the church established
this principle in 1830: "Let all thy garments be plain, and their beauty the
beauty of the work of thine own hands, . . . contract no debts with the
world." . . . By the time the Great Basin was reached the revelation was
given wide application. The Mormon people were asked to manufacture
their own iron, produce their own cotton, spin their own silk, and grind
their own grain. And they must do this without borrowing from "outsiders."
Self-sufficiency was a practical policy, they believed, because God had
blessed each region with all of the resources which were necessary for the
use of the people and the development of the region.

6. *Unity and Cooperation.*   The one quality required to successfully
execute the economic program of the church, as often learned by its absence, was unity. Unity, as first enjoined in a revelation given in January
1831, was a high Christian virtue: "I say unto you, be one; and if ye are
not one, ye are not mine." The symbols of unity were a strong central organization and self-forgetting group solidarity: The participants in the
sublime task of building the Kingdom were to submit themselves to the
direction of God's leaders and to display a spirit of willing cooperation. Cooperation, as a technique of organization by which migrations were effected,
forts erected, ditches dug, and mills constructed, came to be an integral part
of this principle. Cooperation meant that everyman's labor was subject to
call by church authority to work under supervised direction in a cause
deemed essential to the prosperity of the Kingdom.

While unity and cooperation characterized the early church, it remained for Brigham Young to develop the technique of unified action and
combined endeavor to its fullest extent. It was his aim that the church come
to represent one great patriarchal family:

"I will give you a text: Except I am one with my good brethren, do
not say that I am a Latter-day Saint. We must be one. Our faith must be
concentrated in one great work—the building up of the kingdom of God on
the earth, and our works must aim to the accomplishment of that great
purpose.

"I have looked upon the community of Latter-day Saints in vision and
beheld them organized as one great family of heaven, each person perform-

ing his several duties in his line of industry, working for the good of the whole more than for individual aggrandizement; and in this I have beheld the most beautiful order that the mind of man can contemplate, and the grandest results for the upbuilding of the kingdom of God and the spread of righteousness upon the earth. . . . Why can we not so live in this world?"

His deeds matched his words. He instituted countless programs to achieve unity and facilitate cooperation. These included cooperative arrangements for migration, colonization, construction, agriculture, mining, manufacturing, merchandising—and, in fact, for every realm of economic activity.

The Mormon passion for unity and solidarity, strengthened and tempered as it was by years of suffering and persecution, at once provided both the means and the motive for regional economic planning by church authorities in the Great Basin. The means was provided by the willingness of church members to submit to the "counsel" of their leaders and to respond to every call, spiritual and temporal. The motive was provided by the principle of oneness itself, which was regarded as of divine origin, and whose attainment required planning and control by those in authority.

7. *Equality.* One final aspect of the church's economic program was that which pertained to justice in distribution. It should be obvious that developmental principles, such as those previously discussed, were the major emphasis of Mormon economic policy. In "working out the temporal salvation of Zion," to use a contemporary expression, the formulators of church policy centered primary attention on production and the better management of the human and natural resources under their jurisdiction. Nevertheless, early Mormonism, influenced by its own necessities and the democratic concepts of the Age of Jackson, was distinctly equalitarian in theology and economics, and this had significant influences on church policies and practices in the Great Basin.

The Latter-day Saint doctrine on equality was pronounced within a few months after the founding of the church: "If ye are not equal in earthly things, ye cannot be equal in obtaining heavenly things." There was an earnest and immediate attempt to comply with the spirit of this revelation. In May 1831, when the New York converts to the infant church began to arrive at the newly established gathering place of Kirtland, Ohio, the Lord is reported to have inspired Joseph Smith to instruct that land and other properties be allotted "equal according to their families, according to their circumstances, and their wants and needs." The revelation went on further to say: "And let every man . . . be alike among this people, and receive alike, that ye may be one." In a subsequent revelation to the Saints in Ohio the Prophet instructed: "In your temporal things you shall be equal, and this not grudgingly, otherwise the abundance of the manifestations of the Spirit shall be withheld." When the stewardship system was tried in Jackson County, Missouri, similar instructions were given: "And you are to be equal, or in other words, you are to have equal claims on the properties, for the benefit of managing ... your stewardships, every man according to his wants and needs, inasmuch as his wants are just."

Brigham Roberts

Brigham Roberts, the official historian of the Mormon Church, distinguishes between the early doctrines of stewardship and consecration and the principle of community of goods. His history also suggests the way in which the first contacts with the Salt Lake Valley reinforced the earlier revelations.

The Doctrine of Stewardship*

"*Stewardships:* Every man is made accountable unto the Lord a 'steward over his own property, or that which he has received by consecration, as much as is sufficient for himself and family.' But no community of goods is contemplated: 'Thou shalt not take thy brother's garment: thou shalt pay for that which thou shalt receive of thy brother.' If more is obtained in the management of the stewardship than is necessary for his support, the surplus is to be given into the Lord's store house."

Such was the law given to the church in Ohio. Of its excellence as constituting or recognizing both personal and community moral obligations, comment is unnecessary. The statement of it is its own vindication. One thing should be remarked, however, in respect of the law of consecration mentioned above. It was this law which doubtless led many to suppose that the Latter-day Saints sought to establish community of goods, and malice at different times has charged also community of wives. But community of goods is not involved in the principles of consecration and stewardship as above set forth, or subsequently developed either in doctrine or practice.

---

* From Brigham H. Roberts, *Comprehensive History of the Church of Jesus Christ of Latter-day Saints* (6 vols., Salt Lake City: Church of Jesus Christ of Latter-day Saints, 1930), I, 246–247. Reprinted by permission of the publisher.

The principle underlying this doctrine of the church is recognition of the Lord as Creator, Proprietor and Owner of the earth and the fulness thereof, and man as but a steward in his possessions. The earth is the Lord's by proprietary right. His because he created it, and sustains it from age to age by his power, and makes it fruitful by his bounty. By the act of consecration, according to the above law, and as afterwards developed, a man visibly and actually recognized God as proprietor of the earth; and by receiving back from such consecration a stewardship from God's visible agency, the church, he acknowledged himself but a steward over that which he possesses, but he is accountable to God only for his management of that stewardship. If from that management there arose beyond what was needful for his personal use and that of his family, that surplus could again be consecrated to the Lord's store house to be used in the granting of other stewardships or developing enterprises involving community interests. In other words the surplus product of the community's industry was to be made available for community interests.

The Founding of Salt Lake City*

The day following the arrival of President Brigham Young in Salt Lake valley was the Lord's Day—the Christian Sabbath [1847]. Accordingly religious services were held both in the forenoon and in the afternoon; and a number of the apostles addressed the assembled Pioneers. The sacrament of the Lord's Supper was administered, the emblems used being broken bread and water.

The burden of the discourses seems to have been expressions of gratitude that the Lord had led them to so goodly a land. Not a single death had occurred, and only a very few of their cattle or horses had been lost. "The brethren were exhorted," says Wilford Woodruff, "to hearken to counsel, do away with selfishness, live humbly, and keep the commandments of God, that they might prosper in the land.... There was a universal feeling of satisfaction with the valley from the men that spoke upon the subject; said they were joyfully disappointed, that the whole appearance was altogether better throughout the valley than they had anticipated, or even dreamed of. At the close of the meeting President Young, though feeble, addressed the assembly for a few moments, and informed the brethren that they must not work on Sunday, nor hunt, nor fish on that day; and there should be no person dwell among us who would not observe these rules: they might go

---

* Roberts, *Comprehensive History*, III, 268–270.

and dwell where they pleased but they should not dwell with us. In a word, the law proclaimed in the Salt Lake valley that day, was the law of God; and men were admonished to keep that law. The ten commandments and the Christian ethics were practically proclaimed to be in force in the new home of the saints. It was upon this occasion also that Brigham Young proclaimed the "land law" of the community, namely, that—

"No man should buy or sell land. Every man should have his land measured off to him for city and farming purposes, what he could till. He might till it as he pleased, but he should be industrious and take care of it."

The principle of this first "land law" of Utah will be recognized as identical with that which actuated the great leader at Garden Grove, when he said there, in effect, that no man should hold more land than he could cultivate; "and that if a man would not till his land, it should be taken from him."

Subsequently it was announced there would be no private ownership in the water streams; that wood and timber would be regarded as community property. It was also determined that only "dead timber" should be used as fuel, thus hoping to foster the growth of timber as its scarcity was the most serious obstacle then in view to the settlement of the valley. On these three laws or regulations, the prevention of monopoly in land, community ownership of the water, and of the timber, rested the prosperity of the early colonies in Utah. It was a necessary act of justice under the circumstances, this "land law," and the other regulations mentioned. There was a community of nearly 20,000 Latter-day Saints on the banks of the Missouri river and en route across the plains; they were engaged in a common purpose: they were united as exiles by the same decree of eviction from their homes—from their country. To permit the Pioneers, or the advanced companies of such a community to seize upon and monopolize the resources of the valleys to which they were migrating, would be a manifest injustice, hence these mandates issued from their wisest men take on the nature of statesmanlike measures, wholly justifiable and absolutely necessary to safeguard the interest of all.

Brigham Young

In the first of the excerpts below—a discourse delivered in the Tabernacle at Salt Lake City in 1855—Brigham Young (1801–1877) recalls the ways in which the first revelations on stewardship and surplus property occasionally faltered in the face of human foibles. The other excerpts, dealing with stewardship and consecration, are selected from Young's writings over a long period of time.

Discourse on Surplus Property*

When the revelation which I have read was given in 1838, I was present, and recollect the feelings of the brethren. A number of revelations were given on the same day. The brethren wished me to go among the Churches, and find out what surplus property the people had, with which to forward the building of the Temple we were commencing at Far West. I accordingly went from place to place through the country. Before I started, I asked brother Joseph, "Who shall be the judge of what is surplus property?" Said he, "Let them be the judges themselves, for I care not if they do not give a single dime. So far as I am concerned, I do not want anything they have."

Then I replied, "I will go and ask them for their surplus property"; and I did so; I found the people said they were willing to do about as they were counselled, but, upon asking them about their surplus property, most of the men who owned land and cattle would say, "I have got so many hundred acres of land, and I have got so many boys, and I want each one of them to have eighty acres, therefore this is not surplus property." Again, "I have got so many girls, and I do not believe I shall be able to give them more than forty acres each." "Well, you have got two or three hundred acres left." "Yes, but I have a brother-in-law coming on, and he will depend on me for a living; my wife's nephew is also coming on, he is poor, and I shall have to furnish him a farm after he arrives here." I would go on to the

---

* From Brigham Young and others, *Journal of Discourses* (1855), reported by G. D. Watt (photolithographed, Los Angeles: Church of Jesus Christ of Latter-day Saints, 1956), II, 306–307. Reprinted by permission of the publisher. Young is here referring to his experiences in the community of Far West in 1838.

next one, and he would have more land and cattle than he could make use of to advantage. It is a laughable idea, but is nevertheless true, men would tell me they were young and beginning the world, and would say, "We have no children, but our prospects are good, and we think we shall have a family of children, and if we do, we want to give them eighty acres of land each; we have no surplus property." "How many cattle have you?" "So many." "How many horses, &c?" "So many, but I have made provisions for all these, and I have use for every thing I have got."

Some were disposed to do right with their surplus property, and once in a while you would find a man who had a cow which he considered surplus, but generally she was of the class that would kick a person's hat off, or eyes out, or the wolves had eaten off her teats. You would once in a while find a man who had a horse that he considered surplus, but at the same time he had the ringbone, was broken-winded, spavined in both legs, had the pole evil at one end of the neck and a fistula at the other, and both knees sprung.

This is the description of surplus property that some would offer to the Lord. Such have been the feelings of a great many men. They would come to me and say, "Brother Brigham, I want to pay my tithing; please come outside here, I wish to show you a horse I have got. I want to raise fifty dollars on this horse, and the balance I am willing to turn in on tithing. If you will pay me twenty dollars in money, ten in store pay, and so much on another man's tithing, and so much on my own, you shall have the horse for eighty dollars"; when I could get as good a one for forty. I make no such trades. Some of our brethren would actually take a horse worth no more than forty dollars, pay fifty, and give credit on tithing for thirty.

I mention these things to illustrate the feelings of many of the people, for they do not understand the spirit they are of. When a man wishes to give anything, let him give the best he has got. The Lord has given to me all I possess: I have nothing in reality, not a single dime of it is mine.

Discourses on Stewardship and Consecration*

There is another revelation . . . stating that it is the duty of all people who go to Zion to consecrate all their property to the Church of Jesus

* From John A. Widtsoe, ed., *Discourses of Brigham Young* (Salt Lake City: Church of Jesus Christ of Latter-day Saints, 1954), pp. 179–182. Reprinted by permission of the publisher.

Christ of Latter-day Saints. This revelation was referred to at the April Conference in 1854. It was one of the first commandments or revelations given to this people after they had the privilege of organizing themselves as a Church, as a body, as the Kingdom of God on the earth. I observed then, and I now think, that it will be one of the last revelations which the people will receive into their hearts and understanding, of their own free will and choice, and esteem it as a pleasure, a privilege, and a blessing unto them to observe and keep most holy.

I have said, and say today, that according to the age of the people we have improved as fast as the church of Enoch. I trust we improve faster, for we have not as much time as they had. In some of the first revelations which were given to this Church, the Order of Enoch was given for a pattern to this people; and Enoch patterned after the heavens. In the commencement of the Church, the Latter-day Saints could not receive it, and they were driven from city to city, as the Lord said they should be, through the mouth of his servant Joseph, until they should be willing to receive this Order.

Will the time ever come that we can commence and organize this people as a family? It will. Do we know how? Yes; what was lacking in these revelations from Joseph to enable us to do so was revealed to me. Do you think we will ever be one? When we get home to our Father and God, will we not wish to be in the family? Will it not be our highest ambition and desire to be reckoned as the sons of the living God, as the daughters of the Almighty, with a right to the household, and the faith that belongs to the household, heirs of the Father, his goods, his wealth, his power, his excellency, his knowledge and wisdom?

I will say, first, that the Lord Almighty has not the least objection in the world to our entering into the Order of Enoch. I will stand between the people and all harm in this. He has not the least objection to any man, every man, all mankind on the face of the earth turning from evil and loving and serving him with all their hearts. With regard to all those orders that the Lord has revealed, it depends upon the will and doings of the people, and we are at liberty, from this Conference, to go and build up a settlement, or we can join ourselves together in this city, do it legally—according to the laws of the land—and enter into covenant with each other by a firm agreement that we will live as a family, that we will put our property into the hands of a committee of trustees, who shall dictate the affairs of this society.

And when this people become one, it will be one in the Lord. They will not look alike. We will not all have grey, blue, or black eyes. Our features will differ one from another, and in our acts, dispositions, and efforts to accumulate, distribute, and dispose of our time, talents, wealth, and whatever the Lord gives to us, in our journey through life, we will differ just as much as in our features. The point that the Lord wishes to bring us to is to obey his counsel and observe his word. Then every one will be dictated so that we can act as a family. . . .

I have looked upon the community of Latter-day Saints in vision and beheld them organized as one great family of heaven, each person performing his several duties in his line of industry, working for the good of the whole more than for individual aggrandizement; and in this I have beheld the most beautiful order that the mind of man can contemplate, and the grandest results for the upbuilding of the Kingdom of God and the spread of righteousness upon the earth. Will this people ever come to this order of things? Are they now prepared to live according to that patriarchal order that will be organized among the true and faithful before God receives his own? We all concede the point that when this mortality falls off, and with it its cares, anxieties, love of self, love of wealth, and love of power, and all the conflicting interests which pertain to this flesh, that then, when our spirits have returned to God who gave them, we will be subject to every requirement that he may make of us, that we shall then live together as one great family; our interest will be a general, a common interest. Why can we not so live in this world?

Two Mormon Settlers

The feeling of devotion and sacrifice, often at the base of the most co-operative Mormon experiences, was nowhere more dramatically revealed than in the handcart brigades of 1856. In that year and for several years thereafter, Mormons who had been gathered from the East and England made the last lap of their journey from the Missouri settlements to Salt Lake by constructing two-wheeled carts and, in the words of Ann Hafen, "propelled by blood of the human heart," pushed and pulled their way to Zion. The following are first-hand accounts of the 1856 migration: the first is by Daniel McArthur, captain of one of the companies; the second is by Elder Millen Atwood.

The 1856 Handcart Migration*

[Daniel McArthur's account]

On the 24th of July [1856], at 12 o'clock, we struck our tents and started for the plains, all in the best of spirits. Nothing but the very best of luck attended us continually. Our train consisted of 12 yoke of oxen, 4 wagons, and 48 carts; we also had 5 beef and 12 cows; flour, 55 lbs, per head, 100 lbs. rice, 550 lbs. sugar, 400 lbs. dried apples, 125 lbs. tea, and 200 lbs. salt for the company. On the 28th of August, we arrived at Laramie, and on the 2nd of September we met the first provision wagons from the Valley. On Deer Creek we got 1000 lbs. of flour, which caused the hearts of the saints to be cheered up greatly. On the 14th we camped at Pacific Spring Creek, and there I took in 1000 lbs. of more flour, so as to be sure to have enough to do me until we got into the Valley, for I was told that that would be the last opportunity to get it. On the 20th we reached Fort Bridger, and on the 26th of September, we arrived in this Valley, with only the loss of 8 souls. 7 died, and one, a young man, age 20 years, we never could tell what did become of him. We brought in our 48 carts, 4 wagons, 12 yokes of oxen, save one, which we had left at Fort Bridger, 10 cows, (one cow died and one we left at Fort Bridger,) and the 5 beeves, we ate, of course. We laid still 5 Sundays and three week days all day, besides other short stops while traveling from the Missouri River here.

My company was divided into two divisions and Brother Truman Leonard was appointed captain over the first division and Brother Spencer Crandall over the second. We had six tents in each division and a president over each tent, who were strict in seeing that singing and prayer was attended to every morning and night, and that peace prevailed. I must say that a better set of saints to labor with I never saw. They all did the best they could to forward our journey. When we came to a stream, no matter how large it might be, the men would roll up their trousers and into it they would go, and the sisters would follow, if the men were smart enough to get ahead of them, which the men failed many times to do. If the water was high enough to wet the things on the carts, the men would get one before the cart and one behind it and lift it up slick and clean, and carry it across the stream.

---

* From *Journal History,* September 26, 1856, and *Deseret News,* November 16, 1856; reprinted by permission of the Secretary to the First Presidency, Church of Jesus Christ of Latter-day Saints. A complete printing of these documents can be found in LeRoy R. and Ann W. Hafen, *Handcarts to Zion* (Glendale, Calif.: Arthur Clark Co., 1960), pp. 214–255.

I will state a couple of incidents that happened in one day, and one other circumstance that took place. On the 11th of August a man came to camp pretending to be starved nearly to death, and wished me to give him some provisions, for he had had nothing for many days but what he had hunted for. So I gave him bread and meat enough to last him some four or five days and he acted as though he had met with some friends indeed. He said, that he had been robbed by some Californians somewhere near Fort Bridger, with whom he was in company on their way to the States, and on the 16th, while crossing over some sand hills, Sister Mary Bathgate was badly bitten by a large rattlesnake, just above the ankle, on the back part of her leg. She was about a half a mile ahead of the camp at the time it happened, as she was the ring leader of the footmen or those who did not pull the handcarts. She was generally accompanied by Sister Isabella Park. They were both old women, over 60 years of age, and neither of them had ridden one inch, since they had left Iowa camp ground. Sister Bathgate sent a little girl back to me as quickly as possible to have me and Brothers Leonard and Crandall come with all haste, and bring the oil with us, for she was bitten badly. As soon as we heard the news, we left all things, and, with the oil, we went post haste. When we got to her she was quite sick, but said that there was power in the Priesthood, and she knew it. So we took a pocket knife and cut the wound larger, squeezed out all the bad blood we could, and there was considerable, for she had forethought enough to tie her garter around her leg above the wound to stop the circulation of the blood. We then took and anointed her leg and head, and laid our hands on her in the name of Jesus and felt to rebuke the influence of the poison, and she felt full of faith. We then told her that she must get into the wagon, so she called witnesses to prove that she did not get into the wagon until she was compelled to by the cursed snake. We started on and traveled about two miles, when we stopped to take some refreshments. Sister Bathgate continued to be quite sick, but was full of faith, and after stopping one and a half hours we hitched up our teams. As the word was given for the teams to start, old Sister Isabella Park ran in before the wagon to see how her companion was. The driver, not seeing her, hallooed at his team and they being quick to mind, Sister Park could not get out of the way, and the fore wheel struck her and threw her down and passed over both her hips. Brother Leonard grabbed hold of her to pull her out of the way, before the hind wheel could catch her. He only got her out part way and the hind wheels passed over her ankles. We all thought that she would be all mashed to pieces, but to the joy of us all, there was not a bone broken, although the wagon had something like two tons burden on it, a load for 4 yoke of oxen. We went right to work and applied the same medicine to her that we did to the sister who was bitten by the rattlesnake, and although quite sore for a few days, Sister Park got better, so that she was on the tramp before we got into this Valley, and Sister Bathgate was right by her side, to cheer her up. Both were as smart as could be long before they got here, and this is what I call good luck, for I know that nothing but the power of God saved the two sisters and they traveled together, they rode together, and suffered together. Sister Bathgate has got married since she arrived in the Valley. While we were leading our handcart companies through the States and on the plains, we were called tyrants and slave drivers, and everything else that could be thought of, both by Gentiles and apostates.

[Elder Millen Atwood's account]

. . . I did not go to England for gold or silver, but to preach the gospel and gather the poor. We started home with a goodly number on board the ship Thornton, and they were of the class that br. Brigham wrote for when stating, "if they have not a sixpence in the world, they are the ones to bring here." The people that came from where I was laboring were perfectly destitute; we had to buy every thing for them, even to their tin cups and spoons. And let me tell you, the fare that they had on the plains was a feast to them.

They never regretted having to leave their homes, and they are not insensible of the liberality which has been extended to them by the people of these valleys. They have prayed and fasted day after day, and night after night, that they might have the privilege of uniting with their brethren and sisters in these mountains. Many bore testimony to the gentiles that the day would come, although their heads were silvered o'er with age, when they should see br. Brigham in the Valleys of the Mountains. They had borne that testimony so long that it had become like "sounding brass and a tinkling cymbal" to the wicked around them, who said that their way never would be opened. But the Lord opened the way in a manner they looked not for, and they were willing to draw a hand cart, or to take a bundle on their shoulders, or to come in any other way that might be counseled in order to enjoy the blessings you enjoy this day [i.e., the settlers already in Utah].

If you could hear the prayers, and see the tears for the privilege of enjoying what you do this day, you never would feel that you have done too much in assisting them.

I will here say, to those who have come from England and been in these valleys some time, that it seems to your friends that are still there as though you have forgotten them and the promises you made to them at the last shaking of the hand. But when br. Brigham offered his property so liberally, and the word came that they should gather from England, it ran like fire in dry stubble and the hearts of the poor saints leapt with joy and gladness; they could hardly contain themselves.

Will they be willing to pull a hand cart? Yes. I felt it; and I felt that it was the right way, and that it would gather more people than any other that had been adopted, and I have never, since I have been in this church, seen the Scriptures so forcibly fulfilled, as I have seen them this season.

With all their wagons and animals they have scarcely brought one blind or lame man to these mountains, but we have gathered up the lame, the blind and those who had not walked a step for years, and brought them on litters or hand carts to this place.

I never enjoyed myself better than in crossing the plains in a hand cart company. The Spirit of the Lord did accompany us, and the brethren and sisters enlivened the journey by singing the songs of Zion. They would travel 16, 18, 20, 23, or 24 miles a day and come into camp rejoicing, build their fires, get their suppers, rest, and rise fresh and envigorated in the morning.

I have seen some so tired in England, after traveling only 5 or 6 miles to a conference, that they would have to go to bed and be nursed for a week. We stimulated the hand cart companies with the words of br. Brigham, which went through me like lightning. He said, "If they would rise up in the name of the Lord, nothing doubting, no power should stop them in their progress to reach this place." It was in his words that they trusted to perform the journey, and they were determined to see his words fulfilled.

I have walked day by day by the side of the hand carts as they were rolling, and when the people would get weary I have seen them by dozens on their knees by the road side crying to the Lord for strength, and there are scores now in this city who walked from Iowa city to Fort Bridger, and some who were weak and feeble at the start grew stronger every day.

So long as you kept the bundle on the hand cart and stimulated them to lay hold of it, they were filled with the Holy Spirit and it seemed as though angels nerved them with strength; we could out-travel the cattle and might have camped 15 miles ahead of them every night if we had had the provisions with us. I told br. Brigham that I believed we could beat ox, horse, or mule teams.

The gentiles prophesied, as we came along, that we should never see the Valleys of the Mountains, and laughed us to scorn, and ridiculed the idea of men and women's traversing 1200 miles with hand carts, and they marveled to see the saints travel on so cheerfully. I said to them, I defy you and your rulers, with all your gold, to gather up a set of men, women, and children that will travel with hand carts; you have not the influence to do that, but when br. Brigham speaks the word, see how they go.

They were astonished, and wanted to know what kind of a doctrine we preached to them to make them willing to undertake such a task. I told them that we administered the same kind of medicine to all, and it united them together.

The Saints found, however, a wide difference between singing about going to Zion, and actually going. You would almost have thought that they would take wings and fly like doves to their windows, but when they really got into the work, the tune was a little different; but the great majority stuck to it, and those who were good for nothing left us at Florence.

We have not suffered a thousandth part as much as you think we have. Since I have arrived I have heard such tales of woe, though I do not know who could have told them to you. I know that br. Brigham and the honest in heart here have suffered more in their spirits than we have in our bodies. We did not suffer much; we had a little bit of snow, but that was nothing; and we had enough to eat as long as it lasted, and when that was gone you furnished us more; we fared first rate.

Some that met us would gaze on us, and tears would run down their cheeks, while we were smiling, laughing and singing, and wondered what they were crying for; but after they had been two or three days with us, they would tell us that they had altered their notions. I am in for hand carts, any way; and if I had a father or mother in old Babylon I would like to see them roll a hand cart across the plains. . . .

I was surprised when I saw the relief wagons loaded with garments, stockings, shoes, blankets and quilts that had been liberally contributed and sent out to minister to us. I never saw the like, and I marveled and wondered where it all came from. . . .

I am sorry that you have been put to so great expense in the mountains, in consequence of the lateness of this year's immigration; but had you sent loads of gold and silver they would not have been received with such gratefulness as were the clothing, etc. I never saw such a sight.

I am thankful to you for what you have done for us, and to br. Brigham; he has borne the heat and burden of the day, with his brethren. To think that he had done so much to get the companies part way, and then did so much more to get them in, I could hardly keep from weeping.

Charles H. Brough

Once the Mormons were in the Salt Lake Valley and faced with an unyielding, arid terrain, their cooperative ideals flowered magnificently in such practical matters as the development and control of irrigation water. The old Anglo-Saxon legal concept of riparian rights—that is, that the use of the water goes to him who owns the banks of the stream and no other—

did not conform to the Mormon ideas of justice as seen in the doctrine of stewardship. The early Spaniards in the arid Southwest, although they held dissimilar ideals, nevertheless had also abandoned the riparian-rights theory. Charles Brough's treatise on irrigation suggests the innovations of law and practice adopted by the Mormons as they faced new conditions in Utah.

Irrigation in Utah*

Early in the economic history of the Mormons the dominant church encouraged the practical application of the principle that the water right should be inseparable from the land. This is to-day the real key to their industrial system. To the pioneer, water was not only the basis of wealth, but of human existence; the irrigation canal was the first and highest of public utilities. Naturally the ownership and administration of these canals was the first problem to be solved in forming an irrigation system. Monopolies of water in the interest of speculative holders were not tolerated; it was resolved that canals should be so constructed that no interest would ever be paid on water stocks or bonds. A destitute people having no resources save the genius of their leader and the labor of their own hands, resolved to associate and organize their efforts to bring the water on as the people of Holland were compelled to cooperate to keep the water out.

Head-works and dams were constructed by co-operative labor organized and controlled by church authority. That labor should constitute the basis of stock in every canal was the governing principle of Utah colonization. No money was necessary and but little was in circulation. Each farmer became an owner of shares in the canals constructed, in proportion to the diligence of himself and his sons and the strength of his oxen or mules. The lumberman felled the trees of the native mountain forests and furnished materials for flumes, gates and bridges; while the skilled mason mixed the mortar and stones for walling the cuts and fills, and assisted in building aqueducts to carry water to his home and farm the remainder of his days. Inasmuch as a monopoly in water was dreaded by the pioneer, it was provided that all irrigation works should be constructed at public expense and transferred to the farmers dwelling in the particular districts watered. Canals thus constructed by the combined labor of the farmers required no high engineering skill. The virtue of this system of cooperation lay in the fact that it enabled the people to obtain water without

---

* From Charles H. Brough, *Irrigation in Utah* (Baltimore: Johns Hopkins University, 1898), pp. 12–17.

delay and without going into debt; the evil, the fact that it involved the building of many little ditches which will some day necessitate a complete reconstruction of canal systems. For when an undertaking was too great for an individual to complete, labor associations were formed to do the work under the co-operative system, and hundreds of small creeks from which water could cheaply be diverted were thereby constructed by the association for the benefit of the individual.

This method of associated industry which the pioneers learned from the necessity of co-operating in the building of canals and in tilling the soil, without which they could not have produced the first potato or the first ear of corn, was carried throughout their entire economic structure. In every settlement the principle of co-operation was exemplified in the organization of mercantile corporations and banks. This was probably due to the fact that the band of Mormons who settled Salt Lake Valley contained no rich men and represented no considerable capital collectively. . . .

The village community was made the unit in the formation of the Mormon land system. Forts, erected for protection against Indian depredation, were the nuclei around which the crude log cabins were built. When the Indians were finally driven away, and it became possible to erect dwelling houses, town plats were laid out and were drawn by lot. As early as the twenty-seventh of July, 1847, the Council, composed of the president and twelve apostles, decided to build the city. According to a systematic plan it was agreed by the Council that the sites of all the Saints' cities should be laid out in blocks or squares of ten acres, and in lots of an acre and a quarter; the streets to be eight rods wide, with sidewalks of twenty feet. . . .

During the year 1847 the influx of settlers assumed such large proportions that it was deemed necessary to lay out sites for farm villages. The principle adopted in this system of colonization was to enclose a half-mile square, to be selected in the midst of a tract of five or six thousand acres to be irrigated. This half-mile square was usually located near the centre of the valley and near the mountain stream, from which water was diverted into canals on each side at a sufficient elevation to command the irrigable lands. The half a square mile was laid out in blocks of four acres, each block being subdivided into lots of an acre each. On these lots the farmers were to have their homes, while their farms were located on the outlying lands, which were divided into lots ranging from two acres up to twenty acres. Under this system the advantages of town life were blended to a considerable degree with the charms of rural existence. Farm life under such conditions involved no isolation.

The fact that the original town sites were located on some living mountain stream, having a sufficient flow of water to supply the demands for irrigation in the fields, and for culinary purposes in the settlement, had an important effect on the customary law regulating the control and distribution of water. For before the system of priority of rights was introduced, the city and town authorities, by common consent, assumed the powers of controlling and distributing the water. When no regularly constituted council existed the entire community constituted a committee or directory, and employed a watermaster on an annual salary, or with the understanding that the distributor should be paid by levying an assessment on the ratio of acreage under cultivation. The duties of the watermaster consisted in equitably distributing the water among the users, deciding disputes as to the proportionate share of each user, and levying such taxes as were necessary to keep the canals and dams in repair. . . .

Leonard Arrington

In this following selection Professor Arrington succinctly analyzes the relation of Mormon ideas to other American currents. In the process, he reveals the difficulty of weighing the relative importance of the earlier ideals as brought to the frontier, and the effects of the West on those ideals.

Mormon Ideals and Economic Practices*

It should be obvious that in establishing their institutions and in meeting their first problems in the Great Basin the Mormons relied primarily on their own early ideals and experiences. The careful planning which preceded the development of their great city, the patriarchal husbanding of resources and sharing of burdens, the pooling of productive efforts, the nature of their property institutions—all these might have been predicted long before the Mormons reached the Great Basin. The pattern had been foreshadowed in Jackson County, Kirtland, Far West, and Winter Quarters, and it had been formally incorporated in Mormon theology. Moreover, in acknowledging, as the first colonists in the Salt Lake Valley acknowledged, the social responsibility of government (in this case a theocracy) to

* From Leonard J. Arrington, *Great Basin Kingdom: An Economic History of the Latter-day Saints, 1830–1900* (Cambridge, Mass.: Harvard University Press, 1958), pp. 62–63. Copyright, 1958, by The President and Fellows of Harvard College. Reprinted by permission of the publishers.

arrange and supervise their economic life, the Mormons were recalling the policies and practices of early Americans in Massachusetts, where many of their ancestors were born; in Pennsylvania, where their first prophet was baptized and given the priesthood; and in Missouri, where their first economic experiments were tried. Far from being unique, the spirit and technique of Mormon colonization and organized activity were common, if not typical, in the age which produced Mormonism.

Yet, Mormon economic institutions *were* unique in the contemporary American West. To be sure, there was the same hunger, the same improvisation, the same struggle for success, as in all Western settlements. But the unity, homogeneity, joint action, and group planning all stamped the Mormon frontier as unique—as a contrast with the scattered, specialized, exploitative, "wide open" mining, cattle, lumber, and homestead frontiers with which historians have familiarized us.

Hardly enough has been said in the present chapter to explain the cause of this uniqueness, which historians have variously attributed to the geography, early Mormon experiences, and/or Mormon religious beliefs. But the character of Mormon economic organization, as early as 1847–1849, and more certainly in the succeeding half-century, suggests the feasibility of regarding Mormon institutions as the more typically early American, and the individualistic institutions of other Westerners as the more divergent. The Mormon response to the problems imposed by the settlement of the Great Basin—a response which becomes ever clearer in succeeding decades —suggests that Mormon economic policies bore a greater resemblance to those of the ante-bellum northeast than did the economic policies of the West during the years when the West was won. Isolated as they were from American thought-currents after 1847, and under the necessity of continued group action to solve the many problems which plagued them, the Mormons were not affected by the growing accommodation to the private corporation, rugged individualism, Social Darwinism, and other concepts which account for the rise of laissez-faire after 1850. It may yet be conceded that the well-publicized conflicts and differences between the Mormons and other Westerners and Americans were not so much a matter of plural marriage and other reprehensible peculiarities and superstitions as of the conflicting economic patterns of two generations of Americans, one of which was fashioned after the communitarian concepts of the age of Jackson, and the other of which was shaped by the dream of bonanza and the individualistic sentiments of the age of laissez-faire.

If the Mormon pattern was reminiscent, it was also prophetic. For it was precisely this pattern of central direction, cooperation, and long-run planning which, as the result of the failure of individuals, the success of large corporations, and the impositions of government, came to characterize national policy with respect to the West in the twentieth century.

In the years which followed the initial settlement in the Salt Lake Valley, the Mormons would demonstrate some of the advantages of their collective institutions. In 1849–1850 they gathered enough "seed corn" to finance a whole decade of growth.

ADDITIONAL READINGS

Leonard Arrington's *Great Basin Kingdom* (Cambridge, Mass., 1958) purports to be an economic history, but it so skillfully weaves ideas and events that it is one of the best single volumes available on the Mormons. Thomas F. O'Dea's *The Mormons* (Chicago, 1957) is a general treatment from the standpoint of a sociologist. For an unusually revealing collection of documents, see William Mulder and A. R. Mortensen, *Among the Mormons: Human Accounts by Contemporary Observers* (New York, 1958). Leonard H. Creer, *The Founding of an Empire* (Salt Lake City, 1947), and Nels Anderson, *Desert Saints* (Chicago, 1942), are generally sympathetic; but Fawn Brodie, *No Man Knows My History: The Life Story of Joseph Smith* (New York, 1945), seems unwilling to admit the possibility of religious revelation.

9

THE MINING
FRONTIER

The foremost Western stereotype, along with the cowboy, is the miner. The picture usually takes the form of a lonely, gritty prospector wandering with a mule and a pick or stooping beside a stream with a pan of gravel. Like the trapper, the miner is seen as an individualist, a renegade from civilization, a man whose moral code is buried deep within him, subject to no external inspection. The cultural baggage he carries with him, his concepts of morality and religion, of law and government—these are minimal. Does this stereotype of the independent individual, free of all restraints and bondage, have any relevance to the actual Western miner?

To begin with, it is not surprising that the miner should play a large part in the popular notion of the trans-Mississippi West. He entered the scene with great fanfare in the gold Rush of 1849. Gold had been discovered in California the year before; the President had mentioned it in his message to Congress at the end of 1848; and the next spring from all over the world they began to come—Englishmen and Sydney Ducks, Chinese and Chileans, Missourians and Sonorans. By the end of 1849, 100,000 people were in California; and not many of them remained in San Francisco or the sleepy backwater of Los Angeles.

If California had been alone, the mining frontier would have little broad significance, and television serials would lose a key type. But within ten years after the California rush, there were strikes along Cherry Creek in Colorado; and a new fever produced Denver, Boulder, Central City, and Leadville—duplicating scenes of California's Hangtown and Poker Flat. Almost simultaneously, the earliest strikes were made on the Comstock Lode in Nevada, where Virginia City and Reno were to mushroom. Not much later Tucson and the mines along the Gila River in Arizona sprang up. Between 1855 and the last year of the Civil War, the great Northwest (Washington, British Columbia, Idaho, Montana) was also washed by waves of miners. Soon the Fraser River, Idaho City, a new Virginia City, and Helena were likewise involved. Gold in the Black Hills of Dakota in the 1870s drew other thousands—and so it went. Mining activity in the West from the 1850s to the 1880s was a constant source of excitement.

As one center after another was opened, certain patterns developed. For one thing, no area remained for long the domain of the lonely prospector. Within a few years of the first rush in any locale, smaller men were bought out, and larger corporate interests, based often on Eastern and European capital, moved in. By the time the Colorado and Nevada fields opened, the California Mother Lode had become well organized and capitalized; and the individual prospector was forced on, glad to have another place to go. Over and over this pattern was repeated, and it explains a good deal of the restlessness, even bitterness, in the mining story.

Accompanying the movement from one mining frontier to another was the parallel problem of establishing some kind of law and order for each new area. Other settlements, of course, were faced with problems of law and order (what cowtown story does not include a marshal?); but in the mines the problems were dramatically focused. Every miner was immediately concerned with the legal standing of his claim. How much land (hence gold) could he usurp? Close on these questions came water rights. How much of the river could one miner divert for his own sluice boxes? And once he had extracted an ounce of gold or silver—at the cost of strained back, and hands aching from ice water—who would prevent theft, not to mention murder? The possibility of social breakdown was imminent on every mining frontier. It was, as historian Alan Valentine has said, "a crude society, threatened by the law of the jungle, working its way painfully back to law and order."

In an established society the forms of law have evolved through generations. Here there was no such time. One resort was to what Dame Shirley (one woman on the scene, some of whose letters follow) called "their majesties the mob." Judge Lynch was swift and certain. In the mines or nearby areas such action often took the form of Vigilance Committees, whose validity and justification have haunted historians ever since. Some, like Valentine, have called these committees (such as that of San Francisco in 1851) "a unique nobility of motive and restraint." Josiah Royce drew a broader moral: "the people who forget the divine order of things have to learn thereof anew some day, in anxiety and pain." To the more recent historian John Caughey, however, the resorts to extralegal action expressed simply "the vengeful, bestial quality that characterizes lynchings, which is what they really were." The forms and principles of law had been ignored.

The principles, however, were not long in following; and lynch law was either avoided or gradually overcome. From the states the miner had brought a long Anglo-Saxon tradition of self-government, the doctrine of the natural rights of man, and experience with state and national constitutions. Within a short time he, like most settlers, demanded similar forms in his new areas. As one Westerner observed, "Congregate a hundred Americans anywhere beyond the settlements and they immediately lay out a city, form a State constitution and apply for admission into the Union, while twenty-five of them become candidates for the United States Senate." The miner, then, brought with him a high level of political incentive and acumen. In addition, from the Spanish legal tradition he accepted the idea that a claim should be valid only as long as it was being worked and that water should pertain to all the land of an area, not only to the banks of the stream. And he came to understand that the individual in society is subject to the laws of society and cannot entirely divorce himself from the restraints of government.

Sarah Royce

When Josiah Royce was preparing to write his history of California (see p. 188), he asked his mother—who, with her husband and baby, had joined the gold Rush of 1849—to write her reminiscences. She was a woman of great stamina, representing nineteenth-century Protestantism at its best and adding a mystical sense that enabled her to worship God on the plains in a burning bush. She is a striking illustration of the way in which culture and ideas were carried into the West.

Recollections of the Gold Rush*

In the morning of that day I had taken my last look at the waters that flowed eastward, to mingle with the streams and wash the shores where childhood and early youth had been spent; where all I loved, save, O, so small a number, lived; and now I stood on the almost imperceptible elevation that, when passed, would separate me from all these, perhaps forever. Through what toils and dangers we had come to reach that point; and, as I stood looking my farewell, a strong desire seized me to mark the spot in some way, and record at least one word of grateful acknowledgment. Yes, I would make a little heap of stones, and mark on one of them, or on a stick, the word "Ebenezer."†

Nobody would notice or understand it; but my Heavenly Father would see the little monument in the mountain wilderness, and accept the humble thanks it recorded. So I turned to gather stones. But no stone could I find, not even pebbles enough to make a heap,—and no stick either, not a bush or a shrub or a tree within reach. So I stood still upon the spot till the two wagons and the little company had passed out of hearing; and when I left not a visible sign marked the place. . . .

Just in the heat of noon-day we came to where the sage bushes were nearer together; and a fire, left by campers or Indians, had spread for some distance, leaving beds of ashes, and occasionally charred skeletons of bushes to make the scene more dreary. Smoke was still sluggishly curling up here and there, but no fire was visible; when suddenly just before me to my right a bright flame sprang up at the foot of a small bush, ran rapidly up it, leaped from one little branch to another till all, for a few seconds, were ablaze together, then went out, leaving nothing but a few ashes and a little smouldering trunk. It was a small incident, easily accounted for, but to my then over-wrought fancy it made more vivid the illusion of being a wanderer in a far off, old time desert, and myself witnessing a wonderful phenomenon. For a few moments I stood with bowed head worshiping the God of Horeb, and I was strengthened thereby. . . .

---

* Reprinted by permission of Yale University Press from Sarah Royce, *A Frontier Lady: Recollections of the Gold Rush and Early California,* edited by Ralph Henry Gabriel (New Haven: Yale University Press, 1932), pp. 26–114 *passim.* Copyright 1932 by Yale University Press.

† The reference is to Ebenezer, stone of help, a place a few miles north of Jerusalem, where Samuel set up a stone to commemorate a victory over the Philistines: "Then Samuel took a stone, and set it between Mizpeh and Shen, and called the name of it Ebenezer, saying, Hitherto hath the Lord helped us."

[*Later, at Weaverville, in the mines:*] Still, there was a lurking feeling of want of security from having only a cloth wall between us and out of doors. I had heard the sad story (which, while it shocked, reassured us) of the summary punishment inflicted in a neighboring town upon three thieves, who had been tried by a committee of citizens and, upon conviction, all hung. The circumstances had given to the place the name of Hang-Town. We were assured that, since then, no case of stealing had occurred in the northern mines; and I had seen, with my own eyes, buck-skin purses half full of gold-dust, lying on a rock near the road-side, while the owners were working some distance off. So I was not afraid of robbery; but it seemed as if some impertinent person might so easily intrude, or hang about, in a troublesome manner.

But I soon found I had no reason to fear. Sitting in my tent sewing, I heard some men cutting wood up a hill behind us. One of them called out to another "Look out not to let any sticks roll that way, there's a woman and child in that tent." "Aye, aye, we won't frighten them" was the reply, all spoken in pleasant, respectful tones. A number of miners passed every morning and afternoon, to and from their work; but none of them stared obtrusively. One, I observed, looked at Mary with interest a time or two, but did not stop, till one day I happened to be walking with her near the door, when he paused, bowed courteously and said, "Excuse me madam, may I speak to the little girl? We see so few ladies and children in California, and she is about the size of a little sister I left at home." "Certainly," I said, leading her towards him. His gentle tones and pleasant words easily induced her to shake hands, and talk with him. He proved to be a young physician, who had not long commenced practice at home, when the news of gold discovery in California induced him to seek El Dorado, hoping thus to secure, more speedily, means of support for his widowed mother and the younger members of the family. His partner in work was a well educated lawyer; and another of their party was a scientist who had been applying his knowledge of geology and mineralogy, in exploring; and had lately returned from a few miles south with a report so favorable they intended in a day or two to go and make a claim on his newly discovered ground. Here, then, was a party of California miners, dressed in the usual mining attire, and carrying pick, shovel and pans to and from their work; who yet were cultured gentlemen.

I soon found that this was by no means a solitary instance. But a much larger number of the miners belonged to other very valuable classes of society. Merchants, mechanics, farmers were all there in large numbers. So that in almost every mining camp there was enough of the element of order, to control, or very much influence, the opposite forces. These facts soon became apparent to me, and, ere long, I felt as secure in my tent with the curtain tied in front, as I had formerly felt with locked and bolted doors. There was, of course, the other element as elsewhere; but they themselves knew that it was safer for law and order to govern; and, with a few desperate exceptions, were willing, to let the lovers of order enjoy their rights and wield their influence. And the desperate exceptions were, for the time, so over-awed by the severe punishment some of their number had lately suffered, that, for a while, at least, in those early days, life and property were very safe in the mines; unless indeed you chose to associate with gamblers and desperados, in which case you of course constantly risked your money and your life. But, the same is true, in the heart of New York, Philadelphia, or London. . . .

[*Still later, in San Francisco:*] Any newcomer into San Francisco in those days had but to seek, in the right way, for good people, and he could find them. But in the immense crowds flocking hither from all parts of the world there were many of the worst classes, bent upon getting gold at all hazards, and if possible without work. These were constantly lying in wait, as tempters of the weak. A still greater number came with gold-getting for their ruling motive, yet intending to get it honestly, by labor or legitimate business. They did not at all intend, at first, to sacrifice their habits of morality, or their religious convictions. But many of them bore those habits, and held those convictions too lightly; and as they came to feel the force of unwonted excitement and the pressure of unexpected temptation, they too often yielded, little by little, till they found themselves standing upon a very low plane, side by side with those whose society they once would have avoided. It was very common to hear people who had started on this downward moral grade, deprecating the very acts they were committing, or the practices they were countenancing; and concluding their weak lament by saying "But *here* in California we *have* to do such things." Never was there a better opportunity for demonstrating the power and truth of Christian principle, than was, in those days, open to every faithful soul, and, never, perhaps, were there in modern, civilized, society more specious temptations to laxity of conduct. And thus it came to pass, that in this our early California life, while we had the pleasure of associating with those who were true to their convictions, earnest in their religious life, and faithful and lovely in the domestic circle, yet, on the other hand, we often met people, who had let loose the reins of moral government over themselves and families; and consented that others should do so. . . .

In the social life of San Francisco, one of the sensations of that year, was an entertainment, got up for the benefit of a Benevolent Society which, even in that early day, had been organized months before, and had done, and continued doing, works of mercy, which cheered and saved many a lonely wanderer. The entertainment was conducted by the ladies of the different churches, of which there were, in the city, already four. Every thing went prosperously on the day of the festival, and in the evening a large crowd gathered for social enjoyment. Introductions, and cordial greetings were turning strangers into friends, and making many, hitherto lonely, hearts feel, that even in California there was society worth having, when there entered the room a man, prominent for wealth and business-power, bearing upon his arm a splendidly dressed woman, well known in the city as the disreputable companion of her wealthy escort. With cool assurance he proceeded to make her and himself quite at home; but in a few minutes he was waited upon by a committee of gentlemen, who called him aside, and told him they were sent, by the lady-managers to say that they declined to receive as an associate, or to have introduced to their daughters, one who stood in the relation occupied by his companion, and they respectfully requested him to invite her to withdraw with him. Of course there was nothing for him to do but to comply; and all went on again pleasantly. It was reported that he had previously boasted that he could introduce "Irene" any where in San Francisco, but the events of that evening proved to him, as well as to others, that while Christian women would forego ease and endure much labor, in order to benefit any who suffered, they would not welcome into friendly association any who trampled upon institutions which lie at the foundation of morality and civilization.

Dame Shirley

In 1851 another New England woman, Louise Amelia Knapp Clappe (1819–1906), who described herself as "a shivering, frail, home-loving little thistle," began writing a series of long letters, over the name Dame Shirley, from the mining towns of Rich Bar and Indian Bar along the Feather River in California. As later published, they are some of the most vivid and intimate pictures we have of life in a mining camp. Bret Harte used them as raw material for his stories; and Josiah Royce, along with countless succeeding historians, considered them among the most valuable of his sources.

Letters from the California Mines*

From our Log Cabin, Indian Bar,
October 20, 1851

... The great man—officially considered—of the entire river, is the "Squire," as he is jestingly called. It had been rumored for some time, that we were about to become a law and order loving community; and when I requested an explanation, I was informed that a man had gone all the way to Hamilton, the county seat, to get himself made into a Justice of the Peace. Many shook their wise heads and doubted—even if suited to the situation, which they say he is not—whether he would *take* here; and certain rebel spirits affirmed that he would be invited to *walk over the hill* before he had been in the community twenty-four hours; which is a polite way these free-and-easy young people have, of turning out of town an obnoxious individual. Not that the "Squire" is particularly objectionable, *per se,* but in virtue of his office, and his supposed ineligibility to fill the same. Besides, the people here wish to have the fun of ruling themselves. Miners are as fond of playing at law-making and dispensing, as French novelists are of "playing at Providence." They say, also, that he was not elected by the voice of the people, but that his personal friends nominated and voted for him unknown to the rest of the community. This is, perhaps, true. At least I have heard some of the most respectable men here observe, that had they been aware of the Squire's name being up as candidate for an office, which though insignificant elsewhere, is one of great responsibility in a mining community, they should certainly have gone against his election.

Last night I had the honor of an introduction to *"His* Honor." Imagine a middle-sized man, quite stout, with a head disproportionately large, crowned with one of those immense foreheads eked out with a slight baldness (wonder if according to the flattering popular superstition, he has *thought* his hair off?) which enchant phrenologists, but which one *never* sees brooding above the soulful orbs of the great ones of the earth; a smooth, fat face, grey eyes and prominent chin, the *tout ensemble* characterized by an expression of the utmost meekness and gentleness, which expression contrasts rather funnily with a satanic goatee, and you have our good "Squire."

---

* From Dame Shirley (Louise Amelia Knapp Clappe), "Letters," *The Pioneer* (San Francisco), II (Sept. 1854), 154–155; II (Oct. 1854), 214–216; IV (Aug. 1855), 108–109.

You know, N., that it takes the same *kind* of power—differing of course in degree—to govern twenty men that it does to rule a million, and although the "Squire" is sufficiently intelligent and the kindest hearted creature in the world, he evidently does *not* possess that peculiar tact, talent, gift or whatever it is called, which makes Napoleons, Mohammeds and Cromwells, and which is absolutely necessary to keep in order such a strangely amalgamated community, representing as it does the four quarters of the globe, as congregates upon this river.

However, I suppose that we must take the "goods the Gods provide," satisfied that if our "King Log" does no good; he is too sincerely desirous of fulfilling his duty, to do any harm. But I really feel sorry for this "mere young Daniel come to judgment," when I think of the gauntlet which the wicked wits will make him run when he tries his first cause.

However, the "Squire" may, after all, succeed. As yet he has had no opportunity of making use of his credentials in putting down Miner's Law, which is of course the famous code of Judge Lynch. In the mean time, we all sincerely pray that he may be successful in his laudable undertaking, for justice in the hands of a mob, however respectable, is at best a fearful thing.

From our Log Cabin, Indian Bar,
October 29, 1851

Well, My dear N., our grand "Squire," whom I sketched for you in my last letter, has at length had an opportunity to exercise (or rather to try to do so) his judicial power upon a criminal case. His first appearance as Justice of the Peace, took place a week ago, and was caused, I think, by a prosecution for debt. On that momentous occasion, the proceeding having been carried on in the bar-room of the Empire, it is said that our "Young Daniel" stopped the court twice in order to treat the jury!

But let me tell you about the trial which has just taken place. On Sunday evening last, Ned Paganini rushing wildly up to our cabin, and with eyes so enormously dilated that they absolutely looked *all* white, exclaimed, "that 'Little John' had been arrested for stealing four hundred dollars from the proprietor of the Empire; and that he was at that very moment undergoing an examination before the 'Squire,' in the bar-room of the Humboldt, where he was apprehended while betting at monte." "And, added Ned, with a most awe-inspiring shake of his cork-screws, "there is no doubt but that he will be hung!"

Of course I was inexpressibly shocked at Ned's news, for "Little John," as he is always called, (who, by the way, is about the last person—as every one remarked—that would have been suspected), seemed quite like an acquaintance, as he was waiter at the Empire when I boarded there. I hurried F. off as quickly as possible, to inquire into the truth of the report. He soon returned with the following particulars:

It seems that Mr. B. who on Sunday morning wished to pay a bill, on taking his purse from between the two matresses of the bed whereon he was accustomed to sleep, which stood in the common sitting-room of the family, found that four hundred dollars in gold dust was missing. He did not for one moment suspect "Little John," in whom himself and wife had always placed the utmost confidence—until a man who happened to be in the bar-room towards evening, mentioned casually "that 'Little John' was then at the Humboldt betting," or to speak technically,—" 'bucking' away large sums at monte." Mr. B., who knew that he had no money of his own, immediately came over to Indian Bar and had him arrested upon suspicion. Although he had lost several ounces, he had still about a hundred dollars remaining. But as it is impossible to identify gold-dust, Mr. B. could not swear that the money was his.

Of course, the prisoner loudly protested his innocence; and as he was very drunk, the "Squire" adjourned all further proceedings until the next day—placing him under keepers for the night.

On the following morning I was awakened very early by a tremendous "aye"—so deep and mighty that it almost seemed to shake the cabin with its thrilling emphasis. I sprang up and ran to the window, but could *see* nothing, of course—as our house stands behind the Humboldt; but I could easily understand from the confused murmur of many voices, and the rapidly succeeding "ayes" and "noes," that a large crowd had collected in front of the latter. My first apprehension was expressed by my bursting into tears and exclaiming—

"Oh! F., for God's sake rise; the mob are going to hang 'Little John!' "

And my fear was not so absurd as you might at first imagine, for men have often been executed in the mines, for stealing a much smaller sum than four hundred dollars.

F. went to the Humboldt and returned in a few minutes to tell me that I might stop weeping, for John was going to have a regular trial. The crowd was merely a miners' meeting, called by Mr. B. for the purpose of having the trial held at the Empire for the convenience of his wife, who could not walk over to Indian Bar to give her evidence in the case. However, as her deposition could easily have been taken, malicious people *will* say that it was for the convenience of her husband's *pockets*—as it was well known that at whichever house the trial took place, the owners thereof would make a handsome profit from the sale of dinners, drinks, etc., to the large number of people who would congregate to witness the proceedings. Miners are proverbial for their reverence to the sex. Of course, everything ought to yield where a lady is concerned, and they all very properly agreed *nem con,* to Mr. B.'s request.

The "Squire" consented to hold the court at Rich Bar, although many think that thereby he compromised his judicial dignity, as his office is on Indian Bar. I must confess I see not how he could have done otherwise. The miners were only too ready (so much do they object to a Justice of the Peace) to take the case *entirely* out of his hands, if their wishes were not complied with; which, to confess the truth, they *did,* even after all his concessions! though they *pretended* to keep up a sort of mock respect for his office.

Everybody went to Rich Bar. No one remained to protect the calico shanties, the rag huts and the log cabins, from the much talked of Indian attack—but your humble servant and Paganini Ned.

When the people, the mighty people, had assembled at the Empire, they commenced proceedings by voting in a president and jury of their own; though they kindly consented (how *very* condescending!) that the "Squire" might *play at judge,* by sitting at the side of *their* elected magistrate! This honor, the "Squire" seemed to take as a sort of salvo to his wounded dignity, and with unprecedented meekness *accepted* it. A young Irishman from St. Louis was appointed counsel for John, and a Dr. C acted for the prosecution,—neither of them, however, were lawyers.

The evidence against the prisoner was: that he had no money previously; that he had slept at the Empire a night or two before; and that he knew where Mr. B. was in the habit of keeping his gold dust; with a few other circumstances equally unimportant. His only defense was, of course to account for the money, which he tried to do by the following ingenious story:

He said that his father, who resides at Stockholm (he is a Swede) had sent him two months previously, five hundred dollars through the express, which had been brought to him from San Francisco by a young man whose name is Miller; that he told no one of the circumstance, but buried the money (a common habit with the miner) on the summit of a hill about half a mile from Indian Bar; that being intoxicated on Sunday morning, he had dug it up for the purpose of gambling with it; and that Mr. M. who had gone to Marysville a week before, and would return in a fortnight, could confirm his story. When asked if he had received a letter with the money, he replied that he did; but having placed it between the lining and the top of his cap, he had unfortunately lost it. He earnestly affirmed his innocence, and through his counsel, entreated the Court, should he be condemned, to defer the execution of his sentence until the arrival of Miller, by whom he could prove all that he had stated. Notwithstanding the florid eloquence of W., the jury brought in a verdict of guilty, and condemned him to receive thirty-nine lashes at nine o'clock the following morning, and to leave the river, never to return to it, within twenty-four hours; a "claim" of which he owned a part, to be made over to Mr. B., to indemnify him for his loss. His punishment was very light on account of his previous popularity and inoffensive conduct. In spite of his really ingenious defense, no one has the least doubt of his guilt, but his lawyer and the "Squire;" they as firmly believe him an innocent and much injured man. . . .

From our Log Cabin, Indian Bar,
August 4, 1852

. . . The state of society here has never been so bad as since the appointment of a Committee of Vigilance. The rowdies have formed themselves into a company called the "Moguls," and they parade the streets all night, howling, shouting, breaking into houses, taking wearied miners out of their beds and throwing them into the river, and in short, "murdering sleep," in the most remorseless manner. Nearly every night they build bonfires fearfully near some rag shanty, thus endangering the lives, (or I should rather say the property—for as it is impossible to sleep, lives are emphatically safe) of the whole community. They retire about five o'clock in the morning; previously to this blessed event posting notices to that effect, and that they will throw any one who may disturb them into the river. I am nearly worn out for want of rest, for truly they "make night hideous" with their fearful uproar. Mr. O_____, who still lies dangerously ill from the wound received, on what we call the "fatal Sunday," complains bitterly of the disturbance; and when poor Pizarro was dying, and one of his friends gently requested that they would be quiet for half an hour and permit the soul of the sufferer to pass in peace, they only laughed and yelled and hooted louder than ever, in the presence of the departing spirit, for the tenement in which he lay, being composed of green boughs only, could of course shut out no sounds. Without doubt if the "Moguls" had been sober, they would never have been guilty of such horrible barbarity as to compel the thoughts of a dying man to mingle with curses and blasphemies; but alas! they were intoxicated, and may God forgive them, unhappy ones, for they knew not what they did. The poor, exhausted miners, for even well people cannot sleep in such a pandemonium, grumble and complain, but they—although far outnumbering the rioters—are too timid to resist. All say "It is shameful; something ought to be done; something *must* be done," etc. and in the mean time the rioters triumph. You will wonder that the Committee of Vigilance does not interfere; it is said that some of that very Committee are the ringleaders among the "Moguls."

I believe I have related to you everything but the duel—and I will make the recital of this as short as possible, for I am sick of these sad subjects, and doubt not but you are the same. It took place on Tuesday morning at eight o'clock, on Missouri Bar, when and where that same Englishman who has figured so largely in my letter, shot his best friend. The duelists were surrounded by a large crowd, I have been told, foremost among which stood the Committee of Vigilance! The man who received his dear friend's fatal shot, was one of the most quiet and peaceable citizens on the Bar. He lived about ten minutes after he was wounded. He was from Ipswich, England, and only twenty-five years of age, when his own high passions snatched him from life. In justice to his opponent, it must be said, that he would willingly have retired after the first shots had been exchanged, but poor Billy Leggett, as he was familiarly called, insisted upon having the distance between them shortened, and continuing the duel until one of them had fallen.

There, my dear M., have I not fulfilled my promise of giving you a dish of horrors? And only think of such a shrinking, timid, frail thing, as I *used* to be "long time ago," not only living right in the midst of them, but almost compelled to hear if not see the whole. I think that I may without vanity affirm, that I have "seen the elephant." "Did you see his tail?" asks innocent Ada J., in her mother's letter. Yes, sweet Ada, the "entire Animal" has been exhibited to my view.

Charles H. Shinn

Charles Shinn (1852–1924) grew up in California during the Gold Rush; and when at the age of thirty he went East to finish his college education at Johns Hopkins, he capitalized on his early experiences by writing a dissertation on mining camps as a study in American frontier government. He saw that the "habit of law and regulation was planted in these Argonauts before they reached the diggings," and he concluded with great admiration for the way miners learned to govern themselves.

California Mining Camps*

There was a very remarkable example of the gold-seekers' methods
of settling serious disputes which once occurred in the northern part of
California. It fairly deserves to be termed one of the most important and
interesting of litigations in the early history of the mines. In many respects
it is even entitled to rank as the unique example of a higher type of organized effort to do the best thing possible under each and every circumstance than is shown in the history of any other mining camp of the
period. . . .

Scotch Bar is rather indefinitely located by my informant as "in the
Siskiyou-Klamath region." It was a highly prosperous camp, "booming,"
as the miners said; and the fame of its rich placers had already extended
to Trinity, Shasta, and Butte, attracting traders, prospectors, and parasites
of the camp. Exactly what local laws and local officers the camp had, we
do not know; but probably much the same that were known to districts
in the central part of the state. It is likely that they had elected a justice
of the peace, allowing him to settle their disputes over boundaries and to
keep a record of their claims. At least, so it appears; the camp had been
peaceable, law-abiding, and contented; the miners had dwelt together in
concord, much in the spirit of the Arcadian days of '48; and it was "a
royally good camp to live in."

Some time early in 1851, a discovery of some very "rich gravel," or
mining ground, was made, and made in such a way, also, that two
equally strong parties of prospectors laid claim to it at the same time.
There were about a dozen men in each party, and both groups were entirely honest in their belief of the justice of their respective claims. Each
clan at once began to increase its fighting numbers by enlistments from
the rest of the camp, till twenty or thirty men were sworn to each hostile
assembly. The ground in dispute was so situated that it was best worked
in partnership, and thirty claims of the ordinary size allowed in the district
would occupy all the desirable territory of the new find. So there were
two rival companies ready to begin work, and no law whatever to prevent
a pitched battle.

It began to look more and more like fighting. Men were asked to join,
and bring their bowies, revolvers, and shotguns. Men were even forced
to refuse the honor, against their wills, because, forsooth, there were
no more weapons left in camp. The two opposing parties took up their sta-

---

* From Charles H. Shinn, *Mining Camps: A Study in American Frontier Government* (New York: Charles Scribner's Sons, 1884), pp. 219–231 *passim*.

tions on the banks of the gulch; there was further and excited talk; at last there were eight or ten shots interchanged, fortunately injuring no one. But by this time the blood of the combatants was fairly roused; the interests at stake were very large; neither side proposed to yield; and the next minute there probably would have been a hand-to-hand conflict, except for an unlooked-for interference.

The camp, the commonwealth, the community at large, had taken the field the very moment the first shot was fired. Dozens and hundreds of men, five minutes before mere spectators of the difficulty, at once compelled a parley, negotiated a truce, and urged a resort to legal methods. The moment this compromise was suggested, the combatants laid aside their weapons. They knew there was no legal authority within twenty miles, and not even in the camp itself any force able to keep them from fighting; for persuasion was the only argument used, and it is not supposable that the rest of the miners would have actually fought to prevent fighting. It was a victory of common sense, a triumph of the moral principles learned in boyhood in New England villages and on Western prairies. "Men more thoroughly fearless never faced opposing weapons"; but the demand for a fair and full trial in open court found an answering chord in every bosom. Both parties willingly agreed to submit to arbitration; but not to the ordinary arbitration of the "miners' court," or of the "miners' committee," or of the "miners' alcalde" ... They thought out a better plan, and adopted it after a few moments' discussion.

The rude and often biased jury of the camp was repudiated by both contestants alike. None of the ordinary forms of tribunal known to the mining region seemed to them entirely adequate to this momentous occasion. They chose a committee, and sent it to San Francisco. There they had three or four of the best lawyers to be found, engaged for each party; and they also engaged a judge of much experience in mining cases. It was a great day at Scotch Bar when all this legal talent arrived to decide the ownership of the most valuable group of claims on the river—claims that had been lying absolutely idle, untouched by anyone, guarded by camp opinion and by the sacred pledges of honor, ever since the day of the compact between the rival companies.

Well, the case was tried with all possible formality, and as legally as if it had occurred within the civil jurisdiction of a district court. It is not reported in any of the California law-books; but no mining case ever commanded better talent or elicited more exhaustive and brilliant arguments. The lawyers and judge were there to settle the case; the entire camp wanted it settled; both parties to the dispute were anxious to find out who the real owners were. In order to show the childlike sense of fairness the miners had, we should mention that before the trial began, it was arranged by mutual consent that the winners should pay costs. To the losers, it was

sufficient to have failed to prove title to such rich claims: they must not
be made still poorer.

Now, in ordinary cases of camp rule there is often too much compromise: one claimant gets less than he deserves, while the other gets more.
But in this justly famous Scotch Bar case there was in the end a verdict
squarely for one side and squarely against the other. The defeated party
took it placidly, without a murmur; nor then, nor at any other time, were
they ever heard to complain. The cheerfulness of their acceptance of the
verdict was not the least gratifying episode of the famous trial.

"Ah! it was a great case," writes our informant . . . "The whole camp
was excited over it for days and weeks. At last, when the case was decided,
the claim was opened by the successful party; and when they reached bed-
rock, and were ready to 'clean up,' we all knocked off work, and came down
and stood on the banks, till the ravine on both sides was lined with men.
And I saw them take out gold with iron spoons, and fill pans with solid
gold, thousands upon thousands of dollars. Ah! it was a famous claim,
worth hundreds of thousands of dollars."

On the bank, along with these hundreds of spectators, stood the defeated contestants, cheerful and even smiling: it was not their gold, any
more than if it had been in Africa. And the successful miners brought their
gold out on the bank, divided it up among themselves—so many pounds
apiece—and each went to his tent to thrust the treasure under his blankets
till a good opportunity arrived for sending it to San Francisco.

The community capable of that Scotch Bar case was a community
which could be trusted to the uttermost. Put it down on a desert island, and
it would organize a government, pick out its best men, punish its criminals,
protect its higher interests, develop local institutions; and soon, unless its
natural surroundings forbade, there would be a healthy, compact, energetic
state, with capital city, seaports, commerce, navy, and army. Put it down
on a new continent, and it would eventually possess, control, and develop
all its resources and energies; doing the work that Rome did for Italy, that
the Puritans did for New England, and through New England for the
United States. And if the evidence of travelers, of the pioneers themselves,
and of the institutions they organized can be trusted, there were many such
camps in California. The Siskiyou region did not monopolize that habit of
self-control, of acceptance of the situation, of submitting questions to the
best obtainable courts, and of abiding by their decisions. From Klamath to
Colusa, from Siskiyou to Fresno, from Lake Bowman to Trinity Peak,
manhood and honesty ruled the camps of the miners. Some were ruled better than others, but all were ruled well. . . .

Cases of lynch law occur from time to time in almost every frontier
community, and too often in older communities also. But the difference
between the true miner courts of the gold era, and such cases of mob law,
is fundamental and generic. Lynch law, in the plain, everyday acceptance

of the term, is the work of an association of men who have determined to violently expedite, or to suddenly change the course of, judicial procedure in one individual case. They announce no new laws, create no new system, add nothing whatever to the jurisprudence of the land. The moment the piece of work they were banded together to do is accomplished, they separate, and the association ceases to exist. They keep no records of their proceedings; the names of their leaders are sedulously concealed; and the regular officers of the law are often, in the discharge of their duty, brought into open collision with the lynchers. The utmost that may be said for them is that they often, though unintentionally, compel better administration of the laws; but, on the whole, lynch law is manifestly selfish, cowardly, passionate, un-American.

In every important particular the organizations of the typical mining camps which we have been considering offer sharply outlined contrasts. Camp law has never been the enemy of time-tried and age-honored judicial system, but its friend and forerunner. Axe of pioneer and pick of miner have leveled the forests, and broken down the ledges of rock, to clear a place for the stately structures of a later civilization. Rude mountain courts, rude justice of miner camps, truth reached by short cuts, decisions unclouded by the verbiage of legal lexicons, a rough-hewn, sturdy system that protected property, suppressed crime, prevented anarchy—such were the facts; and on these, frontier government rests its claims to recognition as other than mob law, and better than passionate accident.

Later illustrations of vigilantes' justice than those of California can readily be found. When, after a reign of terror almost unexampled in American frontier history, the tried and true miners and merchants of Montana organized during the winter of 1863–4 and in a few weeks hung twenty-four desperadoes and murderers, they performed a solemn duty laid upon them as American citizens. The present peace, order, and prosperity of that empire in the high Rockies, the "land of the silver bow," as its children love to call it, are the result of this acceptance of weighty responsibilities. Not until nearly a hundred persons had been waylaid, robbed, and slain in various parts of the Territory by members of a fully organized band of assassins, did society accept the challenge, and supply the absence of civil authority with the military firmness of the Vigilantes. It is a matter of history that this organization, like that of San Francisco, never hung an innocent man, and that, when its work was done, it quietly disbanded.

In studying the nature of the mining camps of California we are irresistibly compelled to think of the whole race of American pioneers, from the days of Boone and Harrod to the days of Carson and Bridger; heroic forest chivalry, heroic conquerors of the prairies, heroic rulers of the mountain wilderness, ever forcing back the domains of savage and wild beast. Well did one of the most eloquent of American lecturers once exclaim:

"Woe to the felon upon whose track is the American borderer! Woe to the assassin before a self-empanneled jury of American foresters! No lie will help him, no eloquence prevail; no false plea can confuse the clear conceptions or arrest the judgment of a frontier court."

When the pioneers of the newer West pushed into California, adding the leaven of such ideas to the mass of ancient Spanish civilization; when youth and energy from older communities of the Atlantic states, and adventurers from every land under the sun, joined in the famous gold rush of 1849—the marvel of marvels is that mob law and failure of justice were so infrequent, that society was so well and so swiftly organized.

Rodman Paul

In comparison with Shinn, Professor Rodman Paul, modern historian of the mining frontier, holds a much less happy picture of law and order in such settlements. In one of his articles he contrasts the ways Americans and Britishers acted in their respective mining areas. By "Old Californians" he is referring to former Americans who moved into British gold fields like those in Australia or British Columbia.

Old Californians*

... If the "old Californians" and other Americans were always present and apparently influential in showing greenhorns how to mine and in supplying them with goods, it is strange that they did not also convert the British dominions to their careless ways in regard to law and order.... One need only turn to Mark Twain's satire in *Roughing It* to see how inadequate western governors, judges and juries, and police could be, and how insecure were life and property as a result. Or again, the fortune Senator William Stewart made as an attorney in mining litigation on the Comstock Lode suggests the carelessness with which American miners drafted their mining rules and kept their records of claims.

---

* From Rodman W. Paul, " 'Old Californians' in British Gold Fields," *Huntington Library Quarterly*, XVII (1954), 166–172. Reprinted by permission.

Within the British Empire a much higher degree of security seems to have prevailed. The evidence is clearest on the score of law and order; it is difficult to discover much discussion of the effectiveness of British colonial legal precautions in preventing disputes over ownership of mining claims. In so far as law and order are concerned, there seems to have been a degree of success that appears remarkable when compared with the American record. In British Columbia Governor Douglas claimed that in the period of almost two years, from November, 1858, to August, 1860—the height of the Fraser River boom—only two serious crimes were committed by white men. In the Klondike rush also, the verdict seems to be that on the whole civil government was successful and the Northwest Mounted Police did well, although there were several lynchings and miners' juries. By contrast, just across the boundary line in the American Yukon, shootings, robbery, and rule by gamblers and gangsters were prevalent for a long time.

The case of Australia is especially interesting in view of Australia's background as a former penal colony. One Australian writer claims that his country was free from what he terms "the same orgies as disgraced the gold-fields of California." A more careful Australian historian, G. V. Portus, concludes that on the whole unexpectedly good order was maintained. There were, he tells us, always swindlers, harlots, dishonest gold-buyers, and illegal liquor sellers, but apparently the police were able to control serious crime, and either there was no resort to lynch law and popular justice, or else such extra legal action was too rare to be reported.

On the other hand, Australia's gold-rush history is marred by the famous episode of the Eureka Stockade, near Ballarat, Victoria, in 1854. On this occasion long-smoldering discontent among the miners broke out into open defiance of the established authorities. The miners built a stockade, commandeered arms, and even proclaimed themselves an independent republic. The governor, a naval officer of many years' experience, acted with vigor. He assembled 430 soldiers and police, and at just the right moment this force struck as ruthlessly as if it were dealing with a foreign enemy. The stockade was carried at bayonet point; four soldiers and thirty rebels were killed and 120 rebels were taken prisoner. Then, when the revolt had been broken, the chief causes of discontent were removed by legislative reforms.

Perhaps this episode will serve to suggest important differences between American practice and arrangements under the British Empire. Australia was the first part of the British Empire to suffer a gold rush, the date being 1851. Australia was then a pastoral colony with a population of several hundred thousand people, all of whom were penned into a narrow strip between the mountains and the sea on the eastern and southeastern sides of that vast continent. By great good fortune New South Wales, the province that contained more than half of Australia's total population, was the scene of Hargraves' sensational discovery. New South Wales was the oldest colony and the one most fully equipped with the institutions and agents that make for a strong government, including administrative officers, judges, police, and soldiers, and an embryonic representative legislature.

The initial discovery occurred at Bathurst, which was across a difficult mountain range from Sydney, in a primitive region that had been occupied by sheepmen during the preceding thirty-five years. To control the sheepmen's use of these wild transmontane Crown lands, statutes of the 1830's established a system of licenses, that the sheepmen must obtain for a small fee. Commissioners of Crown Lands were appointed to keep order in these remote pastoral districts, and a corps of Border Police was recruited to help them.

Here, as applied to sheepmen before the gold rush, was the system that was to be used in mineral regions throughout Australasia and western British North America. New South Wales was the first to try it. It promptly appointed Gold Commissioners to be resident representatives of authority in the diggings. Police were supplied to back up the Commissioners, and all miners were supposed to purchase a license.

This arrangement for maintaining law and order worked surprisingly well in New South Wales. It functioned less effectively when gold was discovered in Victoria Province, which was newer and was very inadequately staffed with administrative officers, police, and soldiers. Mention has already been made of the revolt at the Eureka Stockade, near Ballarat, Victoria. One of the causes of that outbreak was discrimination against the miners in the electoral franchise, but a more important one was the hated license fee, which was being widely evaded at the time. Following the revolt the license fee was reduced to £1 per annum and was rechristened a "miner's right," presumably because the right to vote henceforth went with it. The revenue lost by this change was made up by an export tax on gold.

The Australian use of Gold Commissioners appointed from the provincial capital, and of supporting police and a system of licenses, is very suggestive. The way in which troops were used to break the revolt at the Eureka Stockade is even more so. Unquestionably there was a degree of authoritarianism in the government of the Australian fields that was completely absent in similar diggings in the United States.

Upon turning from Australia to British Columbia in 1858, one finds the same use of Gold Commissioners, police, and licenses, together with one or two instances in which there was resort to what few military forces were available. Yet the atmosphere seems less authoritarian than in Australia, presumably because the colony was so new and tiny and the machinery of government so slight. A sense of firm authority was certainly present in the strong personality of Governor James Douglas, but along with it went a fine English spirit of compromise. For example, before Douglas's Gold Commissioners were able to assert themselves, the Americans in the Fraser

River camps had already set up their familiar local rules and local mining boards to regulate mining claims. Douglas wisely allowed them to continue this practice, provided the Gold Commissioners were allowed to have a hand in the matter henceforth and provided each set of local rules was submitted to the governor for approval.

It is interesting to note that the miners' attempts to govern themselves in British Columbia were confined to mining matters. There was no attempt to enforce criminal law through miners' juries and lynchings. Here again a strong personality had much to do with it. Judge Matthew Begbie, the head of the judiciary in British Columbia, is universally described with such adjectives as "fearless," "stern," and "upright," although it is admitted that at times he was arbitrary to the point of being unreasonable.

In the Yukon [Canada] authority was imposed only after a preliminary period of neglect by the Canadian government. But once imposed, it was upheld by the Northwest Mounted Police, who seem to have shown a fine balance between tolerance of petty uproar, gambling, and drunkenness, and a firm repression of crime and of miners' meetings when the miners wanted to govern themselves. The police also collected dues or royalties from each miner. One suspects, however, that control was less tight in the Yukon than on other mining frontiers, for there are reports of miners' meetings to protest the collection of the royalty, to demand bigger claims, and even to handle civil disputes.

Despite this partial exception, the paradox remains: on the one hand Americans, especially Californians, were prominent on every Anglo-Saxon mining frontier. As technologists and teachers of mining technology, as suppliers of machinery, goods, and services, they were omnipresent, energetic, effective, and ingenious. Yet as members of the political community they bowed to the will of the tiny little group of appointed officials sent out from distant provincial capitals—and these officials were "foreigners" from the point of view of the Americans. By so bowing they won a greater security for life and property than had existed in the Sierra Nevada or Rocky Mountains. This paradox of technological and economic dominance accompanied by political submission is not easy to explain. . . .

Perhaps all that was needed in the United States was to give law and order a trial in order to make it work in the mining states and territories. The responsible character of the San Francisco vigilance committees suggests that there was a reservoir of determined citizens who would have supported a more effective regime if they had had a chance. On the other hand, Americans were prone to be so preoccupied with their businesses that they could not spare time for matters of government.

Certainly a part of the credit should go to the British tradition of respect for law and order. Much should be assigned to the individual governors and judges who set the tone for the entire frontier staff beneath them and indeed for much of the average man's attitude towards government in general. Not all of the officials were able; some were distinctly weak. But, taken as a group, they appear in a very favorable light when compared with American western officials. It does violence to one's faith in the democratic process to realize that one reason for this was that they were appointed rather than elected, that they represented distant rather than local rule, and furthermore that in several notable instances they were appointed after long service in such authoritarian organizations as the Royal Navy and the Hudson's Bay Company. The picture does not improve for the United States if one restricts the comparison on the American side to territorial officials appointed from Washington. Low standards for holders of Federal office, ridiculously low remuneration, and lack of support from Washington undermined the resolution of all save the most courageous.

Thus one is forced to conclude that the democratic Americans of the nineteenth century still had much to learn about frontier government from the empire that once had ruled their country.

ADDITIONAL READINGS

Two of the best histories of the California mining frontier are *Gold Is the Cornerstone* by John Caughey (Berkeley, 1948) and *California Gold: The Beginnings of Mining in the Far West* by Rodman Paul (Cambridge, Mass., 1947). For an analysis of the widespread corporate activity behind the stereotype of the lonely miner, see Clark Spence, *British Investments and the Mining Frontier, 1860–1901* (Ithaca, 1958). For one example of many books on mining areas outside of California (in this case Colorado), see G. F. Willison, *Here They Dug the Gold* (New York, 1931). An interesting reprint of a first-hand account of Nevada is Dan De Quille's *The Big Bonanza* (New York, 1947). Relative to law and order, one might begin with Hubert Howe Bancroft's *Popular Tribunals* (2 vols., San Francisco, 1887). More recent general studies are *Frontier Justice* by Wayne Gard (Norman, 1949) and *Vigilante Justice* by Alan Valentine (New York, 1956).

10

THE CATTLE FRONTIER

In the popular mind the cattle frontier—although in large part a matter of economics, of business, of connecting cow with consumer—is associated with a single heroic type, the cowboy. Tall in the saddle, fast on the draw, booted and spurred; independent and free as a prairie wind; unfailingly courteous and protective toward women, including "soiled doves"; loyal unto death to his *compadres;* at home on the range, at ease at high noon, lean and limber and forever young, this national hero lopes tirelessly through the mass imagination, so encased in clichés that neither truth nor parody can reduce the reverence or dim the delight that he generates within an admiring public. Surely no other frontier figure sums up the Western experience in so satisfying a fashion for so many Americans.

The partly playful sketch above, of course, is closer to myth than to reality. It ignores the industry that nurtured the hero; it fails to distinguish another frontiersman, the range entrepreneur or cattleman; and it stresses the romantic and individualistic features of range society at the expense of its cooperative and corporate character. A first step toward forcing the cowboy into reasonable perspective, and recovering the conditions that produced both him and his boss, is to trace the rise and development of the cattle frontier.

The cradle of the cattle kingdom, as Walter Prescott Webb unforgettably describes it in *The Great Plains,* lay in a diamond-shaped pocket at the southern tip of Texas. Here conditions of grass and water, mildness of climate and remoteness from the Great Plains haunts of the Indians made the living easy for cattle and men alike. Mexican *ranchero*s and Texans vied for control of the region, but after their revolution the Texans pushed the Mexicans south of the Rio Grande and added hundreds of head of Spanish stock to their own American breeds. Between the Texas revolution and the Civil War, cattle bred with abandon; by 1860 Texas had an estimated 3,500,000—an explosive increase from the approximately 100,000 of a generation earlier. There were of course cattle in the East, many more than in Texas; but they were widely scattered in small clusters on individual farms, "incidents of agriculture," in Webb's words. The essential difference between the cattle industry in the East and the industry that arose west of the 98th meridian was not in the number raised but in the method of handling them.

Before the Civil War there were intermittent efforts to market Texas cattle by water and by land in New Orleans, in California, and in Chicago; but these were small-scale attempts that met with losses or only mild success. In the immediate post-war years—with Texan returnees in search of economic opportunity, with countless cattle bringing only from $3.50 to $4.50 per head at home, with growing demand for beef in urban centers and on Indian reservations creating markets in the East at ten times the Texas figure, with railroads nosing out into the frontier—all the elements were at hand for launching the cattle business on a large scale, provided a way could be found to get seller and buyer together at a point from which the beef might be transported to Eastern slaughter houses.

By 1866, problem and opportunity were clearly defined; but it took an Illinois livestock shipper, Joseph G. McCoy, to bring the Eastern buyer and the Texan drover together. The point of intersection was Abilene, near the railhead of the Kansas Pacific and the first of the Western cow towns. McCoy also secured favorable rates from the Hannibal and St. Joe Railroad for shipments from the Missouri River to Illinois, helping to shift the hub of the cattle business from St. Louis to Chicago. By the close of 1867, some 35,000 head of longhorns had been trailed from Texas to Abilene and shipped East, most of them via the Kansas Pacific. Over the next decade and a half, nearly 5,000,000 head were moved north over routes such as the Chisholm Trail, the Dodge City Trail, and the Goodnight-Loving Trail, that shifted with the advancing railheads ever to the west.

The discussion thus far has followed Webb's classic account, with the Texas historian's understandable emphasis on the Southwest. This interpretation, however, needs mild modification. Even before the advent of the Texas herds, the cattle business of the high plains was under way on road ranches that provided fresh cattle for the exhausted stock of migrants coming west along the emigrant trails in the two decades before the Civil War. Another source of cattle on the northwestern frontier was the stock of animals that the freighting companies wintered on the range. Farther to the north and west, in Montana, need for beef in the mines encouraged an incipient cattle business. In short, although the major influx of stock into the Great Plains region was made up of rangy Texas longhorns, these herds did not move into a vacuum but mingled with sturdier breeds brought in from the East and, a little later, from Oregon. Moreover, not all the cattle trailed up from Texas were fit to ship to Eastern markets. Those that were not wintered on the northern ranges and formed one basis for ranching ventures in the North.

By 1885, the cattle frontier stretched from southern Texas north and west, overspreading the Great Plains region. The result was a relatively small business in beef done on a sweeping scale and establishing for a moment in American history a distinctive and very logical way of life.

On the cattle frontier, adaptation rather than innovation was the rule. In the first place, the influence of Spain was strong. There were Spanish cattle and Spanish saddles and the *sombrero*. Some Spanish terms, such as *remuda,* were appropriated outright. More often (as with "chaps," from *chaparejos;* "lariat," from *la reata;* "cayuse," from *caballo*), they were abbreviated or twisted out of shape. On the other hand, the roundup was probably derived from small, seasonal gatherings of stock in the mountainous regions of border and Southern states. At any rate, however ingenious and self-reliant the cowboy may have been on the open range or when trailing herds, he was not essentially an innovator.

As for the rugged individualism so often associated with the frontier, the cattleman (as distinguished from the cowboy) found this a luxury that he could indulge only as long as he preserved genuine isolation. As the range filled up and cow camps crowded one another, individual roundups by each owner meant working the same herds over and over again, a practice that prevented the stock from gaining weight. The answer was the formation of stockgrowers' associations in the 1870s and 80s to establish range regulations and organize one large roundup for a group of owners over a wide area, or district. Roundup committees exercised what amounted to military control over movements of men and cattle. In this way frontier individualism gradually gave way to economic necessity; and on the Plains, where laws were often either inadequate or nonexistent, a system of cooperation and control evolved that provided substantial stability for the range-cattle industry. Cattlemen's associations were effective, too—first in discouraging Indian depredations and, more important, in keeping cattle thieves or "rustlers" in rein.

The cowboy's existence was at once freer and more circumscribed than the stockman's. He maintained a curious balance between freedom and responsibility, between self-reliance and dependence. During the trail drive and on the open range, as far as strictly personal rights were concerned, the herder was a law unto himself; and if he was short in stature or underweight, he *did* have an "equalizer" strapped around his waist or handy in his saddlebags. Men were careful not to infringe on each other's privacy or to probe into the personal history of others. Quite commonly, in instances of sudden death on the cattle frontier, the friends and associates of the dead man had no idea whom to notify, being absolutely ignorant of their comrade's past. On the other hand, working cattle was a dangerous activity and required close cooperation and mutual dependence, much of it assumed and implicit. Then too, whether riding trail or working on one of the ranches, the cowboy was an employee hired for wages; and the authority of the foreman or trail boss was not likely to be questioned or challenged. Nevertheless, a "top hand" could quit at any time, enjoying somewhat the same kind of mobility that characterized the lumberjack. When the food or the discipline or the setting ceased to please him, he could simply move on.

The day of the cattle frontier was short. It was brought to a close by a combination of circumstances including overstocking; fencing with barbed wire; wicked winters and protracted droughts; the introduction of blooded stock too expensive for small, independent operators to afford; the extension of railroads and the rise of towns; and other pressures of population and progress. In addition, the invasion of large Eastern and foreign investors not only contributed to overstocking and artificially high prices but also established terms of competition that tended to drive out the small rancher. At any rate, by the late 1880s the open range was constricting or gone, the trail drives intermittent, and the last roundup was just around the turn of the century. The cattle frontier was finished, an era was ended and a kingdom lost.

George C. Duffield

Of the two primary activities on the cattle frontier, the trail drive and the roundup, first-hand accounts of the former are hard to come by. Unlike the immigrants along the overland trails, the drovers seldom kept diaries. Thus, the classic accounts of the "long drive" up from Texas are generally reminiscences or descriptions that tend to telescope the experience and focus on a dramatic episode or two—a dry drive, perhaps, or a stampede through a stormy night. The following selection, from a trail-drive diary of 1866 by George C. Duffield (1824–1908), provides quite a different dimension by suggesting the confusion, monotony, and grinding day-by-day discouragement of a long drive. Later drives—after trailing cattle out of Texas became organized and regularized—were doubtless less chaotic and more successful.

Diary of a Cattle Drover*

March 20th. Struck out to make a trade crossed the Cherokee and stopped for the night at a Mr. Barbers contracted for 1000 Head of Beeves at 12$ p. head.

26th. started at 8 A.M for Galveston via Buffalo Bayou Brazos Colorado R R Arrived at Richmond for Dinner and to Harrisburg at 2 P M distance 80 Miles. From Alleytown to Richmond on the Brazos River the Road ran through the Most beautiful Prairie that I ever laid eyes on Pasture was abundant and the Prairie was literally covered with tens of thousands of cattle Horses and Mules. . . . From Rich to this place the country is Level good grass and thousands of cattle . . . Left at 3 for Galveston and arrived at 7 P.M Country level. put at Island City Hotel Fare 5$ gold pr day.

April 5th. Started for Sansaba with two wagons and 5 yoke Oxen and Seven hands Travelled 12 Miles and camped. Rained hard during the night

15th. Returned to Camp found 4 new hands had come to Camp Making 20 in all. It Rained hard while we were gone and the River rose. great sport and Men wet crossing.

16th. Lay round Camp had two Horse races won two bits on each went in swimming—fishing and had a gay day—all the Fish to eat we want.

21. Rode to Mr. Harrells where Boys were hearding Cattle for Him. slept by cattle pen—cattle stampeded and 150 got away.

23rd. Packed up for off Travelled six Miles to first pen and camped Rode 15 More to Mr. Montgomerys.

24th. back over the mountains to Camp at Harrels Recd 241 cattle and finished Branding Pen hearded all night.

27th. finished Branding Started for Salt Creek with 835 Beeves Landed safe.

May 1st. Travelled 10 miles to Corryell co Big Stamped lost 200 head of cattle

2ond. Spent the day hunting and found but 25 Head it has been Raining for three days these are dark days for me.

3rd. day Spent in hunting cattle found 23 hard rain and wind lots of trouble.

4th. Continued the hunt found 40 head day pleasant Sun shone once more. Heard that the other Herd has stampeded and lost over 200.

---

* From "Driving Cattle from Texas to Iowa, 1866: George C. Duffield's Diary," *Annals of Iowa* (published by the Iowa State Department of History and Archives), Third Series, XIV (April 1924), 241–262. By permission.

5. Cloudy damp Morning rode 16 Miles and back to see the other Boys found them in trouble with cattle all scattered over the country.

7th. Hunt cattle is the order of the day—found most of our Cattle and drove 12 miles and camped on a large creek in Bosque Co.

8th. All 3 heards are up and ready to travel off together for the first time travelled 6 miles rain pouring down in torrents and here we are on the banks of a creek with 10 or 12 ft water and raising crossed at 4 Oclock and crossed into the Bosque Bottom found it 20 ft deep Ran my Horse into a ditch and got my Knee badly sprained—15 Miles.

9th. Still dark and gloomy River up everything looks *Blue* to me no crossing to day cattle behaved well.

13th. Big Thunder Storm last night Stampede lost 100 Beeves hunted all day found 50 all tired. Every thing discouraging.

14th. Concluded to cross Brazos swam our cattle and Horses and built Raft and Rafted our provisions and blankets &c over Swam River with rope and then hauled wagon over lost Most of our Kitchen furniture such as camp Kittles Coffee Pots Cups Plates Canteens &c &c.

15. back at River bringing up wagon Hunting Oxen and other *lost* property. Rain poured down for one Hour. It does nothing but rain got all our *traps* together that was not lost and thought we were ready for off dark rainy night cattle all left us and in morning not one Beef to be seen.

16th. Hunt Beeves is the word—all Hands discouraged and are determined to go 200 Beeves out and nothing to eat.

18th. Everything gloomey four best hands left us got to Buchanon at noon and to Rock Creek in Johnston Co distance 14 [miles].

20th. Rain poured down for two hours Ground in a flood Creeks up —Hands leaving Gloomey times as ever I saw drove 8 miles with 5 hands (359 Head) passed the night 6 miles S.W. from Fort Worth in Parker Co.

22nd. This day has been spent in crossing the West Trinity and a hard and long to be remembered day to me we swam our cattle and Horses. I swam it 5 times upset our wagon in River and lost Many of our cooking utencils again drove 3 miles and camped.

23rd. Travelled 10 Miles over a beautiful Prairie country such as I expected to see before I came here stopped for dinner on Henrietta Creek and then on to Elisabeth Town and creek and stopped for the night—Hard rain that night and cattle behaved very bad—ran all night—was on my Horse the whole night and it raining hard.

24th. Glad to see Morning come counted and found we had lost none for the first time—feel very bad. travelled 14 miles crossed Denton Creek.

29th. Moved up to River and after many difficulties got all my Drove over but 100.

30th. worked in River all day and 50 Beeves on this side of River yet —am still in Texas.

31st. Swimming Cattle is the order We worked all day in the River and at dusk got the last Beefe over—and am now out of Texas—This day will long be remembered by men—There was one of our party Drowned to day (Mr Carr) and several narrow escapes and I among the no.

June [1]st. Stampede last night among 6 droves and a general mix up and loss of Beeves. Hunt Cattle again Men all tired and want to leave. am in the Indian country am annoyed by them believe they scare the Cattle to get pay to collect them—Spent the day in separating Beeves and Hunting —Two men and Bunch Beeves lost—Many Men in trouble. Horses *all* give out and Men refused to do anything.

2ond. Hard rain and wind Storm Beeves ran and had to be on Horse back all night Awful night. wet all night clear bright morning. Men still lost quit the Beeves and go to Hunting Men is the word—4 P.M. Found our men with Indian guide and 195 Beeves 14 Miles from camp. almost starved not having had a bite to eat for 60 hours got to camp about 12 M *Tired*

5th. Oh! what a night—Thunder Lightning and rain—we followed our Beeves *all* night as they wandered about—put them on the road at day break found 90 beeves of an other mans Herd travelled 18 Miles over the worst road I ever saw and come to Boggy Depot and crossed 4 Rivers It is well Known by that name We hauled cattle out of the Mud with oxen half the day

8th. traveled 4 miles and camped for the day to [wait] for 12 Beeves that is in another Heard. this is another gloomey evening and I tremble for the result of this night—Thunder and rain all night was in the saddle until day light am almost dead for sleep.

10th. Feel much refreshed this morning and am ready for the duties of the day crossed Elk and Canion Creeks and camped near S. Fork of Canadian.

12th. Hard Rain and Wind Big stampede and here we are among the Indians with 150 head of Cattle gone hunted all day and the Rain pouring down with but poor success Dark days are these to me Nothing but Bread and Coffee Hands all Growling and Swearing—every thing wet and cold Beeves gone rode all day and gathered all but 35 Mixed with 8 other Herds Last night 5000 Beeves stampeded at this place and a general mix up was the result

14th. Last night there was a terrible storm Rain poured in torrents *all* night and up to 12 M today our Beeves left us in the night but for *once* on the whole trip we found them *all* together near camp at day break. all the other droves as far as I can hear are scattered to the four winds our Other Herd was all gone. We are now 25 Miles from Ark River and it is Very High we are water bound by two creeks and but Beef and Flour to eat. am not Homesick but Heart sick.

18th. Nice day went to Ft Gibson got some coffee and Beefe. River very High but falling. Gloomey prospect out of Money and provisions got back to camp and found the Indians had been there and claimed and tried to take some of our cattle The Indians are making trouble stampeeding cattle here. We expect it. Cook dinner under a tree on the A K River Bank with two Ladies

19th. Good day 15 Indians come to Herd and tried to take some Beeves. Would not let them. Had a big muss One drew his Knife and I my revolver. Made them leave but fear they have gone for others they are the Seminoles.

23rd. worked all day hard in the River trying to make the Beeves swim and did not get one over. Had to go back to Prairie Sick and discouraged. Have *not* got the *Blues* but am in *Hel of a fix*. Indians held High Festival over stolen Beef all night. lost 2 Beeves mired and maby more.

25th. We hired 20 Indians to help us cross. We worked from Morning until 2 Oclock and finally got them over with a loss of 5 and camped near the *old* Mission between the Ark River and the Verdigris.

27th. Beautiful Bright Morn appearnce of warm day My Back is Blistered badly from exposure while in the River and I with two others are Suffering very much I was attacked by a Beefe in the River and had a very narrow escape from being hurt by Diving this day has been very warm travelled 10 Miles and rested.

July 9th. Still cloudy followed a man that drove off one of My Beeves and got him. Other Herd came up and went on. it camped 1½ Miles from us and that night at 9 Oclock it stampeded and ran one Mile and over. the next Morning.

18th. Spent the day trying to settle up with partners preparitory to starting around Kansas to get Home Horse stolen last night.

23rd. finished our settlement and divided our Beeves—drove 3 Miles and camped for the night Made a contract with Mr. Bumbarger of Honey Grove Fanin Co Texas and Mr. Augustus Goff of Paris Lamar Co Texas who had 300 Stock cattle—to go through together and join Herds—

29th. Sunday Excitement in camp thought our Horses and oxen were stolen but found them after many troubles we got down the Mountain and across the Creek weather very *Hot* Travelled 8 miles Lost my coat and went back after it. Osages visited our camp Are great Beggars.

30th. Drove 6 Miles and crossed Verdigris had to give the Indians a Beefe for the right of way. Indians saucy Went Bathing 5 miles in afternoon and camp.

August 1st. No trouble last night but lost a Cow have travelled about 10 Miles today and while I sit here in the grass in the Broad prairie the Rear of the Herd is coming up Weather pleasant and no flies.

3rd. All right but 2 men one down with Boils and one with Ague Travelled about 10 Miles over high Rocky Peaks and 2 creeks with fine grass.

8th. Come to Big Walnut cattle stampeded and ran by 2 farms and

the People were very angry but we made it all right was visited by Many
Men was threatened with the Law but think we are all right now (Plenty
of vegetables)

10. Separating cattle is the business of the day. Appearances of rain
(no rain).

22d. We have travelled about 20 miles today and camped on Mill Creek
I am on herd tonight it is now 11 oclock a beautiful moonlight night but
cool. I have to stand half the night the day was *cold* and some rain—There
is but little timber in all this country none only on the water courses there
are some fine springs I have a severe pane in my neck

31st. Last night was one of those old fashioned rainy stormey thundering nights just such as we used to have in Texas was up with the cattle all
night They travelled where they pleased but we stuck too them until morning. Today we crossed Big Muddy and camped on North fork of Nimehah
It commenced raining at dark and rained all night was up with cattle until
midnight and then went to bed found them all in the morning.

October 3rd. Taylor and I left the Herd and started for Home.

Joseph G. McCoy

*Joseph G. McCoy (1837–1915) is the pioneer historian of the cattle
frontier, and the only historian who was a participant in those early days.
His descriptions of the cattle trade are generally authoritative, objective,
and thorough. His judgments about Southwestern cattlemen are less objective, perhaps in part because he sustained heavy financial loss in the business.
As one of the excerpts below makes clear, McCoy saw clearly that livestock
men must act in concert to protect themselves from exorbitant freight and
storage charges at the hands of "conscienceless corporations." First published in 1874, the heyday of the cattle frontier, McCoy's book remains an
indispensable source in the history of the cattle industry.*

Cattle Trade of the West and Southwest*

Fully seventy-five thousand cattle arrived at Abilene during the summer of 1868; and at the opening of the market in the spring, fine prices were realized and snug fortunes were made by such drovers as were able to effect a sale of their herds.

It was the custom to locate herds as near the village as good water and plenty of grass could be found. As soon as the herd is located upon its summer grounds, a part of the help is discharged, as it requires less labor to hold than to travel. The camp was usually located near some living water or spring where sufficient wood for camp purposes could be easily obtained. After selecting the spot for the camp, the wagon would be drawn up; then a hole dug in the ground, in which to build a fire of limbs of trees or driftwood gathered to the spot; and a permanent camp instituted by unloading the contents of the wagon upon the ground. And such a motley lot of assets as come out of one of those camp carts would astonish one and beggar minute description: a lot of saddles and horse blankets, a camp kettle, coffee pot, bread pan, battered tin cups, a greasy mess chest, dirty, soiled blankets, an ox yoke, a log chain, spurs and quirts, a coffee mill, a broken-helved ax, bridles, picket ropes, and last, but not least, a side or two of fat, mastfed bacon; to which add divers pieces of rawhide in various stages of dryness. A score of other articles not to be thought of will come out of that exhaustless camp cart. But one naturally inquires what use would a drover have for a rawhide, dry or fresh? Uses infinite; nothing breaks about a drover's outfit that he cannot mend with strips or thongs of rawhide. He mends his bridle or saddle or picket rope, or sews his ripping pants or shirt, or lashes a broken wagon tongue, or binds on a loose tire with rawhide. In short, a rawhide is a concentrated and combined carpenter and blacksmith shop, not to say saddler's and tailor's shop, to the drover. Indeed, it is said that what a Texan cannot make or mend with a rawhide is not worth having or is irretrievably broken into undistinguishable fragments. . . .

The life of the cowboy in camp is routine and dull. His food is largely of the regulation order, but a feast of vegetables he wants and must have, or scurvy would ensue. Onions and potatoes are his favorites, but any kind of vegetables will disappear in haste when put within his reach. In camp,

---

* From Joseph G. McCoy, *Historic Sketches of the Cattle Trade of the West and Southwest* (Kansas City, Mo.: Ramsey, Millett and Hudson, 1874), pp. 131–342 *passim.*

on the trail, on the ranch in Texas, with their countless thousands of cattle, milk and butter are almost unknown; not even milk or cream for the coffee is had. Pure shiftlessness and the lack of energy are the only reasons for this privation, and to the same reasons can be assigned much of the privations and hardships incident to ranching. It would cost but little effort or expense to add a hundred comforts, not to say luxuries, to the life of a drover and his cowboys. They sleep on the ground, with a pair of blankets for bed and cover. No tent is used, scarcely any cooking utensils, and such a thing as a camp cook stove is unknown. The warm water of the branch or the standing pool is drunk; often it is yellow with alkali and other poisons. No wonder the cowboy gets sallow and unhealthy, and deteriorates in manhood until often he becomes capable of any contemptible thing; no wonder he should become half civilized only, and take to whiskey with a love excelled scarcely by the barbarous Indian.

When the herd is sold and delivered to the purchaser, a day of rejoicing to the cowboy has come, for then he can go free and have a jolly time; and it is a jolly time they have. Straightway after settling with their employers, the barber shop is visited, and three to six months' growth of hair is shorn off, their long-grown sunburnt beard "set" in due shape and properly blacked. Next a clothing store of the Israelitish style is "gone through" and the cowboy emerges a new man in outward appearance, everything being new, not excepting the hat, and boots with star decorations about the tops; also a new ——, well, in short, everything new. Then for fun and frolic! The barroom, the theater, the gambling room, the bawdy house, the dance house, each and all come in for their full share of attention. In any of these places an affront or a slight, real or imaginary, is cause sufficient for him to unlimber one or more "mountain howitzers" invariably found strapped to his person, and proceed to deal out death in unbroken doses to such as may be in range of his pistols, whether real friends or enemies, no matter; his anger and bad whiskey urge him on to deeds of blood and death.

The cowboy enters the dance with a peculiar zest, not stopping to divest himself of his sombrero, spurs, or pistols; but just as he dismounts off of his cow pony, so he goes into the dance. A more odd, not to say comical, sight is not often seen than the dancing cowboy. With the front of his sombrero lifted at an angle of fully forty-five degrees, his huge spurs jingling at every step or motion, his revolvers flapping up and down like a retreating sheep's tail, his eyes lit up with excitement, liquor, and lust, he plunges in and "hoes it down" at a terrible rate in the most approved yet awkward country style, often swinging his partner clear off of the floor for an entire circle, then "balance all," with an occasional demoniacal yell near akin to the war whoop of the savage Indian. All this he does, entirely oblivious to the whole world and the balance of mankind. After dancing furiously, the entire "set" is called to "waltz to the bar," where the boy is required to treat his partner and, of course, himself also; which he does not hesitate to do time and again, although it costs him fifty cents each time. Yet if it cost ten times that amount he would not hesitate; but the more he dances and drinks, the less common sense he will have, and the more completely his animal passions will control him. Such is the manner in which the cowboy spends his hard-earned dollars. And such is the entertainment that many young men—from the North and the South, of superior parentage and youthful advantages in life—give themselves up to; and often more, their lives are made to pay the forfeit of their sinful foolishness.

After a few days of frolic and debauchery the cowboy is ready, in company with his comrades, to start back to Texas, often not having one dollar left of his summer's wages. To this rather hard-drawn picture of the cowboy there are many creditable exceptions—young men who respect themselves and save their money, and are worthy young gentlemen. But it is idle to deny the fact that the wild, reckless conduct of the cowboys while drunk, in connection with that of the worthless northern renegades, [has] brought the personnel of the Texan cattle trade into great disrepute, and filled many graves with victims—bad men and good men—at Abilene, Newton, Wichita, and Ellsworth. But by far the larger portion of those killed are of that class that can be spared without detriment to the good morals and respectability of humanity It often occurs when the cowboys fail to get up a mêlée and kill each other by the half dozen, that the keepers of those "hell's half acres" find some pretext arising from business jealousies or other causes, to suddenly become belligerent, and stop not to declare war but begin hostilities at once. It is generally effective work they do with their revolvers and shotguns, for they are the most desperate men on earth. Either some of the principals or their subordinates are generally "done for" in a thorough manner, or wounded so as to be miserable cripples for life. On such occasions there are few tears shed, or even inquiries made, by the respectable people, but an expression of sorrow is common that active hostilities did not continue until every rough was stone dead. . . .

In concluding the numerous sketches of Texan ranchmen and drovers, we offer a few reflections on the general character of southwestern cattlemen. In doing so we are not animated by other motives than a desire to convey a correct impression of that numerous class as a whole—reflections and impressions based upon close observation and a varied experience of seven or eight years spent in business contact and relation with them. They are, as a class, not public spirited in matters pertaining to the general good, but may justly be called selfish, or at least indifferent to the public welfare. They are prodigal to a fault with their money when opportunity offers to gratify their appetites or passions, but it is extremely difficult to induce them to expend even a small sum in forwarding a project or enterprise that has other than a purely selfish end in view. In general they entertain strong suspicions of northern men and do not have the profoundest confidence in each other. They are disposed to measure every man's action and prompting motives by the rule of selfishness, and they are slow indeed to believe that other than purely selfish motives could or ever do prompt a man to do an act or develop an enterprise. If anything happens [to] a man, especially a northern man, so that he cannot do or perform all that they expect or require of him, no explanation or reasons are sufficient to dispel the deep and instant conviction formed in their breasts that he is deliberately trying to swindle them, and they can suddenly see a thousand evidences of his villainy—in short, instantly vote such an one a double-dyed villain. Their reputation is widespread for honorably abiding [by] their verbal contracts, for the very nature of their business and the circumstances under which it is conducted, renders an honorable course imperative; and, as a rule, where agreements or contracts are put into writing, they will stand to them unflinchingly, no matter how great the sacrifice. But when the contract or understanding is verbal only and not of the most definite nature, their consciences are fully as pliant as are those of any other section. A promise made as to some future transaction is kept or broken as their future interests may dictate. Nor are they any more brave, or more fond of facing death's cold pellets on an equal footing with their adversaries, than are men in general from other sections of the country. True, their habits of life and the necessities and exposed nature of their business renders the daily use and carrying of firearms imperative; hence their habitual use of the pistol renders them fair to good shots. Besides, the habit of settling their disputes, often very trifling, with the revolver (which, with some, is considered the first and only legitimate law, argument, or reason) has given to the denizens of the Lone Star State a name and reputation abroad for universal, genuine bravery, not warranted by the facts. They are just as brave, but no more so, than are the men of other sections.

They are almost invariably convivial in habit, preferring as a rule the strongest liquors, and take them "straight." Nevertheless, it is rare indeed that a drover is a confirmed drunkard or sot. They think, act, and conduct their business in an independent, self-reliant manner, seldom seeking or following the advice of others. Each man seems to feel himself an independent sovereign and as such capable of conducting his affairs in his own way, subject to nobody or nothing save the wishes, tastes, and necessities of himself. They are, in common with all stockmen, universal lovers of the ladies, and as a class present a discouraging field for a Shaker missionary. Indeed, they are specially noteworthy as being obedient to the first commandment. Sanguine and speculative in temperament, impulsively generous in free sentiment, warm and cordial in their friendships, hot and hasty in anger, with a strong innate sense of right and wrong, with a keen sense for the ridiculous and a general intention to do that that is right and honorable in their dealings, they are, as would naturally be supposed when the manner of their life is considered, a hardy, self-reliant, free, and independent class, acknowledging no superior or master in the wide universe.

It is true that live stock men are, or have been heretofore, entirely unorganized, and as a result thereof they are not correctly informed as to the extent or magnitude of the business in which they are engaged. Nor do the stockmen of one state, as a class or as a rule, have any definite knowledge of the number engaged in like business in any other state or territory. This might be truthfully said of most stockmen as to their adjoining counties and often townships. Nor do they know or have any good means of informing themselves as to the number of live stock—hogs, cattle, or sheep—that are being prepared for market, or that are likely to be put upon the market at any given time in the future. And when they are prepared or ready to market their stock, if the nearest and most convenient means of transportation chooses to ask them exorbitant rates of freight, they submit, and although they will complain piteously about the extortion, they do nothing to prevent its repetition. Indeed, it has often been said that every stockman was an independent sovereignty in and of himself, and preferred to act for himself alone, free and independently, even if he does pay dearly for the privilege of so doing. It is idle to question the proposition that if stockmen would organize, they could have at least a part of the say in fixing rates of freight, yard charges, feed charges, commissions, and other incidental expenses to which the business is inevitably subjected. It would be next to impossible for railroads to effect and maintain combinations which the stockmen could not break. Corporations, by combination, would not successfully put up and maintain the price of freight fully thirty-three per cent over rates charged previous years, and that, too, when live stock is selling at prices ranging from twenty-five to fifty per cent below those realized in former years. No such outrage could or would be attempted successfully, or tolerated, if live stock men would act in concert to obtain that, that they desire and of a right ought to have. Neither could stockyard companies insolently mistreat and abuse live stock, or charge exorbitant and outrageous prices for yardage, hay, corn, or for other services rendered; they would not dare to do it. But as matters now stand, the live stock men, entirely unorganized, each one by himself and for himself only, are subjected to the arbitrary restrictions and extortionate charges of conscienceless corporations. A stockman or shipper sees himself wronged, and his stock abused, neglected, and otherwise mistreated, but feels himself powerless as to remedies, and usually does nothing but mutter curses, not loud, but deep; then pass along, only to have the same outrages repeated as often as he attempts to go to market.

The only remedy suggested to the mind of the author for these and many other abuses and grievances is in organization. Then a potent protest that could and would be enforced and respected would issue against offending parties, and they be compelled to do right and act fairly with their patrons; or in the event of their persisting in oppressive practices, such retributive justice could be meted out to them as would compel a change in their conduct and manner of doing business, or the business would be taken entirely from them. Again, if the stockmen were properly associated together, a statistical bureau would be established for gathering and disseminating such information as would enable the members of the association to form correct estimates as to the amount of stock in every section of the country, and the probable number that would be marketed each month of the year. It is not difficult for the practical cattleman to see wherein such information would be of inestimable value in forming business calculations, and a correct judgment of the probable future status of the business and markets. Besides, a great aid to both buyers and sellers would be thus created, and a general business register of the wants or desires of live stock men would exist, to which any member might refer at his pleasure; and thus save much time and money which would otherwise be spent in rambling over the country seeking, without knowing just where to look, for that which he desired. The advantages of organization or association are so numerous and so great that it is time spent idly to urge them upon the attention of thinking, discerning live stock men. But if they continue to bear without effort to remedy, the many evils, abuses, and extortions which have been heaped upon them in the past, then are they degenerate dunghills and unfit to bear the proud distinction to which as a class they aspire.

But we hope and apprehend the day is not distant when there will be found organizations of live stock men in every state and in many counties, all of which may be made auxiliary to a general or national association. When that day does come, live stock men will be subjected to fewer losses, and be able to conduct their business in an intelligent, systematic manner, just as is every other industry or vocation in the United States. It is in no sense for the lack of intelligence among stockmen that effectual organization has not before been effected, but from a habit of doing and acting in an independent, individual capacity. The benefits to accrue from association are not thought of or realized; but the day now is, when their numbers and their interest alike, behoove them to organize for their own mutual benefit, information, and strength. . . .

. . . let no one delude himself with the idea that cattle ranching— either breeding and rearing, or only wintering and fatting, or handling live stock in any manner peculiar to the West—is a business wherein the poetic or sentimental aspects of life or labor abound to any alarming extent. Indeed, it is a life and business which, aside from its phase of independent freedom, has few other aspects than those of diligent labor, watchfulness, care, and risk, combined with great self-denial, privations, and lonely hardships. He must be the servant of his herds, to attend to and provide for their every want. When the weather is stormiest, and a comfortable seat in a snug corner by a warm fire would be most congenial to feelings, and perchance health also, then is the very time the would-be successful ranchman must be out with his herds and to them give double ordinary attention with extra feed and shelter. Anyone can attend live stock in fine weather, when the sun shines out mild and warm, and the stock can and will feed and care for itself. But when the cold, driving storm sweeps across the plains, piercing the animal world by its chilling blasts, then is when it requires the "man to the manor born," or one adapted by nature and stimulated by a love of the vocation. A man must have a natural adaptation and taste for the business and the life, to succeed. It is not a vocation wherein starched shirts, fashionable-cut broadcloth, polished boots, faultless set mustache, or latest style of hairdressing will flourish or scarce be in order for a single day. But long-legged stogy boots, huge spurs, strong corduroy pants, a thick, colored, woolen shirt, a leather belt around the waist, no suspenders, a sombrero or other broadbrimmed hat, a soldier overcoat, and a pair of heavy blankets constitute the make-up, the necessary habiliments, the usual personal outfit of the practical ranchman or cowboy. And the daily fare almost of necessity is meager and of the commonest varieties of food, cooked in the simplest style of the art usually by one of the men who knows but little about culinary matters, and is not overanxious to learn more than he already knows, be that ever so little. However, death from dyspepsia is never feared by the ranchman, for his daily labor and exercise give him a sharp appetite and a vigorous digestion.

If a young, energetic man, one who desires to make a name and a fortune for himself, and to be one among the substantial men of the new and great West, can make up his mind to endure the privations, hardships, and lonely life of labor and exposure incident to a ranchman's life, there are great opportunities offered and to be had for the taking in the broad, free West. Lands are cheap, the climate mild, the natural advantages good and great. The stock with which to begin is abundant and at reasonable prices. The process and means of improvement in blood, as well as in numbers, are at hand. The plainest and best of results invariably attend every effort made in crossing Durham bulls with Texan heifers and cows. An improved animal is obtained of nearly or quite double the value of the Texan. As a paying, reliable, certain occupation, there is none that is more so than stock ranching. But it requires time, labor, patience, energy, grit, and perseverance to make the beginning, and to carry it through to any profitable fruition.

Theodore Roosevelt

*Easterner of Easterners by heritage, upbringing, and education,
Theodore Roosevelt (1858–1919) nevertheless was deeply influenced by
the American West. The pull of far frontiers was reflected politically in
the Roosevelt administration's record in conservation; physically in his
advocacy of "the strenuous life"; and intellectually in much of his own
writing, including his six-volume* Winning of the West *and the book on
ranch life from which the following description of cattlemen and the
roundup is taken. Although Roosevelt saw both cowboy and stockman
through romantic eyes, he was able, by virtue of participation on his own
ranch in Dakota Territory in the 1880s, to describe the everyday activities
of his heroes graphically and realistically.*

The Roundup*

Cattle-ranching can only be carried on in its present form while the
population is scanty; and so in stock-raising regions, pure and simple,
there are usually few towns, and these are almost always at the shipping
points for cattle. . . .

A true "cow town" is worth seeing,—such a one as Miles City, for
instance, especially at the time of the annual meeting of the great Montana
Stock-raisers' Association. Then the whole place is full to overflowing,
the importance of the meeting and the fun of the attendant frolics, especially the horse-races, drawing from the surrounding ranch country
many hundreds of men of every degree, from the rich stock-owner worth
his millions to the ordinary cowboy who works for forty dollars a month.
It would be impossible to imagine a more typically American assemblage,
for although there are always a certain number of foreigners, usually
English, Irish, or German, yet they have become completely Americanized;
and on the whole it would be difficult to gather a finer body of men, in spite
of their numerous shortcomings. The ranch-owners differ more from each
other than do the cowboys; and the former certainly compare very favorably with similar classes of capitalists in the East. Anything more foolish

---

* From Theodore Roosevelt, *Ranch Life and the Hunting Trail* (New York:
The Century Company, 1920), pp. 7–71 *passim*. This account was first published in
1888.

than the demagogic outcry against "cattle kings" it would be difficult to imagine. Indeed, there are very few businesses so absolutely legitimate as stock-raising and so beneficial to the nation at large; and a successful stock-grower must not only be shrewd, thrifty, patient, and enterprising, but he must also possess qualities of personal bravery, hardihood, and self-reliance to a degree not demanded in the least by any mercantile occupation in a community long settled. Stockmen are in the West the pioneers of civilization, and their daring and adventurousness make the after settlement of the region possible. The whole country owes them a great debt.

The stock-growers of Montana, of the western part of Dakota, and even of portions of extreme northern Wyoming,—that is, of all the grazing lands lying in the basin of the Upper Missouri,—have united, and formed themselves into the great Montana Stock-growers' Association. Among the countless benefits they have derived from this course, not the least has been the way in which the various round-ups work in with and supplement one another. At the spring meeting of the association, the entire territory mentioned above, including perhaps a hundred thousand square miles, is mapped out into round-up districts, which generally are changed but slightly from year to year, and the times and places for the round-ups to begin refixed so that those of adjacent districts may be run with a view to the best interests of all. . . .

The captain or foreman of the round-up, upon whom very much of its efficiency and success depends, is chosen beforehand. He is, of course, an expert cowman, thoroughly acquainted with the country; and he must also be able to command and to keep control of the wild rough-riders he has under him—a feat needing both tact and firmness.

At the appointed day all meet at the place from which the round-up is to start. Each ranch, of course, has most work to be done in its own round-up district, but it is also necessary to have representatives in all those surrounding it. A large outfit may employ a dozen cowboys, or over, in the home district, and yet have nearly as many more representing its interest in the various ones adjoining. Smaller outfits generally club together to run a wagon and send outside representatives, or else go along with their stronger neighbors, they paying part of the expenses. A large outfit, with a herd of twenty thousand cattle or more, can, if necessary, run a round-up entirely by itself, and is able to act independently of outside help; it is therefore at a great advantage compared with those that can take no step effectively without their neighbors' consent and assistance.

If the starting-point is some distance off, it may be necessary to leave home three or four days in advance. Before this we have got everything in readiness; have overhauled the wagons, shod any horse whose forefeet are tender,—as a rule, all our ponies go barefooted,—and left things in order at the ranch. Our outfit may be taken as a sample of every one else's. We have a stout four-horse wagon to carry the bedding and the food; in its rear a mess-chest is rigged to hold the knives, forks, cans, etc. All our four team-horses are strong, willing animals, though of no great size, being orginally just "broncos," or unbroken native horses, like the others. The teamster is also cook: a man who is a really first-rate hand at both driving and cooking—and our present teamster is both—can always command his price. Besides our own men, some cowboys from neighboring ranches and two or three representatives from other round-up districts are always along, and we generally have at least a dozen "riders," as they are termed,—that is, cowboys, or "cowpunchers," who do the actual cattle-work,—with the wagon. Each of these has a string of eight or ten ponies; and to take charge of the saddle-band, thus consisting of a hundred odd head, there are two herders, always known as "horse-wranglers"—one for the day and one for the night.

At the meeting-place there is usually a delay of a day or two to let every one come in; and the plain on which the encampment is made becomes a scene of great bustle and turmoil. The heavy four-horse wagons jolt in from different quarters, the horse-wranglers rushing madly to and fro in the endeavor to keep the different saddle-bands from mingling, while the "riders," or cowboys, with each wagon jog along in a body. The representatives from outside districts ride in singly or by twos and threes, every man driving before him his own horses, one of them loaded with his bedding. Each wagon wheels out of the way into some camping-place not too near the others, the bedding is tossed out on the ground, and then every one is left to do what he wishes, while the different wagon bosses, or foremen, seek out the captain of the round-up to learn what his plans are.

There is a good deal of rough but effective discipline and method in the way in which a round-up is carried on. The captain of the whole has as lieutenants the various wagon foremen and in making demands for men to do some special service he will usually merely designate some foreman to take charge of the work and let him parcel it out among his men to suit himself. The captain of the round-up or the foreman of a wagon may himself be a ranchman; if such is not the case, and the ranchman nevertheless comes along, he works and fares precisely as do the other cowboys.

There is no eight-hour law in cowboy land: during round-up time we often count ourselves lucky if we get off with much less than sixteen hours; but the work is done in the saddle, and the men are spurred on all the time by the desire to outdo one another in feats of daring and skillful horsemanship. There is very little quarreling or fighting; and though the fun often takes the form of rather rough horse-play, yet the practice of carrying dangerous weapons makes cowboys show far more rough courtesy to each other and far less rudeness to strangers than is the case among, for instance, Eastern miners, or even lumbermen. When a quarrel may very probably result fatally, a man thinks twice before going into it.

The method of work is simple. The mess-wagons and loose horses, after breaking camp in the morning, move on in a straight line for some few miles, going into camp again before midday; and the day herd, consisting of all the cattle that have been found far off their range, and which are to be brought back there, and of any others that it is necessary to gather, follows on afterwards. Meanwhile the cowboys scatter out and drive in all the cattle from the country round about, going perhaps ten or fifteen miles back from the line of march, and meeting at the place where camp has already been pitched. The wagons always keep some little distance from one another, and the saddle-bands do the same, so that the horses may not get mixed.

The speed and thoroughness with which a country can be worked depends, of course, very largely upon the number of riders. Ours is probably about an average round-up as regards size. The last spring I was out, there were half a dozen wagons along; the saddle-bands numbered about a hundred each; and the morning we started, sixty men in the saddle splashed across the shallow ford of the river that divided the plain where we had camped from the valley of the long winding creek up which we were first to work.

In the morning the cook is preparing breakfast long before the first glimmer of dawn. As soon as it is ready, probably about 3 o'clock, he utters a long-drawn shout, and all the sleepers feel it is time to be up on the instant, for they know there can be no such thing as delay on the round-up, under penalty of being set afoot. . . . The meal is not an elaborate one; nevertheless a man will have to hurry if he wishes to eat it before hearing the foreman sing out, "Come, boys, catch your horses"; when he must drop everything and run out to the wagon with his lariat. When all are saddled, many of the horses bucking and dancing about, the riders from the different wagons all assemble at the one where the captain is sitting, already mounted. He waits a very short time—for laggards receive but scant mercy—before announcing the proposed camping-place and parceling out the work among those present. If, as is usually the case, the line of march is along a river or creek, he appoints some man to take a dozen others and drive down (or up) it ahead of the day herd, so that the latter will not have to travel through other cattle; the day herd itself being driven and guarded by a dozen men detached for that purpose. The rest of the riders are divided into two bands, placed under men who know the country, and start out, one on each side, to bring in every head for fifteen miles back. The captain then himself rides down to the new camping-place, so as to be there as soon as any cattle are brought in.

Meanwhile the two bands, a score of riders in each, separate and make their way in opposite directions. The leader of each tries to get such a "scatter" on his men that they will cover completely all the land gone over. This morning work is called circle riding, and is peculiarly hard in the Bad Lands on account of the remarkably broken, rugged nature of the country. The men come in on lines that tend to a common center— as if the sticks of a fan were curved. As the band goes out, the leader from time to time detaches one or two men to ride down through certain sections of the country, making the shorter, or what are called inside, circles, while he keeps on; and finally, retaining as companions the two or three whose horses are toughest, makes the longest or outside circle himself, going clear back to the divide, or whatever the point may be that marks the limit of the round-up work, and then turning and working straight to the meeting-place. Each man, of course, brings in every head of cattle he can see.

When the men on the outside circle have reached the bound set them, —whether it is a low divide, a group of jagged hills, the edge of the rolling, limitless prairie, or the long, waste reaches of alkali and sage brush, —they turn their horses' heads and begin to work down the branches of the creeks, one or two riding down the bottom, while the others keep off to the right and the left, a little ahead and fairly high up on the side hills, so as to command as much of a view as possible. . . . All the cattle are carried on ahead down the creek; and it is curious to watch the different behavior of the different breeds. A cowboy riding off to one side of the creek, and seeing a number of long-horned Texans grazing in the branches of a set of coulees, has merely to ride across the upper ends of these, uttering the drawn-out "ei-koh-h-h," so familiar to the cattle-men, and the long-horns will stop grazing, stare fixedly at him, and then, wheeling, strike off down the coulees at a trot, tails in air, to be carried along by the center riders when they reach the main creek into which the coulees lead. . . . Every little bunch of stock is thus collected, and all are driven along together. At the place where some large fork joins the main creek another band may be met, driven by some of the men who have left earlier in the day to take one of the shorter circles; and thus, before coming down to the bottom where the wagons are camped and where the actual "round-up" itself is to take place, this one herd may include a couple of thousand head; or, on the other hand, the longest ride may not result in the finding of a dozen animals. As soon as the riders are in, they disperse to their respective wagons to get dinner and change horses, leaving the cattle to be held by one or two of their number. If only a small number of cattle have been gathered, they will all be run into one herd; if there are many of them, however, the different herds will be held separate.

As soon as, or even before, the last circle riders have come in and have snatched a few hasty mouthfuls to serve as their mid-day meal, we begin to work the herd—or herds, if the one herd would be of too unwieldy size. The animals are held in a compact bunch, most of the riders forming a ring outside, while a couple from each ranch successively look the herds through and cut out those marked with their own brand. It is difficult, in such a mass of moving beasts,—for they do not stay still, but keep weaving in and out among each other,—to find all of one's own animals: a man must have natural gifts, as well as great experience, before he becomes a good brand-reader and is able really to "clean up a herd"— that is, be sure he has left nothing of his own in it.

All this time the men holding the herd have their hands full, for some animal is continually trying to break out, when the nearest man flies at it at once and after a smart chase brings it back to its fellows. As soon as all the cows, calves, and whatever else is being gathered have been cut out, the rest are driven clear off the ground and turned loose, being headed in the direction contrary to that in which we travel the following day. Then the riders surround the next herd, the men holding cuts move them up near it, and the work is begun anew.

As soon as all the brands of cattle are worked, and the animals that are to be driven along have been put in the day herd, attention is turned to the cows and calves, which are already gathered in different bands, consisting each of all the cows of a certain brand and all the calves that are following them. If there is a corral, each band is in turn driven into it; if there is none, a ring of riders does duty in its place. A fire is built, the irons heated, and a dozen men dismount to, as it is called, "wrestle" the calves. The best two ropers go in on their horses to catch the latter; one man keeps tally, a couple put on the brands, and the others seize, throw, and hold the little unfortunates.

Every morning certain riders are detached to drive and to guard the day herd, which is most monotonous work, the men being on from 4 in the morning till 8 in the evening, the only rest coming at dinner-time, when they change horses.

From 8 in the evening till 4 in the morning the day herd becomes a night herd. Each wagon in succession undertakes to guard it for a night, dividing the time into watches of two hours apiece, a couple of riders taking each watch. This is generally chilly and tedious; but at times it is accompanied by intense excitement and danger, when the cattle become stampeded, whether by storm or otherwise. The first and the last watches are those chosen by preference; the others are disagreeable, the men having to turn out cold and sleepy, in the pitchy darkness, the two hours of chilly wakefulness completely breaking the night's rest.

But though there is much work and hardship, rough fare, monotony, and exposure connected with the round-up, yet there are few men who do not look forward to it and back to it with pleasure. The only fault to be found is that the hours of work are so long that one does not usually have enough time to sleep. The food, if rough, is good: beef, bread, pork, beans, coffee or tea, always canned tomatoes, and often rice, canned corn, or sauce made from dried apples. The men are good-humored, bold, and thoroughly interested in their business, continually vying with one another in the effort to see which can do the work best. It is superbly health-giving, and is full of excitement and adventure, calling for the exhibition of pluck, self-reliance, hardihood, and dashing horsemanship; and of all forms of physical labor the easiest and pleasantest is to sit in the saddle.

"Teddy Blue" Abbott

There has been some pungent writing about horses, men, and cattle. One thinks immediately of the two Charlies—Siringo and Russell—or of Will James or Ross Santee. Of the same high order are the reminiscences of E. C. ("Teddy Blue") Abbott (1860–1939), as set down with apparent fidelity by Helena Huntington Smith. E. C. Abbott, born in Norfolk, England, came with his father to Nebraska in 1871. He spent about seven years tending his father's cattle around Lincoln, and grew up with the men who came from Texas with them. In 1883 Abbott came up the trail from Texas to Montana, where he remained as a cattleman for the last fifty years of his life. Helena Huntington Smith met "Teddy Blue" in 1937 while she was in Montana gathering materials for a Western novel. As she came to know the rancher, she discovered that he had a partly finished book of his own; and, supplementing his manuscript with the results of thorough and frequent interviews, she produced a convincing collaboration. In the following excerpts, Abbott captures effectively the experience of the trail herds and tends to sustain the ambivalent impression of the cowboy as at once royally independent and fiercely loyal to his outfit. To appreciate the full flavor of "Teddy Blue's" forthrightness, one must read the book in its entirety.

Recollections of a Cowpuncher*

When my father got over here in '71 the Texas trail had only been in existence three or four years, but it was a big business already, and a steady stream of herds was moving north. . . . By 1880 Texas cattle had got as far north as Miles City, Montana, and Texas cowboys with them. The name cowpuncher came in about this time, when they got to shipping a lot of cattle on the railroad. Men would go along the train with a prod pole and punch up cattle that got down in the cars, and that was how it began. It caught on, and we were all cowpunchers on the northern range, till the close of range work. . . .

Those first trail outfits in the seventies were sure tough. It was a new business and had to develop. Work oxen were used instead of horses to pull the wagon, and if one played out, they could rope a steer and yoke him up. They had very little grub and they usually run out of that and lived on straight beef; they had only three or four horses to the man, mostly with sore backs, because the old time saddle eat both ways, the horse's back and the cowboy's pistol pocket; they had no tents, no tarps, and damn few slickers. They never kicked, because those boys was raised under just the same conditions as there was on the trail—corn meal and bacon for grub, dirt floors in the houses, and no luxuries. In the early days in Texas, in the sixties, when they gathered their cattle, they used to pack what they needed on a horse and go out for weeks, on a cow-hunt, they called it then. That was before the name roundup was invented, and before they had anything so civilized as mess wagons. And as I say, that is the way those first trail hands were raised. Take her as she comes and like it. They used to brag that they could go any place a cow could and stand anything a horse could. It was their life.

Most of all them were Southerners, and they were a wild, reckless bunch. For dress they wore wide-brimmed beaver hats, black or brown with a low crown, fancy shirts, high-heeled boots, and sometimes a vest. Their clothes and saddles were all homemade. Most of them had an army coat with cape which was slicker and blanket too. Lay on your saddle blanket and cover up with a coat was about the only bed used on the Texas trail at first. A few had a big buffalo robe to roll up in, but if they ever got good and wet, you never had time to dry them, so they were not popular. All had a pair of bullhide chaps, or leggins they called them then. They

---

* From E. C. ("Teddy Blue") Abbott and Helena Huntington Smith, *We Pointed Them North: Recollections of a Cowpuncher* (Norman: University of Oklahoma Press, 1955), pp. 5–213 *passim*. Copyright 1955 University of Oklahoma Press. Reprinted by permission.

were good in the brush and wet weather, but in fine weather were left in the wagon.

As the business grew, great changes took place in their style of dress, but their boots and cigarettes have lasted nearly the same for more than sixty years. In place of the low-crowned hat of the seventies we had a high-crowned white Stetson hat, fancy shirts with pockets, and striped or checkered California pants made in Oregon City, the best pants ever made to ride in. Slickers came in too. In winter we had nice cloth overcoats with beaver collars and cuffs. The old twelve-inch-barrel Colt pistol was cut down to a six- and seven-and-a-half-inch barrel, with black rubber, ivory, or pearl handle. The old big roweled spurs with bells give place to hand-forged silver inlaid spurs with droop shanks and small rowels, and with that you had the cowpuncher of the eighties when he was in his glory.

In person the cowboys were mostly medium-sized men, as a heavy man was hard on horses, quick and wiry, and as a rule very good-natured; in fact it did not pay to be anything else. In character their like never was or will be again. They were intensely loyal to the outfit they were working for and would fight to the death for it. They would follow their wagon boss through hell and never complain. I have seen them ride into camp after two days and nights on herd, lay down on their saddle blankets in the rain and sleep like dead men, then get up laughing and joking about some good time they had had in Ogallala or Dodge City. Living that kind of a life, they were bound to be wild and brave. In fact there was only two things the old-time cowpuncher was afraid of, a decent woman and being set afoot.

In the eighties, conditions on the trail were a whole lot better than they were in the seventies. Someone had invented mess boxes to set up in the hind end of the wagon; they had four-horse teams to pull it, lots of grub, and from six to eight horses for each man to ride; and the saddles had improved. When I was on the trail in '83, we didn't have hardly a sore-backed horse all the way up to Montana, and the trail bosses had got the handling of a herd down to a science.

After some experience in the business, they found that about 2,000 head on an average was the best number in a herd. After you crossed Red River and got out on the open plains, it was sure a pretty sight to see them strung out for almost a mile, the sun flashing on their horns. At noon you would see the men throw them off the trail, and half the crew would go to dinner while the other half would graze them onto water. No orders were given; every man knew his place and what to do. The left point, right swing, left flank, and right drag would go in to dinner together. The first men off would eat in a hurry, catch up fresh horses, and go out on a lope to the herd. It sure looks good, when you are on herd and hungry, to see the relief come out on a lope.

Eleven men made the average crew with a trail herd. The two men in the lead were called the point men, and then as the herd strung out there would be two men behind them on the swing, two on the flank, and the two drag drivers in the rear. With the cook and horse wrangler and boss, that made eleven. The poorest men always worked with the drags, because a good hand wouldn't stand for it. I have seen them come off herd with the dust half an inch deep on their hats and thick as fur in their eyebrows and mustaches, and if they shook their head or you tapped their cheek, it would fall off them in showers. That dust was the reason a good man wouldn't work back there, and if they hired out to a trail outfit and were put with the drags, they would go to the boss and ask for their time. But the rest of them were pretty nearly as bad off when they were on the side away from the wind. They would go to the water barrel at the end of the day and rinse their mouths and cough and spit and bring up that black stuff out of their throats. But you couldn't get it up out of your lungs.

Going into a new country, the trail boss had to ride his tail off hunting for water. But he would come back to the wagon at night. Lots of times he would ride up on a little knoll and signal to the point—water this way, or water that way. And that is when you will see some trail work, when they are going to turn the herd. If they're going to turn to the right the man on the right point will drop back, and the man on left point will go ahead and start pushing them over, and the men behind can tell from their movements what they want to do. By watching and cutting the curve, you can save the drags two or three hundred yards. It's the drags you have to protect—they are the weak and sore-footed cattle—and that's what counts in the management of a herd.

There is quite an art, too, to watering a herd. You bring them up and spread them out along the bank, with the lead cattle headed downstream. The leads get there first, and of course they drink clear water, and as the drags keep coming in they get clear water, too, because they are upstream.

Oh, those trail bosses know their business, and their business was to get their herd through in good shape; that was all they thought about. . . .

But when you add it all up, I believe the worst hardship we had on the trail was loss of sleep. There was never enough sleep. Our day wouldn't end till about nine o'clock, when we grazed the herd onto the bed ground. And after that every man in the outfit except the boss and horse wrangler and cook would have to stand two hours' night guard. Suppose my guard was twelve to two. I would stake my night horse, unroll my bed, pull off my boots, and crawl in at nine, get about three hours' sleep, and then ride two hours. Then I would come off guard and get to sleep another hour and a half, till the cooked yelled, "Roll out," at half past three. So I would get maybe five hours' sleep when the weather was nice and everything smooth and pretty, with cowboys singing under the stars. If it wasn't so nice, you'd be lucky to sleep an hour. But the wagon rolled on in the morning just the same. . . .

[*E. C. "Teddy Blue" Abbott hires out as hand for the A. J. Davis, S. T. Hauser, and Granville Stuart outfit. Later Abbott married one of Stuart's daughters.*] Everything that grub line rider had told us about the D H S sounded good to me, and I found out he hadn't exaggerated. It was a wonderful outfit, very well run, and the best I ever knew for a cowboy to work for. Granville Stuart fed well, never asked his men to work too hard, took a great interest in their welfare, and was always willing to help them when they were in trouble.

But he did more than that for them. Of all the big stockmen I ever knew or heard about, he was the fairest and the best friend to the cowpunchers. A great many of the big men in the cattle business were opposed to letting the cowboys own cattle, because they thought if a man was allowed to have his own little bunch, with his own brand on them, it would encourage him in branding mavericks and other forms of stealing.

Granville Stuart never agreed with this. In '85 or '86, at the stock association meeting at Miles City, he made quite a speech, in which he tried very hard to get all the members to allow their cowpunchers to own cattle on the range. He said that 99 per cent of them were honest men, that if they were allowed to buy mavericks and own cattle it would give them a chance to get ahead and give them an interest in the range, that this would do more than anything else to stop rustling, since the boys were on the range all the time. He was voted down at the time, but he was right. The few outfits that did allow their men to own cattle never had any cause for complaint. Mr. Stuart himself stuck to his policy, against the opposition of some of his own partners. . . .

Another thing about cowpunchers, they were the most independent people on earth. That was why certain customs were followed on the range that you wouldn't find with any other class of men who worked for wages. For example, once a string of horses had been turned over to you, no one, not even the boss, could ride one of them without your permission, though they were his horses. I remember when Con Kohrs, the big, long-legged old Dutchman who was president of the D H S company after the hard winter, came up to the ranch one time and asked the foreman to get him a horse. And the first man the foreman went to said: "Hell no, he can't ride none of my horses." That fellow wasn't aiming to disoblige anybody; he just didn't like to have anybody else riding his horses. Once when Bill Burnett was foreman at the D H S, he came near quitting because Granville Stuart sold a horse out of his string. He asked for his time, but it was just a misunderstanding and was straightened out. Those things were a matter of etiquette, and as I told you, Granville Stuart didn't know a whole lot about the cattle business when he started. If he had gone to the man first and said: "I've got a chance to get a good price for that horse," the man would have said go ahead.

But if they were independent, they were proud too, and that independence and that pride made for the best results in a cow outfit. To tell the truth, it wasn't thinking about the owners' money that made them so anxious to turn out their herd in good shape. What they cared about was the criticism of other cowpunchers. They didn't want to hear it said, "That's a hell of an outfit"—so they made it a point to prove the opposite. But that sensitiveness on their part and that belief that their outfit was the best on earth was all to the advantage of the owners, and that was why John Clay was such a fool when he made that speech before the feeders' convention in Illinois, in 1914, attacking the old-time cowpunchers.

"The chief obstacle of the range at that time," he said, "was the cowboys, who were mostly illiterate, uncivilized; who drank and thieved and misbranded cattle, and with a kind of rough loyalty, never told on one another in their crimes."

John Clay was a hard-fisted, money-loving Scotchman who had no understanding of the kind of men who worked on the range. "A kind of rough loyalty" to each other—yes, they had that, in money matters, too. A real cow outfit had only one pocketbook. I've seen them come off herd, when one man had only forty or fifty dollars, and the others would lend him a hundred dollars to go to town. He'd pay it back sooner or later. They were all like a bunch of brothers. And if they weren't, they were no use as an outfit and the boss would get rid of them.

Joseph Nimmo, Jr.

The most informative government document dealing with the early range- and ranch-cattle industry is the report by Joseph Nimmo, Jr., Chief of the Bureau of Statistics, to the United States Treasury Department in February 1885. The Nimmo report is in large part a statistical record concerning grazing lands, cattle shipments, market information, foreign investments, and the like, along with appended statements on prevailing conditions by prominent cattlemen. The report is particularly significant for purposes of this text, because it describes and sums up the situation as the cattle frontier was coming to a close.

Report on the Cattle Industry *

The expression "range and ranch cattle" in this report applies to cattle which, from the time they are dropped until they are shipped to market, seek their own food, water, and shelter, as did the buffalo, the deer, and the elk before them, and which are subject only to the restraints of herding.

The distinction between the "range" and the "ranch" cattle business herein observed, is that the former designation applies to the raising and fattening of cattle upon public lands, or upon unfenced lands generally, where the herds of different proprietors freely range and intermingle; whereas the "ranch" cattle business is carried on within inclosures, belonging to cattlemen on which only their own cattle graze.

The very fact that the range-cattle business is most profitably carried on in a large way, and that its successful prosecution involves organization and co-operative work, appears to have suggested at an early day the conduct of the business under corporate ownership and management. Accordingly this has been one of the marked features of the enterprise almost from the beginning.

Incorporated companies, chartered under the laws of this country as well as under the laws of foreign countries, are now extensively engaged in the cattle business from Southern Texas to the northern border line of the United States.

The raising of cattle in Texas had its origin long before the admission of that State into the Union. The original or native cattle of Texas are of Spanish and Mexican origin. Their most distinctive physical characteristics are long horns, large and vigorous lungs, small intestinal organization, and small bones.

Texas cattle exhibit some of the marked self-reliant traits of the wild animal, being strong in the instinct of seeking food and water, and of self-protection against the inclemency of the weather. In the language of the herdsmen they are good "rustlers," which means that they know how and where to find food and water and have the alertness and spirit to seek them upon the vast plains and in valleys and mountain fastnesses where they roam, and even beneath the snows which in the winter, at times, in the more northerly regions, cover their feeding grounds.

Upon her admission into the Union Texas retained the ownership of

---

* From Joseph Nimmo, Jr., *The Range and Ranch Cattle Traffic in the Western States and Territories* (Washington, D.C.: U.S. Treasury Dept., February 1885), House Executive Document No. 267, 48th Cong., 2d Sess., pp. 9–13, 25–26, 49–50.

her public lands. These lands have been surveyed and divided into townships, sections, and quarter sections in a manner quite similar to that in
which the public lands of the United States have been laid out. Texas has,
however, pursued a less conservative policy in regard to the disposition
of her public lands than has the United States, and the result is, that the
ownership of vast areas has been freely acquired for ranch purposes by
individuals and corporations. In a few instances single individuals have
acquired the ownership of upwards of 250,000 acres. The result of this is
that with the exception of the extreme western and extreme northern
portions of the State, where herds range on the public domain, the cattle
business of Texas has become largely a ranch business.

Twenty-five years ago Texas cattle were slaughtered in immense
numbers for their hides and tallow. Then the average value of three-year-
old steers on the ranch or range was only from $3.50 to $4.50 a head. But
a great change has taken place in the cattle interests of that State within
a comparatively brief period. Railroads have been constructed, whereby
the markets of Kansas City, Saint Louis, and Chicago have been opened
to the Texas cattle trade.

During the last twenty years another movement from Texas has
sprung up and has attained great commercial importance, viz., the driving
of young cattle north, to stock the newly opened ranges of the vast Northwestern Territories, including also the Indian Territory, New Mexico, and
Colorado. It is estimated that the total number thus driven north, composed mainly of yearling and two-year-old steers, has, since the beginning of the movement, amounted to about 3,000,000.

The opening of these new and enormous commercial possibilities to
the cattle-owners of Texas has developed a vast amount of wealth, and
has, of course, greatly stimulated the cattle industry of that State. Cattle
which about the year 1868 were worth only $4.50 a head advanced in
value to $15 and $18 per head. The lands of Texas also greatly appreciated
in value, and the general prosperity of the State attracted to it hundreds
of thousands of immigrants from other States and from foreign countries. The opportunities for gain and the wild fascination of the herdsman's
life have also drawn to Texas many young men of education and of fortune in the Northern States, and even scions of noble families in Europe.
This has also been the case throughout the entire range and ranch cattle
area of the United States.

Soon after this discovery of the possibilities of the great dry area of
the north for pasturage, the range and ranch cattle trade of Texas de-
bouched upon a territory three times as large as its original habitat.

Already the range and ranch business of the Western and Northwestern States and Territories has assumed gigantic proportions. The total
number of cattle in this area, east of the Rocky Mountains and north of

New Mexico and Texas, is estimated at 7,500,000, and their value at $187,500,000.

The secretary of the Wyoming Stock-Growers' Association has recently reported that since its organization in 1873 it has increased from ten members, representing an ownership of 20,000 cattle, valued at $350,-000, to a membership of 435 in 1885, representing an ownership of 2,000,000 head of cattle, valued at $100,000,000.

With the exception of the small percentage of lands the title to which has been secured under the provisions of the homestead and pre-emption laws of the United States, the desert-land acts, or the timber-culture acts, the cattle upon the northern ranges feed upon the public lands of the United States, their owners being simply tenants by sufferance upon such lands.

The range cattle business of the western and northwestern portions of the great cattle area of course differs widely in the various localities and sections as to its profitableness. This is due to differences of conditions as to water supply, the quantity and quality of grasses, shelter, the number of calves produced, extent of winter losses, and the management of herds. As a rule the business has yielded very large profits. This is clearly indicated by the very large amounts of capital which have been invested in it during the last fifteen years. Large fortunes have been made at the business within a comparatively brief period. Hundreds of men who embarked in the business a few years ago, with exceedingly limited means, are now ranked as "cattle kings." In certain instances women also have successfully engaged in the enterprise, and two or three of their number have already won the soubriquet of "cattle queen."

But like all enterprises yielding extraordinary results in the beginning, competition has in many sections already reduced the average profits approximately to the limits usually attained in commercial enterprises.

Mr. E. V. Smalley states that the usual profits on long-established ranges in Wyoming and Montana vary from 20 to 30 per cent. per annum on the capital invested. The following is from his statement, in Appendix No. 1:

"The average cost of raising a steer on the ranges, not including interest on the capital invested, is usually estimated by the large stock-owners at from 75 cents to $1.25 a year. Thus a steer four years old ready for market has cost the owner $4 or $5 to raise. When driven to the railroad he is worth from $25 to $45. A recent estimate, approved by a number of Wyoming ranchmen, places the profit at the end of the third year on a herd consisting of 2,000 cows with 1,000 yearlings, and 35 short-horn bulls, representing in all, with ranch improvements and horses, an investment of about $70,000, at $40,000."

The completion of the Northern Pacific Railroad, and the construction of other railroads in the Territories during the past two or three years, caused the price of range cattle to advance. Thus large profits were realized from the sale of herds.

Generally it is found that the average cost per head of the management of large herds is much less than that of small herds. The tendency in the range cattle business of late years has therefore been toward a reduction in the number of herds, and generally toward the consolidation of the business in the hands of individuals, corporations, and associations. It is stated that a single cattle company in Wyoming advertises the ownership of ninety different brands, each one of which formerly represented a herd constituting a separate property.

In opposition to the tendency toward consolidation, there is also the tendency toward separate ownerships on the part of homestead, pre-emption, and "desert-land" settlers, through the privileges afforded them under the public land laws of the United States.

The range and ranch cattle business of the North has provided an enormous outlet for young cattle from the great State of Texas, the most prolific breeding ground in this country, and it has also provided quite extensively a market for young cattle from the dairy States of the West, and from the State of Oregon and Washington Territory, to be matured and fattened on the northern ranges. It has also added very largely to the beef supply of this country, and thus has exerted a most important influence in placing that very nutritious and desirable article of food within the reach of the laboring classes. It has, besides, afforded a large amount of profitable traffic to transcontinental railroads, and been the means of greatly encouraging railroad construction throughout the Territories, thereby largely increasing their population and wealth. At the same time it has been highly promotive of both the internal and the foreign commerce of the United States.

The northern range-cattle business has also been perhaps the most efficient instrumentality in solving the Indian problem, by occupying lands throughout that extensive region over which formerly the Indians roamed, and upon which for centuries the buffalo and other wild animals fed. By this means a vast area, which, but a few years ago, was apparently a barren waste, has been converted into a scene of enterprise and of thrift, and now supplies a large and profitable employment both to capital and to labor. Thus the scope of the national industries has been greatly enlarged and the national wealth increased.

Already the range and ranch cattle industry has passed through two or three successive stages of development, and it appears to be now in a transition state. That in the future it will largely increase, no one who has studied the subject with any degree of care can for a moment doubt. Evidently it is yet too early to attempt to throw around it the constraints of artificial conditions. Its best and most natural development for the good of the country must come as the result of a growth conformed to its relationships to co-ordinate branches of industry throughout the vast area where now, to a great extent, it occupies the attitude of a pilgrim upon the public lands of the United States. The difficulties of which the cattlemen complain are largely a result of this fact. But the methods of pioneer life are never those of organized society, and it is yet too early to attempt to set bounds to future development.

ADDITIONAL READINGS

For reliable and readable accounts of the range-cattle industry see Ernest S. Osgood, *The Day of the Cattleman* (Minneapolis, 1929); Edward E. Dale, *The Range Cattle Industry* (Norman, 1930); Louis Pelzer, *The Cattlemen's Frontier* (Glendale, 1936); and chapters in Walter Prescott Webb's *The Great Plains* (Boston, 1931) and Fred A. Shannon's *The Farmer's Last Frontier* (New York, 1945). J. Frank Dobie provides an engaging description of wild-cattle roundups along the Rio Grande in *A Vaquero of the Brush Country* (Dallas, 1929). First-hand accounts of trail riders are conveniently assembled in *Trail Drivers of Texas,* edited by J. Marvin Hunter (Nashville, 1925). *Log of a Cowboy,* by Andy Adams (Boston, 1903), is fictionalized but convincing. Down-to-earth and honest are the original notes of Bruce Siberts, recorded by Walker D. Wyman in *Nothing but Prairie and Sky: Life on the Dakota Range in the Early Days* (Norman, 1954). W. Turrentine Jackson has done careful work on the Wyoming Stockgrowers' Association in a series of articles, one of which is "The Wyoming Stock Growers' Association: Political Power in Wyoming Territory, 1873–1890," *Mississippi Valley Historical Review* (March 1947).

As for the cowboy, there is the breezily interpretive book by Joe B. Frantz and Julian E. Choate, Jr., *The American Cowboy: The Myth and the Reality* (Norman, 1955); and the popular book by Charles A. Siringo, *A Texas Cowboy, or Fifteen Years on the Hurricane Deck of a Spanish Pony* (New York, 1885). For more serious studies see Philip A. Rollins, *The Cowboy* (New York, 1922); E. Douglas Branch, *The Cowboy and His Interpreters* (New York, 1926); and Carl C. Rister, *Southern Plainsmen* (Norman, 1938). Lewis Atherton aims to separate the cattlemen from the cowboys in *The Cattle Kings* (Bloomington, Indiana, 1961).

II

RED MEN AND WHITE

There is general consensus among anthropologists that man moved into North America from eastern Asia—perhaps by land bridge, perhaps in hide boats—anywhere from fifteen to twenty thousand years ago. From successive infiltrations over the centuries, the continent was lightly sprinkled with peoples of Mongolian ancestry until, on the threshold of the sixteenth century, there were perhaps a million native inhabitants within the present continental limits of the United States.

The Indian, then, was one of the "givens" of the American frontier experience. Along with the elements and the untrammeled wilderness, he was part of the savagery to which, for a time, the frontiersman succumbed. Although early reactions to the first Americans stressed exotic and romantic factors, soon the image of the Indian as a "Child of Nature" or "Noble Savage" gave way to a view that mingled fear with contempt. By the time the moving frontier was ascending the Missouri River early in the nineteenth century, decades of border warfare had bred the widespread conviction that only dead Indians were good.

The Indians of the trans-Mississippi West who played significant roles on the American frontier may be classified within six culture areas. (1) The Pacific Northwest Coast peoples lived along a strip roughly one hundred miles broad, extending from the panhandle in southeastern Alaska through British Columbia, Washington, and Oregon, to the northwestern corner of California. They included such groups as the Kwakiutl, Haida, Nootka, and Chinook. (2) The Plateau culture area, embracing land drained by the Columbia River system and most of the Fraser River drainage as well, included parts of future British Columbia, Alberta, Washington, Idaho, Oregon, and Montana. Here lived the Flatheads, the Nez Percé, and the Cayuse, among others. (3) The Plains area stretched from central Alberta all the way south to the Mexican border and was bounded on the west by the Rocky Mountains and on the east by the Missouri River. Fighting Indians such as the Blackfoot, Sioux, Cheyenne, and Comanche claimed this territory. (4) The California culture area, including about two thirds of the future state, was small, but its peoples varied widely in physical type and speech. The so-called Mission Indians were the best-known representatives of the area. (5) Modocs, Paiutes, and Utes, among others, inhabited the Great Basin culture area: all of Nevada and Utah, plus parts of California, Oregon, Idaho, Wyoming, and Colorado. (6) The Oasis culture area took in most of Arizona, New Mexico, all of the Mexican states of Sonora and Sinaloa, and the western parts of Chihuahua and Durango. Because the land was largely desert, the Indians clustered around oasis-like spots near streams. In this region lived Pueblo peoples such as the Zuñi and the Hopi, as well as the more restless Navajos and Apaches.

The tendency to lump all Western Indians together, and to dismiss their downfall with the easy generalization that a backward and barbaric people had to give way before a dynamic and superior race, obscures the fact that the Western Indian's reaction to the white tide varied widely and sharply among and within representatives of the six culture areas.

The Indians of the Pacific Northwest Coast—with their intensely individualistic, often megalomaniac striving for wealth and position, and their encouragement of conspicuous display—seem almost to have embraced destruction as their contacts with European maritime traders rendered virtually pathological the competition that lay at the heart of their culture. With an unprecedented flood of blankets, trinkets, and metal utensils, particularly copper, pouring into Indian hands, the precisely calibrated scale of social rank disintegrated. Moreover, close commercial and social contacts exposed the coastal tribes to European diseases such as measles, smallpox, and scarlet fever with frightening effects. The Chinooks of the lower Columbia, for example, once some 15,000 strong, were reduced to approximately 1,500 before the middle of the nineteenth century, largely through the ravages of the white man's maladies.

At the other end of the scale were the Pueblo peoples of the Oasis culture area. Their communal and controlled way of life—along with deferred and limited relationships with whites, due to the isolation and austerity of their environment—contrasts dramatically with the aggressive individualism and vulnerability to maritime commercial currents of the Northwest Coast groups. This combination of remoteness and a disciplined and integrated way of life permitted the Pueblo peoples to maintain their customs and their cultural integrity perhaps better than was true of any other Indians in the American West. In fact, there have been and are

Americans who claim to find a harmony and unity among these Oasis types that seems to be missing in the dominant modern American culture.

The Indians of the Plains area mustered stiff resistance to white encroachment. By the time the fingers of American expansion were probing their homeland, they were potentially a formidable foe. The introduction of the horse by the Spanish increased the dependence of the Plains peoples on buffalo and made them the most nomadic of all Indians. Their cultural pattern emphasized warfare and individual feats of courage, and their diet and way of life gave them stamina and physical prowess. However, by the time these people awakened to the threat of the white migrations, the huge buffalo herd so essential to Indian existence had been cut in two by the transcontinental railroad; and bands of buffalo hunters were methodically reducing the beasts to a point just short of extinction. Nevertheless, there were flurries of fierce resistance. The ambushing of Captain William Feterman's command by the Sioux and the last stand of Colonel Custer against the same foe were simply two famous episodes in the desperate efforts of the Plains Indians to hold on to their homelands.

If there was diversity in the way the Indian met the white advance, there was a unity too. Whether along the rain-wrapped Pacific Northwest Coast or in the long, sun-drenched stretch of the New Mexico Valley or on the wind-whipped Plains country, the Indian shaped his living to the land, establishing a kind of equilibrium with nature. Young Joseph, the Nez Percé chief, epitomized the fundamental conflict in point of view between red man and white in a few phrases:

We were like deer. They were like grizzly bears. We had a small country. Their country was large. We were contented to let things remain as the Great Spirit Chief made them. They were not; and would change the rivers and mountains if they did not suit them.

Government policy toward the Indian in the nineteenth century was vacillating, confused, and opportunistic. It could scarcely have been otherwise. The federal departments exercising jurisdiction over Indian affairs (first the War Department and then, after 1849, the Department of the Interior), as well as Congress, were sensitive to popular pressures: settlers clamoring for more land, or miners howling over being barred by Indians from potential pay dirt, or cattlemen demanding right-of-way through Indian territory, or humanitarians pleading for preservation of Indian rights. Although most of the time the official ideal of the federal government was peace, the outcome was violence. And in the wake of that violence there were dead Indians, plenty of them. Still the red man's total fate was not annihilation; it was concentration on selected islands or reservations apart from the American mainstream. Here, as a kind of displaced and second-class American, the Indian lived; and if he failed to thrive he did increase, so that by mid-twentieth century his numbers were substantially greater than when the frontier closed in the 1890s. Meanwhile, friends of the Indian differed as to what was right for him as well as to how it was to be achieved. Some aimed toward ultimate assimilation; others were committed to restoring and sealing off the culture of the Indian groups to guard against further white contamination; some wanted the best of both approaches. The problem persists.

The selections that follow are intended to illustrate diversity among Indian groups in the trans-Mississippi West; to sample attitudes of both sides while in the throes of cultural clash; and to point up processes of cultural change and adaptation so far as they relate to the themes that run through this book.

Black Elk

This description of a buffalo hunt is taken from the autobiography of Black Elk (1863–1933), Holy Man of the Oglala Sioux, as told to fellow-mystic John G. Neihardt. Neihardt belongs to a fast-shrinking fraternity of men who lived with and won the trust of the American Indian while the Indian was still in touch with his peoples' experience in the late nineteenth century. Author of Song of Hugh Glass *(1915),* Song of the Indian Wars *(1925), and* Song of Jed Smith *(1941), Neihardt is poet-in-residence at the University of Missouri.*

*The Buffalo Hunt**

One morning the crier came around the circle of the village calling out that we were going to break camp. The advisers were in the council tepee, and he cried to them: "The advisers, come forth to the center and bring your fires along." It was their duty to save fire for the people, because we had no matches then.

---

* From *Black Elk Speaks, Being the Life Story of a Holy Man of the Oglala Sioux as Told to John G. Neihardt* (New York: William Morrow and Company, 1932), pp. 53–59. Copyright 1961 by University of Nebraska Press. Reprinted by permission.

"Now take it down, down!" the crier shouted. And all the people began taking down their tepees, and packing them on pony drags.

Then the crier said: "Many bison, I have heard; many bison, I have heard! Your children, you must take care of them!" He meant to keep the children close while traveling, so that they would not scare the bison.

Then we broke camp and started in formation, the four advisers first, a crier behind them, the chiefs next, and then the people with the loaded pony drags in a long line, and the herd of ponies following.

When the sun was high, the advisers found a place to camp where there was wood and also water; and while the women were cooking all around the circle I heard people saying that the scouts were returning, and over the top of a hill I saw three horsebacks coming. They rode to the council tepee in the middle of the village and all the people were going there to hear. I went there too and got up close so that I could look in between the legs of the men. The crier came out of the council tepee and said, speaking to the people for the scouts: "I have protected you; in return you shall give me many gifts." The scouts then sat down before the door of the tepee and one of the advisers filled the sacred pipe with chacun sha sha, the bark of the red willow, and set it on a bison chip in front of him, because the bison was sacred and gave us both food and shelter. Then he lit the pipe, offered it to the four quarters, to the Spirit above and to Mother Earth, and passing it to the scouts he said: "The nation has depended upon you. Whatever you have seen, maybe it is for the good of the people you have seen." The scouts smoked, meaning that they would tell the truth. Then the adviser said: "At what place have you stood and seen the good? Report it to me and I will be glad."

One of the scouts answered: "You know where we started from. We went and reached the top of a hill and there we saw a small herd of bison." He pointed as he spoke.

The adviser said: "Maybe on the other side of that you have seen the good. Report it." The scout answered: "On the other side of that we saw a second and larger herd of bison."

Then the adviser said: "I shall be thankful to you. Tell me all that you have seen out there."

The scout replied: "On the other side of that there was nothing but bison all over the country."

Then the crier shouted like singing: "Your knives shall be sharpened, your arrows shall be sharpened. Make ready, make haste; your horses make ready! We shall go forth with arrows. Plenty of meat we shall make!"

Everybody began sharpening knives and arrows and getting the best horses ready for the great making of meat.

Then we started for where the bison were. The soldier band* went first, riding twenty abreast, and anybody who dared go ahead of them would get knocked off his horse. They kept order, and everybody had to obey. After them came the hunters, riding five abreast. The people came up in the rear. Then the head man of the advisers went around picking out the best hunters with the fastest horses, and to these he said: "Good young warriors, my relatives, your work I know is good. What you do is good always; so to-day you shall feed the helpless. Perhaps there are some old and feeble people without sons, or some who have little children and no man. You shall help these, and whatever you kill shall be theirs." This was a great honor for young men.

Then when we had come near to where the bison were, the hunters circled around them, and the cry went up, as in a battle, "Hoka hey!" which meant to charge. Then there was a great dust and everybody shouted and all the hunters went in to kill—every man for himself. They were all nearly naked, with their quivers full of arrows hanging on their left sides, and they would ride right up to a bison and shoot him behind the left shoulder. Some of the arrows would go in up to the feathers and sometimes those that struck no bones went right straight through. Everybody was very happy.

Standing Bear Speaks:

I remember that hunt, for before that time I had only killed a calf. I was thirteen years old and supposed to be a man, so I made up my mind I'd get a yearling. One of them went down a draw and I raced after him on my pony. My first shot did not seem to hurt him at all; but my pony kept right after him and the second arrow went in half way. I think I hit his heart, for he began to wobble as he ran and blood came out of his nose. Hunters cried "Yuhoo!" once when they killed, but this was my first big bison, and I just kept on yelling "Yuhoo!" People must have thought I was killing a whole herd, the way I yelled. When he went down, I got off my horse and began butchering him myself, and I was very happy. All over the flat, as far as I could see, there were men butchering bison now, and the women and the old men who could not hunt were coming up to help. And all the women were making the tremolo of joy for what the warriors had given them. That was in the Moon of Red Cherries [July]. It was a great killing.

Black Elk Continues:

When the butchering was all over, they hung the meat across the horses' backs and fastened it with strips of fresh bison hide. On the way

---

* The organized military or police force of the camp.

back to the village all the hunting horses were loaded, and we little boys
who could not wait for the feast helped ourselves to all the raw liver we
wanted. Nobody got cross when we did this.

During this time, women back at camp were cutting long poles and
forked sticks to make drying racks for the meat. When the hunters got
home they threw their meat in piles on the leaves of trees.

Then the advisers all went back into the council tepee, and from all
directions the people came bringing gifts of meat to them, and the advisers
all cried "Hya-a-a-a!," after which they sang for those who had brought
them the good gifts. And when they had eaten all they could, the crier shouted
to the people: "All come home! It is more than I can eat!" And people from
all over the camp came to get a little of the meat that was left over.

The women were all busy cutting the meat into strips and hanging it
on the racks to dry. You could see red meat hanging everywhere. The people feasted all night long and danced and sang. Those were happy times.

Ruth Benedict

*The following passage from an essay by Ruth Benedict (1887–1948).
widely known anthropologist, shows succinctly the presence of intensely individualistic competition on the one hand, and close cooperation and group
loyalty on the other, among the Dakota Blackfeet.*

Competition and Cooperation
among the Blackfeet*

. . . It is ironic that nations which exalt personal profit as the one way
in which to keep the wheels of industry moving should in wartime eradicate
or conceal the profit motive and trust again in group loyalty. In this major
emergency we turn away from the competitive motive. In spite of all decla-
rations of learned writers that working for profit is the only incentive upon

---

* From Ruth Benedict, "Primitive Freedom," *Atlantic Monthly*, CLXIX (June
1942), 762–763.

which society can depend, in war we know it is too weak and too expensive. We invoke again coöperation for the common good and the defense of our country. And it is a commonplace that men like war. For peace, in our society, with the feeling we have then that it is feeble-minded to strive except for one's own private profit, is a lonely thing and a hazardous business. Over and over men have proved that they prefer the hazards of war with all its suffering. It has its compensations.

The moral is not that war is therefore an inevitable human need, but that our social order starves men in peacetime for gratifications they get only in time of war. Many Indians of the great Mississippi plains, on the other hand, set up war and peace in reverse. Their peace-time dealings with their fellow tribesmen were arranged in joint-stock-company fashion with pooled profits and limited liability. Their primitive guerrilla warfare, however, was a field in which private advantage could be safely sought at the expense of an enemy they did not even count as 'human.' The Dakota Indians were brave and inveterate followers of the warpath. They were feared by all neighboring tribes. But the state had no stake in their exploits; no armies were sent out for political objectives, and the idea of establishing their sovereignty over another tribe had not occurred to them. Young men on the warpath accumulated long lists of standardized exploits—for getting away with an enemy's horse picketed in his camp circle, for touching a fallen enemy who was still alive, for taking a scalp, for bringing a slain or wounded tribesman from the enemy's lines, for having a horse shot under one. These coups, as the voyageurs called them, they totaled up and used for vying with their fellows. The warpath and all that went with it was competitive. A man joined a war party for no reasons of patriotism, but because he wanted to make his mark. When the party got to enemy country, each man put on his finest regalia and the feather headdress, each feather of which was insignia of a coup he had previously taken. When the party returned to its home camp, those who had coups to their credit were extravagantly acclaimed by all those families who could in any way claim relationship to the heroes. To their dying day warriors boasted competitively of their accumulated coups. A hundred or more counting sticks were kept in the council house, and men 'won' who had the right to take up the greatest number of sticks and tell their exploits.

Life within the Dakota tribe, on the other hand, and all dealings within the community, rested solidly on mutual advantage and group loyalty. The large family connections, the band, even the whole tribe, was a coöperating group where mutual support brought every man honor. The worst thing that could be said of a Dakota was: 'He thinks more of what he owns than he does of people.' They took it literally and in great giveaways they showed how much they 'cared for people'; obviously, too, giving lavishly raised the giver's own standing in the tribe. *Noblesse oblige* they took literally too. A person who had risen high and who had a strong and prosperous family must be by that token the most generous and the most willing to give all kinds of assistance. It was an essential part of his honorable status. The Dakota had tied group loyalty inextricably to times of peace.

Commissioner of Indian Affairs

In 1877 several bands of Nez Percé (whose leaders—Joseph, Ollicut, Looking Glass, Too-hul-hul-sote, White Bird, and Yellow Bull—had never signed the treaty that confined other Nez Percé peoples to a reservation at Lapwai, Idaho Territory) engaged United States Army troops in a running fight over some 1,500 miles before they were finally pinned down in the Bear Paw Mountains, Montana Territory, just short of the Canadian border and freedom. This resistance movement was preceded by several years of negotiation in the effort to persuade the non-treaty Nez Percé to accept the Lapwai reservation. In the report of the Civil and Military Commission reproduced in part here, the essential incompatibility between white and Indian attitudes comes through clearly; and Joseph is revealed, albeit indirectly, as an adroit and accomplished spokesman for his race.

Chief Joseph and the Commissioner*

Information of the assembling of the commission at Lapwai, Idaho, on or about November 8 [1876], had been seasonably forwarded to Agent Monteith, at Lapwai, with instructions to lose no time in sending for the non-treaty Nez Percé Indians, and especially for Joseph and his band, to be there at that time. A large number of treaty Indians had already arrived from Kamiah and other points, but no reliable tidings had been received from Joseph. . . . An appointment was finally secured for a council to be convened in the church at Lapwai, near the agency, on Monday, November

---

*From D. H. Jerome, O. O. Howard, Wm. Stickney, and A. C. Barstow, "Report of Civil and Military Commission to Nez Percé Indians, Washington Territory and the Northwest," to J. Q. Smith, Commissioner of Indian Affairs, December 1, 1876, in *Annual Report of the Commissioner of Indian Affairs to the Secretary of the Interior* (Washington, D.C.: 1877), pp. 211–217.

13, 1876, at 12 m., nearly a week after the arrival of the commissioners.

A few moments before the appointed hour the head of his well-mounted column was seen from the agency turning a point in the road. With military precision and order it massed itself in front of, but at considerable distance from the church. As he entered the church with his band, it was evident that their ranks were considerably swelled by the addition of other prominent non-treaty Indians, as also by some malcontents among those who acknowledged themselves bound by the treaties. The commission occupied the platform of the church. Joseph and his band, sixty or seventy in number (including malcontents,) after an exchange of salutations by himself and a few of his headmen with the commission, took seats upon our left, the treaty-Indians filling the right and center of the house.

From the first it was apparent that Joseph was in no haste. Never was the policy of masterly inactivity more fully inaugurated. He answered every salutation, compliment, and expression of good-will, in kind, and duplicated the quantity. An alertness and dexterity in intellectual fencing was exhibited by him that was quite remarkable.

He is in the full vigor of his manhood; six feet tall, straight, well formed, his voice musical and sympathetic, and his expression usually calm and sedate, when animated marked and magnetic.

When, in answer to suggestions and general inquiry, no grievance was stated, the commission plied him with questions touching his occasional occupation of Wallowa Valley, and the irritations and disturbances consequent thereon with the white settlers; he answered, he had not come to talk about land, and added that these white settlers had first informed him of the appointment of this commission, expressing their belief that on its assembling all these troubles would be settled, and they (the whites) would retire from the valley. In this, and the following interviews, which were long drawn out, Joseph maintained his right to Wallowa Valley and including Imnaha Valley, where he and his band spend most of their time. As Joseph did not move upon and occupy this reservation, said order was revoked June 10, 1875. This tract embraces a territory equal to 1,425 square miles, and is larger than the present reservation.

The commission answered that a part of the valley had already been surveyed and opened to settlement; that if, by some arrangement, the white settlers in the valley could be induced to leave it, others would come; that the State of Oregon, in whose territory the valley is located, is inviting the white race from the four corners of the earth to come in and occupy its hills and valleys, and would not be long willing so large a territory should be left to the exclusive (and that but occasional) use of so small a band; and if it were, could hardly prevent the permanent settlement of such immense tracts of land which he and his band merely visit for a brief season annually for hunting and fishing; and that in the conflicts which may arise in the future, as in the past, between him and the whites, the President might not be able to justify or defend him.

As against his claim of right to the valley, the commission stated that under the law of nations the title of our government to this whole country, drained by the Columbia, by right of discovery and occupation, had been admitted by other great nations; that notwithstanding this, the government had always sought to extinguish the Indians' possessory title, whatever that may be; that in respect to this Wallowa Valley, the President claimed that he extinguished the Indian title to it by the treaty of 1863, which bore the signatures of a majority of their chiefs and headmen; but in a spirit of generosity he was disposed, rather than press his rights to issue, to treat for an adjustment of present differences: that owing to the coldness of the climate the Wallowa Valley is not a suitable location for an Indian reservation, and is now in part settled by white squatters for grazing purposes. Consequently, we suggested a willingness to set apart suitable lands for tillage and pasture for himself and his band upon the present reservation; to aid him in the erection of houses, in fencing their land, in procuring farming implements and other helps to peaceful industries, and to habits of life consonant with the spirit of the age, together with the privileges now enjoyed by the treaty-Indians; and to secure such rights and privileges for fishing and hunting as would be consistent with a settled pastoral, rather than a nomadic life.

The reply to all such suggestions, seriously made and oft repeated both by Joseph and his brother, was to the effect that the "Creative Power," when he made the earth, made no marks, no lines of division or separation upon it, and that it should be allowed to remain as then made. The earth was his mother. He was made of the earth and grew up on its bosom. The earth, as his mother and nurse, was sacred to his affections, too sacred to be valued by or sold for silver and gold. He could not consent to sever his affections from the land that bore him. He was content to live upon such fruits as the "Creative Power" placed within and upon it, and unwilling to barter these and his free habits away for the new modes of life proposed by us. Moreover, the earth carried chieftainship, (which the interpreter explained to mean law, authority, or control,) and therefore to part with the earth would be to part with himself or with his self-control. He asked nothing of the President. He was able to take care of himself. He did not desire Wallowa Valley as a reservation, for that would subject him and his band to the will of and dependence on another, and to laws not of their own making. He was disposed to live peaceably. He and his band had suffered wrong rather than do wrong. One of their number was wickedly slain by a white man during the last summer, but he would not avenge his death. But unavenged by him, the voice of that brother's blood, sanctifying the ground, would call the dust of their fathers back to life, to people the land in protest of this great wrong.

The serious and feeling manner in which he uttered these sentiments was impressive. He was admonished that in taking this position he placed himself in antagonism to the President, whose government extended from ocean to ocean; that if he held to this position, sooner or later there would come an issue, and when it came, as the weaker party, he and his band would go to the wall; that the President was not disposed to deprive him of any just right or govern him by his individual will, but merely subject him to the same just and equal laws by which he himself as well as all his people were ruled.

We pointed him to the fact that the wild, nomadic habits of the Indians cut off most of their offspring in infancy and many of their aged before their time; that warm, permanent homes, comfortable clothing, and better food, made sure at regular seasons, would as certainly promote happiness as they would longevity.

He and his band have fallen under the influence of the "dreamers," (Smohollah), a modern spiritualistic mysticism, known of late among the Indians of this region, and represented in his band by his "medicine-man" or magician, who is understood to have great power over him and the whole band. We had waited long for his coming, as we thought very needlessly, and did not think it best to wait longer, with hope of shaking his resolve, buttressed, as we knew it to be, in a new-fangled religious delusion and kept alive by a kind of wizard, who allowed no word to enter his ear except also strained through his own.

We thought it best to close the conference and leave him to his reflections, with the request that if he came to a better mind he communicate with the agent.

Owing to the lateness of the season and the delays attending our interviews with Joseph and his band, we have been able to visit only the Umatilla, Yakama, Nez Percé, Puyallup, and Neah Bay reservations. From these comparatively limited means of information we have collated much useful knowledge.

All the Indians in Oregon and the Territories of Washington and Idaho could be well accommodated with sufficient arable land suitable in soil and climate for comfortable homes upon the Nez Percé and Yakama reservations alone. Here they would also find ample pasture-lands for all their herds, supplies of pine, fir, and other timber suitable for building, fencing, and fuel, streams filled with fish, and mountains teeming with game.

Upon the Nez Percé reservation at Lapwai is one saw-mill and one grist-mill, and the same at Kamiah. At Yakama are two saw-mills and one grist-mill. These mills have abundant capacity to saw the lumber and grind the grain for all the Indians in the said State and Territories, nor need any additional expense be incurred for the construction of agency buildings. .

In view of these important facts, we earnestly recommend that a system of reducing the existing number of agencies be entered upon at once, as far as the same can be effected without violation of existing treaties, believing such action would not only result in a large saving to the Government, but in promoting the true and highest interests of the Indians. For in the interest of the Indian, in order to change his habits of life and render him speedily self-supporting, there is required, as Agent Wilbur well says, "patient and constant perseverance, instructing, correcting, and reproving. This needs to be done everywhere—from house to house, from camp to camp, on the mountains, at their fisheries, on the week-day and on the Sabbath. They are grown-up children, and must be personally educated to work."

Such tutelage cannot be accomplished by allowing the Indians to be scattered without governmental direction and aid, as will be the case at the expiration of the present treaties, or to roam at will, as thousands are doing in the valley of the Columbia to-day. The government should, in our judgement, assume and exercise a plain duty, viz, treat the Indians as its wards, and exercise over them the necessary and wholesome authority.

Chief Joseph

The Indian point of view has seldom been expressed more forcefully or poignantly than in "Chief Joseph's Own Story," printed first in the North American Review *for April 1879, parts of which appear below. Joseph died in 1904 on the Colville reservation in the state of Washington. Already, at the time of his death, he was the embodiment of the Noble Savage; and his stature has not been diminished over the years.*

*The Indian's Point of View**

My friends, I have been asked to show you my heart. I am glad to have a chance to do so. I want the white people to understand my people. Some of you think an Indian is like a wild animal. This is a great mistake.

---

* From "Chief Joseph's Own Story," *North American Review* CXXVII (April 1879), 415–433 *passim.*

I will tell you about our people, and then you can judge whether an Indian is a man or not. I believe much trouble and blood would be saved if we opened our hearts more. I will tell you in my way how the Indian sees things. The white man has more words to tell you how they look to him, but it does not require many words to speak the truth. What I have to say will come from my heart, and I will speak with a straight tongue. Ah-cum-kin-i-ma-me-hut (the Great Spirit) is looking at me, and will hear me.

My name is In-mut-too-yah-lat-lat (Thunder-traveling-over-the-mountains). I am chief of the Wal-lam-wat-kin band of Chute-pa-lu, or Nez Percés (nose-pierced Indians). I was born in eastern Oregon, thirty-eight winters ago. My father was chief before me. When a young man he was called Joseph by Mr. Spalding, a missionary. He died a few years ago. There was no stain on his hands of the blood of a white man. He left a good name on the earth. He advised me well for my people.

Our fathers gave us many laws, which they had learned from their fathers. These laws were good. They told us to treat all men as they treated us; that we should never be the first to break a bargain; that it was a disgrace to tell a lie; that we should speak only the truth; that it was a shame for one man to take from another his wife, or his property, without paying for it. We were taught to believe that the Great Spirit sees and hears everything, and that He never forgets; that hereafter He will give every man a spirit-home according to his deserts; if he has been a good man, he will have a good home; if he has been a bad man, he will have a bad home. This I believe, and all my people believe the same.

The first white men of your people who came to our country were named Lewis and Clarke. They also brought many things that our people had never seen. They talked straight, and our people gave them a great feast, as a proof that their hearts were friendly. These men were very kind. They made presents to our chiefs and our people made presents to them. We had a great many horses of which we gave them what they needed, and they gave us guns and tobacco in return. All the Nez Percés made friends with Lewis and Clarke, and agreed to let them pass through their country, and never to make war on white men. This promise the Nez Percé have never broken. . . .

Next there came a white officer (Governor Stevens) who invited all the Nez Percé to a treaty council. After the council was opened he made known his heart. He said there were a great many white people in the country, and many more would come; that he wanted the land marked out so that the Indians and white men could be separated. If they were to live in peace it was necessary, he said, that the Indians should have a country set apart for them, and in that country they must stay. My father, who represented his band, refused to have anything to do with the council, because he wished to be a free man. He claimed that no man owned any part of the earth, and a man could not sell what was not his own.

Mr. Spalding took hold of my father's arm and said: "Come and sign the treaty." My father pushed him away and said: "Why do you ask me to sign away my country? It is your business to talk to us about spirit matters, and not to talk to us about parting with our land." Governor Stevens urged my father to sign his treaty, but he refused. "I will not sign your paper," he said, "you go where you please, so do I; you are not a child, I am no child; I can think for myself. No man can think for me. I have no other home than this. I will not give it up to any man. My people would have no home. Take away your paper. I will not touch it with my hand." ...

The United States Government again asked for a treaty council. My father had become blind and feeble. He could no longer speak for his people. It was then I took my father's place as chief. In this council I made my first speech to white men. I said to the agent who held the council:

"I did not want to come to this council, but I came hoping that we could save blood. The white man has no right to come here and take our country. We have never accepted presents from the Government. Neither Lawyer nor any other chief had authority to sell this land. It has always belonged to my people. It came unclouded to them from our fathers, and we will defend this land as long as a drop of Indian blood warms the hearts of our men."

The agent said he had orders, from the Great White Chief at Washington, for us to go upon the Lapwei reservation, and that if we obeyed he would help us in many ways. "You must move to the agency," he said. I answered him: "I will not. I do not need your help; we have plenty, and we are contented and happy if the white man will let us alone. The reservation is too small for so many people with all their stock. You can keep your presents; we can go to your towns and pay for all we need; we have plenty of horses and cattle to sell, and we won't have any help from you; we are free now; we can go where we please. Our fathers were born here. Here they lived, here they died, here are their graves. We will never leave them." The agent went away, and we had peace for awhile. ...

For a short time we lived quietly. But this could not last. White men had found gold in the mountains around the land of the winding water. They stole a great many horses from us, and we could not get them back because we were Indians. ... We could have avenged our wrongs many times, but we did not. Whenever the Government has asked us to help them against other Indians we have never refused. When the white men were few and we were strong we could have killed them off, but the Nez Percés wished to live at peace. ...

In the treaty councils the commissioners have claimed that our country had been sold to the Government. Suppose a white man should come to me and say, "Joseph, I like your horses, and I want to buy them." I say to him, "No, my horses suit me, I will not sell them." Then he goes to my neighbor, and says to him: "Joseph has some good horses. I want to buy them, but he refuses to sell." My neighbor answers, "Pay me the money, and I will sell you Joseph's horses." The white man returns to me and says, "Joseph, I have bought your horses, and you must let me have them." If we sold our lands to the Government, this is the way they were bought. . . .

Year after year we have been threatened, but no war was made upon my people until General Howard came to our country two years ago and told us that he was the white war-chief of all that country. He said: "I have a great many soldiers at my back. I am going to bring them up here, and then I will talk to you again. I will not let white men laugh at me the next time I come. The country belongs to the Government, and I intend to make you go upon the reservation."

I remonstrated with him against bringing more soldiers to the Nez Percé country. He had one house full of troops all the time at Fort Lapwei. . . .

When the party arrived there General Howard sent out runners and called all the Indians to a grand council. I was in that council. I said to General Howard, "We are ready to listen." He answered that he would not talk then, but would hold a council next day, when he would talk plainly. I said to General Howard: "I am ready to talk today. I have been in a great many councils, but I am no wiser. We are all sprung from a woman, although we are unlike in many things. We cannot be made over again. You are as you were made, and as you were made you can remain. We are just as we were made by the Great Spirit, and you cannot change us; then why should children of one mother and one father quarrel?—why should one try to cheat the other? I do not believe that the Great Spirit Chief gave one kind of men the right to tell another kind of men what they must do."

General Howard replied: "You deny my authority, do you? You want to dictate to me, do you?" . . .

In the council General Howard informed us in a haughty spirit that he would give my people thirty days to go back home, collect all their stock, and move on to the reservation, saying, "If you are not here in that time, I shall consider that you want to fight, and will send my soldiers to drive you on." . . .

When I returned to Wallowa I found my people very much excited upon discovering that the soldiers were already in the Wallowa Valley. We held a council, and decided to move immediately to avoid bloodshed. . . .

We gathered all the stock we could find, and made an attempt to move. We left many of our horses and cattle in Wallowa, and we lost several hundred in crossing the river. All my people succeeded in getting across in safety. Many of the Nez Percés came together in Rocky Cañon to hold a grand council. . . .

Again I counseled peace, and I thought the danger was past. We had not complied with General Howard's order because we could not, but we intended to do so as soon as possible. I was leaving the council to kill beef for my family when news came that the young man whose father had been killed had gone out with several hot-blooded young braves and killed four white men. He rode up to the council and shouted: "Why do you sit here like women? The war has begun already."

[*The Indians engaged the troops in a series of running battles that ended in early October when Colonel Nelson Miles coming from the East cornered the Nez Percés in the Bear Paw mountains of Montana Territory about thirty miles south of the Canadian border.*]

On the fifth day I went to General [*sic*] Miles and gave up my gun, and said, "From where the sun now stands I will fight no more."

[*Although promised that they would be sent to Lapwei, the Nez Percés were routed first to Bismarck, then to Kansas, then to Indian Territory in the Southwest.*]

At last I was granted permission to come to Washington and bring my friend Yellow Bull and our interpreter with me. I am glad we came. I have shaken hands with a great many friends, but there are some things I want to know which no one seems able to explain. I cannot understand how the Government sends a man out to fight us as it did General Miles and then breaks his word. Such a Government has something wrong about it. I cannot understand why so many chiefs are allowed to talk so many different ways, and promise so many different things. I have seen the Great Father Chief (the President); the next Great Chief (Secretary of the Interior); the Commissioner Chief (Hayt); the Law Chief (General Butler); and many other law chiefs (Congressmen), and they all say they are my friends, and that I shall have justice, but while their mouths all talk right I do not understand why nothing is done for my people. I have heard talk and talk, but nothing is done. Good words do not last long until they amount to something. Words do not pay for my dead people. They do not pay for my country, now overrun by white men. They do not protect my father's grave. They do not pay for my horses and cattle. Good words will not give me back my children. Good words will not make good the promise of your War Chief, General Miles. Good words will not give my people good health and stop them from dying. Good words will not get my people a home where they can live in peace and take care of themselves. I am tired of talk that comes to nothing. . . .

I know that my race must change. We cannot hold our own with the white men as we are. We only ask an even chance to live as other men live. We ask to be recognized as men. We ask that the same law shall work alike on all men. If the Indian breaks the law, punish him by the law. If the white man breaks the law, punish him also.

Let me be a free man—free to travel, free to stop, free to work, free to trade where I choose, free to choose my own teachers, free to follow the religion of my fathers, free to think and talk and act for myself—and I will obey every law, or submit to the penalty.

Whenever the white man treats the Indian as they treat each other, then we shall have no more wars. We shall be all alike—brothers of one father and one mother, with one sky above us and one country around us, and one government for all. Then the Great Spirit Chief who rules above will smile upon this land, and send rain to wash out the bloody spots made by brothers' hands upon the face of the earth. For this time the Indian race are waiting and praying. I hope that no more groans of wounded men and women will ever go to the ear of the Great Spirit Chief above, and that all people may be one people.

In-mut-too-yah-lat-lat has spoken for his people.

Young Joseph

Elwell S. Otis

Even among contemporaries, it is easier to find sympathetic accounts of the American Indian than harsh or unfavorable appraisals. Here an army officer, despite more than a trace of ambivalence, renders in 1878 a generally arrogant and severe judgment on the red man.

The Indian Question*

The white man has misconceived his red brother, ever since the two first met upon the continent. Misjudging his mental powers and his moral qualities, he has viewed him as one having like sentiments and desires as himself, but wanting the knowledge necessary to improve his condition.

Said the Indian Commission a few years since, while in conference at Washington: "It is our opinion that if the present peace policy can be persisted in for four years longer, the Indian problem will be placed in a fair way of solution," and it gave as reasons why that policy had not been successful, "the laxity in the enforcement of the laws when the Indians

---

* From Elwell S. Otis, Lt. Colonel, U.S. Army, *The Indian Question* (New York: Sheldon and Company, 1878), pp. 228–283 *passim*.

were the complainants and the whites the aggressors," also that the agents and missionaries had been "defeated in their purposes by thieves and robbers who were allowed to live among the Indians." These abuses corrected and slight impediments removed, and the interesting nomad would, it is inferred, be seen clothed and in his right mind, engaged in agriculture and acquiring the virtues of the thrifty husbandman. Such expectations were unreasonable, and could not have been predicated upon a fair consideration of all circumstances.

What qualities then does this American Indian lack, that he is so little impressed by the efforts which have been put forth for his amelioration? He has the same physical properties, the same senses, the same elementary mental powers which we possess, but here the parallel ceases. Although equally if not more skilled in the use of the senses than the white man, he lacks the faculty of abstraction, and consequently his imagination, reason and understanding, are of a very low order. He is almost entirely destitute of the moral qualities, and his religious nature is of that kind which presumes the existence of a Supreme Being, simply to account for facts and occurrences beyond his comprehension. His conceptions of that Divinity are extremely vague and uncertain. It may be one and indivisible, or it may exist in many and antagonistic forms. . . . His Divinity has none of the attributes of goodness, for he, in his utter ignorance of virtues, is unable to imagine their existence. It is only propitiated by substantial material gifts, and may be persuaded to assist in enterprises of the most wicked character.

Like all savage people, the Indian has not the slightest conception of definite law as a rule of action. He is guided by his animal desires. He practices all forms of vice, and even to a great extent those crimes which are pronounced as against nature. He takes little thought except for the present, knows nothing of property in the abstract, and has not therefore any incentive to labor further than to supply immediate wants. Instead of making an effort for moral improvement he strives to strengthen his vicious propensities. He eats the raw liver of ferocious beasts to augment his ferocity, wounds and bruises his person to increase his animal courage, boasts in council of his brutalities, parades them as deeds of approved valor and as examples worthy of imitation.

The brief picture here presented is intended to portray the members of the wild tribes, and is not overdrawn, although they exhibit to us in their superstitious ceremonies and in their councils of state, and even in the hospitalities of their lodges, certain qualities which do not appear to harmonize with the character we have so quickly sketched. It is the manifestation of these traits, such as reverence for the Great Spirit, respect for the dead, affection for those within the family relation, hospitable reception of strangers, admiration for mental endowments, and an occasional display of cunning sagacity and rich imagery of language, which has made the Indian a psychological and metaphysical enigma to many. And indeed to the casual observer of Indian life and manners, our representations would appear paradoxical at best. How shall the seeming inconsistencies be reconciled?

The Indian possesses of course the natural instincts, the general characteristics of humanity, among which is an innate love for kindred and a desire for fellowship. The superstitious observances which attend his mode of worship, if such it can be denominated, the rite of burial, and indeed all religious ceremonies from the sun dance to the exorcism of evil spirits, have been handed down by tradition through countless generations. From whence they proceed, whether borrowed and adapted to circumstances, or whether of native birth and growth, the natural product of the Indian mind, endeavoring to account for existence and cause, cannot be ascertained. So analogous, however, are many of their ceremonies to those practiced in eastern Asia, many centuries ago, so similar are many of their traditions to those long since extant in the old world, that the conclusion is almost forced, that they are in substance of foreign origin. The slaughter of horses over the grave of a relative reminds one of the action of Achilles at the tomb of Patroclus. The act of piercing the ears of children is suggestive of the Jewish rite of circumcision. The conjurations of the medicine man assimilate the sorceries spoken of in ancient history, and the traditions and crude mythology of the Indians, contain much which might be ascribed to the Asiatic pagans.

But from whatever source their ceremonies may be derived, they have become the inheritance of the tribes and have been practiced successive years without variation. They are found to be, when examined, characteristic of those who maintain them, and are attended with cruelty or with a repulsive indelicacy shocking to moral sensibility. Reverence when analyzed becomes a superstitious dread of an unappeased vindictive Deity. The beautiful service of sepulture is an observance repellant to the civilized because of the bloody scenes which accompany it.

The Indian is sometimes called a statesman and an orator. His dignified bearing in council, the beautiful metaphors and rich imagery with which his efforts at oratory often abound, challenge admiration. Language is the embodiment of thought. It mirrors the mind, though it does not reveal intention nor morals. While, therefore, manifestations of the highest excellence which the red man has attained may be witnessed in the proceedings of their great tribal gatherings, no correct opinion of their moral condition can be gained. He is a keen observer of nature, and its objects supply him with figures to illustrate and impress his primitive ideas. With the Indian oratory is an art, the result of study and repeated practice. Few acquire it and they become the leading spirits of the tribe. The maiden speeches of the young chiefs about to assume control of the movements of their people, are generally miserable failures. After a few years of trial some become fluent declaimers and fervent exhorters. Fortunately for their reputations, their ideas are few and simple, and they can by their labor, be frequently reproduced with increased adornment.

The efforts of years secure a dress which is rich and oftentimes brilliant. Still it must be remembered that before the speech obtains our criticism, it is embellished by the imagination of the poetical interpreter.

Considering then fairly the character of the superstitious observances maintained by the Indians, also the nature of their mental productions, neither their devout and religious tendencies, nor their arts and accomplishments, are incompatible with that degree of savagery which is destitute of moral principle and the knowledge of abstract right. These deficiencies, together with that spirit of communism which is prevalent among all tribes, and which is due as well to an undeveloped idea in regard to property, as any desire for common ownership, make the reception and understanding of our American civilization very improbable. . . .

It is well known that no portion of the Indian population can much longer maintain itself after its old customs of life, for wild game can only be found in sufficient quantities for its subsistence in small sections of the country. It is well known that it is impossible to improve the Indian while in a nomadic state, and that in such condition he is a constant source of menace to pioneers, and to the frontier settlements. It is also well known that much of the country now rendered insecure and unremunerative because roamed over by irresponsible tribes, is sought by our citizens for occupation, and that it is desirable that routes of travel be opened through the same which can be safely journeyed over by the public. In fine, it is well understood that imperative necessity and the interests of both races demand, that the entire Indian population shall be permanently located either individually by tribes or collectively, and that it be compelled to conform to the laws of the country. It might also be stated as a fact, that this population must be compelled to work for its food, which must in future be largely gained through agricultural toil, for neither charity, gratitude nor justice, requires the Government to feed it in idleness, and its own well-being and prosperity calls upon it to labor for its own maintenance and support.

The question of the future relationship of the white and red races to each other, cannot be satisfactorily determined. Very likely, the idea that a large civilized Indian nation might be created, and preserved, within the country, has been entirely abandoned. That has given way to the hope that Indian communities may be perpetuated, and made similar, in action and intention, to white societies. Speculation, however, based upon tendencies as shown in the past, might lead to the belief that such a hope cannot be realized.

We have in mind more particularly, that gradual absorption of the Indian stock, which has been in progress since the discovery of America, and which is even more noticeable in Mexico, and in some of the South

American provinces, than in the United States. But even with us, it has been so rapidly progressing, as to raise a strong presumption, that the Indian race will, in a few generations, be practically absorbed. In eighteen hundred and seventy-six, the Commissioner of Indian Affairs reported, that nearly one-sixth of the Indian population of the United States, exclusive of Alaska, was made up of mixed bloods; and his figures show, that only about one half of the Cherokees, Creeks, Choctaws, Chickasaws and Seminoles are of pure extraction. These estimates are approximative, and really enumerate the mixed bloods at too low a rate. At many of the agencies, a large number of the half and quarter breeds there dwelling seem to be almost entirely ignored.

The gradual absorption of our Indian stock will assuredly continue, and it is probable, that it will be finally merged in the great body of our white population. The question whether the unity of the two races will produce vigorous physical organisms, is still debatable; and the psychological inquiry, whether the product will be mentally and morally of an inferior order, is still unsettled in the minds of many. Our own opinions upon the latter subject are decided. . . . The cross will be an inferior being, both in mind and morals, when viewed in the light of our civilization, or rather, when measured by the rules prescribed by our civilization, as tests of nature and quality.

However much such an ultimate result is to be deplored, the effect will scarcely be perceptible upon our institutions, except in those sections of country where the Indians shall have been collected in masses. They are now in numbers, only as one to ninety of our entire white population; and indeed as one to twelve of our colored population. In nineteen hundred, the ratio of Indians to whites, even if the two races can be restrained from much intermingling, will be about as one to one hundred and seventy-five. Whatever view therefore, may be taken of this social problem no decided effect can be produced upon our national character. It is only in the event that Indians are collected in large bodies (which certainly, in so far as attempted, seems to have encouraged amalgamation,) that any danger is to be apprehended. Should a course of action, having for its object the concentration of the tribes, be persistently and successfully prosecuted, we shall have, within the heart of the United States, an element which will there prolong social disorder for generations to come. If scattered throughout the interior, its evil effects will, in a short time, be neutralized.

Helen Hunt Jackson

Helen Hunt Jackson (1830–1885) was converted to the cause of the American Indian at a Boston tea party in 1879, when she heard Standing Bear and Bright Eyes discourse on the sufferings of the Plains Indians. In a book published two years later, she denounced American treatment of the Indians under a title that stuck: A Century of Dishonor. *Mrs. Jackson went on to rescue the Mission Indians of Southern California briefly from oblivion through the sentimental and largely false-to-life novel* Ramona. *The passages included here come from the general indictment of federal Indian policy with which she concluded* A Century of Dishonor.

A Century of Dishonor*

There are [as of 1880] within the limits of the United States between two hundred and fifty and three hundred thousand Indians, exclusive of those in Alaska. The names of the different tribes and bands, as entered in the statistical tables of the Indian Office Reports, number nearly three hundred. One of the most careful estimates which have been made of their numbers and localities gives them as follows: "In Minnesota and States east of the Mississippi, about 32,500; in Nebraska, Kansas and the Indian Territory, 70,650; in the Territories of Dakota, Montana, Wyoming, and Idaho, 65,000; in Nevada and the Territories of Colorado, New Mexico, Utah, and Arizona, 84,000; and on the Pacific slope, 48,000.

Of these, 130,000 are self-supporting on their own reservations, "receiving nothing from the Government except interest on their own moneys, or annuities granted them in consideration of the cession of their lands to the United States."†

This fact alone would seem sufficient to dispose forever of the accusation, so persistently brought against the Indian, that he will not work.

There is not among these three hundred bands of Indians one which has not suffered cruelly at the hands either of the Government or of white

---

* From Helen Hunt Jackson, *A Century of Dishonor: A Sketch of the United States Government's Dealings with Some of the Indian Tribes* (Boston: Roberts Brothers, 1891), pp. 336–342.

† Annual Report of Indian Commissioner for 1872.

settlers. The poorer, the more insignificant, the more helpless the band, the more certain the cruelty and outrage to which they have been subjected. This is especially true of the bands on the Pacific slope. These Indians found themselves of a sudden surrounded by and caught up in the great influx of gold-seeking settlers, as helpless creatures on a shore are caught up in a tidal wave. There was not time for the Government to make treaties; not even time for communities to make laws. The tale of the wrongs, the oppressions, the murders of the Pacific slope Indians in the last thirty years would be a volume by itself, and is too monstrous to be believed.

It makes little difference, however, where one opens the record of the history of the Indians; every page and every year has its dark stain. The story of one tribe is the story of all, varied only by differences of time and place; but neither time nor place makes any difference in the main facts. Colorado is as greedy and unjust in 1880 as was Georgia in 1830, and Ohio in 1795; and the United States Government breaks promises now as deftly as then, and with an added ingenuity from long practice.

One of its strongest supports in so doing is the wide-spread sentiment among the people of dislike to the Indian, of impatience with his presence as a "barrier to civilization," and distrust of it as a possible danger. The old tales of the frontier life, with its horrors of Indian warfare, have gradually, by two or three generations' telling, produced in the average mind something like an hereditary instinct of unquestioning and unreasoning aversion which it is almost impossible to dislodge or soften.

There are hundreds of pages of unimpeachable testimony on the side of the Indian; but it goes for nothing, is set down as sentimentalism or partisanship, tossed aside and forgotten.

President after president has appointed commission after commission to inquire into and report upon Indian affairs, and to make suggestions as to the best methods of managing them. The reports are filled with eloquent statements of wrongs done to the Indians, of perfidies on the part of the Government; they counsel, as earnestly as words can, a trial of the simple and unperplexing expedients of telling truth, keeping promises, making fair bargains, dealing justly in all ways and all things. These reports are bound up with the Government's Annual Reports, and that is the end of them. It would probably be no exaggeration to say that not one American citizen out of ten thousand ever sees them or knows that they exist, and yet any one of them, circulated throughout the country, read by the right-thinking, right-feeling men and women of this land, would be of itself a "campaign document" that would initiate a revolution which would not subside until the Indians' wrongs were, so far as is now left possible, righted.

To assume that it would be easy, or by any one sudden stroke of legislative policy possible, to undo the mischief and hurt of the long past, set the Indian policy of the country right for the future, and make the Indians at once safe and happy, is the blunder of a hasty and uninformed judgment. The notion which seems to be growing more prevalent, that simply to make all Indians at once citizens of the United States would be a sovereign and instantaneous panacea for all their ills and all the Government's perplexities, is a very inconsiderate one. To administer complete citizenship of a sudden, all round, to all Indians, barbarous and civilized alike, would be as grotesque a blunder as to dose them all round with any one medicine, irrespective of the symptoms and needs of their diseases. It would kill more than it would cure. Nevertheless, it is true, as was well stated by one of the superintendents of Indian Affairs in 1857, that, "so long as they are not citizens of the United States, their rights of property must remain insecure against invasion. The doors of the federal tribunals being barred against them while wards and dependents, they can only partially exercise the rights of free government, or give to those who make, execute, and construe the few laws they are allowed to enact, dignity sufficient to make them respectable. While they continue individually to gather the crumbs that fall from the table of the United States, idleness, improvidence, and indebtedness will be the rule, and industry, thrift, and freedom from debt the exception. The utter absence of individual title to particular lands deprives every one among them of the chief incentive to labor and exertion—the very mainspring on which the prosperity of a people depends."

All judicious plans and measures for their safety and salvation must embody provisions for their becoming citizens as fast as they are fit, and must protect them till then in every right and particular in which our laws protect other "persons" who are not citizens.

However great perplexity and difficulty there may be in the details of any and every plan possible for doing at this late day anything like justice to the Indian, however hard it may be for good statesmen and good men to agree upon the things that ought to be done, there certainly is, or ought to be, no perplexity whatever, no difficulty whatever, in agreeing upon certain things that ought not to be done, and which must cease to be done before the first steps can be taken toward righting the wrongs, curing the ills, and wiping out the disgrace to us of the present condition of our Indians.

Cheating, robbing, breaking promises—these three are clearly things which must cease to be done. One more thing, also, and that is the refusal of the protection of the law to the Indian's rights of property, "of life, liberty, and the pursuit of happiness."

When these four things have ceased to be done, time, statesmanship, philanthropy, and Christianity can slowly and surely do the rest. Till these four things have ceased to be done, statesmanship and philanthropy alike must work in vain, and even Christianity can reap but small harvest.

"Teddy Blue" Abbott

In this vignette, "Teddy Blue" Abbott (represented at greater length in Chapter 10, "The Cattle Frontier") captures the collapse of a way of life.

The Dispossessed*

One day I rode down to Claggett, which was on the Missouri River at the mouth of the Judith River. A party of Assiniboine Sioux was just coming across the river on the ferry, seven lodges of them, and they was bent on a celebration. They had killed three bear in the Bear Paw Mountains, on the north side of the river, and they had sold the hides and meat to the captain of the steamboat *Rosebud* for seventy-five dollars, and they was going to spend it for grub and clothes and ammunition and whisky.

The fellow that had the ferry was rowing the Indians across in a little boat, and I sat down in the shade of a big cottonwood tree to watch them. Pretty soon along come a big Indian, and I said, "How," and he said, "How," and he sat down beside me. He knew a little English, and I knew some Sioux and some sign, and he had been drinking and wanted to talk. I asked him where they were going, and he said they were going down the river with their women and just lay around, fishing and drinking whisky.

So we talked awhile about what they were going to do down there and then we got on the subject of the old days. I said: "You fellows used to have a pretty good time."

He said, "Yes," and then he described the way they used to live before the white man came. They would go down a creek and camp where there was good grass and water, run a bunch of buffalo down and skin them and get the meat—then when the grass got a little short, they would just move on to a place where there was new grass, and keep that up, no troubles or worries, and when one wife got old, they'd marry another one.

Coming back up Dog Creek, I met Russell (Charles M. Russell, the cowboy artist). I said: "God, I wish I'd been a Sioux Indian a hundred years ago," and I told him the story.

---

* From E. C. ("Teddy Blue") Abbott and Helena Huntington Smith, *We Pointed Them North: Recollections of a Cowpuncher* (Norman: University of Oklahoma Press, 1955), pp. 144–146. Copyright 1955 University of Oklahoma Press. Reprinted by permission.

He said: "Ted, there's a pair of us. They've been living in heaven for a thousand years, and we took it away from 'em for forty dollars a month."

Another time I got talking to some of these Indians and one old fellow offered me his wife, for twenty-two dollars. This was not to keep, you understand, just a temporary arrangement. Twenty-two dollars was too high. A dollar and a half was more like it. Of course he made a big talk about her being his favorite wife and so forth, but that was all bull. Most of the Indian tribes was doing a regular business of that kind with the white men, and some of them, especially the Crows and Sioux, had got so low they would offer you their wives. But the way they did it in most of the camps, they had special tepees for the purpose, and certain squaws that was just like sporting women among the whites. Only among the Indians it never seemed to hurt their chances for marrying afterwards.

The Gros Ventres, Crows, and Sioux, and I think the Blackfeet were all doing this kind of business. But never the Northern Cheyennes, nor the Pawnees, down in Nebraska. You couldn't touch one of their women unless you married her with a priest.

ADDITIONAL READINGS

A recent general work on the Indian from the anthropological standpoint and with an extensive bibliography is *Indians of North America* by Harold E. Driver (Chicago, 1961). *Indians of the Americas* (New York, 1947) is a sympathetic interpretation by John Collier, superintendent of the Bureau of Indian Affairs under the New Deal. The development of Indian policy between 1830 and 1854 is treated in James C. Malin's "Indian Policy and Westward Expansion," University of Kansas *Bulletin* (1921). Standard on our later Indian policy is Loring B. Priest's *Uncle Sam's Step-children: The Reformation of United States Indian Policy, 1865–1887* (New Brunswick, New Jersey, 1942).

For reliable works on Indians of the Southwest, see Ruth M. Underhill, *The Navajos* (Norman, 1956); Edward E. Dale, *The Indians of the Southwest* (Norman, 1949); and C. L. Sonnichsen, *The Mescalero Apaches* (Norman, 1959). A recent account of the annihilation of the buffalo herds is by Mari Sandoz, *The Buffalo Hunters: The Story of the Hide Men* (New York, 1954). The authority on the Cheyenne is George B. Grinnell, author of *The Fighting Cheyennes* (New York, 1915) and *The Cheyenne Indians* (2 vols., New Haven, 1923). The Sioux wars are carefully treated by George E. Hyde in *Red Cloud's Folk: A History of the Oglala Sioux* (Norman, 1937) and *A Sioux*

Chronicle (Norman, 1956). The controversial Custer is dealt with competently by F. Van de Water in *Glory Hunter: A Life of General Custer* (Indianapolis, 1934). The autobiography of a seasoned frontier fighter, *General George Crook: His Autobiography* (Norman, 1946), has been well edited by Martin F. Schmitt.

For useful accounts of Chief Joseph, see L. V. McWhorter, *Hear Me, My Chiefs! Nez Percé History and Legend* (Caldwell, Idaho, 1952); and Francis Haines, *The Nez Percés: Tribesmen of the Columbia Plateau* (Norman, 1955).

12

ROADS, RIVERS, AND RAILS

In the middle of the nineteenth century, the American frontier vaulted to the Pacific slope; and the question of maintaining contacts with the settled and civilized East, always a problem in the westward advance, suddenly stood out in bold and urgent relief. The fact that in the 1850s the nation felt the frightening pull of North-South tension over the spread of slavery simply underscored the need to bind the Far West securely to the Union. Well before the crisis at Ft. Sumter a transportation network was taking shape, spreading through Western valleys and on Western waters; providing mail, freight, and passenger service between the Eastern frontier fringe and California and the Pacific Northwest; linking islands of settlement—in New Mexico, in the Salt Lake Valley, in mountain mining camps of Nevada and Colorado, and in the Inland Empire—with society east of the Mississippi. Before the Civil War transportation in the West was predominantly a matter of roads and rivers rather than rails. After Appomattox, railroads, moving quickly ahead of the frontier line, came on strong.

A roll call of the chief figures in Western transportation between the 1840s and the 1880s suggests the prominence of the individual in the struggle to constrict the wide-open spaces of the West: William H. Russell, Alexander Majors, William B. Waddell, Henry Wells, William G. Fargo, and John Butterfield in the wagon freight and stagecoach business; John Mullan, Jesse Applegate, Levi Scott, and Samuel K. Barlow, road builders; John C. Ainsworth, Robert Thompson, William Ladd, and Simeon Reed, the "Big Four" of Columbia River steamboating; Asa Whitney, George Wilkes, Stephen A. Douglas, and Thomas Hart Benton, promoters of a Pacific railroad; Theodore Judah, Leland Stanford, Charles Crocker, Collis P. Huntington, and Mark Hopkins of the Central Pacific; General Grenville Dodge of the Union Pacific; Northern Pacific's Henry Villard; and Jim Hill of the Great Northern. In the same long breath, it must be added that the contributions made by transportation tycoons were nearly always possible only through generous public subsidies, such as mail contracts to stagecoach companies, military contracts for the supply of Western army posts, and land grants and loans to the railroads. Although the federal government was the most conspicuous grantor of lands to the railroads, ambitious towns, cities, and states probably played a larger part in providing the necessary subsidies.

Westerners sought to solve their transportation problems on both a regional and a national or cross-country front. Acutely aware of their isolation from population centers and Eastern markets, they hungered first of all for long-range connections across the mountains and plains. All too aware of the vast distances in the West—since many of them had come the long, weary way across the continent—they tended to look to the federal government for mail service and for military protection along the Western trails. While they waited, however, they set about to meet needs closer to home. Californians, for example, largely because they had to have supplies for the mines, developed stagecoach lines that coalesced in the California Stage Company. Under James Birch the company achieved a near monopoly of the coaching business in California and the Oregon country, operating more than 2,500 miles of stage routes. In the Pacific Northwest a toll road, established by Samuel K. Barlow and Philip Foster in 1846, ran south of Mt. Hood into the Willamette Valley and eliminated the dangerous passage down the Columbia, which had been the last leg of the Oregon Trail. That same year the Old South Road or Applegate Trail entered the Oregon Territory from the south, permitting emigration from California. Private enterprise was behind the monopoly of steamboat traffic on the Columbia that developed in the 1860s under the Oregon Steam Navigation Company. OSN sternwheelers ploughed the waters of the Columbia River system from Astoria at the mouth to Lewiston on the Snake with railroad portages at the Cascades and The Dalles. Carrying mail, wheat, lumber, and passengers, the company enjoyed a rising financial power uncommon in Western history—especially since, unlike most frontier enterprises, the OSN was completely home-owned.

Stage coaches, wagon trains, toll roads, short-line railroads of both portage and feeder variety, sternwheelers—these were significant and picturesque features of Far Western transportation; but the dominant dream was of a transcontinental railroad. It is not surprising that the idea of a Pacific railroad was advanced during the expansionist decade of the 1840s. Several general plans competed for the attention of Congress. Two of them were inspired by the desire to reach the western rim of the continent, tie in with the China trade, and complete the "passage to India." Asa Whitney sought a donation from the federal government of a 60-mile-wide swath of land from Lake Michigan to the mouth of the Columbia or to Puget Sound. George Wilkes's idea was that the federal government should sell its lands and construct its own road. A third scheme, advanced by Stephen A. Douglas, had a continental focus and subordinated the maritime motive. Douglas favored the forming of a chain of new territories from Iowa to the Pacific Coast on the theory that settlement ought to pull the railroad west rather than the other way around. No promoter of Western transportation was more visionary than William Gilpin, who saw a central railroad as the key to uniting Asiatic trade and culture with the economic growth of the American agrarian heartland to produce the highest civilization in the history of man. Like Douglas, Gilpin was an ardent advocate of continental as opposed to maritime policy. He sharply criticized a governmental design that, in his view, sought to extend the shell of maritime (hence Atlantic-seaboard) influence around the continent rather than driving straight through the country's heart to the Western sea, thereby uniting land and ocean commerce and pulling the opulence of the Orient through the nation's center from west to east. Gilpin's vision of a Pacific railroad thus united features of Whitney's dream of encompassing Asiatic trade and Douglas's idea of westward extension of territories, with its focus on the farmer's West.

Congressional action on the building of railroads was put off pending the running of government surveys, a number of which were authorized in 1853. Despite identification and investigation of three feasible routes —a northern, central, and southern—the sectional controversy effectively blocked legislation until the South had left the Union. A Pacific Railroad Act could then be passed in 1862, authorizing two railroad companies: the Union Pacific to build west from Council Bluffs, and the Central Pacific to build east from Sacramento until the two should meet.

Before the nineteenth century closed, there were five major transcontinental lines: Union Pacific (1869), Northern Pacific (1883), Southern Pacific (1883), Santa Fe (1883), and Great Northern (1893). Most of these lines were financed and built by means of a fascinating mixture of private initiative and public support. The scale of construction was so large, the initial investments so heavy, the challenge of distance and terrain so great, the sprawl of territory to be traversed so empty of settlers, and the prospects for immediate and lucrative returns so remote that the task was clearly too formidable for private interests to undertake unaided. Consequently, the federal government was disposed to be generous with grants of lands and loans. At the same time, the dominant *laissez-faire* philosophy of the age prevented the government from supervising or regulating the enterprises, so that the railroad corporations had something approaching *carte blanche* in the use of subsidies and the management of their affairs.

It is not easy to generalize about the results. The sins of the giant railroads are well known: shoddy construction; exploitation of labor, particularly of the Chinese; false-front construction companies; reckless overexpansion, ending in bankruptcies; evasion of taxes; high and discriminatory freight rates; and withholding of lands from ordinary settlers for unconscionably long periods. Nevertheless, the tracks were laid and the continent was spanned—not once but, by 1906, half a dozen times. There was energy and vision as well as corruption and greed. There was prudent and skillful management, too. In fact, Jim Hill—by careful initial building with attention to easier curves and lower grades, by cautious financing, and by the device of adding feeder lines where he saw profitable traffic—was able to reach Puget Sound without benefit of federal land grant. Moreover, while the other major lines were going through receivership, Hill's road maintained regular dividends throughout the depression decade of the 1890s. It is true that Western railroads received nearly half a billion dollars in land value, but over the years the federal government realized savings of equal amount through a reduction of 50 per cent from the ordinary rates for shipment of its supplies and personnel. Finally, of course, there was the incalculable public service provided by stitching together the trans-Mississippi West with strands of steel, nourishing coastal ports and Rocky Mountain cities, and giving Western rail transportation a key role in the burgeoning and increasingly complex national economy.

It should be noted that problems of trans-Mississippi travel and communication called forth innovation. The Pony Express and the use of Chinese contract labor in laying track are examples in point. Nevertheless, the system of transportation in the West was largely the logical extension of earlier patterns of wagon roads, stage routes, steamship lines, and Eastern railroads. The total achievement is complex and impressive, involving as it did imagination as well as avarice, ingenuity as well as inefficiency, initiative as well as dependence, service as well as exploitation. In truth, transportation tamed the West.

W. Turrentine Jackson

In 1952 W. Turrentine Jackson, professor of history at the University of California (Davis), published a study of road surveys and construction undertaken by the federal government in the trans-Mississippi West between 1846 and 1869. In his book Professor Jackson traced and assessed the national government's contribution to western transportation; in the process, he modified significantly the previously held impression that private citizens, highly charged with pioneering zeal and entrepreneurial energy, were primarily responsible for laying out the transportation pattern of the American West in the pre-Pacific Railroad era. The selection that follows is from the closing chapter of Jackson's book.

Wagon Roads West*

The American frontiersman expressed his individualism by seeking an untrod path into the wilderness for a new home. Yet the pioneers' individualism and adaptability did not preclude their willingness to call upon the government for practical help in solving problems of migration and transportation. When projects, because of size or financial outlay, were beyond the means of private enterprise or the collective action of a western community, the resources and sponsorship of the national government were unhesitatingly demanded. Local groups constantly besieged Congress with requests for roads and other internal improvements. In the process localism was broken down, and a great desire to expand national power soon permeated most western communities. The pioneer became a nationalist as well as an individualist. . . .

Over the protest of a militant minority, the Democratic party platform of 1840 incorporated some fundamental concepts on the question of internal improvements. First, the party proclaimed its belief in a federal government of limited and expressed powers, to be strictly construed, and warned against the inexpediency of doubtful constitutional action. Moreover, it was felt that the Constitution did not confer on the national government the power to carry out a general system of internal improvements. In view of this policy of the major political party, only those road projects which were the exception to the general rule were likely to receive federal support. Throughout the 1840's a process was inaugurated to wear down gradually the reservations of congressmen by pressure of interested groups, chiefly from the West. Those improvements declared and proved necessary to the execution of a specific power of Congress, such as the maintenance of post roads, were most certain to gain approval. Even so, constructions within state boundaries were closely scrutinized and usually rejected by the strict constructionists attempting to preserve State rights in the federal

---

* From W. Turrentine Jackson, *Wagon Roads West: A Study of Federal Road Surveys and Construction in the Trans-Mississippi West, 1846–1869* (Berkeley: University of California Press, 1952), pp. 319–328. Reprinted by permission.

system. Westerners successfully placed emphasis upon the exclusive power of Congress to make regulations for the territories of the United States. Military roads were also justified on the basis of providing for the common defense, a criterion early approved by President Monroe. The recognition that Congress possessed power in the territories not admissible in the states, plus the responsibility for the common defense, usually proved an unbeatable combination in securing a majority vote in both houses of Congress. Territorial delegates, introducing road legislation, never failed to describe the improvement as a *military* road. Every effort was made in the 1840's and 1850's to avoid a discussion of constitutionality. Once the project was launched, no serious question about its legality was likely to arise, and funds for its continuation or expansion were more easily obtained.

With emphasis upon national defense as a constitutional justification of the federal road program, these projects were assigned to the Secretary of War. The United States Army thus became the government's road builder. The year 1846 signalized the establishment of the "Great West." The Oregon country below the forty-ninth parallel was incorporated into the United States, and a state of war was declared to gain the northern Mexican provinces for an expanding democracy. The responsibilities of the United States Army thereby became manifestly greater; the purposes, scope, and methods of the military-road program of the federal government were revolutionized. . . .

One of the most important activities in the trans-Mississippi West, 1846–1869, was topographical exploration for trails and roads that were to become avenues of migration, communication, and commerce. The dominant roles were played by agents of the national government, either as officers of the United States Army or civilian employees of the Interior Department. As a result of federal appropriations, the old established emigrant and trade routes known as the Santa Fe, Oregon, and California trails were shortened and improved. New ways of migration were opened. The emigrants' interest was always of paramount importance to the military road builders as well as to the civilian contractors. Wood for the camp fires, grass for the animals, and water for both men and beast were essential. Where they were known to be inadequate, adjustments were made, as in the digging of artesian wells and the construction of water tanks in New Mexico Territory.

The Argonaut of 1849–1850 was often indebted to an Army surveyor who had examined and reported upon a route of travel to California. One of the most popular avenues was the Marcy–Simpson trail along the banks of the Canadian River. Between El Paso and San Diego, many traveled along much of Cooke's wagon road. In the 1859 rush to the Colorado Rockies, the routes of Stansbury and Bryan were sometimes followed across the Kansas and Nebraska plains, either going to or returning from the Pike's Peak region. When the mining frontier moved to Idaho and Montana in the early 1860's, prospecting parties and freighters from both east and west used the Army's Mullan road to reach the sites of the latest discoveries. . . .

The road program did not facilitate the demands of a mobile population to the exclusion of the settler. Just as the military roads had provided an access to the agricultural lands of Iowa and Arkansas, so the pioneers in Nebraska and Kansas pushed westward along the pathway of similar surveys to take up farm land. The rich agricultural resources of the Rogue and Umpqua river valleys in southern Oregon were made easily accessible to the homeseeker. Lumbermen in the upper Mississippi Valley of Minnesota, in Oregon between the Willamette and Columbia rivers, and along the Puget Sound of Washington were indebted to federal road surveyors who penetrated the evergreen forests. Improved transportation facilities accelerated the volume of land sales and in some areas were a contributing factor to the pattern of settlement. Many frontier communities used these wagon roads to move products of the farm and forest to market and thereby laid the foundations for the earliest commerce of the region.

Before the Civil War, at least one, if not both, of the termini of most federal roads was at a military installation. Although the Indian-fighting Army was never so fortunate as to conduct its campaigns along military road surveys in the trans-Mississippi West, these improvements did provide a way for new recruits and supply trains dispatched to western outposts, and a continuous connection between the forts or Indian agencies and the population centers.

Many entrepreneurs engaged in mail deliveries under the subsidy of a government contract or carrying freight to the western forts for War Department compensation, received additional, though indirect, aid in using roads already explored and surveyed at federal expense. The freighting companies, such as Russell, Majors & Waddell whose headquarters were at Leavenworth, made extensive use of the roads laid out from the Kansas forts into the Great Basin and to the New Mexico settlements on the upper Rio Grande. The Pony Express, and later, the transcontinental telegraph followed, for the most part, the Simpson survey across western Utah Territory. The Pacific wagon road, located and partly improved by the Interior Department west of El Paso across New Mexico Territory, was traveled extensively by the stage and mail coaches on the San Antonio–San Diego route and by the Butterfield Overland Service. The government of the United States thus provided continuous and sustaining support for many businessmen whose financial success and promotional publicity brought them fame as builders of the West.

The federal engineers made a direct contribution to the location of the highways and railroads of the late nineteenth and twentieth centuries. As trained explorers and topographers, government surveyors succeeded in finding the natural passages for transportation routes along the river val-

leys, across the plains, or through the mountain passes. These were surveyed and mapped, and recommended for wagon travel. When the railroad
reconnaissances were authorized in 1853, they represented not an innovation but a continuation of federal aid to transportation and communication
along the established policy. It was inevitable that modern communication
lines should follow, to a large extent, the recommendations of those who
first scientifically examined the terrain of the trans-Mississippi West.

The Oregon Steam Navigation Company

*The Oregon Steam Navigation Company was organized in 1860 by
individuals and companies operating competing steamboat lines and portage roads on the Columbia and Willamette, who agreed to cooperate in
order to survive. Elements of strife and competition did not disappear,
however; for between 1860 and 1865, the OSN was divided within itself:
one group was committed to a program of long-range improvement and
expansion designed to make Portland the shipping center for the Columbia
and its tributary valleys, while others in the company wanted quick profits
and large dividends for the purpose of stock manipulations. The "building" group—led by Captain John C. Ainsworth, Robert R. Thompson,
Simeon G. Reed, and William S. Ladd—prevailed over the "profit-taking"
interests, among whom Daniel and Putnam Bradford were prominent.
There were also outside interests to worry about—notably, the Pacific
Mail Steamship Company, headed by Ben Holladay, and the California
Steam Navigation Company. Both of these companies offered passenger
and freight service between San Francisco and Portland, but their rates
were high and their vessels so decrepit that, according to the Portland
Oregonian, "the very rats long ago instinctively quit them." The weak link
in the route from San Francisco to the Idaho mines via Portland was the
ocean voyage; and as long as inferior service at high cost prevailed along
the coast, the OSN was at a disadvantage in competition with the rival
route overland from San Francisco by way of Red Bluff and Chico to
the "diggings" in Owyhee and Boise. The "building four" of OSN, seeking to expand their enterprise, decided to build and buy on the Atlantic
coast an ocean-going steamer to provide the kind of service needed to
bring increased traffic to their Columbia river fleet. In the process, they*

maneuvered the Bradford brothers out of the company. Most of the correspondence that follows bears on the negotiations for building and acquiring the steamship Oregonian, *and the internal contest that accompanied them. In addition, the letters yield some clear impressions of Western business policy and philosophy, as well as significant details of the company's operations. The OSN maintained its monopoly on the Columbia for two decades; finally, in 1880, it sold all interests to the Oregon Railroad and Navigation Company.*

Correspondence*

Daniel Bradford to Simeon G. Reed

Sheffield Mass
Feby 22d, 1865

... Your letter of Jany 14th was very entertaining & satisfactory as regards the doings—You again refer to the time you was talking in the board of getting rid of the opposition and that you had all agreed to say nothing to any outsider—on the point I want to ask you one question— Did you not all the time you was talking opposition in the board consult Capt A [J. C. Ainsworth, one of the charter members of the OSN and president during all but one year of the company's life] and did he not know every move which was made I know your answer will be yes— Now in the position I occupy toward the company am I not entitled to as much or more confidence than Capt Ainsworth I don't propose to be a cypher with the O. S. N. Co wether I am with them or against them and tis very annoying to one who has been as intimately connected with the company as I have to get news of importance in the companies affairs from *outsiders* Mr. Holliday [sic] informed me of the whole transaction before it was a week old so much for your d＿＿d secrets. Ainsworth in writing me a short time since says "You know I can't live without steamboats and I am about to purchase the "Couch" "Belle" & if so shall take possession in 1st Jany" Now what was the use of that humbug had he not better have said nothing about them. This is just the rock the company has all along split on two or three amongst the board or large outside owners have always had a smart secret from those entitled to know everything and in every instance it has been the cause of jealousies

---

* From Dorothy O. Johansen and Frank B. Gill, "A Chapter in the History of the Oregon Steam Navigation Company: The Ocean Steamship *Oregonian*," *Oregon Historical Quarterly*, XXXVIII (March 1937), 5–23 *passim;* (September 1937), 308–311, 313–314; (December 1937), 404; XXXIX (March 1938), 58, 61. Reprinted by permission of Oregon Historical Society.

and heart burnings and have always proved to the disadvantages of the Co—Let the board of Directors have as many secrets as they please & keep their actions to themselves, but let it be with the entire board & to the exclusion of *all* outsiders. . . .

John Wesley Ladd to S. G. Reed

New York June 2d 1865
Friday 11 A.M.

I have just this moment received and read your letter of April 22d. Where it has been I don't know but Wells Fargo & Co say it came overland. I have written William [William S. Ladd, John Wesley Ladd's elder brother, a member of the board of directors of the company] pretty fully which he will probably read you.

Bradford knows there is a movement on foot to build Steamers but thinks it is being made by the Citizens of Portland with Corbett [prominent Portland merchant] at the head, he knows nothing more from me and of course will not till we are advised by the official action of the board when he will probably be informed by Put [Putnam Bradford, Daniel's brother] and will of course rush to me for comparison of notes. All I know of the matter will of course be received at the same time his advices are, and shall then know how much to impart and how much to keep from him. I dont suppose it [is] the design of the Company to keep from Bradford the *fact* that the Co are to build a Steamer—if it is, I don't see how it can be done, as Put is on the board—I hope the company will out of courtesy to Dan ask him to render such assistance as he can, it certainly can do no harm and may result in good, the matter of future elections and management need not be alluded to, and would suggest that in the company's *official* correspondence, it will be policy to write only of such matters as can be shown to Dan—if you deem best—this would in all probability secure his assistance here and he would not feel as though he had been entirely left out.

Fifth Avenue Hotel
New York Wednesday
Eve June 14th 1865

On the 2d Inst. I received your interesting letter of April 22d giving me pretty fully your views of the past and prospective management of the Compn's affairs, an account of how the agreement between you four [Reed, Thompson, Ainsworth, and Ladd] to secure the future management, was brought about; as also your opinion of the several parties named. I am glad you took the trouble to write me so full an account, I had supposed that all the differences heretofore existing between Bradford & Co [portage railroad at the Cascades on north bank of Columbia] and the Company had been amicably settled and that nothing remained between them. Dan had told me of the matter left to arbitration and though he expressed some disappointment that the award was no larger yet he led me to believe that he should abide by it without a murmer. I also got the impression that there was nothing further which could ever come up between Bradford & Co and the O.S.N. Co. that no more "bones were to be picked."

I believe now as I did when I wrote William, i.e. "Bradford is with us just so long as he beleives it his interest to be, and no longer" I beleive too that he rather likes to sit quietly down, have others do the work and he reap the reward, notwithstanding this I had thought his interest and our own were identical, that the successful management of the company was his, as *it has been, and is,* our first and foremost object—and when Wm. wrote me of the probable change and of the agreement made, I was very much surprised. You and William are on the spot know all the "ins and outs" know the character of all the parties much better than I do and of course see through the true state of circumstances, while I am only acquainted with some few general features and scarcely any details, and am certainly in no wise capable of saying *who* in the Co. are most capable and most likely to manage it successfully and profitable, taking this view of it, I am perfectly satisfied with what has been done and know perfectly well that neither you or William could be induced to do anything which you beleived predjudicial to the best interests of the company. So you will find me not only willing but glad to give all the support I can towards carrying out any policy which may be decided upon. . . . I have been gaining all the information I can so to be prepared to go ahead when ordered to. I have got so far as to know pretty well what steamers have been built for different trades—what many have cost—their size capacity speed and owners. One thing pretty certain there have been no steamers yet built here which will fill the bill . . . Labor and building materials are gradually falling, iron and metal has come down good deal—labor 75c to 1.00 per day, but lumber for ship building hasn't fallen and isn't likely to till another year so many think—the production has been light on account of those formally engaged in getting it out, having gone to the war —and it will be a year before new can be got to market—the consumption on the other hand will be light and I think it will be lower in a month.

Daniel Bradford to S. G. Reed

Metropolitan Hotel
New York July 2 1865

I propose to write you a letter altho I am rather shakey today as I go on the principle no one is entitled to receive letters unless he writes—by the last steamer I recd a letter from you dated in Portland in Dec 8th & mailed in San Fran Jan 4th of course your news was not late—still I

notice all you had to say about your election and I am confidant tis now
an old story and you are all moving along in the regular course of business.
One thing I can see being far removed from the daily circumstances which
arise amongst you, that little things which at the time cause excitement,
jealousies & heart-burnings do in fact amount to just nothing at all only so
far as they annoy at the time—Our company has fought itself to its present
position against stronger obstacles than can ever again occur and wether
an Ainsworth a Ruckle John Brown or Pete Snook is its Executive it
will live & succeed and I truly wish I had money to buy more stock for if
it is not worth & will sell for 100 cts on the dollar before next summer
passes then I am no judge—I say again we can at this distance see things
more clearly than you can on the spot & I have yet to see any place that I
could put my money as satisfactorily as the O.S.N. Co stock at even par
value—So Mr. Thompson [R. R. Thompson, one of the original incorpora-
tors and a powerful figure in the company] bartered you at 70 cts for the
whole of his stock he was very smart for he well knew neither you or
any set of men in Portland had the *cash money* to see him if you had
asked him two weeks time he would not have been there—I believe he
understands the game of Poker? This was only a tantrum and by this
time 'tis forgot—all I have got to say is you managers stick to your business & it will come out all right. . . .

Simeon G. Reed to J. W. Reed and D. F. Bradford

Office Oregon Steam Nav. Co.

Portland, July 13, 1865

At a meeting of the Board of Directors of the O.S.N. Co. held on the
7th inst., present Ruckel, Thompson, Ladd and Reed, it was resolved
"that the company should take immediate steps in the Atlantic states to
procure the building of an ocean steamer." Having this morning listened
to a letter by W. S. Ladd and addressed to you, in which he states many
of the causes that actuated us in this matter. I shall not attempt to enlarge
on them, or go much into the details, but suffice it to say that after a
thorough canvassing, and looking to what we conceive to be the true
interest of the company, the building of a suitable ocean steamer owned,
and controlled by this company to run between Portland and San Francisco, was deemed a measure of vital importance, and one entirely within
our scope, although in carrying out this project we may be compelled to
forego anything like large dividends for the next six months, yet I am firm
in the belief that in the end accomplished, we will all be repaid fourfold by
the additional security and enhanced value of what we already have. On
the 10th inst. we paid a dividend of one-half of one per cent and expect
to be able to continue paying like monthly dividends through the season,
with a possibility of their being increased to one per cent should business

continue good. The enclosed financial statement will show you upon what our calculations are based, and I would here remark that our company is entirely free and clear of debt, with additional amounts already earned and due from the different agents which do not appear in the statement.

I am aware of nothing in the future management of the company's business, outside the building of this ship that will involve any large expenditure of money. Our idea of the cost of a suitable ship laid down in San Francisco ranges from $250,000 to $300,000 in currency, and with what we have already in hand, with several months of business before us, the way seems clear for paying dividends, building our ship and not come out in debt. . . .

Simeon G. Reed to J. W. Ladd

Portland   July 25th   1865

I have just written an official letter to Bradford and yourself accompanied by the drawing of the ships forwarded by "WF & Co" [Wells, Fargo] which go ford today. The matter alluded to in that letter as a subject for the "Board" to take under consideration is this. Through Rev. Mr. Pearne who arrived this steamer from the States, we get in substance as follows, which information he (Pearne) obtained semi-confidentially from Capt. Lapidge. That two (2) Steamships were to be constructed in New York to run between Portland and San Francisco. . . .

In my letters to you both private and official I have always favored and advocated the policy of this company building and owning a ship suitable for the trade between here and San Francisco, in order to protect ourselves and take our chances as against any such old "Tubs" as Holliday or the "C S N Co" [California Steam Navigation Company] now have and I have little faith that either of these above named parties intended building a ship so long as their old ones would answer a purpose or at any rate for some time to come. But this new programme puts matters in a different light to me *at least*. If these two ships are to be built by Dall and others, for our company to start in and build one, making three new ships of large carrying capacity, and together with the old ones now in the trade, it strikes me we should have a "merry time" with them and *possibly* with so many "irons in the fire" some of them might get burnt. Then again we must leave "no stone unturned" to divert all the Boise and Owyhee trade this way and one of the *strongest* arguments in favor of this route is an extended line of water communication as against land transportation by any other route. Hence the building of a steam boat on Snake River *early* in the spring to run from Olds Ferry to a point above (some 120 miles) 30 miles equidistant from Owyhee and Boise City is not a matter of choice but necessity—To be sure it would [be] desirable for our Company to own and controll a ship running between Portland and San

Fran°, but the main object would be accomplished if first class ships of ample accomodations were in the trade although they might be owned and controlled by others, and I have never supposed that the parties now in the trade would quietly subside without something of an effort on their part, but did suppose and do still that the right kind of a ship would command the greater part of the trade and travel but with two new ships and ours making a third, we would be engaged in a three cornered fight against steamboat men and capitallist, and if nothing more we as a company would in my judgment be hazarding what we already have with the chance of a fight on our hands for a year or more, and then perhaps—well I wont say it—I dont know—

At any rate I should say "go slow" make no contracts, or any positive engagements, but find out the truth of these reports as we are now in a position to stop where we are or go ahead, as may seem best. But bear in mind this is not an official letter, but by next steamer we will have time to canvas matters, have a meeting of the "Board" and you will then receive the result of our deliberation in an official form. . . .

Portland, Augt. 3d 1865

J. W. Ladd
  Dr Sir

Yesterday morning we were apprised (by Telegraph from Jacksonville) of the loss of the Steamer "Bro Jonathan" off Crescent City with all on Board save (so far as heard from) one boat load consisting of 3 women and 3 children and the balance (17 in all) comprised of negros flunkies and fireman—She left San Frano two days previous, and struck the reef off Crescent City about mid-day, and as we are advised, sunk in 45 minutes with all on board except the Boat load as above stated. . . . This sad disaster has cast a gloom on our whole community—The supposition here is that the "Jonathan" had encountered strong head winds against which she could make but little headway, and was folowing along in shore to avoid them. . . . Now we come to matters of Steamships. I wrote you on the 25th ulto relitave to this matter and certain information obtained, upon which I expressed my views at some length, and advocated the policy of "going slow" && all of which I contend was right, and sound policy, but since the date of that letter we have talked these matters over among ourselves, and in the meantime obtained information bearing on the subject, besides an event has transpired in the loss of the "Bro Jonathan" both of which have a direct bearing on the question. The information I refer to is regarding the Chico and other routes via way of the Sacramento River, showing us that we must depend upon our own resources to divert the trade & travel this way. Have our office and our agent in San Frano receive freight direct for Wallula or Umatilla, and sell tickets through to Idaho City and Owyhee (if necessary) regulating and controlling the rates to suit any immegency. Then the "Jonathan" will deter people from travelling or even shipping freight on these *old ships,* and the wants of the community will *demand* new and a better class of Steamers for the trade. And *if* we are compelled to carry fgts & passengers at *low* or even *loosing* rates, it will increase the business and act as a feeder to our river route. Something will continually be transpiring either for or against the project of building a Steamer, and taking every-[thing] into consideration it is deemed advisable to *go on* with building the Steamer. . . .

D. F. Bradford to R. R. Thompson

Sheffield, Mass.
May 9th 1866

By last nights mail I was most agreeably surprised to receive yr favor dated Mch 19th. I am indebted to you for the Commencement of Correspondence and hope it may lead to the interchange of ideas which may prove of mutual advantage to both as our great interests are so identical our united opinion in matters relating to the Nav Co should carry great weight & that there may be unity in our views it is well & pleasant to compare our thoughts even though 'tis done by "Pen write"

I have often thought & think so now if I only had the board set down in some room in New York & let me talk to them I might change their ideas somewhat in reference to business I do not propose to find any fault with the Company in their action or judgment but it Seems to me we do things wrong. . . . For the repayment of the Capital invested, dividends from monies earned or the advanced sale of Stock are the only Sources— Enterprises involving large sums of money are originated and brought into shape by men who are supposed to have a large amount of brains & Some money they supplying the former in unlimited quantities and look to the mass for the latter—Now my notion is brains should be paid for as well as the use of money and whilst in the management of other parties money we should in all respects be strictly just but it should not debar the brains from taking advantage of Knowledge gained in the management of the business and make money as the opportunity offers. The managers of stock companies in the main make as much or more in the manipulation of stock than from the dividends. The original owners of our Cos Stock have made money by the increase of the value of the stock or in other words by the doubleing up of stock caused by force of circumstances—Have you or I been paid in dividends for the business we put in the hands of the company & Capital invested I say no, and why? By a careful study of large stock Companies both here & in California I find there are none who have done there work so well so permanent as we—

Are we working for future generations or for a few dollars to spend ourselves as we pass along? Our pride is gratified when a Stranger remarks
what a splendid wharf magnificent boats grand this, grand that, but does
that pay dividends? Had we managed the California Co. we would have
had as fine a warehouse both at San Fran & Sacremento as stone & brick
could build, they content themselves with a wharf at the former place and
the levee at the latter ... The fact is we are working for Glory, and as
though we were to live for all time and not for money at the present time
—You ask how this should be changed—I say let the present owners and
managers have an eye only to making dividends, by that I mean to spend
as little as possible on repairs—Make dividends you & I large owners
can go into the market & sell stock[,] much or little as we see fit[,] when
we show our stock is in demand—let your property if necessity does not
demand repairs depreciate but make your dividends being inside we know
what is the value of the stock we sell from time to time reduce our stock
Now perhaps opposition comes or great repairs are needed dividends
cease the stock drops you are on the inside you know when to buy—you
buy back your stock which you may have sold a short time before at 10 20
or 30 pr ct less than you got for it ... Our pride has made our business a
pet, it has all grown up like a child under our fostering care and we cannot bear to see it suffer or grow ragged although sucking the very life
blood from us—Our company has much to be proud of all we have done
redownds to our credit but now is the time for us to make our money for
the many years of labor we have bestowed on this business—And in doing
this will not retard the growth of the Company or the laudable enterprise
of placeing boats on all the inland waters of Oregon—but let the dividends
of some new owners do it—let us by dividends paid us & sales of our stock
—get even on the company and at the same time secure us from haveing
our "Eggs all in one basket" I have for some time intended to write Ladd
or Ainsworth the embodiment of the foregoing as being my views of how
we as a company should act so as to allow large stock holders to dispose
of some of their shares Scatter the stock & by our knowledge try to
make as much or more from buying & selling as from dividends—I dont
know how this will suit Ainsworth he has such a holy horror of debt I
am afraid he would prefer the Company to have immense sinking fund
even although stockholders had to borrow money to live on because the
policy of the company demands at the present time the actual status must
not be known—Please let Ladd & Ainsworth get these ideas from you &
thus I be saved from writing them over ...

J. C. Ainsworth to S. G. Reed

May 11, 1866

Business is frightfully dull, May, unless business improves very much,
will not much more than pay expenses. We have curtailed expenses in

every way possible, I find the C. S. N. Co. in connection with the Pacific Railroad are offering every inducement to parties who will ship for Idaho via Sacramento River, both have offered to carry freight free as far as their lines extend, this, of course, is hearsay, but it comes very credibly endorsed, what it all means, I am not exactly prepared to say, but that we will ultimately get the trade, I have not the slightest shadow of a doubt, I may look at it as did the boy after the woodchuck, but not less confidently. . . .

You say that Bradford wants dividends if we have to borrow money to make them, *I am not on it*. I think our goose is a good one, and do not mean to kill her by trying to force two eggs at once. It is impossible for any one to judge from that standpoint, as to what is the best policy for us to pursue, I feel confident that both Bradford and "Wes" would fully endorse everything we have done were they here to see for themselves. Every day brings its changes, even you will require posting up when you return . . .

Editors' note: The plans of Ainsworth, Thompson, Reed and Ladd to get rid of Bradford and other troublesome stockholders and themselves to control the destiny of the Oregon Steam Navigation Company . . . were slowly worked out. Alvinza Hayward, of Hayward, Coleman & Co., the owner of a famous gold mine in Amador County, California, and a man of much wealth, was persuaded to lend his name to the four directors of the Oregon company. It was given out that Mr. Hayward wished to control the O.S.N. property, and the stockholders who were not parties to the scheme were invited to sell out.

J. C. Ainsworth to J. W. Ladd

May 18, 1867

Your favor per "Idaho" duly received and contents noted; also your telegram saying that "Mine" [code word for the OSN's *Oregonian*] could be sold for $350,000 and asking what we thought. In reply to this we telegraphed to get ultimatum, and we would say yes or no. As yet we have not heard what that ultimatum was. I am decidedly of the opinion if we can do no better that it is prudent to accept rather than go into a fight, but the price named is too low, and under any other circumstances would not be entertained for a moment. . . .

Editors' note: [The *Oregonian* was sold at a loss in June of 1867. However, the purchasing company, the North American Steamship Company, was shortly to succumb to the kind of competition forecast in a Portland *Oregonian* editorial of August 13, 1868] : "Railroads vs. Steamships: The days of steamships as the means of passenger transportation between the Atlantic and Pacific States are nearly ended. Already the overland communication between San Francisco and New York City is more than a week shorter than by steamer via Panama, and any of the cities west of the Lakes may be reached by rail and stage in less than half the time required by the steamship route. ... It is now almost certain that during next year the great railway track across the continent will be completed, and then farewell to the glory of the steamships . . ."

William Gilpin

In a kind of apostolic succession, the idea of a pathway across the continent was passed along from Thomas Jefferson to Thomas Hart Benton to William Gilpin (1813–1894). More than any other promoter of a way west, Gilpin was a participant in the frontier experience. After service in the Seminole War, he resigned his commission in 1838 and went to St. Louis to edit the Missouri Argus *and pump for the re-election of Benton and Lewis Linn to the United States Senate. Ever restless, in 1843 Gilpin left for Oregon, where he participated briefly in the revision of the provisional government. Soon afterward he served with Doniphan's Missouri Volunteers in the Mexican War and then fought Indians in the Rockies. In 1861 he was appointed governor of the newly created Colorado Territory. Balancing his liking for action, Gilpin wrote enthusiastically and prophetically about the American West in articles, books, and published addresses. In the following selection, Gilpin—speaking at a mass meeting in Independence, Missouri, in the fall of 1849—urges the authorization of a Pacific railroad to run by the central route through South Pass to the mouth of the Columbia. The excerpts included here represent a very small proportion of Gilpin's rambling, hour-and-a-half-long address.*

Observations on the Pacific Railroad*

It is with profound pleasure, Mr. Chairman, that I address my fellow-citizens here assembled, to respond approvingly to the National

---

* From William Gilpin, *The Central Gold Region: The Grain, Pastoral, and Gold Regions of North America with Some New Views of Its Physical Geography; and Observations on the Pacific Railroad* (Philadelphia: Sower, Barnes & Co., 1860), pp. 145–171 *passim*.

[Railroad] Convention at St. Louis. . . . I greet with enthusiastic joy these civic movements of the people to consummate, with the great works of peace, what war and exploration have opened. Diplomacy and war have brought to us the completion of our territory and peace. From this we advance to the RESULTS. These results are, for the present, the imperial expansion of our Republic to the other ocean, fraternity with Asia, and the construction across the centre of our territory, from ocean to ocean, of a great iron pathway, specially national to us, international to the northern continents of America, Asia, and Europe. . . .

Up to the year 1840, the progress whereby twenty-six States and four Territories had been established and peopled, had amounted to a solid strip of twenty-five miles in depth, added annually, along the western face of the Union from Canada to the Gulf. This occupation of wild territory, accumulating outward like the annual rings of our forest trees, proceeds with all the solemnity of a Providential ordinance. It is at this moment sweeping onward to the Pacific with accelerated activity and force, like a deluge of men, rising unabatedly, and daily pushed onward by the hand of God. . . .

. . . From this very spot [Independence] had gone forth a forlorn hope to occupy Oregon and California; Texas was thus annexed, the Indian country pressed upon its flanks, and spy companies reconnoitering New and Old Mexico. . . . Thus, then, *overland* sweeps this tide-wave of population, absorbing in its thundering march the glebe, the savages, and the wild beasts of the wilderness, sealing the mountains and debouching down upon the seaboard. Upon the high Atlantic sea-coast, the pioneer force has thrown itself into ships, and found in the ocean-fisheries food for its creative genius. The whaling fleet is the *marine* force of the pioneer army. These two forces, by land and sea, have worked steadily onward to the North Pacific. They now reunite in the harbors of Oregon and California, about to bring into existence upon the Pacific a commercial grandeur identical with that which has followed them upon the Atlantic. . . .

To the American people, then, belongs this vast interior space, covered over its uniform surface of 2,300,000 square miles, with the richest calcareous soil, touching the snows towards the north, and the torrid heats towards the south, bound together by an infinite internal navigation, of a temperate climate, and constituting, in the whole, the most magnificent dwelling-place marked out by God for man's abode. As the complete beneficence of the Almighty has thus given to us, the owners of the continent, the great natural outlets of the Mississippi to the Gulf, and the St. Lawrence to the North Atlantic, so is it left to a pious and grateful people, appreciating this goodness, to construct through the gorge of the Sierra Madre [Rockies], a great artificial monument, an iron path, a NATIONAL Railway to the *Western* Sea. . . .

At this moment the *maritime policy,* planned with dark genius, and pursued with scrupulous selfishness, palls our march. Nothing behind us in history at all rivals in rapidity of growth, in wealth, power, and splendor, those States masking the seaboard, and called at home *"the Old Thirteen."* Here are cities surpassing, at one century old, those of a thousand years, upon the old continents! The States have swelled as fast. This admirable greatness is due to the mastery of the continent which they exercise by majorities in the national councils; to the immense income of revenue which they thus collect and use, and to their monopoly of all foreign commerce. A new and rival seaboard—*"a New Thirteen"*—would halve and distribute all of these. It was *foreseen* how progress, travelling centrally across the continent, was striding point blank to this consummation. To retard this, indefinitely, arose the *maritime policy,* invented by sophistry, and sustained by metaphysics.

Within the young States, the public glebe has been held by the central government and withheld from taxation. Thus is State revenue cut off. These public lands are held at a tyrannical price, the sales made cash, donations of homestead rights, pre-emption, and graduation refused. Savages ejected from the older States, have been bought up and planted as a wall along the western frontier and across the line of progress. These are metaphysically called foreign nations. Recently there has been given to the soldiers of the nation a bounty of $100 in money or $200 in land. This is legislative declaration that the price is 100 per cent above their highest value. The revenue raised from the customs is collected at the seaports, where the expenses of collection are disbursed. The heavy part of this revenue is paid by the agriculturists of the west, who are the consumers. $3,000,000 annually of direct land revenue is exclusively paid by these latter. But where is this splendid income of $40,000,000, thus levied for the most part from western industry, expended? To the navy is devoted $9,000,000 (all upon the tide-waters of the seaboard). To the civil list $5,000,000—all *there* also. To *seaboard* improvements, viz.: customhouses, mints, harbors, breakwaters, fortifications, navy-yards, lighthouses, coast survey, post-offices, armories, &., $2,500,000. All this too is upon the *tide-water.* To the army $5,000,000—this is expended on a military academy, ordnance foundries, four artillery regiments, engineers— *all* upon the *seaboard.* True it is that a few stingy details of cavalry and infantry are posted in shanties upon the western frontier, and a largess of half a million sowed among the Indians. But the single fortress of "Old Point Comfort," has cost more than the sum total of western military structures. Thus do we come at one cardinal item of maritime power —$40,000,000 collected annually from thirty States, of which $39,000,000 is annually paid out to *thirteen only!* Such is the *income* which *maritime policy* secures to itself by taxation. . . . With these maritime States, too, rests the political mastery of the continent, because they have as yet always had the majority of the Houses of Congress, and still retain that in the House of Representatives, in spite of the accession of Texas, Iowa, and Wisconsin, which have changed the Senate. It is the decennial census of 1850 which will give in the thirty-third Congress a majority to this great indigenous American people, residing within the mountains in the great basins of the continent. To them will belong the glorious task to give to the public domain its true, patriotic use, and root out the scorching tyranny, of which it is now the engine. To make taxation and the expenditures of revenue national, and equal among the States and people. To pay, not grind, the pioneers. To reverse the uses of the national wilderness, so that its glebe shall be the beneficent fountain of great roads, unlimited agriculture, population, commerce, and rich States. To give us maritime rivalry and a new seaboard. To reconcile the white man and the Indian, now kept by infamous laws in a state of implacable feuds and mutual piracy. . . .

The *maritime policy* blends the double object of blocking up the interior, and extending the seaboard in a shell around the continent. For this the navy is enormously increased and the army emasculated. Enterprises in the central States are marred, but those of the seaboard sustained directly from the National Treasury. Of this let us take a recent illustration.

A proposition was submitted to the Twenty-ninth Congress, early in its first session (1845–'46) to carry onward to the coast of California and Oregon, and to Santa Fe, *monthly,* the mail which comes tri-weekly to our city of Independence. A law authorizing the Postmaster-General to let the contract for such an extended mail route to the lowest bidder, in the ordinary way, was alone required. Contractors were ready to execute the whole undertaking for $50,000 per annum, carrying the mails in *fifteen days,* making the time from ocean to ocean *twenty-five* days. This proposition, admirable for its practicability, its economy in time and cost, was belabored by orators and suppressed. To this hour all overland mails are prohibited by statute.* At this same session of this same Congress, and under the promptings of these orators, the Government was, by statute, made the partner with ship-building companies of New York city. To construct four mail steamers, the sum of $1,250,000 was *advanced* to these companies, to whom was also given the monopoly of future government transportation for ten years. The transportation of *our* mails through the Isthmus is confided to the *Spaniards* of New Granada! All this enormous expenditure has produced at the end of four years, an uncertain monthly mail, *outside* of our country, and exposed to the hostilities of the whole world, which traverses 9000 miles of *sterile* ocean in fifty

---

* Not until 1857 did Congress authorize an overland mail. The contract was awarded to John Butterfield, who used the southern route until 1861 when the line was shifted to the central route.

days! In the interval the contracts have been doubled in amount by doubling
the size and cost of the ships. It is a condition of these contracts that
these "mail steamers" may be appraised and purchased by Government
for the Navy. Thus is the Navy *clandestinely* increased by eight or a dozen
war steamers.

Thus, whilst we may transport the domestic mails between our distant people and seaboards through the heart of our territories, every inch
upon our own soil, and 1000 miles from any foreign foe or frontier—
whilst this can be done and is offered to be done, by our citizens, for
prices at which the mails will yield remunerating revenues—whilst this
admits of an increase to daily mails at any time, and a reduction of time
to one-half—whilst this allows of innumerable way mails, telegraphs, and
the most intimate domestic intercourse—involves neither increase of military force nor expenditures by sea or land, and avoids the possibility of
foreign interference or molestation—opening roads and crowding them
with population and settlements—concentrating to the seaport where it
reaches the Pacific, the American shipping and business on that ocean,
at once creating a great American emporium. Instead of all this, which is
sensible and natural, and understood by our people, whose *cardinal right*
it is to have the circulation of their domestic thoughts and business
through home channels which are short, safe, and expeditious! Yes, instead of this, we are taxed millions, to have our letters sent 9000 miles in
fifty days, under the equator, by sea, through foreign nations, exposed to
delay, dangers, and destruction in every form, ruffling the jealousies of
rival nations, and exposed to their cannon—and all this to fill the maws
of maritime speculators and political ambition. . . .

The experience gained from the great works constructed by the
last generation in digging through the Alleghenies routes for commerce
to the Atlantic, settles for us the rules that shall guide *us* across the Sierra
Madre [Rockies] to the Pacific. In 1818 the State of New York cut
through the low and narrow ridge between Rome and Syracuse, the former
on an affluent of the Hudson, the latter of Lake Ontario. Thus the *first*
expenditures, perforating the dividing mountain, let through that infant
commerce, which in thirty years has grown to such a grandeur of quantity
and profit, that this great thoroughfare is itself quadrupled in capacity and
lengthened out to Montreal, to Boston, to New York city and into Pennsylvania, towards the east. Westward, it reaches through Ohio and Indiana
to the Ohio river, and by the Illinois and Wisconsin rivers to the Missouri
and Mississippi. What the single State of New York, of 1,200,000 population, accomplished by her own intrinsic bravery and resources, undismayed
by ridicule and unappalled by the *then* experimental character of such
works in a republic and upon our continent:—just such a work now invites
the national bravery, power, and wealth of this imperial republic; namely:
to lay, over the dividing barrier of the Sierra Madre, along the floor of

its natural tunnel at the South Pass, *an iron pathway,* which, descending the grades of the Platte and Columbia to the highest points of navigation, shall let through the first infant stream of that supreme Oriental commerce, whose annually expanding flood will, during our generation, elongate its arms and fingers through all the States and to every harbor of the two seaboards. . . .

It is, then, I repeat, through the heart of our Territories, our population, our States, our farms and habitations, that we need this broad current of commerce. Where passengers and cargo may, at any time or place, embark upon or leave the vehicles of transportation. . . . This central railroad is an essential domestic institution, more powerful and permanent than law, or popular consent, to thoroughly complete the great systems of fluvial arteries which fraternize us into one people; to bind the two seaboards to this one nation, like ears to the human head; to radicate the foundations of the UNION so broad and deep, and render its structure so solid, that no possible force or stratagem can shake its permanence; and to secure such scope and space to progress, that prosperity and equality shall never be impaired or chafe for want of room.

What, sirs, are these populous empires of Japan and China, now become our neighbors? They are the most ancient, the most highly civilized, the most polished of the earth. It was from Sinim [China] that the Judean king Solomon imported the architects, the mechanics, the furniture of his gorgeous temple. . . . Hence came the climax of all human inventions, *letters and figures,* which fix language and numbers, making them eternal . . . Tea, sugar, the peach produced from the wild almond, the orange from the sour lime, the apple from the crab, the fruits, the flowers, the vegetables of our gardens, are the *creations* of Chinese *horticultural* science. The horse, cattle, the swine and poultry of our farms, come to us from thence. . . . Hence also came gunpowder, the magnetic needle, and calomel. The paints, varnish, and tools of the art have come, and the remedies used in pharmacy.*

. . . Such as *Progress* is to-day, the same has it been for ten thousand years. It is the stream of the human race flowing from the east to the west, impelled by the same divine instinct that pervades creation. . . .

. . . It is by the rapid propagation of new States, the immediate occupation of the broad platform of the continent, the aggregation of the Pacific Ocean and Asiatic commerce, that inquietude will be swallowed up, and the murmurs of discontent lost in the onward sound of advancement. Discontent, distanced, will die out. The immense wants of the Pacific will draw off, over the Western outlets, the overteeming crops of the Missis-

---

* This paean to the Chinese has a bitter and ironic ring in the light of the subsequent use of contract coolie labor in the building of the Central Pacific Railroad.

sippi Valley. Thus will the present seaboard States resume again their once profitable monopoly of the European market, relieved from the competition of the interior States. The cotton and rice culture of Georgia and the Carolinas will revive. The tobacco of Virginia and Maryland will again alone reach Europe. Ships withdrawn from the Northern States to the Pacific, will regenerate the noble business of nautical construction in New England and New York. The established domestic manufactures of clothing and metals will find, in our great home extension, that protection which they in vain seek to create by unequal legislation, nocuous and impracticable in our present incomplete and unbalanced geographical form. Thus calmly weighed and liberally appreciated, does this great Central Railroad minister to the interests, and invite the advocacy and co-operation of every section of our territory, and every citizen of our common country.

Grenville Dodge

As the preceding selection suggests, the need for a transcontinental railroad became apparent immediately after the Mexican War, but in the intensifying sectional conflict and with the assumption that only one road could be afforded, neither North nor South would allow the other the benefit of the line. It was hoped that the engineers might take the question out of politics altogether, but surveys following 1853 showed at least four feasible crossings. Not until the South seceded was it possible to settle the route; and in 1862 Congress passed the first Pacific railroad bill, accepting the middle passage. The Central Pacific Railroad, under the leadership of "the Big Four"—Huntington, Stanford, Hopkins, and Crocker—built eastward from Oakland; the Union Pacific Railroad built westward from Omaha; the two eventually met at Promontory, Utah, in 1869. The government subsidized the construction by granting a 400-foot right-of-way, ten alternate sections of land for each mile (later increased to twenty), and loans from $16,000 to $48,000 per mile, depending on the topography of the country. But it was nevertheless a Herculean task. Grenville Dodge (1831–1916), a general who had earlier served in the West, was chief engineer for the Union Pacific after 1866; his account of the construction gives some measure of the accomplishment.

How We Built the Union Pacific*

The organization for work on the plains away from civilization was as follows: Each of our surveying parties consisted of a chief, who was an experienced engineer, two assistants, also civil engineers, but without personal experience in the field, besides axe men, teamsters and herders. When the party was expected to live upon the game of the country a hunter was added. Each party would thus consist of from eighteen to twenty-two men, all armed. When operating in a hostile Indian country they were regularly drilled, though after the Civil War this was unnecessary, as most of them had been in the army. Each party entering a country occupied by hostile Indians was generally furnished with a military escort of from ten men to a company under a competent officer. The duty of this escort was to protect the party when in camp. In the field the escort usually occupied prominent hills commanding the territory in which the work was to be done, so as to head off sudden attacks by the Indians. Notwithstanding this protection, the parties were often attacked, their chief, or some of their men killed or wounded, and their stock run off.

In preliminary surveys in the open country a party would run from eight to twelve miles of line in a day. On location in an open country three or four miles would be covered, but in a mountainous country generally not to exceed a mile. All hands worked from daylight to dark, the country being reconnoitered ahead of them by the chief, who indicated the streams to follow, and the controlling points in summits and river crossings. The party of location that followed the preliminary surveys, had the maps and profiles of the line selected for location and devoted its energies to obtaining a line of the lowest grades and the least curvature that the country would admit.

The location party in our work on the Union Pacific was followed by the construction corps, grading generally 100 miles at a time. That distance was graded in about thirty days on the plains, as a rule, but in the mountains we sometimes had to open our grading several hundred miles ahead of our track in order to complete the grading by the time the track should reach it. All the supplies for this work had to be hauled from the end of the track, and the wagon transportation was enormous. At one time we were using at least 10,000 animals, and most of the time from 8,000 to 10,000 laborers. The bridge gangs always worked from five to twenty miles ahead of the track, and it was seldom that the track

---

* From Grenville Dodge, *How We Built the Union Pacific Railway* (Washington, D.C.: Government Printing Office, 1910), pp. 15–38 *passim*.

waited for a bridge. To supply one mile of track with material and supplies required about forty cars, as on the plains everything—rails, ties,
bridging, fastenings, all railway supplies, fuel for locomotives and trains,
and supplies for men and animals on the entire work, had to be transported from the Missouri River. Therefore, as we moved westward, every
hundred miles added vastly to our transportation. Yet the work was so
systematically planned and executed that I do not remember an instance
in all the construction of the line of the work being delayed a single week
for want of material. Each winter we planned the work for the next
season. By the opening of spring, about April 1st, every part of the
machinery was in working order, and in no year did we fail to accomplish
our work. . . .

The law of 1862 provided that the Union Pacific and Central Pacific
should join their tracks at the California State line. The law of 1864
allowed the Central Pacific to build 150 miles east of the state line, but
that was changed by the law of 1866, and the two companies allowed to
build, one east and the other west, until they met. The building of 500
miles of road during the summers of 1866 and 1867, hardly twelve months'
actual work, had aroused great interest in the country, and much excitement, in which the Government took a part. We were pressed to as speedy
a completion of the road as possible, although ten years had been allowed
by Congress. The officers of the Union Pacific had become imbued with
this spirit, and they urged me to plan to build as much road as possible
in 1868. . . .

We made our plans to build to Salt Lake, 480 miles, in 1868, and to
endeavor to meet the Central Pacific at Humboldt Wells, 219 miles west
of Ogden, in the spring of 1869. I had extended our surveys during the
years 1867 and 1868 to the California State line, and laid my plans before the company, and the necessary preparations were made to commence work as soon as frost was out of the ground, say about April 1st.
Material had been collected in sufficient quantities at the end of the track
to prevent any delay. During the winter ties and bridge timber had been
cut and prepared in the mountains to bring to the line at convenient
points, and the engineering forces were started to their positions before
cold weather was over that they might be ready to begin their work as
soon as the temperature would permit. I remember that the parties going
to Salt Lake crossed the Wasatch Mountains on sledges, and that the
snow covered the tops of the telegraph poles. We all knew and appreciated
that the task we had laid out would require the greatest energy on the
part of all hands. About April 1st, therefore, I went onto the plains myself
and started our construction forces, remaining the whole summer between Laramie and the Humboldt Mountains. I was surprised at the
rapidity with which the work was carried forward. Winter caught us in
the Wasatch Mountains, but we kept on grading our road and laying our

track in the snow and ice at a tremendous cost. I estimated for the company that the extra cost of thus forcing the work during that summer and winter was over $10,000,000, but the instructions I received were to go on, no matter what the cost. Spring found us with the track at Ogden, and by May 1st we had reached Promontory, 534 miles west of our starting point twelve months before. Work on our line was opened to Humboldt Wells, making in the year a grading of 754 miles of line.

The Central Pacific had made wonderful progress coming east, and we abandoned the work from Promontory to Humboldt Wells, bending all our efforts to meet them at Promontory. Between Ogden and Promontory each company graded a line, running side by side, and in some places one line was right above the other. The laborers upon the Central Pacific were Chinamen, while ours were Irishmen, and there was much ill-feeling between them. Our Irishmen were in the habit of firing their blasts in the cuts without giving warning to the Chinamen on the Central Pacific working right above them. From this cause several Chinamen were severely hurt. Complaint was made to me by the Central Pacific people, and I endeavored to have the contractors bring all hostilities to a close, but, for some reason or other, they failed to do so. One day the Chinamen, appreciating the situation, put in what is called a "grave" on their work, and when the Irishmen right under them were all at work let go their blast and buried several of our men. This brought about a truce at once. From that time the Irish laborers showed due respect for the Chinamen, and there was no further trouble. . . .

The track laying on the Union Pacific was a science. Mr. W. A. Bell, in an article on the Pacific Railroads, describes, after witnessing it, as follows:

"We, pundits of the far East, stood upon that embankment, only about a thousand miles this side of sunset, and backed westward before that hurrying corps of sturdy operators with a mingled feeling of amusement, curiosity and profound respect. On they came. A light car, drawn by a single horse, gallops up to the front with its load of rails. Two men seize the end of a rail and start forward, the rest of the gang taking hold by twos, until it is clear of the car. They come forward at a run. At the word of command the rail is dropped in its place, right side up with care, while the same process goes on at the other side of the car. Less than thirty seconds to a rail for each gang, and so four rails go down to the minute. Quick work, you say, but the fellows on the Union Pacific are tremendously in earnest. The moment the car is empty it is tipped over on the side of the track to let the next loaded car pass it, and then it is tipped back again, and it is a sight to see it go flying back for another load, propelled by a horse at full gallop at the end of sixty or eighty feet of rope, ridden by a young Jehu, who drives furiously. Close behind the first gang come the gaugers, spikers and bolters, and a lively time they make of it. It is a grand 'Anvil Chorus' that those sturdy sledges are playing across the plains. It is in a triple time, three strokes to the spike. There are ten spikes to a rail, four hundred rails to a mile, eighteen hundred miles to San Francisco —twenty-one million times are they to come down with their sharp punctuation, before the great work of modern America is complete."

Robert S. Henry

Because the federal land grants were indispensable to the launching of most Western railroads, it is important that the government's contribution in this form be seen in balanced perspective. For years it was generally assumed that great chunks of the public domain were handed to American railroads as unequivocal subsidies. In an article written in 1945, Robert S. Henry, railroad man and historian, challenged this traditional view in the area where it was most effectively advanced and perpetuated—textbooks in American history. Henry's analysis, much of which appears below, provides a needed corrective. Note that he confines his treatment to the federal land grants, since they were the central target of attack. Recent work in the history of railroad finance indicates that state and local aid, private and public, was more important to railroad growth than was national aid.

Government's Contribution to the Railroads*

In 1850, the United States government had a public domain of approximately 1,400,000,000 acres, vacant, unoccupied, and, for lack of transportation, largely unusable and unsalable. Between that year and the end of 1871, the government undertook to use a portion of this land to encourage and assist the building of railroads in vacant or sparsely settled sections, in the same way in which previously it had aided the building of wagon roads and canals. The resulting series of transactions

---

*From Robert S. Henry, "The Railroad Land Grant Legend in American History Texts," *Mississippi Valley Historical Review,* XXXII (September 1945), 171–172, 182–189, 193. Reprinted by permission.

came to be known as the Federal railroad land grants, a subject frequently mentioned in high school and college texts which are the first, last, and only works on the history of their country read by many, if not most, Americans. . . .

A balanced story of the Federal land grant transactions requires reasonably correct answers to these questions, at the very least:

How much land was granted to railroads, and what proportion was this of the whole public domain?

What proportion of the railroad mileage of the country received land grants from the government?

What was this land worth?

What were the terms and conditions of the grants? Were they gifts, or did the government get as well as give?

The first of these questions, purely a matter of recorded fact, deals with the amount of land granted to railroads by the United States government. In the standard general work on the subject, Donaldson's *Public Domain,* published by the government in 1884, the total amount of land that would be necessary to fulfill all the acts granting lands to railroads was estimated at 155,504,994 acres. The amount of land actually patented to railroads, however, fell substantially short of this acreage, for a variety of reasons—noncompletion of the lines or other failure to comply with the conditions of the grants, or lack of sufficient acreage within the designated limits to fulfill the terms of the grants. The acreage to which the railroads actually received title appears in the annual reports of the Commissioner of the General Land Office, the latest such report showing a total of 131,350,534 acres. . . .

The second, and equally simple, question deals with the extent of railroad mileage, the construction of which was aided by the government's land grants. Such grants were made in aid of a total of 18,738 miles of railroad line—less than 8 per cent of the total mileage of railroads built in the United States. The fact that more than 92 per cent of all the railroad mileage in the United States was built without the aid of an acre of Federal land grants is nowhere brought out in the texts examined . . .

The same tendency to exaggerate the government's financial part in railroad building appears in the treatment of the bond aid extended to six of the companies chartered to build the pioneer "Pacific" railroads. The government made a loan of its bonds to these railroads, in the total amount of $64,623,512. The roads were to pay 6 per cent interest on the bonds and to pay them off. During the long period of development and light traffic they were not always able to meet these charges, but in the final settlement in 1898 and 1899 the government collected $63,023,512 of principal plus $104,722,978 in interest—a total repayment of $167,746,-490 on an intial loan of $64,623,512. . . . Thirty-four of the thirty-seven

texts examined mention the bond aid to these Pacific roads. In one-third
of the works, it is not made clear whether the financial assistance referred to was a loan or a gift. Three describe the aid definitely as gifts—
which they were not. Twenty-one refer to the transactions as loans, but
only four mention the fact that the loans were repaid, while three make
the positively erroneous statement that the loans were never repaid.

One measure of the value of the lands granted—though no one
would contend that it is the correct one—would be the cost to the government of acquiring them, which, according to Donaldson, was an average of
23.3 cents an acre. On that basis, the 131,351,000 acres which the railroads received could be said to be worth less than $31,000,000.

Another possible measure is the standard "minimum" price at which
the government offered the public domain for sale in the land grant period.
This price was $1.25 an acre, though the government was never able to
realize even this figure as an average selling price. But if the new railroad
companies had bought from the government the 131,350,534 acres actually
received, and had paid the full established price, the lands would have
cost them $164,188,167. . . .

A more correct measure of value is the one applied in all ordinary
transfers between buyer and seller—the worth of the land granted and received at the time of sale. During the period in which the land grants
were being made to the railroads, the average sale price of government
lands in the land grants states was less than $1 an acre. Applying that price
to the lands granted to the railroads gives a value as of the time of the
grants, of less than $130,000,000.

It is sometimes contended that the measure of value in this case
should be the amount finally realized by the railroads on their lands, after
the roads had been built and after years of colonizing, advertising, sales
effort, and development costs had been put upon them. There is no more
basis for setting up such a measure of value than there would be for putting it at the 23 cents an acre which it cost the government to acquire
the lands in the first place, but because the point is raised in some of the
works examined, it may be noted that the average realizations of the railroads from their Federal land grants, plus the estimated value of the lands
remaining unsold, was put at $3.38 an acre according to one government
study, while in another report, including both state and Federal grants,
the average is $2.81 an acre. . . .

The real contribution of the Federal land grants to the spread of the
rails in the West and the newer South was not the cash realized upon
them, but the fact that they furnished a basis of credit which got the job
started and made it possible to get it done. The land grant acreage could
be certified, patented, and sold only as the railroad itself was completed,
in sections, and then could be sold mostly on long time credit. The selling
price had to be low to get it sold at all, and the expense of sale was neces-

sarily high. The net realizations from the sales, particularly during the period of construction, were but a tiny fraction of the cost of building the railroads. Thus, the Auditor of Railroad Accounts of the Department of the Interior reported that up to 1880 the several companies going to make up the five pioneer "Pacific" routes had sold only $36,383,795 worth of land. "The lands have been sold in small tracts, some for cash, but most of them on time," the Auditor wrote in describing the sales of one of the several companies concerned. The cost up to that time of building the several Pacific routes is shown in the same report as having been $465,584,029. This, the Auditor thought and so reported, was excessive, or at least much more than similar roads could have been built for when the report was made. Even the lesser figure of $168,045,000, which he estimated as enough to reproduce the roads, however, was considerably more than four times the realizations from land sales up to that date. Looking to the future, the Auditor estimated that the value of the railroad lands unsold in 1880 was $78,889,940, making a total estimated value for all lands sold and to be sold of $115,273,735, as against a total estimated cost of the several "Pacific" railroads, to completion, of $634,165,613. The Auditor thought that similar railroads could be built for $286,819,300, but even this figure is more than double the estimated total realizations from the lands granted to the "Pacific's." . . .

. . . Were the Federal land grants gifts? Or were they trades by which the government got, as well as gave, direct consideration? . . .

While the conditions of the several grants vary, in the overwhelming majority of cases the Acts of Congress making grants to railroads adopted the phraseology of the earlier canal and wagon road grants in requiring that the railroad to be built should "be and remain a public highway for the use of the government of the United States, free from toll or other charge upon the transportation of any property or troops of the United States." The effect of this clause, as finally determined by the Supreme Court, was that the government was entitled to the use of the roadbed without toll, by analogy to the free right of passage for its vehicles or boats over grant-aided wagon roads and canals, but that this did not extend so far as to require the railroad company to provide and operate without charge the engines, cars, and other equipment needed for transportation over the railroads.

Under a formula subsequently worked out by the United States Court of Claims, the deduction from ordinary charges on account of this provision of the land grant acts was established at 50 per cent. Still later, by a series of Acts of Congress, the same percentage of deduction from commercial rates was made applicable to the limited number of land grant roads whose grants did not contain the "toll-free" provision in this form, while even railroads which received no land grant whatever from the government have long since entered into "equalization agreements" by which they also undertake to handle government traffic at the same rates applying by law on the land grant lines. Compensation for handling mail on land grant lines was fixed by Act of Congress in 1876 at 80 per cent of the rates applying on other railroads.

In the Transportation Act of 1940, the Congress eliminated these provisions in so far as they applied to mail pay and to rates on the government's civilian passenger and freight traffic. Deductions of 50 per cent were continued, however, on the charges for transportation of military and naval and not for civil uses. . . .

Thus it is that although less than 10 per cent of railroad mileage received grants of land, either Federal or state, the whole railroad system of the nation has paid for them a direct monetary return far exceeding the value of the lands granted.

"It is probable," said the Congressional Committee report already referred to, "that the railroads have contributed over $900,000,000 in payment of the lands which were transferred to them under the Land Grant Acts. This is double the amount received for the lands sold by the railroads plus the estimated value of such lands still under railroad ownership. Former Commissioner Eastman estimated that the total value of the lands at the time they were granted . . . was not more than $126,000,-000." . . .

Almost without exception, however, the history textbooks have failed to develop the major and essential fact that, whatever may have been its shortcomings, the land-grant policy touched off national and individual energies which in a few short years accomplished the greatest engineering, construction, and colonization project ever undertaken up to that time, a project which transformed the West from a wilderness to a civilized community and welded the nation into one.

ADDITIONAL READINGS

Fundamental to an understanding of American transportation, Western or otherwise, is George R. Taylor's *The Transportation Revolution, 1815–1860* (New York, 1951). A readable history of the express companies is *Old Waybills* by Alvin F. Harlow (New York, 1934). More scholarly is Oscar O. Winther's *Via Western Express and Stage Coach* (Stanford, California, 1945). LeRoy R. Hafen's *The Overland Mail, 1849–1869* (Cleveland, 1926) and Roscoe and

Margaret Conklings' *The Butterfield Overland Mail, 1858–1869* (Glendale, California, 1947) are competent. Raymond W. and Mary L. Settle, in *Empire on Wheels* (Stanford, California, 1949), tell the story of Russell, Majors and Waddell. *Wells Fargo, Advancing the American Frontier,* by Edward Hungerford (New York, 1949), and *The Pony Express Goes Through,* by Howard R. Driggs (New York, 1935) are popular treatments. See also Arthur Chapman, *The Pony Express* (New York, 1932).

Randall Mills, in *Sternwheelers up Columbia* (Palo Alto, California, 1947), deals affectionately with steam navigation in the Pacific Northwest. See also Louis C. Hunter, *Steamboats on Western Rivers* (Cambridge, 1949). The role of the Army Engineers in transportation is the theme of Forest G. Hill, *Roads, Rails and Waterways* (Norman, Oklahoma, 1957).

The best general works on Western railroads are *The Story of the Western Railroads,* by Robert E. Riegel (New York, 1926); and *They Built the West: An Epic of Rails and Cities,* by Glenn C. Quiett (New York, 1934). For individual railroads, see Richard C. Overton, *Burlington West* (Cambridge, 1941); L. L. Waters, *Steel Rails to Santa Fe* (Lawrence, Kansas, 1950); Stuart Daggett, *Chapters in the History of the Southern Pacific* (New York, 1922); James B. Hedges, *Henry Villard and the Railways of the Northwest* (New Haven, 1930); Oscar Lewis, *The Big Four* (New York, 1938); and Stewart Holbrook, *James J. Hill* (New York, 1955).

13

CITIES AND
SMALL TOWNS

Denver, Salt Lake, Seattle, San Francisco—such Western cities were themselves lures, commercial magnets that attracted businessmen much as cheap land drew the farmer. Each major city tended to develop in its own direction, distinct in subtle ways from others and especially from Eastern cities, and each therefore attracting different kinds of people. San Francisco, for example, facing the Orient, long had a brawling, lusty flavor that no Eastern metropolis could match.

Cities cannot support themselves; they must be linked to rural areas for their food and sustenance. Therefore, urban development required a transportation system, and the building of the transcontinental railroad had vital significance to the growth of Western cities. The termini of railroads or key junction points mushroomed. Many another center, begun with equal hopes but not finally favored with a rail connection, withered like forgotten fruit on the vine. Brigham Young had this fact in mind when he fought so hard for the transcontinental line to run directly through Salt Lake, but topography was against him. Salt Lake grew for other reasons—as a religious and agricultural center; but cities like Seattle and Los Angeles waited for their full development until the railroads came.

If the cities managed to encourage differences among themselves, the small towns in the West had little individualized, distinctive flavor. Many a European traveler commented on their sameness; one Main Street looked like another—the same bank, the same drugstore, the same jerry-built houses. In contrast with European villages, which cherished special idiosyncrasies, the monotony of American towns even today must be admitted. And the West had much to do with this; for it was restless, it was building for a day, and its progress came during a limited span of history. There was no time for the slow growth of varying styles of architecture and contrasting tastes in planning. True, nineteenth-century cities were rapidly expanding elsewhere too; but the builders of Western towns usually moved on and, as critics pointed out, seldom looked backward to see their structures crumbling. It all happened so fast! The founder of Spokane, built on vacant land, saw his purchase become within his own lifetime a city of 100,000 people.

Like Spokane, most of the towns and cities of the West grew haphazardly by accretions of individuals, with little community planning or cohesion. This pattern had typified Western growth from the Southern colonies in the seventeenth and eighteenth centuries, but it was not the pattern characteristic of early New England. There communities were founded as a result of group enterprise, usually centering in a church congregation and based upon a religious covenant. Such foundations did not have widespread counterparts in the West of the nineteenth century; but there were some, usually revolving around religious sects (for example, the Bruderhof in the Dakotas, the Icarian settlements in Texas and Iowa and California, and the Amana society of Iowa), which either moved intact or branched out. They stand, of course, in the long line of communal and utopian experiments that had their zenith in the Fourieristic phalanxes of the 1840s. Fourierist communities got as far west as Wisconsin, and in the 1820s Indiana had witnessed the blighted hopes of Robert Owen's New Harmony. But these latter were based on secular ideals and lasted only a few years at the most. Amana is an example of the religious strain and hence is closer to the earlier New England concept.

The small town in America, though its covenanted base was weakened, continued to protect some elements of group consciousness; in this sense it must be set abruptly apart from the city. The isolated individual could be found on a farm or he could hide amid "the lonely crowd" in a big city, but it was not easy to insulate oneself from the citizens of a small town. There one grew up in bonds of what Lewis Atherton calls "togetherness." Clinging to countless holdovers from the covenanted community, the Middle Western and Far Western small town, like its counterparts elsewhere, had an inestimable effect on American life and thought.

Samuel Bowles

Samuel Bowles (1826–1878), editor of the Springfield (Massachusetts) Republican, strong voice against slavery, and one of the founders of the Republican party, traveled west with Representative Schuyler Colfax in the summer of 1865. In his subsequent account of this trip, he gives some interesting descriptions of Western cities and their importance.

Some Western Cities*

We find that neither the graces nor the culture of life are confined to the East. They flourish here [in Denver] among the Rocky Mountains as beautifully as in the parlors of Boston, or the sweet groves of the Connecticut valley.

Most agreeable of all our experiences here are the intelligent, active, earnest, right-minded and right-hearted young men and women we meet; people, many of whom have been here for years, but, instead of losing anything of those social graces that eastern towns and cities are wont to think themselves superior in, have not only kept even pace in these, but gained a higher play for all their faculties, and ripened, with opportunity and incentive and necessary self-reliance, into more of manhood and womanhood. Everywhere, too, I find old friends and acquaintances from the Connecticut valley; and nowhere do I find them forgetting old Massachusetts, or unworthy her parentage. I see less drunkenness; I see less vice here among these towns of the border, and of the Rocky Mountains, than at home in Springfield; I see personal activity and growth and self-reliance and social development and organization, that not only reconcile me to the emigration of our young people from the East to this region, but will do much to make me encourage it. To the right-minded, the West gives open opportunity that the East holds close and rare; and to such, opportunity is all that is wanted, all that they ask. . . .

Salt Lake City, Saturday, June 17

In the "great and glorious future" of our Fourth of July orations, when polygamy is extinct, the Pacific Railroad built, and the mines devel-

---

* From Samuel Bowles, *Across the Continent: A Summer's Journey to the Rocky Mountains, the Mormons, and the Pacific States, with Speaker Colfax* (Springfield, Mass.: S. Bowles & Co., 1868), pp. 50–51, 98–103, 182–183.

oped, Salt Lake City will be not only the chief commercial city of the mountains, the equal of St. Louis and Chicago, but one of the most beautiful residence cities and most attractive watering-places on the Continent. Its admirable location and early development secure the one; its agreeable climate for eight months in the year, at least, and the surpassing beauty of its location, with its ample supply of water, its fruits and vegetables, will add the second; and joining to all these circumstances, its snow-capped mountains, its hot sulphur springs, and its Great Salt Lake, and we have the elements of the third fact. There are two principal sulphur springs, one hot enough (one hundred and twenty degrees) to boil an egg, which is four miles from the center of the city, and the other just the right temperature for a hot bath, (ninety degrees,) which is close to the city, and is already brought into a large enclosure for free bathing purposes. Both these streams are large enough for illimitable bathing; the water is as highly sulphurized and as clear as that of the celebrated Sharon Springs; and its use, either for drinking or for baths, most effective in purifying the blood and toning up the system. Other and smaller springs of the same character have been found in the neighborhood.

Then the Lake opens another field of attractions; it is a miniature ocean, about fifteen miles from the city, fifty miles wide by one hundred long,—the briniest sheet of water known on the Continent,—so salt that no fish can live in it, and that three quarts of it will boil down to one quart of fine, pure salt,—but most delicious and refreshing for bathing, floating the body as a cork on the surface,—only the brine must be kept from mouth and eyes under the penalty of a severe smarting;—with its high rocky islands and crestfull waves and its superb sunsets, picturesque and enchanting to look upon; while its broad expanse offers wide space for sailing, and every chance for sea-sickness. Count up all these features for a watering-place; and where will you find a Newport, a Saratoga or a Sharon that has the half of them? So, ye votaries of fashion, ye rheumatic cripples, ye victims of scrofula and ennui, prepare to pack your trunks at the sound of the first whistle of the train for the Rocky Mountains for a season at Salt Lake City.

The city is regularly laid out into squares of ten acres each, and these into lots of one acre and a quarter, only farther subdivided in the business or more thickly populated streets. The building material is mostly sun-dried bricks, (called adobe,) covered with plaster, and the houses are generally of one story, covering much space and with as many front doors as the owner has wives. A few of the newer stores are built of stone, and are elegant and capacious within and without.

There are very large mercantile interests here. Several firms do a business of a million dollars or more each, a year, and keep on hand stocks of goods of the value of a quarter of a million. They frequently have subsidiary stores in other parts of the Territory to the number of four or six. Their freights are enormous, and sometimes their goods are a year on the way hither. One firm has just received a stock of goods, costing one hundred thousand dollars, that was bought in New York last June. It got caught on the Plains by early snow, last fall, and had to winter on the way. Another leading merchant paid one hundred and fifty thousand dollars for freights last year. One lot of goods, groceries, hardware, dry goods, everything, was found to have cost, on reaching here, just one dollar a pound, adding to original purchase the cost of freighting, which from New York to this point averages from twenty-five to thirty cents a pound. It of course requires large capital and courage to enter upon the mercantile business here under such circumstances. Prices, too, must rule high; and when the supply is short, as it was last year, and the demand large, great profits are realized; and again, with an overstocked market and a small sale, there is danger of heavy losses. One concern made seventy-five per cent profit last year, but this season promises poorly; and the stocks on hand cannot, in many cases, be sold for their cost. . . .

There are not many absolutely poor; and the general scale of living is generous. In the early years of the Territory, there was terrible suffering for the want of food; many were reduced to the roots of the field for sustenance; but now there appears to be an abundance of the substantial necessaries of life, and as most of the population are cultivators of the soil, all or nearly all have plenty of food. And certainly, I have never seen more generously laden tables than have been spread before us at our hotel or at private houses. A dinner to our party this evening by a leading Mormon merchant, at which President Young and the principal members of his council were present, had as rich a variety of fish, meats, vegetables, pastry and fruit, as I ever saw on any private table in the East; and the quality and the cooking and the serving were unimpeachable. All the food, too, was native in Utah. The wives of our host waited on us most amicably, and the entertainment was, in every way, the best illustration of the practical benefits of plurality, that has yet been presented to us.

Later in the evening we were introduced to another, and perhaps the most wonderful, illustration of the reach of social and artificial life in this far off city of the Rocky Mountains. This was the Theater, in which a special performance was improvised in honor of Speaker Colfax. The building is itself a rare triumph of art and enterprise. No eastern city of one hundred thousand inhabitants,—remember Salt Lake City has less than twenty thousand,—possesses so fine a theatrical structure. It ranks, alike in capacity and elegance of structure and finish, along with the opera-houses and academies of music of Boston, New York, Philadelphia, Chicago and Cincinnati. In costumes and scenery, it is furnished with equal richness and variety, and the performances, themselves, though by amateurs, by merchants and mechanics, by wives and daughters of citizens, would have done full credit to a first-class professional company. There was first a fine and elaborate drama, and then a spectacular farce, in both which were introduced some exquisite dancing, and in one some good singing also. I have rarely seen a theatrical entertainment more pleasing and satisfactory in all its details and appointments.

Portland, by far the largest town of Oregon, stands sweetly on the banks of the Willamette, twelve miles before it joins the Columbia River, and one hundred and twenty miles from where the Columbia meets the Pacific Ocean. Ships and ocean steamers of highest class come readily hither; from it spreads out a wide navigation by steamboat of the Columbia and its branches, below and above; here centers a large and increasing trade, not only for the Willamette valley, but for the mining regions of eastern Oregon and Idaho, Washington Territory on the north, and parts even of British Columbia. Even Salt Lake, too, has taken groceries and dry goods through this channel, and may yet find it advantageous to buy more and continuously; such are the attained and attainable water communications through the far-extending Columbia.

The population of Portland is about seven thousand; they keep Sunday as we do in New England, and as no other population this side of the Missouri now does; and real estate, as you may infer, is quite high,—four hundred dollars a front foot for best lots one hundred feet deep on the main business street, without the buildings. In religion, the Methodists have the lead, and control an academic school in town and a professed State university at Salem; the Presbyterians are next with a beautiful church and the most fashionable congregation, and favor a struggling university under Rev. S. H. Marsh, (son of President Marsh of the Vermont university,) located twenty miles off in the valley; perhaps the Catholics rank third, with a large Sisters of Charity establishment and school within the city. Governor Gibbs, the present chief magistrate of the State, resides here, and though a lawyer, owns and runs a successful iron foundry that imports its material from England, though undeveloped iron mines are thick in neighboring hills;—a single daily paper has two thousand five hundred circulation, with a weekly edition of three thousand more; and altogether Portland has the air and the fact of a prosperous, energetic town, with a good deal of eastern leadership and tone to business and society and morals.

Mark Twain

When Mark Twain (1835–1910), himself the son of a restless Western land speculator, came to Nevada Territory in 1861, he intended to stay but a few months; but his Western jaunt lasted nearly seven years. During that time he came of age as a writer and earned his first reputation; later he capitalized on the adventure in Roughing It *(1872). From that book comes the following description of his experiences in San Francisco (about 1864–65). Note that many of the problems of urban areas—unemployment, poverty, loneliness—were no different in the West than anywhere else. Twain does not discuss the question as such, but one can understand the conclusions of many recent historians that, because city problems were so universally similar, Western cities in planning their institutions relied heavily on previous Eastern experience.*

San Francisco*

For a few months I enjoyed what to me was an entirely new phase of existence—a butterfly idleness; nothing to do, nobody to be responsible to, and untroubled with financial uneasiness. I fell in love with the most cordial and sociable city in the Union. After the sage-brush and alkali deserts of Washoe, San Francisco was Paradise to me. I lived at the best hotel, exhibited my clothes in the most conspicuous places, infested the opera, and learned to seem enraptured with music which oftener afflicted my ignorant ear than enchanted it, if I had had the vulgar honesty to confess it. However, I suppose I was not greatly worse than the most of my countrymen in that. I had longed to be a butterfly, and I was one at last. I attended private parties in sumptuous evening dress, simpered and aired my graces like a born beau, and polked and schottisched with a step peculiar to myself—and the kangaroo. In a word, I kept the due state of a man worth a hundred thousand dollars (prospectively,) and likely to reach absolute affluence when that silver-mine sale should be ultimately achieved in the East. I spent money with a free hand, and meantime watched the stock sales with an interested eye and looked to see what might happen in Nevada....

---

* From Mark Twain (Samuel Clemens), *Roughing It* (Hartford, Conn.: American Publishing Co., 1872), pp. 419, 428–430.

For a time I wrote literary screeds for the *Golden Era.* C. H. Webb had established a very excellent literary weekly called the *Californian,* but high merit was no guaranty of success; it languished, and he sold out to three printers, and Bret Harte became editor at $20 a week, and I was employed to contribute an article a week at $12. But the journal still languished, and the printers sold out to Captain Ogden, a rich man and a pleasant gentleman who chose to amuse himself with such an expensive luxury without much caring about the cost of it. When he grew tired of the novelty, he re-sold to the printers, the paper presently died a peaceful death, and I was out of work again. I would not mention these things but for the fact that they so aptly illustrate the ups and downs that characterize life on the Pacific coast. A man could hardly stumble into such a variety of queer vicissitudes in any other country.

For two months my sole occupation was avoiding acquaintances; for during that time I did not earn a penny, or buy an article of any kind, or pay my board. I became a very adept at "slinking." I slunk from back street to back street, I slunk away from approaching faces that looked familiar, I slunk to my meals, ate them humbly and with a mute apology for every mouthful I robbed my generous landlady of, and at midnight, after wanderings that were but slinkings away from cheerfulness and light, I slunk to my bed. I felt meaner, and lowlier and more despicable than the worms. During all this time I had but one piece of money—a silver ten cent piece—and I held to it and would not spend it on any account, lest the consciousness coming strong upon me that I was *entirely* penniless, might suggest suicide. I had pawned every thing but the clothes I had on; so I clung to my dime desperately, till it was smooth with handling.

However, I am forgetting. I did have one other occupation beside that of "slinking." It was the entertaining of a collector (and being entertained by him,) who had in his hands the Virginia banker's bill for the forty-six dollars which I had loaned my schoolmate, the "Prodigal." This man used to call regularly once a week and dun me, and sometimes oftener. He did it from sheer force of habit, for he knew he could get nothing. He would get out his bill, calculate the interest for me, at five per cent a month, and show me clearly that there was no attempt at fraud in it and no mistakes; and then plead, and argue and dun with all his might for any sum —any little trifle—even a dollar—even half a dollar, on account. Then his duty was accomplished and his conscience free. He immediately dropped the subject there always; got out a couple of cigars and divided, put his feet in the window, and then we would have a long, luxurious talk about everything and everybody, and he would furnish me a world of curious dunning adventures out of the ample store in his memory. By and by he would clap his hat on his head, shake hands and say briskly :

"Well, business is business—can't stay with you always !"—and was off in a second.

The idea of pining for a dun! And yet I used to long for him to come, and would get as uneasy as any mother if the day went by without his visit, when I was expecting him. But he never collected that bill, at last nor any part of it. I lived to pay it to the banker myself.

Misery loves company. Now and then at night, in out-of-the-way, dimly lighted places, I found myself happening on another child of misfortune. He looked so seedy and forlorn, so homeless and friendless and forsaken, that I yearned toward him as a brother. I wanted to claim kinship with him and go about and enjoy our wretchedness together. The drawing toward each other must have been mutual; at any rate we got to falling together oftener, though still seemingly by accident; and although we did not speak or evince any recognition, I think the dull anxiety passed out of both of us when we saw each other, and then for several hours we would idle along contentedly, wide apart, and glancing furtively in at home lights and fireside gatherings, out of the night shadows, and very much enjoying our dumb companionship.

Finally we spoke, and were inseparable after that. For our woes were identical, almost. He had been a reporter too, and lost his berth, and this was his experience, as nearly as I can recollect it. After losing his berth, he had gone down, down, down, with never a halt: from a boarding house on Russian Hill to a boarding house in Kearney street; from thence to Dupont; from thence to a low sailor den; and from thence to lodgings in goods boxes and empty hogsheads near the wharves. Then, for a while, he had gained a meagre living by sewing up bursted sacks of grain on the piers; when that failed he had found food here and there as chance threw it in his way. He had ceased to show his face in daylight, now, for a reporter knows everybody, rich and poor, high and low, and cannot well avoid familiar faces in the broad light of day.

This mendicant Blucher—I call him that for convenience—was a splendid creature. He was full of hope, pluck and philosophy; he was well read and a man of cultivated taste; he had a bright wit and was a master of satire; his kindliness and his generous spirit made him royal in my eyes and changed his curb-stone seat to a throne and his damaged hat to a crown.

Bertha Shambaugh

The Amana Society (the Community of True Inspiration) was founded in Germany in 1714. Christian Metz led the band across the Atlantic in 1843 to upstate New York, from where, seeking greater isolation, they shortly removed to Iowa. They eventually numbered well over a thousand members, grouped in seven Amana villages, engaged in prosperous farming and industry. In 1932 they abandoned their purely communistic arrangement in favor of a joint-stock corporation, but until that time Amana was a fine modern version of the Puritan covenanted community.

*The Amana Society**

While it is true that Amana That Was had won the distinction of being the oldest and the largest in the long list of communistic ventures on American soil, it is equally true that communism had ever been incidental to the life and thought of the Community. The chief concern of the Community of True Inspiration was spiritual. Some care of the weaker and less gifted Brothers had characterized the early congregations, and always had the effort been made to find opportunity for each member to earn his living according to his calling or inclination. But in all the frank discussion recorded by "the old who no longer are" there is nothing to indicate that the "new spiritual economy" had in any way been influenced by the writings or the teachings of Étienne Cabet or other dreamers of Utopia.

Born of religious enthusiasm in the beginning of the eighteenth century, the Community of True Inspiration was primarily a church, and as such it lived for seven generations. "Common estate and property" and the blending of temporal rule and spiritual authority (both adopted in America under the leadership and the spiritual influence of the inspired prophet Christian Metz) merely carried the old religious ideal of "all that believed were together and had all things in common" to its logical conclusion.

The thousands of pages of manuscript preserved in the archives, "correctly written down from day to day in weal or woe," reveal suffering from persecution, many a spiritual struggle, some "demons of doubt and unbelief," and much grief caused by the "wordly wise and self-willed." But in

---

* From Bertha Shambaugh, *Amana That Was and Amana That Is* (Iowa City: State Historical Society of Iowa, 1932), pp. 351–355. Reprinted by permission.

all this candid recording the real concern was ever for the salvation of the soul. There was no discussion of an economic, social, or political philosophy —only the necessity of preserving "the faith which has love and the bond of peace for its essence and foundation." It is therefore beside the point to discuss Amana's communism as primarily an economic, social, or political venture.

Amana itself has never regarded its communism as the working out of a social theory. It claimed only to be a church brotherhood whose structure, management, and control were born of necessity and circumstance. For generations the Community of True Inspiration had been a church that clothed and fed its members in a material as well as in a spiritual sense. So long as the faith that had brought the members together retained its glow and living power, just so long was it possible to maintain the integrity of the Church. And whatever the cause, whatever the motive, whatever the entering wedge, when the old bond was no longer strong enough to subordinate the *me* spirit to the *we* spirit, the ideal of "Brothers All" began to lose its practical significance.

While the records of the Community refer to the "common estate and property" tenet as absolute communism, the same fundamental law that provided for the "share and share alike" privilege made special provision for the repayment to members receding (either by their own choice or by expulsion) of "moneys paid into the common fund." "And so it seems that the Community never did secure *real* communism, and hasn't got it now," was the criticism of the advocate of pure communism as he pointed out the weakness of the "drawback privilege."

The element of individual freedom in the Community has always been more or less disturbing to the theorist. Admittedly, Amana's village system was not economical. But it fostered a rather precious spirit of independence. While the house in which a family lived was Community property, "home" was ever the sanctuary where its members, old and young, enjoyed a wholesome sphere of privacy and domestic independence. The annual sum of maintenance was received from a common fund "according to justice and equity," but there was little save conscience or public opinion to prevent a member from spending it unwisely—which he sometimes did. A too gentle discipline in a later day of "worldly ways" had made easy a rather liberal interpretation of this sphere of individual freedom, resulting on the part of some in a little private trade on the side and an occasional inexplainable bank account. (All of which was quite foreign to the spirit or intention of the original idealistic group and put an undue strain on the morale of the Community.)

In some of the social experiments in America, communism itself has been the cementing force; but the greatest number and the longest lived (like Amana) have been groups of separatists from the established church. Few have outlived their spiritual leaders. Amana rather miraculously retained its living power and survived its great spiritual leaders by several generations.

But one by one the "witnesses of the great blessings of Inspiration" joined the silent brotherhood. With the passing of each generation and the increasing contact with the outside world, the symbols of the faith and the ideals of the Founders waned and the old commandments lost much of their authoritative character. Perhaps, as in the outside world during the first third of the twentieth century, asceticism was destroyed by ease and material prosperity. Perhaps modern disillusionment had entered the soul of the Community, causing religion to lose its infallibility. At any rate the religious fervor and zeal of the day of pioneering had suffered a decline, and with it went the old willingness to sacrifice personal ideas and ambitions for the common good. The once sacred "covenant and promise collectively and each to the other" had to many become an empty phrase.

To be sure, there were members of the Community who remained loyal to the old interpretation of each bearing his allotted share of "all the labor, cares, troubles and burdens." But there were others to whom communism had come to mean only "free board and dwelling, support and care in old age, sickness and infirmity," the annual sum of maintenance, and the privilege of grumbling.

There were still some, of course, to whom the Church was a living history of all the work and character and ideals that had been associated with it in the past: some to whom the Community remained a precious inheritance and a sacred trust. It is to this faithful devoted group, still making the ancient sacrifice for a spiritual ideal, that the Community of True Inspiration owes its remarkable longevity. The life of every organization comes at last to depend on those few who are ready to do the actual work, who really put their hearts into it, and who let nothing interfere with it. Among those devoted few in Amana have been men of moral power and business ability, whose talents would have made them individually successful in any of the ordinary professions of the outside world.

But disintegrating forces were at work. Amana had been drawn into the circle of the world, and old standards were giving way under the pressure of a scientific, machine age. Members who had wandered far afield spiritually remained for the material blessings and benefits linked with membership. With the loss of the old "solidarity," the number of workers declined and drones multiplied. Amana the Church—Amana the Community of True Inspiration—faced a setting sun. Without its spiritual significance the communism of Amana was as empty as a chrysalis from which the butterfly had flown.

Edgar Watson Howe

The novel The Story of a Country Town, *by Edgar Watson Howe (1853–1937), is based upon memories of childhood in Fairview, a village in northern Missouri in the late 1850s. It is a vivid evocation, and the opening sections are particularly interesting for their comments on the restlessness of the westward movement.*

A Country Town*

Ours was the prairie district, out West, where we had gone to grow up with the country.

I believe that nearly every farmer for miles around moved to the neighborhood at the same time, and that my father's wagons headed the procession. I have heard that most of them gathered about him on the way, and as he preached from his wagon wherever night overtook him, and held camp-meetings on Sundays, he attracted a following of men traveling the same road who did not know themselves where they were going, although a few of the number started with him, among them my mother's father and his family. When he came to a place that suited him, he picked out the land he wanted—which any man was free to do at that time—and the others settled about him.

In the dusty tramp of civilization westward—which seems to have always been justified by a tradition that men grow up by reason of it—our section was not a favorite, and remained new and unsettled after counties and States farther west had grown old. Every one who came there seemed favorably impressed with the steady fertility of the soil, and expressed surprise that the lands were not all occupied; but no one in the great outside world talked about it, and no one wrote about it, so that those who were looking for homes went to the west or the north, where others were going.

There were cheap lands farther on, where the people raised a crop one year, and were supported by charity the next; where towns sprang up on credit, and farms were opened with borrowed money; where the people were apparently content, for our locality did not seem to be far enough west, nor far enough north, to suit them; where no sooner was one stran-

---

* From Edgar Watson Howe, *The Story of a Country Town* (Atchison, Kansas: Howe & Co., 1883), pp. 1–3, 5–7.

ger's money exausted than another arrived to take his place; where men mortgaged their possessions at full value, and thought themselves rich notwithstanding, so great was their faith in the country; where he who was deepest in debt was the leading citizen, and where bankruptcy caught them all at last. On these lands the dusty travelers settled, where there were churches, school houses and bridges—but little rain—and railroads to carry out the crops should any be raised; and when any one stopped in our neighborhood, he was too poor and tired to follow the others.

I became early impressed with the fact that our people seemed to be miserable and discontented, and frequently wondered that they did not load their effects on wagons again, and move away from a place which made all the men surly and rough, and the women pale and fretful. Although I had never been to the country they had left except as a baby in arms, I was unfavorably impressed with it, thinking it must have been a very poor one that such a lot of people left it, and considered their condition bettered by the change, for they never talked of going back, and were therefore probably better satisfied than they had ever been before. A road ran by our house, and when I first began to think about it at all, I thought that the covered wagons traveling it carried people moving from the country from which those in our neighborhood came, and the wagons were so numerous that I was led to believe that at least half the people of the world had tried to live there, and moved away after an unfortunate experience.

On the highest and bleakest point in the county, where the winds were plenty in winter because they were not needed, and scarce in summer for an opposite reason, the meeting-house was built, in a corner of my father's field. This was called Fairview, and so the neighborhood was known. There was a graveyard around it, and cornfields next to that, but not a tree or shrub attempted its ornament, and as the building stood on the main road where the movers' wagons passed, I thought that next to their ambition to get away from the country which had been left by those in Fairview, the movers were anxious to get away from Fairview church, and avoid the possibility of being buried in its ugly shadow, for they always seemed to drive faster after passing it.

High up in a steeple which rocked with every wind was a great bell, the gift of a missionary society, and when there was a storm this tolled with fitful and uncertain strokes, as if the ghosts from the grave lot had crawled up there, and were counting the number to be buried the coming year, keeping the people awake for miles around. Sometimes, when the wind was particularly high, there were a great number of strokes on the bell in quick succession, which the pious said was an alarm to the wicked sounded by the devil, a warning relating to the conflagration which could never be put out, else Fairview would never have been built.

When any one died it was the custom to toll the bell once for every year of the deceased's age, and as deaths usually occur at night, we were frequently wakened from sleep by its deep and solemn tones. When I was yet a very little boy I occasionally went with my father to toll the bell when news came that some one was dead, for we lived nearer the place than any of the others, and when the strokes ran up to forty and fifty, it was very dreary work, and I sat alone in the church wondering who would ring for me, and how many strokes could be counted by those who were shivering at home in their beds.

The house was built the first year of the settlement, and the understanding was that my father contributed the little money necessary, and superintended the work, in which he was assisted by any one who volunteered his labor. It was his original intention to build it alone, and the little help he received only irritated him, as it was not worth the boast that he had raised a temple to the Lord single-handed. All the carpenter's work, and all the plasterer's work, he performed without assistance except from members of his own household, but I believe the people turned out to the raising, and helped put up the frames.

Regularly after its completion, he occupied the rough pulpit (which he built with especial reference to his own size), and every Lord's day morning and evening preached a religion to the people which I think added to their other discomforts, for it was hard and unforgiving. There were two or three kinds of Baptists among the people of Fairview when the house was completed, and a few Presbyterians, but they all became Methodists without revolt or question when my father announced in his first preaching that Fairview would be of that denomination.

He did not solicit them to join him, though he probably intimated in a way which admitted of no discussion that the few heretics yet remaining out in the world had better save themselves before it was too late. It did not seem to occur to him that men and women who had grown up in a certain faith renounced it with difficulty; it was enough that they were wrong, and that he was forgiving enough to throw open the doors of the accepted church. If they were humiliated, he was glad of it, for that was necessary to condone their transgression; if they had arguments to excuse it, he did not care to hear them, as he had taken God into partnership, and built Fairview, and people who worshipped there would be expected to throw aside all doctrinal nonsense. . . .

The only remarkable thing I ever did in my life—I may as well mention it here, and be rid of it—was to learn to read letters when I was five years old, and as the ability to read even print was by no means a common accomplishment in Fairview, this circumstance gave me great notoriety. I no doubt learned to read from curiosity as to what the books and papers scattered about were for, as no one took the pains to teach me, for I remember that they were all greatly surprised when I began to spell words, and pronounce them, and I am certain I was never encouraged in it.

It was the custom when my father went to the nearest post-office to bring back with him the mail of the entire neighborhood, and it was my business to deliver the letters and papers at the different houses. If I carried letters, I was requested to read them, and the surprise which I created in this direction was so pronounced that it was generally said that in time I would certainly become a great man, and be invited to teach school. If I came to a word which I did not understand, I invented one to take its place, or an entire sentence, for but few of the people could read the letters themselves, and never detected the deception. This occupation gave me my first impression of the country where the people had lived before they came to Fairview, and as there was much in the letters of hard work and pinching poverty, I believed that the writers lived in a heavily timbered country where it was necessary to dig up trees to get room for planting. Another thing I noticed was that they all seemed to be dissatisfied, and anxious to get away, and when in course of time I began to write answers to the letters, I was surprised to learn that the people of Fairview were satisfied, and that they were well pleased with the change.

I had never thought this before, for they all seemed as miserable as was possible, and wondered about it a great deal. This gave me fresh reason for believing that the country which our people had left was a very unfavored one, and when I saw the wagons in the road, I thought that at last the writers of the letters I had been reading had arrived, and would settle on some of the great tracts of prairie which could be seen in every direction, but they turned the bend in the road, and went on, as if a look at Fairview had frightened them, and they were going back another way.

It seems to me now that between the time I began to remember, and the time I went out with my father and Jo to work, or went alone through the field to attend the school in the church, that about a year elapsed, and that I was very much alone during the interval, for ours was a busy family, and none of them had time to look after me. My father and Jo went to the fields, or away with the teams, at a very early hour in the morning, and usually did not return until night, and my mother was always busy about the house, so that if I kept out of mischief, no more was expected of me. I think it was during this year (it may have been two years, but certainly not a longer period) that I learned to read, for I had nothing else to do, and no companions, and from looking at the pictures in the books, I began to wonder what the little characters surrounding them meant.

In this I was assisted by Jo, who seemed to know everything, and by slow degrees I put the letters together to make words, and understood them. Sometimes in the middle of the day I slipped out into the field to ask him the meaning of something mysterious I had encountered, and although he would good-naturedly inform me, I noticed that he and my father worked without speaking, and that I seemed to be an annoyance, so I scampered back to my loneliness again. . . .

Beyond the little stream and the pasture was the great dusty road, and in my loneliness I often sat on the high fence beside it to watch for the coming of the movers' wagons, and to look curiously at those stowed away under the cover bows, tumbled together with luggage and effects of every kind. If one of the drivers asked me how far it was to the country town, I supposed he had heard of my wonderful learning, and took great pains to describe the road, as I had heard my father do a hundred times in response to similar inquiries from movers. Sometimes I climbed up to the driver's seat, and drove with him out to the prairie, and I always noticed that the women and children riding behind were poorly dressed, and tired looking, and I wondered if only the unfortunate traveled our way, for only that kind of people lived in Fairview, and I had never seen any other kind in the road.

When I think of the years I lived in Fairview, I imagine that the sun was never bright there (although I am certain that it was), and I cannot relieve my mind of the impression that the cold, changing shadow of the gray church has spread during my long absence, and enveloped all the houses where the people lived. When I see Fairview in my fancy now, it is always from a high place, and looking down upon it, the shadow is denser around the house where I lived than anywhere else, so that I feel to this day that should I visit it, and receive permission from the new owners to walk through the rooms, I would find the walls damp and mouldy because the bright sun and the free air of Heaven had deserted them as a curse.

Lewis Atherton

A careful social history of life in a small Western town is Lewis Atherton's Main Street on the Middle Border, *from which the following selection with its exploration of the term "togetherness" is taken.*

Main Street on the Middle Border*

Since citizens knew the color and shape of every home in town, and could even direct strangers by such means, streets and houses went unmarked until towns grew large enough to obtain house-to-house mail deliv-

---

* From Lewis Atherton, *Main Street on the Middle Border* (Bloomington: Indiana University Press, 1954), pp. 181–186.

ery, at which time federal regulations required people to post street names and house numbers. Here was tangible evidence of the closely knit character of village life, of the satisfaction of being so well-known as to need no identifying numbers, of belonging to a neighborhood, of achieving membership in a community simply by living within its boundaries. Early in the twentieth century, and just before the debunking era, Zona Gale published her popular Friendship Village Love Stories, in which she eulogized village life:

In fellowship! I think that in this simple basic emotion lies my joy in living in this, my village. Here, this year long, folk have been adventuring together, knowing the details of one another's lives, striving a little but companioning far more than striving, kindling to one another's interests instead of practicing the faint morality of mere civility;... The ways of these primal tribal bonds are in my blood, for from my heart I felt what my neighbor felt when she told me of the donation party which the whole village has just given to Lyddy Ember:—"I declare," she said, "it wasn't so much the stuff they brought in, though that was all elegant, but it was the Togetherness of it. I couldn't get to sleep that night for thinkin' about God not havin' anybody to neighbour with."

This imaginary village contained characters like "Little Child," a simple, simpering, and angelic being, and her cat, "Bless-Your-Heart." In Gale's words, " 'I'm breathing,' Little Child soberly announced to me that first day of our acquaintance. And I wonder why I smiled." Mark Twain would have guffawed. Miggy and Peter, romantic lovers, extended the gallery of saccharine portraits which Gale created for Friendship Village. In spite of the obvious limitations of her characters, they appealed to a wide reading audience which idealized village life.

Many small-town citizens were less enamored of the "togetherness" of their existence. When a door-to-door salesman in late summer, 1898, sold sixty dollars' worth of house numbers to Gallatin, Missouri, women, the local editor immediately criticized them for being taken in by the "numbers game," which, in his opinion, was "as covered with moss as lightning-rod deals." According to him, women who disliked to live in country towns used house numbers to show that they understood city ways. Although the editor was correct in saying that not one citizen out of ten knew the names of Gallatin streets, and that residents had no need for signs and numbers to direct them, his sharp criticism of dissatisfied women undoubtedly made them no happier over having to live in a community which assumed the prerogative of telling them how to decorate their homes.

Thoughtful writers have noted the influence of "togetherness" on small-town personalities. In his stories of Winesburg, Ohio, Sherwood Anderson included the half-witted town character, Seth Smollett, the wood chopper, who went out of his way to wheel his cart of wood down Main

Street for the sheer joy of being shouted at and of returning the hoots and catcalls. They proved that he belonged and had a place in local society. Anderson also described the farm boy who, after moving to town with his father to open a store, learned to dread the attitude of Winesburg people. They called his family queer, or, at least, he thought they did. Under the circumstances, he longed to return to farm life:

When we lived out here it was different. I worked and at night I went to bed and slept. I wasn't always seeing people and thinking as I am now. In the evening, there in town, I go to the post office or to the depot to see the train come in, and no one says anything to me.... Then I feel so queer that I can't talk either. I go away. I don't say anything. I can't.

In Anderson's story this boy "escaped" to Cleveland and hid himself in city crowds. Solitude existed on the farm and in cities, but no one could escape the "togetherness" of village life.

Prying eyes, gossip, and pressure toward conformity, which naturally accompanied the "togetherness" of village life, could scarcely have been eliminated in a group which paid that price for membership in a neighborhood—for belonging to a society in its totality. Some loved life in the small town; others found it a severe trial. Hamlin Garland called himself an intellectual aristocrat, incapable of village life, and yet he shared for a time the unalloyed joy of his mother over returning to the village home which he purchased for her:

As I went about the village I came to a partial understanding of her feeling. The small dark shops, the uneven sidewalks, the ricketty wooden awnings were closely in character with the easy-going citizens who moved leisurely and contentedly about their small affairs. It came to me (with a sense of amusement) that these coatless shopkeepers who dealt out sugar and kerosene while wearing their derby hats on the backs of their heads, were not only my neighbors, but members of the Board of Education. Though still primitive to my city eyes, they no longer appeared remote. Something in their names and voices touched me nearly. They were American. Their militant social democracy was at once comical and corrective.

O, the peace, the sweetness of those days! To be awakened by the valiant challenge of early-rising roosters; to hear the chuckle of dawn-light worm-hunting robins brought a return of boyhood's exultation. Not only did my muscles harden to the spade and the hoe, my soul rejoiced in a new and delightful sense of establishment. I had returned to citizenship. I was a proprietor. The clock of the seasons had resumed its beat.

Village people rose early in the morning and set a pace which saw them through a long working day without exhausting their energies. A leisurely tempo with slack periods gave time to enjoy others and to engage in talk, the most pervading of all social activities. Women deserted their canning, washing, and housecleaning to gossip over the back fence or to rock in another's home while they discussed departures from routine patterns of neighborhood and town life. Marriage, birth, accidents, and death were common topics of conversation. Reports on those ill circulated each morning, and rumors of moral derelictions were passed from home to home. Retired farmers, down town for the morning mail, discussed crops and weather, which had shaped their daily activities for so many years, and then deaths and marriages. These were fitted into family and community relationships. Ancestral backgrounds, family connections, property holdings, and highlights of the career of any recently deceased member of the community were recalled and placed in their proper niche in the oral history of the village, thus giving a sense of continuity.

Town loafers who worked intermittently or not at all gathered at another spot to squat against the wall of a business building or to sit hunched over on the ledge extending from the foundation. They alone failed to speak to women passing by on shopping trips to the business section, feigning instead a blindness to matron and girl which was belied by the shifty glance of appraisal and interest in the female body.

At the post office and within the stores conversation was more general and yet more restricted because of the presence of both sexes and of all age groups. Everywhere it concerned people and things. Since art, literature, and abstract ideas were beyond the daily experience of those engaged in making conversation, individuals sought esteem by telling how they had warned another of the proper method of handling some situation which resulted badly through failure to follow seasoned experience. Illness or distress were quickly known and evoked a warmly sympathetic response because people were flesh-and-blood neighbors; wrongdoing or snobbishness aroused an equally quick condemnation for much the same reasons. Gossip served as informal judge and jury, and it sat daily to pass on every individual in the town.

Although this "togetherness" was achieved without numerous, formal social organizations, Europeans have been inclined to call us a nation of joiners and to seek explanations as to why we supposedly dote on organizational activities. In the 1830's Tocqueville suggested that an equalitarian, democratic country required associations to hold society together. In contrast, said Tocqueville, aristocratic societies were somewhat like armies, with relationships clearly defined and recognized by custom or law. In societies committed to equality, in which all were on a common level, men had to band together to accomplish their purposes. In the 1880's James Bryce said that associations were formed, extended, and operated more rapidly in the United States than elsewhere in the world. And this was true in his opinion because Americans were a sympathetic people, capable of such action in spite of nomadic habits which militated against organizational efforts. Still others have traced American interest in joining to the need for associations in which individuals can build their egos by the very act of combining with others and by holding offices of honor. Many observers seem to feel that rank and recognized honors must come either from associations in the American sense or from the clearly defined status of people in aristocratic societies.

The structure and functioning of nineteenth-century mid-western village life confirm European critics in their assumptions that people must have a sense of belonging to the larger society around them and also in their convictions that a mobile, equalitarian age struggles hard to find a sense of permanence and stability. But European critics have misread American history when they assert that we have achieved such ends and must achieve them by being a nation of joiners, for nineteenth-century villagers were satisfied with a limited number of organizations which admitted *all* members of the community. Before automobiles permitted people to seek distant associations, they had to find them locally. "Togetherness" before 1900 came from a few community-wide organizations, from informal community life, and from local association. Americans are not necessarily "joiners"; they do want to "belong."

ADDITIONAL READINGS

For Western towns the entire work of Atherton, excerpted in the foregoing chapter, should be read. A full study of the tendency of Western cities to rely on earlier Eastern urban experience is Richard C. Wade's *The Urban Frontier: the Rise of Western Cities, 1790–1830* (Cambridge, Mass., 1959). An excellent sociological account is *Prairie City* by Angie Debo (New York, 1944). Additional insights can be found in Granville Hicks's *Small Town* (New York, 1946) and William Allen White's *Forty Years on Main Street* (New York, 1937).

14

LAND, THE PLAINS,
AND THE FARMER

$L$and was the lure that never failed, the attraction whose luster seldom tarnished. The immigrant—whether he disembarked from the *Mayflower,* the *Sarah Constant,* or the stinking holds of more recent steerage—was apt to dream of owning land. He would judge the government, royal or democratic, state or federal, largely on the way its land policies benefited him. And governments early found that the distribution of land would provide political tangles and thorns from Cape Cod to the continent's end.

After the Revolution, the question of land control became a sensitive spot in relations between the states and the central government, but in the 1780s the states had begun to cede their Western lands to the central authority. The federal government, on its part, had to determine an equitable system of disposal. There were at least two alternatives. New England—with its Puritan backgrounds and the idea of the cohesive, corporate community—had spawned new settlement on a group basis; that is, the colonial government would survey large tracts, a group (originally a congregation) then would move to the land, and the community thereafter would parcel out the subdivisions. Around the central square would be rows of roughly equal town lots and beyond them farm or meadow plots. Each original settler would receive approximately equivalent shares. It was an orderly system, avoiding conflicts in title and working through a tight-knit community. In the South a more individualistic practice had grown. A settler would seek a patent for land and then himself survey his own boundaries. The piece could be small or large, symmetrical or irregular, depending on how the best acres could be encompassed, and hence could relate to the individual's needs and pleasures. The Southern system suited most frontiersmen and speculators and encouraged more immediate settlement.

The New England system, however, was paralleled in the great Land Ordinance of 1785—the act that set the pattern for Western settlement to the present time. Government surveyors, who preceded the settlers, divided the land into townships of 36 square miles; the townships were blocked into 36 sections, each covering an area of 1 square mile (640 acres). A few sections in each township were reserved (for example, one was set aside for education); the others were thrown open to auction, with a minimum price and sometimes a minimum number of acres. From the Land Ordinance until the Homestead Act of 1862, the price ranged from $1.00 to $2.50 per acre. To make matters worse, the auctions were frequently held in the East, far from the locale of settlement.

Although the New England pattern of prior survey was followed, the New England attention to the congregation or the corporate community hardly remained a significant element. Instead of the congregation, one found the large speculator, who could purchase the minimum-sized tract with no trouble and could then parcel out to the individual settler a few acres which the small farmer could afford. Then, too, the government soon found that its early auctions of small parcels were not financially successful. For purposes of revenue it was better to sell huge tracts to companies, even though the acre price was low.

Thus land speculation and large land companies were conspicuous features, and in their wakes often followed such unsavory practices as the buying of legislative influence and the duping of settlers. So, if the government was hard to find and the company corrupt, it is hardly surprising that settlers frequently avoided them both by simply squatting on the land desired. The Pre-emption Act of 1841 admitted that the squatter did have certain rights. It provided that every adult male could pre-empt 160 acres by erecting a dwelling and making improvements, and when that land came up for sale by the government, the settler would have the first right to buy at the minimum price. Unfortunately, the Pre-emption Act handicapped speculation but little. Speculators simply hired armies of individual squatters to pre-empt lands. In 1862 the Homestead Act, it was felt, by giving land substantially free to those who settled on it, might remedy the situation, but the Homestead Act applied only to surveyed lands; the speculator could still move with his paid squatters ahead of the surveyor and pre-empt the best acres.

Moreover, as some of the following selections make clear, the individual squatter was not always either the hireling of a larger speculator or a pure-minded seeker of ownership in fee simple. Often enough he was himself a speculator, taking land and fulfilling the legal requirements, but with no purpose to stay, desiring only to sell at a profit and then to move on as soon as he possibly could.

In the face of all these forces, the Puritan idea of community, in which men had roots and responsibilities one to another, was to become an anachronism; and the reckless, restless, irresponsible pattern was to triumph.

Such problems of land distribution and settlement were common to the entire westward movement; but when the line of settlement reached the Mississippi-Missouri, the Great Plains beyond presented certain special problems, which had to be solved before farming on the Great Plains became feasible: a special kind of agriculture had to be developed; an unusual set of technological problems had to be solved; some means for the transportation of products had to be found; and a monetary incentive, such as a high market price for grain, was required. In the years immediately following the Civil War, all of these prerequisites materialized for the Great Plains.

The problem of transportation was solved by the thin tracks of the transcontinental railroad as they were laid during the four years following the summer of 1865. The Civil War, by eliminating the South in the councils of the nation, had made possible the choice of routes for the railroad. The war had also produced an advantageous market for wheat; and the price rose.

But the Plains were a more hostile environment than anything the American farmer had previously known. To begin with, rainfall was insufficient for crops, and new approaches to agriculture had to be devised. The technology of windmills pumping water from wells was perfected by the 1870s, but the mills were expensive and required capital. In areas where rainfall was moderate but still not sufficient, dry farming was developed, a technique in which deep plowing and harrowing, properly timed with the rainfall, increased the water capacity of the soil. Barbed wire in the 1870s answered the need for easy, inexpensive fencing materials; but it, too, required an unusual investment for farmers accustomed to wooded areas where split rails were free. Mechanical improvements in chilled-iron and steel plows and finally in machinery like harvesters and threshers were also basic to the fullest agricultural development of the Plains.

On the other hand, the gift of the land itself, substantially free after the Homestead Act of 1862, could, it was assumed, compensate for the additional investments required. This act, a towering landmark in Western history, implied that the public lands were to be given away rather than sold and that the government's compensation would come from increased national prosperity and property value. On the Plains, however, what followed was a disappointment. As the years went by, the farmer began to sing the mournful refrain "Starving to Death on My Government Claim."

Why the disappointment? Partly because the price of wheat began an inexorable decline: in the 1890s it was a fraction of what it had been in the 1860s. The farmers were selling their products in a world market unprotected by tariffs; and the expansion of immense grain areas like the Ukraine and Argentina was for them disastrous. To make matters worse, the technological improvements which they needed on the Plains, their plows and windmills and harvesters, were manufactured in an Eastern market protected by tariffs and were delivered to them by railroads whose rates compounded the injury.

And there was also continuing personal hardship, physical and mental. True, there were some rewards to prairie farming: in the boyhood reminiscences of John Muir or Hamlin Garland are long paeans to the immensity of the sky, the pungency of new-cut hay, the wind-ripples across ripe wheat. But the romance was slim compared with the rigor of life on the Plains—long hours of labor, monotony and isolation, mortgages and rising indebtedness, wasted women's bodies, worn, sallow, and bent. The settlement of the Plains became a saga of blighted hopes.

And the farmer reacted. First, he organized the Patrons of Husbandry (the Grange) where, no longer a "hayseed," he proclaimed himself the "oldest of nobles." This fraternity gave his ego a lift and provided social outlets: the Grange picnic with its buggies and banners and bands was, as Garland said, "a most grateful relief from the sordid loneliness of the farm." The Farmers' Alliances later moved into the same arena and added a more serious political dimension. Finally, in the Populist movement of the 1890s the farmer's cry reached its most piercing level. Suddenly out of the Plains came violent emotion: Mary Lease shouting to raise less corn and more Hell; "Bloody Bridles" Waite, asking that blood drip from the bridles before the farmer cease his crusade; "the sage" Ignatius Donnelly, foreseeing the destruction of the present oligarchic civilization and the final erection of a monstrous "Caesar's column" built of human blood and bones. The protest was against monopoly in the form of railroads and banks; against a monetary system based on gold, hence not elastic enough to provide for an expanding economy; in favor of the free coinage of silver; in favor of the farmer and the working man in general, wherever he may be. Western farmers were joined by other voices, particularly from the agricultural South, men like Tom Watson of Georgia and "Pitchfork" Ben Tillman of South Carolina; and the climax came in 1896, when William Jennings Bryan, the Silver Knight, was nominated by the Populist party as well as his own Democratic party. The Plains echoed in Bryan's every word: "The great cities rest upon our broad and fertile prairies. Burn down your cities and leave our farms, and your cities will spring up again as if by magic; but destroy our farms, and the grass will grow in the streets of every city in the Country." Bryan lost the election, but the prairie farmer had spoken.

To what extent did the experience of Plains settlement affect the character of the farmer? Did he remain the same independent, highly individualistic yeoman whom Jefferson had proclaimed the backbone of democracy? Was the Western version of rural life to persist, like the earlier, as "the best architect of a complete man" (in the words of John Taylor of Caroline)? The selections that follow raise questions about the farmer and the theme of individualism. Does a hard, grim, isolated environment breed self-reliance in men? Or does it as likely produce a desire for cooperative action?

Closely related to any answer is the fact that the Plains farmer, like most men of the nineteenth century, was increasingly involved in larger and larger economic frameworks produced by staple crops, railroads, and wider markets. If the final answer to such dependence was an appeal to stronger government, as in the Ignatius Donnelly selection, then individual freedom had ceased to be defined as the absence of restraint and had come instead to imply perfect conformity to perfect law—i.e., freedom to obey laws which were made in the interests of all men, including the farmer. It was not precisely the individualism, based on weak government, that Jefferson and John Taylor had in mind, but it was a reasonable and understandable answer to a question the frontier had been posing for at least a century.

Horace Greeley

In the summer of 1859 the New York newspaper editor Horace Greeley (1811–1872) traveled across the country from New York to San Francisco. Greeley had long been interested in the West, as his famed epigram, "Go West, young man," attests; his comments must therefore be considered better informed than the shortness of a summer excursion would indicate.

The Kansas Squatter*

There are too many idle, shiftless people in Kansas. I speak not here of lawyers, gentlemen speculators, and other nonproducers, who are in excess here as elsewhere; I allude directly to those who call themselves settlers, and who would be farmers if they were anything. To see a man

---

* From Horace Greeley, *An Overland Journey, from New York to San Francisco, in the Summer of 1859* (New York: C. M. Saxton, Barker & Co., 1860), pp. 64–65, 68–70.

squatted on a quarter-section in a cabin which would make a fair hog-pen, but is unfit for a human habitation, and there living from hand to mouth by a little of this and a little of that, with hardly an acre of prairie broken (sometimes without a fence up), with no garden, no fruit-trees, "no nothing"—waiting for some one to come along and buy out his "claim" and let him move on to repeat the operation somewhere else—this is enough to give a cheerful man the horrors. . . .

As to the infernal spirit of land speculation and monopoly, I think no state ever suffered from it more severely than this. The speculators in broadcloth are not one whit more rapacious or pernicious than the speculators in rags, while the latter are forty times the more numerous. Land speculation here is about the only business in which a man can embark with no other capital than an easy conscience. For example: I rode up the bluffs back of Atchison, and out three or four miles on the high rolling prairie, so as to have some fifteen to twenty square miles in view at one glance. On all this inviting area, there were perhaps half a dozen poor or middling habitations, while not one acre in each hundred was fenced or broken. My friend informed me that every rood I saw was "preëmpted," and held at thirty up to a hundred dollars or more per acre. "Preëmpted!" I exclaimed; "how preëmpted? by living or lying?" "Well," he responded, "they live a little and lie a little." I could see abundant evidence of the lying, none at all of the living. To obtain a preëmption, the squatter must swear that he actually resides on the quarter-section he applies for, has built a habitation and made other improvements there, and wants the land for his own use and that of his family. The squatters who took possession of these lands must every one have committed gross perjury in obtaining preëmption—and so it is all over the territory, wherever a lot is supposed likely to sell soon for more than the minimum price. I heard of one case in which a squatter carried a martin-box on to a quarter-section, and on the strength of that martin-box, swore that he had a house there "eighteen by twenty"—he left the officer to presume the feet. So it is all over; the wretched little slab shanty which has sufficed to swear by on one "claim," is now moved off and serves to swear by on another, when the first swearing is done. I am confident there is not at this hour any kind of a house or other sign of improvement on one-fourth of the quarter-sections throughout Kansas which have been secured by preëmption. The squatter who thus establishes a "claim" sells it out, so soon as practicable, to some speculator, who follows in his wake, getting from $50 to $300 for that which the future bona-fide settler will be required to pay $250 to $1,500 for. Such, in practical operation, is the system designed and ostensibly calculated to shield the poor and industrious settlers from rapacity and extortion; but which, in fact, operates to oppress and plunder the real settler—to pay a premium on perjury—to foster and extend speculation—to demoralize the people, paralyze industry and impoverish the country.

Walter Prescott Webb

Walter Prescott Webb in his classic The Great Plains *uses three criteria for the identification of the Plains environment: (1) a vast, level surface; (2) the absence of trees; and (3) insufficient rainfall for agriculture short of artificial irrigation. His book explores the ways in which this environment influenced those who moved into it, "the modifications that were made by the American timber-dwellers when they emerged from the forests and undertook to make their homes on the Plains. Their effort constitutes a gigantic human experiment with an environment."*

*The Great Plains**

This area, with its three dominant characteristics, affected the various peoples, nations as well as individuals, who came to take and occupy it, and was affected by them; for this land, with the unity given it by its three dominant characteristics, has from the beginning worked its inexorable effect upon nature's children. The historical truth that becomes apparent in the end is that the Great Plains have bent and molded Anglo-American life, have destroyed traditions, and have influenced institutions in a most singular manner.

The Great Plains offered such a contrast to the region east of the ninety-eighth meridian, the region with which American civilization had been familiar until about 1840, as to bring about a marked change in the ways of pioneering and living. For two centuries American pioneers had been working out a technique for the utilization of the humid regions east of the Mississippi River. They had found solutions for their problems and were conquering the frontier at a steadily accelerating rate. Then in the early nineteenth century they crossed the Mississippi and came out on the Great Plains, an environment with which they had had no experience. The result was a complete though temporary breakdown of the machinery and ways of pioneering. They began to make adjustments, and this book is the story of those adjustments.

As one contrasts the civilization of the Great Plains with that of the eastern timberland, one sees what may be called an institutional *fault*

---

* From Walter Prescott Webb, *The Great Plains* (New York: Ginn & Co., 1931), pp. 8–431 *passim*. Reprinted by permission.

(comparable to a geological fault) running from middle Texas to Illinois or Dakota, roughly following the ninety-eighth meridian. At this *fault* the ways of life and of living changed. Practically every institution that was carried across it was either broken and remade or else greatly altered. The ways of travel, the weapons, the method of tilling the soil, the plows and other agricultural implements, and even the laws themselves were modified. When people first crossed this line they did not immediately realize the imperceptible change that had taken place in their environment, nor, more is the tragedy, did they foresee the full consequences which that change was to bring in their own characters and in their modes of life. In the new region—level, timberless, and semi-arid—they were thrown by Mother Necessity into the clutch of new circumstances. Their plight has been stated in this way: east of the Mississippi civilization stood on three legs—land, water, and timber; west of the Mississippi not one but two of these legs were withdrawn,—water and timber,—and civilization was left on one leg—land. It is small wonder that it toppled over in temporary failure....

We see a nation of people coming slowly but persistently through the forests, felling trees, building cabins, making rail fences, digging shallow wells, or drinking from the numerous springs and perennial streams, advancing shoulder to shoulder, pushing the natives westward toward the open country. They are nearing the Plains. Then, in the first half of the nineteenth century, we see the advance guard of this moving host of forest home-makers emerge into the new environment, where there are no forests, no logs for cabins, no rails for fences, few springs and running streams. Before them is a wide land infested by a fierce breed of Indians, mounted, ferocious, unconquerable, terrible in their mercilessness. They see a natural barrier made more formidable by a human barrier of untamed savagery. Upon this barrier of the Great Plains the pioneers threw themselves, armed and equipped with the weapons, tools, ideas, and institutions which had served them so long and so well in the woods that now lay behind them. Inevitably they failed in their first efforts, and they continued to fail until they worked out a technique of pioneering adapted to the Plains rather than to the woodland....

New inventions and discoveries had to be made before the pioneer farmer could go into the Great Plains and establish himself. To the farmer, then, the Great Plains presented an obstacle which he could not, at the time he first confronted it, overcome. In time the Industrial Revolution was to develop agencies that enabled him to go forward and solve the problems of water and fence and extensive agriculture which hitherto had been insoluble. While these inventions and adaptations were being worked out, improved, and perfected, the agricultural frontier stood at ease, or, more aptly, stamped about in uneasiness along the borders of the

Plains country. In the interval of awaiting the Industrial Revolution there arose in the Plains country the cattle kingdom.

The cattle kingdom was a world within itself, with a culture all its own, which, though of brief duration, was complete and self-satisfying. The cattle kingdom worked out its own means and methods of utilization; it formulated its own law, called the code of the West, and did it largely upon extra-legal grounds. The existence of the cattle kingdom for a generation is the best single bit of evidence that here in the West were the basis and the promise of a new civilization unlike anything previously known to the Anglo-European-American experience. The Easterner, with his background of forest and farm, could not always understand the man of the cattle kingdom. One went on foot, the other went on horseback; one carried his law in books, the other carried it strapped round his waist. One represented tradition, the other represented innovation; one responded to convention, the other responded to necessity and evolved his own conventions. Yet the man of the timber and the town made the law for the man of the plain; the plainsman, finding this law unsuited to his needs, broke it, and was called lawless. The cattle kingdom was not sovereign, but subject. Eventually it ceased to be a kingdom and became a province. The Industrial Revolution furnished the means by which the beginnings of this original and distinctive civilization have been destroyed or reduced to vestigial remains. Since the destruction of the Plains Indians and the buffalo civilization, the cattle kingdom is the most logical thing that has happened in the Great Plains, where, in spite of science and invention, the spirit of the Great American Desert still is manifest. . . .

One is struck, incidentally, with the analogy that exists between the history of the South and the history of the Great Plains country, between the cotton kingdom and the cattle kingdom, in their relation to the industrial section of the North. The cotton kingdom of the South and the cattle kingdom of the West took root in the natural conditions of soil and climate which were especially favorable to the development of each respectively; the cotton kingdom expanded because the Industrial Revolution was working far off in the production and operation of textile machinery and particularly because of the invention of the cotton gin, which was being manufactured in New England. The cattle kingdom arose and spread because the Industrial Revolution was working far off in the railroads, which furnished transportation for cattle, and in the packing houses with their automatic machinery and methods of refrigeration which made it possible to carry meat and meat products to all parts of the world. Therefore both kingdoms became tributary to the masters of the Industrial Revolution. Both kingdoms produced what promised to be a distinctive civilization, a thing apart in American life. Both kingdoms were pioneers in their character, the first occupants and users of the soil. And in time both were completely altered by the force that had developed them. One produced the plantation and the Negro slave; the other produced the ranch and the cowboy; but here analogy breaks down, and contrast sets in.

The cotton kingdom became involved in social and political problems from which it undertook to extricate itself by secession. The result was war between an agricultural people and an industrial people, followed by the conquest of the South, a revolution in the theory of government, and the emergence of industrialism triumphant in finance, in politics, and in government. The Industrial Revolution quickly effected in the South a military and a political conquest, but it had not as yet applied itself there to the solution of the economic problems of the section. Prejudice and bitterness on both sides, together with certain inherent difficulties in the problems presented, held the constructive forces of the Industrial Revolution out of the South until comparatively recent times. But in the Plains country there existed no serious political problems; therefore the forces of the Industrial Revolution were applied first and freely to the solution of the peculiar economic problems found there. The South was from the first occupied by agriculture; the West had to wait on the Industrial Revolution; therefore in the Plains the Industrial Revolution had free sway to show what it could do to establish a different kind of agriculture to meet the new conditions.

The Industrial Revolution found itself confronted by four major problems in the Plains country: (1) transportation, (2) fencing, (3) water, and (4) farming. The first was solved by railroads, the second by barbed wire, the third by windmills, and the fourth partly by farm machinery and by a new form of agriculture. Aside from transportation the other problems may be thought of as growing out of agriculture; that is, in this second phase of Plains history the farm may be considered as the unit rather than the range or ranch, which was the unit in the preceding period. Fundamentally, the major problem of agriculture had to do with providing means of utilizing large areas of land. . . .

It has been the good fortune of the people of the humid region to hold the controlling interest in the national government. This fact arises from the very nature of things, from history and from the fact that the humid region supports, and will continue to support, the larger population. The Westerner has belonged to a minority and has been compelled to accept the laws and institutions made for other conditions or, at best, such modifications of the laws as the Eastern senators and representatives could be induced to agree to. About all the Westerner has been able to achieve has come through wheedling, cajolery, threats at radicalism, and the formation of third parties or of alliances with the minority party. The land legislation illustrates the point. . . .

Had anyone, knowing the conditions that the homesteader was to meet on the Great Plains, suggested a homestead of 640, 1280, or 2560 acres as the unit, he would have been considered insane. It required more than twenty years of experimentation to show that in terms of utilization 160 acres of land in the humid region was equivalent in productiveness to 2560 acres in the arid region, but that knowledge and conviction were limited to a few and have probably not yet become general. . . .

In another place mention was made of the grim humor of the dwellers in the Great Plains. A part of it was applied to the Homestead Act, and in this wise: The government is willing to bet the homesteader one hundred and sixty acres of land that he'll starve to death on it in less than five years. Had evasions and fraud been eliminated in the Great Plains, the government would have won most of the wagers.

Albert Greene

Whether this gigantic effort to adapt to new conditions had an effect on the individualism of the settler is a moot point. His isolated environment encouraged self-reliance, of this we can be sure; but it also intensified the kind of cooperation that has always been a part of rural life. The following selection relates the way in which a settler, Albert Greene, benefited from neighborly help in the frontier period of Middle Western settlement. Frontier writings are full of such experiences—bees of all kinds and house or barn raisings; and when machinery came, the system of "changing works," so dramatically explained in the books of Hamlin Garland, required that groups of farmers help the man who momentarily had use of the machine.

Reminiscences*

One of the friends of those early days was Abraham Lincoln. He advised my parents to come to Kansas when this territory was opened to settlement, and at last they took that advice, and, having earned full honors in the hard school of pioneering in Illinois, took a postgraduate course in the great American desert.

For a few weeks we lived in the tent—that is, it was the shelter for

---

* From Albert R. Greene, "In Remembrance," Kansas State Historical Society, *Collections*, XI (1909–10), 482–484.

the sick one and her mother, while the rest of the family and our goods and chattels found accommodations in the open air. The days were warm and dry and the nights balmy and without dew, so that this sort of life was without hardship, but was rather a romantic exhilaration. The first substantial habitation was a cabin on small poles supplied with a roof of bark obtained from a large elm tree which was felled for the purpose, lumber and shingles being unobtainable except at the Missouri river, at prohibitive prices. For this reason there was no floor except natural earth. For the same reason the habitation was without windows, a modicum of light being admitted through the cracks between the logs, and on cloudy days by opening the door. The greater part of one end was occupied by a fireplace, and the chimney was split sticks daubed with mud. The dimensions of this cabin were, as I remember them, ten feet in width and sixteen feet in length. It joined the tent, and the tent had connections with the covered wagon. This cabin and its annex were our quarters for the greater part of our first year in the territory. We were about as well accommodated as the few neighbors who had straggled in from time to time and located above and below us along the creek. At least we were not ostracized by the few who had clapboard roofs and puncheon floors to their houses, and actually entertained (informall) a good deal that first winter. Many of our guests were Indians, who came unannounced, helped themselves to food, and left without a hint of remuneration. Ours was a sort of half-way house between the California and Santa Fe trails, and a convenient stopping place for travelers and prospective settlers who were going across the country. . . .

[Later] a set of house logs were obtained from an adjoining claim, and when they had been hewed ready for the structure we had a raising, the neighbors coming from far and near to lay up the walls, cob-house fashion, ready for the rafters. This kind of work was so common in those days that the qualifications of each settler for the various details were well known, and a sort of informal organization had been effected. Thus there were corner men, and skid men, scorers and hewers, each taking his part and as a matter of course. The man whose house was being raised had nothing to say about it except to indicate the location. The day's work wound up with a big dinner, or, more properly, supper, and then the crowd with many expressions of good will dispersed to their homes. In the same unselfish manner the voluntary labor of the settlers gathered the crops and prepared the winter's wood for their neighbors who from sickness or any other cause were unable to do it for themselves. As for any pay, beyond a good meal when the day's work was done, the suggestion of such a thing would have been resented as an insult.

Hamlin Garland

Hamlin Garland's father moved his family from Wisconsin to Iowa, where Hamlin (1860–1940) spent his boyhood on the Plains. They moved again to homestead a bleak stretch in the Dakota Territory in 1881. Garland as an ambitious youth went East, where he followed the reforming currents of men like Henry George; in 1887, he returned on a visit to the northern prairies. In the following selection from his autobiography, he tells of this visit and its impact upon him.

*A Son of the Middle Border**

To find myself actually on the train and speeding westward was deeply and pleasurably exciting, but I did not realize how keen my hunger for familiar things had grown, till the next day when I reached the level lands of Indiana. Every field of wheat, every broad hat, every honest treatment of the letter "r" gave me assurance that I was approaching my native place. The reapers at work in the fields filled my mind with visions of the past. . . .

Something deep and resonant vibrated within my brain as I looked out upon this monotonous commonplace landscape. I realized for the first time that the east had surfeited me with picturesqueness. It appeared that I had been living for six years amidst painted, neatly arranged pasteboard scenery. Now suddenly I dropped to the level of nature unadorned, down to the ugly unkempt lanes I knew so well, back to the pungent realities of the streamless plain.

Furthermore I acknowledged a certain responsibility for the conditions of the settlers. I felt related to them, an intolerant part of them. Once fairly out among the fields of northern Illinois everything became so homely, uttered itself so piercingly to me that nothing less than song could express my sense of joy, of power. This was my country—these my people. . . .

All that day I had studied the land, musing upon its distinctive quali-

---

ties, and while I acknowledged the natural beauty of it, I revolted from
the gracelessness of its human habitations. The lonely box-like farm-
houses on the ridges suddenly appeared to me like the dens of wild animals. The lack of color, of charm in the lives of the people anguished me.
I wondered why I had never before perceived the futility of woman's life
on a farm.

I asked myself, "Why have these stern facts never been put into our
literature as they have been used in Russia and in England? Why has
this land no story-tellers like those who have made Massachusetts and
New Hampshire illustrious?" ...

Looking at the sky above me, feeling the rush of the earth beneath
my feet I saw how much I had dared and how little, how pitifully little
I had won. Over me the ragged rainclouds swept, obscuring the stars
and in their movement and in the feeling of the dawn lay something illimitable and prophetic. Such moments do not come to men often—but to
me for an hour, life was painfully purposeless. "What does it all mean?"
I asked myself.

At last the train came, and as it rattled away to the north and I drew
closer to the scenes of my boyhood, my memory quickened. The Cedar
rippling over its limestone ledges, the gray old mill and the pond where
I used to swim, the farm-houses with their weedy lawns, all seemed not
only familiar but friendly, and when at last I reached the station (the
same grimy little den from which I had started forth six years before),
I rose from my seat with the air of a world-traveller and descended upon
the warped and splintered platform, among my one time friends and
neighbors, with quickened pulse and seeking eye. ...

As I walked the street I met several neighbors from Dry Run as
well as acquaintances from the Grove. Nearly all, even the young men,
looked worn and weather-beaten and some appeared both silent and sad.
Laughter was curiously infrequent and I wondered whether in my days
on the farm they had all been as rude of dress, as misshapen of form
and as wistful of voice as they now seemed to me to be. "Have times
changed? Has a spirit of unrest and complaining developed in the American farmer?"

I perceived the town from the triple viewpoint of a former resident,
a man from the city, and a reformer, and every minutest detail of dress,
tone and gesture revealed new meaning to me. Fancher and Gammons
were feebler certainly, and a little more querulous with age, and their
faded beards and rough hands gave pathetic evidence of the hard wear
of wind and toil. At the moment nothing glozed the essential tragic futility of their existence.

Then down the street came "The Ragamuffins," the little Fourth of
July procession, which in the old days had seemed so funny, so exciting
to me. I laughed no more. It filled me with bitterness to think that such

a makeshift spectacle could amuse anyone. "How dull and eventless life must be to enable such a pitiful travesty to attract and hold the attention of girls like Ella and Flora," I thought as I saw them standing with their little sister to watch "the parade." . . .

In those few days, I perceived life without its glamor. I no longer looked upon these toiling women with the thoughtless eyes of youth. I saw no humor in the bent forms and graying hair of the men. I began to understand that my own mother had trod a similar slavish round with never a full day of leisure, with scarcely an hour of escape from the tugging hands of children, and the need of mending and washing clothes. I recalled her as she passed from the churn to the stove, from the stove to the bedchamber, and from the bedchamber back to the kitchen, day after day, year after year, rising at daylight or before, and going to her bed only after the evening dishes were washed and the stockings and clothing mended for the night.

Carl Becker

Carl Lotus Becker (1873–1945), one of the most gifted of modern American historians, was born and raised on the Iowa plains. He taught history at Pennsylvania State and at Dartmouth before he returned to the prairies in 1908 to teach at the University of Kansas. He was moved to write his impressions of his fellow Middle Westerners in an essay that might be called a credo of Plains individualism.

*Kansas**

There are those who will tell us, and have indeed often told us, with a formidable array of statistics, that Kansas is inhabited only in small part by New Englanders, and that it is therefore fanciful in the extreme to think of it as representing Puritanism transplanted. It is true, the people of Kansas came mainly from "the Middle West"—from Illinois, Indiana,

---

* From Carl L. Becker, "Kansas," in *Everyman His Own Historian* (New York: Appleton-Century-Crofts, Inc., 1935), pp. 3–11. Copyright, 1935, F. S. Crofts & Co., Inc. By permission of Appleton-Century-Crofts, Inc.

Ohio, Iowa, Kentucky, and Missouri. But for our purpose the fact is of little importance, for it is the ideals of a people rather than the geography they have outgrown that determine their destiny; and in Kansas, as has been well said, "it is the ideas of the Pilgrims, not their descendants, that have had dominion in the young commonwealth." Ideas, sometimes, as well as the star of empire, move westward, and s' it happens that Kansas is more Puritan than New England of to-day. It is akin to New England of early days. It is what New England, old England itself, once was—the frontier, an ever changing spot where dwell the courageous who defy fate and conquer circumstance.

For the frontier is more than a matter of location, and Puritanism is itself a kind of frontier. There is an intellectual "West" as well as a territorial "West." Both are heresies, the one as much subject to the scorn of the judicious as the other. Broad classifications of people are easily made and are usually inaccurate; but they are convenient for taking a large view, and it may be worth while to think, for the moment, of two kinds of people—those who like the sheltered life, and those who cannot endure it, those who think the world as they know it is well enough, and those who dream of something better, or, at any rate, something different. From age to age society builds its shelters of various sorts—accumulated traditions, religious creeds, political institutions, and intellectual conceptions, cultivated and well-kept farms, well-built and orderly cities—providing a monotonous and comfortable life that tends always to harden into conventional forms resisting change. With all this the home-keeping and timid are well content. They sit in accustomed corners, disturbed by no fortuitous circumstance. But there are those others who are forever tugging at the leashes of ordered life, eager to venture into the unknown. Forsaking beaten paths, they plunge into the wilderness. They must be always on the frontier of human endeavor, submitting what is old and accepted to conditions that are new and untried. The frontier is thus the seed plot where new forms of life, whether of institutions or types of thought, are germinated, the condition of all progress being in a sense a return to the primitive.

Now, generally speaking, the men who make the world's frontiers, whether in religion or politics, science, or geographical exploration and territorial settlement, have certain essential and distinguishing qualities. They are primarily men of faith. Having faith in themselves, they are individualists. They are idealists because they have faith in the universe, being confident that somehow everything is right at the center of things; they give hostage to the future, are ever inventing God anew, and must be always transforming the world into their ideal of it. They have faith in humanity and in the perfectibility of man, are likely, therefore, to be believers in equality, reformers, intolerant, aiming always to level others up to their own high vantage. These qualities are not only Puritan, they are American; and Kansas is not only Puritanism transplanted, but Americanism transplanted. In the individualism, the idealism, the belief in equality that prevail in Kansas, we shall therefore see nothing strangely new, but simply a new graft of familiar American traits. But as Kansas is a community with a peculiar and distinctive experience, there is something peculiar and distinctive about the individualism, the idealism, and the belief in equality of its people. If we can get at this something peculiar and distinctive, it will be possible to understand why the sight of sunflowers growing beside a railroad track may call forth the fervid expression, "Dear old Kansas."

Individualism is everywhere characteristic of the frontier, and in America, where the geographical frontier has hitherto played so predominant a part, a peculiarly marked type of individualism is one of the most obvious traits of the people. "To the frontier," Professor Turner has said, "the American intellect owes its striking characteristics. That coarseness and strength combined with acuteness and inquisitiveness; that practical, inventive turn of mind, quick to find expedients; that masterful grasp of material things, lacking in the artistic but powerful to effect great ends; that restless nervous energy; that dominant individualism, working for good and for evil, and withal that buoyancy and exuberance that comes from freedom." On the frontier, where everything is done by the individual and nothing by organized society, initiative, resourcefulness, quick, confident, and sure judgment are the essential qualities for success. But as the problems of the frontier are rather restricted and definite, those who succeed there have necessarily much the same kind of initiative and resourcefulness, and their judgment will be sure only in respect to the problems that are familiar to all. It thus happens that the type of individualism produced on the frontier and predominant in America, has this peculiarity, that while the sense of freedom is strong, there is nevertheless a certain uniformity in respect to ability, habit, and point of view. The frontier develops strong individuals, but it develops individuals of a particular type, all being after much the same pattern. The individualism of the frontier is one of achievement, not of eccentricity, an individualism of fact rising from a sense of power to overcome obstacles, rather than one of theory growing out of weakness in the face of oppression. It is not because he fears governmental activity, but because he has so often had to dispense with it, that the American is an individualist. Altogether averse to hesitancy, doubt, speculative or introspective tendencies, the frontiersman is a man of faith: of faith, not so much in some external power, as in himself, in his luck, his destiny; faith in the possibility of achieving whatever is necessary or he desires. It is this marked self-reliance that gives to Americans their tremendous power of initiative; but the absence of deep-seated differences gives to them an equally tremendous power of concerted social action.

The confident individualism of those who achieve through endurance is a striking trait of the people of Kansas. There, indeed, the trait has in it an element of exaggeration, arising from the fact that whatever has been achieved in Kansas has been achieved under great difficulties. Kansans have been subjected, not only to the ordinary hardships of the frontier, but to a succession of reverses and disasters that could be survived only by those for whom defeat is worse than death, who cannot fail because they cannot surrender. To the border wars succeeded hot winds, droughts, grasshoppers; and to the disasters of nature succeeded in turn the scourge of man, in the form of "mortgage fiends" and a contracting currency. Until 1895 the whole history of the state was a series of disasters and always something new, extreme, bizarre, until the name Kansas became a by-word, a synonym for the impossible and the ridiculous, inviting laughter, furnishing occasion for jest and hilarity. "In God we trusted, in Kansas we busted," became a favorite motto of emigrants, worn out with the struggle, returning to more hospitable climes; and for many years it expressed well enough the popular opinion of that fated land.

Yet there were some who never gave up. They stuck it out. They endured all that even Kansas could inflict. They kept the faith, and they are to be pardoned perhaps if they therefore feel that henceforth there is laid up for them a crown of glory. Those who remained in Kansas from 1875 to 1895 must have originally possessed staying qualities of no ordinary sort, qualities which the experience of those years could only accentuate. And as success has at last rewarded their efforts, there has come, too, a certain pride, an exuberance, a feeling of superiority that accompany a victory long delayed and hardly won. The result has been to give a peculiar flavor to the Kansas spirit of individualism. With Kansas history back of him, the true Kansan feels that nothing is *too much* for him. How shall he be afraid of any danger, or hesitate at any obstacle, having succeeded where failure was not only human, but almost honorable? Having conquered Kansas, he knows well that there are no worse worlds to conquer. The Kansas spirit is therefore one that finds something exhilarating in the challenge of an extreme difficulty. "No one," says St. Augustine, "loves what he endures, though he may love to endure." With Kansans, it is particularly a point of pride to suffer easily the stings of fortune, and if they find no pleasure in the stings themselves, the ready endurance of them gives a consciousness of merit that is its own reward. Yet it is with no solemn martyr's air that the true Kansan endures the worst that can happen. His instinct is rather to pass it off as a minor annoyance, furnishing occasion for a pleasantry, for it is the mark of a Kansan to take a reverse as a joke rather than too seriously. Indeed, the endurance of extreme adversity has developed a keen appreciation for that type of humor, everywhere prevalent in the west, which consists in ignoring a difficulty, or transforming it into a difficulty of precisely the opposite kind. There is a tradition surviving from the grasshopper time that illustrates the point. It is said that in the midst of that overwhelming disaster, when the pests were six inches deep in the streets, the editor of a certain local paper fined his comment on the situation down to a single line, which appeared among the trivial happenings of the week: "A grasshopper was seen on the court-house steps this morning." This type of humor, appreciated anywhere west of the Alleghenies, is the type *par excellence* in Kansas. Perhaps it has rained for six weeks in the spring. The wheat is seemingly ruined; no corn has been planted. A farmer, who sees his profits for the year wiped out, looks at the murky sky, sniffs the damp air, and remarks seriously, "Well, it looks like rain. We may save that crop yet." "Yes," his neighbor replies with equal seriousness, "but it will have to come soon, or it won't do any good." When misfortunes beat down upon one in rapid succession, there comes a time when it is useless to strive against them, and in the end they engender a certain detached curiosity in the victim, who finds a mournful pleasure in observing with philosophical resignation the ultimate caprices of fate. Thus Kansans, "coiners of novel phrases to express their defiance of destiny," have employed humor itself as a refuge against misfortune. They have learned not only to endure adversity, but in a very literal sense to laugh at it as well.

I have already said that the type of individualism that is characteristic of America is one of achievement, not of eccentricity. The statement will bear repeating in this connection, for it is truer of Kansas than of most communities, notwithstanding there is a notion abroad that the state is peopled by freaks and eccentrics. It was once popularly supposed in Europe, and perhaps is so yet, that Americans are all eccentric. Now, Kansans are eccentric in the same sense that Americans are: they differ somewhat from other Americans, just as Americans are distinguishable from Europeans. But a fundamental characteristic of Kansas individualism is the tendency to conform; it is an individualism of conformity, not of revolt. Having learned to endure to the end, they have learned to conform, for endurance is itself a kind of conformity. It has not infrequently been the subject of wondering comment by foreigners that in America, where every one is supposed to do as he pleases, there should nevertheless be so little danger from violence and insurrection. Certainly one reason is that while the conditions of frontier life release the individual from many of the formal restraints of ordered society, they exact a most rigid adherence to lines of conduct inevitably fixed by the stern necessities of life in a primitive community. On the frontier men soon learn to conform to what is regarded as essential, for the penalty of resistance or neglect is extinction: there the law of survival works surely and swiftly.

However eccentric frontiersmen may appear to the tenderfoot, among themselves there is little variation from type in any essential matter. In the new community, individualism means the ability of the individual to succeed, not by submitting to some external formal authority, still less by following the bent of an unschooled will, but by recognizing and voluntarily adapting himself to necessary conditions. Kansas, it is true, has produced its eccentrics, but there is a saying here that freaks are raised for export only. In one sense the saying is true enough, for what strikes one particularly is that, on the whole, native Kansans are all so much alike. It is a community of great solidarity, and to the native it is "the Easterner" who appears eccentric.

The conquest of the wilderness in Kansas has thus developed qualities of patience, of calm, stoical, good-humored endurance in the face of natural difficulties, of conformity to what is regarded as necessary. Yet the patience, the calmness, the disposition to conform is strictly confined to what is regarded as in the natural course. If the Kansan appears stolid, it is only on the surface that he is so. The peculiar conditions of origin and history have infused into the character of the people a certain romantic and sentimental element. Beneath the placid surface there is something fermenting which is best left alone—a latent energy which trivial events or a resounding phrase may unexpectedly release. In a recent commencement address, Mr. Henry King said that conditions in early Kansas were *"hair-triggered."* Well, Kansans are themselves hair-triggered; slight pressure, if it be of the right sort, sets them off. "Every one is on the *qui vive,* alert, vigilant, like a sentinel at an outpost." This trait finds expression in the romantic devotion of the people to the state, in a certain alert sensitiveness to criticism from outside, above all in the contagious enthusiasm with which they will without warning espouse a cause, especially when symbolized by a striking phrase, and carry it to an issue. Insurgency is native in Kansas, and the political history of the state, like its climate, is replete with surprises that have made it "alternatively the reproach and the marvel of mankind." But this apparent instability is only the natural complement of the extreme and confident individualism of the people: having succeeded in overcoming so many obstacles that were unavoidable, they do not doubt their ability to destroy quickly those that seem artificially constructed. It thus happens that while no people endure the reverses of nature with greater fortitude and good humor than the people of Kansas, misfortunes seemingly of man's making arouse in them a veritable passion of resistance; the mere suspicion of injustice, real or fancied exploitation by those who fare sumptuously, the pressure of laws not self-imposed touch something explosive in their nature that transforms a calm and practical people into excited revolutionists. Grasshoppers elicited only a witticism, but the "mortgage fiends" produced the Populist régime, a kind of religious crusade against the infidel Money Power. The same spirit

was recently exhibited in the "Boss Busters" movement, which in one summer spread over the state like a prairie fire and overthrew an established
machine supposed to be in control of the railroads. The "Higher Law"
is still a force in Kansas. The spirit which refused to obey "bogus laws"
is still easily stirred. A people which has endured the worst of nature's
tyrannies, and cheerfully submits to tyrannies self-imposed, is in no mood
to suffer hardships that seem remediable.

Paul Wallace Gates

*Paul Wallace Gates, professor of history at Cornell University, has
written extensively and perceptively of the Western farmer. His essay on
the Homestead Act has become an indispensable commentary on the mis-
understandings and misfortunes which that act engendered.*

*The Homestead Act**

The principle of free homesteads for settlers had long been the goal
for which the West had struggled, and as each succeeding land law, more
liberal than its predecessor, was passed, that goal came constantly nearer
until, in 1862, it was attained. So generous seemed this policy in contrast
with the earlier one of regarding the lands as a source of revenue, and
so significant did it appear prospectively, that it became the subject of
eulogy at the outset. Furthermore, the measure had been sponsored by
the Republican party and when this party was later accused of representing
the interests of large capitalistic combines and of neglecting the farmers,
its leaders pointed to the Homestead Act as a refutation of the accusation.
Consequently there was built up around the law a halo of political and
economic significance which has greatly magnified the importance to be
attributed to it and which has misled practically every historian and econo-
mist who has dealt with land policies. The Homestead Law has been considered the capstone of an increasingly liberal land policy, and to it has

---

* From Paul Wallace Gates, "The Homestead Act in an Incongruous Land
System," *American Historical Review,* XLI (1936), 653–670 *passim.* Reprinted by
permission of the American Historical Association.

been ascribed the rapid settlement of the West and the large percentage of farmer owners in the United States. It has also been regarded as providing an outlet for the discontented and surplus labor of the East with the result that, as compared with European countries, high wage rates have prevailed in that section. The influence of free land has been blithely discussed by writers who have never taken the time to examine the facts with which they dealt so lightly. . . .

It is the purpose of this paper to show that the Homestead Law did not completely change our land system, that its adoption merely superimposed upon the old land system a principle out of harmony with it, and that until 1890 the old and the new constantly clashed. In presenting this view it will appear that the Homestead Law did not end the auction system or cash sales, as is generally assumed, that speculation and land monopolization continued after its adoption as widely perhaps as before, and within as well as without the law, that actual homesteading was generally confined to the less desirable lands distant from railroad lines, and that farm tenancy developed in frontier communities in many instances as a result of the monopolization of the land. . . .

The moderate land reformers of the mid-nineteenth century believed that the enactment of a homestead measure would retard if not end speculation in public lands. They argued that once free homesteads were available to settlers speculators would no longer have a market for their lands and all inducements to purchase in advance of settlement would be ended. Parenthetically, similar arguments have been advanced by certain historians to prove that there was little or no profit in land speculation. The land reformers reckoned too lightly, however, with the astuteness of the speculators who in the past had either succeeded in emasculating laws inimical to their interests or had actually flouted such laws in the very faces of the officials appointed to administer them.

From the outset the cards were stacked against the efficient and successful operation of the Homestead Law. Other acts in existence in 1862 greatly limited its application and new laws further restricting it were subsequently enacted. The administration of the law, both in Washington and in the field, was frequently in the hands of persons unsympathetic to its principle, and Western interests, though lauding the act, were ever ready to pervert it. The existence of the Pre-emption Law and its later variations, the Desert Land Act, the Timber Culture Act, the Timber and Stone Act, the land grants to railroads and states, the cash sale system, the Indian land policy, the acts granting land warrants to ex-soldiers or their heirs, and the Agricultural College Act of 1862, which granted millions of acres of land scrip to Eastern states, tended to make it practically as easy for speculators to engross huge areas of land after 1862 as before. . . .

The railroads were, of course, built through undeveloped regions and, other things being equal, routes were selected which would ensure to the companies the largest amount of what was then considered to be the best agricultural land. When the alternate government sections were finally restored to market settlers were frequently outbid for them by speculators. Moreover, the provision in the Homestead Law which confined the homesteader to eighty acres within the limits of a railroad grant was sufficient to send many homeseekers farther afield. On the railroad sections, of course, no free homesteading was permitted and thus the prospective settler found it necessary to go far from transportation facilities in order to take advantage of the government's bounty. In numerous instances the land policies of the railroads encouraged speculative and large-scale purchases with the result that millions of acres were turned into bonanza farms, such as those found in Dakota Territory, or were rented or leased to incoming settlers who had expected to find free land available to them. . . .

With over 125,000,000 acres of railroad lands, 140,000,000 acres of state lands, 100,000,000 acres of Indian lands, and 100,000,000 acres of Federal lands for sale in large or small blocks, and with the opportunities for evasion of the Homestead and Pre-emption laws and their variations . . . , it is obvious that there were few obstacles in the way of speculation and land monopolization after 1862. As before, it was still possible for foresighted speculators to precede settlers into the frontier, purchase the best lands, and hold them for the anticipated increase in value which the succeeding wave of settlers would give to them. It has heretofore been maintained that the existence of free land after 1862 greatly diminished the speculators' chances of profit and consequently limited their activities. This view will not bear careful scrutiny. Except for the squatters' claims, the speculators were generally able to secure the most desirable lands, that is, those easily brought under cultivation, fertile and close to timber, water, markets, and lines of communication. The subsequent settler had the choice of buying at the speculators' prices, from the land grant railroads which held their alternate tracts at equally high prices, from the states whose land policies were less generous than those of the Federal government, or of going farther afield to exercise his homestead privilege where facilities for social and economic intercourse were limited. . . .

Not only were the best agricultural lands being snapped up by speculators but the richest timber lands remaining in the possession of the United States were being rapidly entered by large dealers during the post-Civil War period. There were three areas in which vast amounts of timber land were still owned by the Federal government, the Lake states, the Gulf states with Arkansas, and the Pacific Coast states. In each of these three regions millions of acres of pine, spruce, hemlock, and fir were available for cash entry and in the Pacific area lands covered with the rich redwood and other trees peculiar to that region had been or were just being brought into the market. In the timber lands of these three sections some of the largest purchases by speculators or lumber men took place. Many thousands of acres in Wisconsin and Michigan were located by Isaac Stephenson, Philetus Sawyer, and Russell A. Alger, influential lumber dealers, who were subsequently to become members of the Senate of the United States. Ezra Cornell located 385,780 acres in the Eau Claire, Wisconsin, land district, 76,180 acres in the Bayfield district, 29,200 in the Stevens Point district, 12,480 acres in Minnesota, and 4000 acres in Kansas, all with Agricultural College scrip of New York. A group of New York magnates, Thomas F. Mason, George B. Satterlee, and William E. Dodge, entered 232,799 acres in the Marquette, Michigan, district, 10,850 acres elsewhere in that state, and 10,359 acres in Wassau, Wisconsin. Francis Palms purchased in Wisconsin and Michigan 286,208 acres, and with Frederick E. Driggs entered in the eighties about 200,000 acres more in the Marquette district. Three Ithaca, New York, lumber dealers, Henry W. Sage, John McGraw, and Jeremiah W. Dwight, like Ezra Cornell benefactors of Cornell University, entered 277,000 acres in Michigan, Wisconsin, and Minnesota, and 75,000 acres in Mississippi, Alabama, and Arkansas. Other large timberland entrymen in the Northwest were Calvin F. Howe of New York who acquired 105,000 acres in Minnesota, Thomas B. Walker who alone and with others acquired 166,000 acres in the St. Cloud, Minnesota, district, George M. Wakefield who accumulated 110,-000 acres in the Marquette district, and Jesse Spaulding and H. H. Porter of Chicago who purchased 113,000 acres in the same district. Fifty-six other persons purchased a total of 1,514,000 acres in Michigan, mostly in the Marquette district. . . .

Further details concerning the widespread speculative activity in public lands—both agricultural and timbered—after the passage of the Homestead Act are unnecessary; it is clear that speculation and land engrossment were not retarded by the act. Homeseekers in the West, being unwilling to go far afield from means of transportation or to settle upon the inferior ' lands remaining open to homestead, and lacking capital with which to purchase farms and to provide equipment for them, were frequently forced to become tenants on the lands of speculators. Thus farm tenancy developed in the frontier stage at least a generation before it would have appeared had the homestead system worked properly. In the states of Kansas and Nebraska, in which large-scale land monopolization has been revealed, sixteen and eighteen per cent respectively of the farms were operated by tenants in 1880, the first year for which figures are available, and in 1890 twenty-eight and twenty-four per cent respectively were operated by tenants. This continued monopolization of the best lands and the resulting growth of farm tenancy led reformers and others who feared the establishment of a landed aristocracy similar to that existing in many European countries to advocate the ending of the cash sales system entirely. Their demands were expressed in petitions to Congress, agitation in the press, and union of effort with other antimonopoly groups which were coming into prominence in the last third of the nineteenth century. Their agitation and the growing seriousness of the monopoly movement led to a series of halting steps toward the abandonment of cash sales, which frequently were offset by movements in the opposite direction.

Ignatius Donnelly

The Populist party, which followed earlier reform movements such as the Grange and the Farmers' Alliances, climaxed the most vigorous political protest of the farmer. One of the Populist leaders, Ignatius Donnelly (1831–1901), the sage of Nininger (his home town), also wrote a novel, Caesar's Column (1890). At one point in the story is imbedded a utopian vision for Western American agriculture.

A Farmer's Reform*

"But what would you do, my good Gabriel," said Maximilian, smiling, "if the reformation of the world were placed in your hands? Every man has an Utopia in his head. Give me some idea of yours."

"First," I said, "I should do away with all interest on money. Interest on money is the root and ground of the world's troubles. It puts one man in a position of safety, while another is in a condition of insecurity, and thereby it at once creates a radical distinction in human society."

"How do you make that out?" he asked.

"The lender takes a mortgage on the borrower's land or house, or goods, for, we will say, one-half or one-third their value; the borrower then assumes all the chances of life in his efforts to repay the loan. If he is a farmer, he has to run the risk of the fickle elements. Rains may drown, droughts may burn up his crops. If a merchant, he encounters all the hazards of trade; the bankruptcy of other tradesmen; the hostility of the

---

*From Ignatius Donnelly, *Caesar's Column* (Chicago: F. J. Schulte & Co., 1890), pp. 116–130 *passim*.

elements sweeping away agriculture, and so affecting commerce; the tempests that smite his ships, etc. If a mechanic, he is still more dependent upon the success of all above him, and the mutations of commercial prosperity. He may lose employment; he may sicken; he may die. But behind all these risks stands the money-lender, in perfect security. The failure of his customer only enriches him; for he takes for his loan property worth twice or thrice the sum he has advanced upon it. Given a million of men and a hundred years of time, and the slightest advantage possessed by any one class among the million must result, in the long run, in the most startling discrepancies of condition. A little evil grows like a ferment—it never ceases to operate; it is always at work. Suppose I bring before you a handsome, rosy-cheeked young man, full of life and hope and health. I touch his lip with a single *bacillus* of *phthisis pulmonalis*—consumption. It is invisible to the eye; it is too small to be weighed. Judged by all the tests of the senses, it is too insignificant to be thought of; but it has the capacity to multiply itself indefinitely. The youth goes off singing. Months, perhaps years, pass before the deadly disorder begins to manifest itself; but in time the step loses its elasticity; the eyes become dull; the roses fade from the cheeks; the strength departs, and eventually the joyous youth is but a shell—a cadaverous, shrunken form, inclosing a shocking mass of putridity; and death ends the dreadful scene. Give one set of men in a community a financial advantage over the rest, however slight—it may be almost invisible—and at the end of centuries that class so favored will own everything and wreck the country. A penny, they say, put out at interest the day Columbus sailed from Spain, and compounded ever since, would amount now to more than all the assessed value of all the property, real, personal and mixed, on the two continents of North and South America." . . .

"But," said Maximilian, with a smile, "it would not take long for your rich men, with their surplus wealth, to establish all those works you speak of. What would you do with the accumulations of the rest?"

"Well," said I, "we should find plenty to do. We would put their money, for instance, into a great fund and build national railroads, that would bring the productions of the farmers to the workmen, and those of the workmen to the farmers, at the least cost of transportation, and free from the exactions of speculators and middlemen. Thus both farmers and workmen would live better, at less expense and with less toil."

"All very pretty," said he; "but your middlemen would starve."

"Not at all," I replied; "the cunning never starve. There would be such a splendid era of universal prosperity that they would simply turn their skill and shrewdness into some new channels, in which, however, they would have to give something of benefit, as an equivalent for the benefits they received. Now they take the cream, and butter, and beef, while some one else has to raise, feed and milk the cow."

"But," said he, "all this would not help our farmers in their present condition—they are blotted off the land."

"True," I replied; "but just as I limited a man's possible wealth, so should I limit the amount of land he could own. I would fix a maximum of, say, 100 or 500 acres, or whatever amount might be deemed just and reasonable. I should abolish all corporations, or turn them back into individual partnerships. Abraham Lincoln, in the great civil war of the last century, gave the Southern insurgents so many days in which to lay down their arms or lose their slaves. In the same way I should grant one or two years' time, in which the great owners of land should sell their estates, in small tracts, to actual occupants, to be paid for in installments, on long time, without interest. And if they did not do so, then, at the end of the period prescribed, I should confiscate the lands and sell them, as the government in the old time sold the public lands, for so much per acre, to actual settlers, and turn the proceeds over to the former owners."

"But, as you had abolished interest on money, there could be no mortgages, and the poor men would starve to death before they could raise a crop."

"Then," I replied, "I should invoke the power of the nation, as was done in that great civil war of 1861, and issue paper money, receivable for all taxes, and secured by the guarantee of the faith and power of five hundred million people; and make advances to carry these ruined peasants beyond the first years of distress—that money to be a loan to them, without interest, and to be repaid as a tax on their land. Government is only a machine to insure justice and help the people, and we have not yet developed half its powers. And we are under no more necessity to limit ourselves to the governmental precedents of our ancestors than we are to confine ourselves to the narrow boundaries of their knowledge, or their inventive skill, or their theological beliefs. The trouble is that so many seem to regard government as a divine something which has fallen down upon us out of heaven, and therefore not to be improved upon or even criticized; while the truth is, it is simply a human device to secure human happiness, and in itself has no more sacredness than a wheelbarrow or a cooking-pot. The end of everything earthly is the good of man; and there is nothing sacred on earth but man, because he alone shares the Divine conscience." . . .

"Government," I replied; "government—national, state and municipal —is the key to the future of the human race.

"There was a time when the town simply represented cowering peasants, clustered under the shadow of the baron's castle for protection. It advanced slowly and reluctantly along the road of civic development, scourged forward by the whip of necessity. We have but to expand the powers of government to solve the enigma of the world. Man separated is man savage; man gregarious is man civilized. A higher development in society requires that this instrumentality of co-operation shall be heightened in its powers. There was a time when every man provided, at great cost, for the carriage of his own letters. Now the government, for an infinitely small charge, takes the business off his hands. There was a time when each house had to provide itself with water. Now the municipality furnishes water to all. The same is true of light. At one time each family had to educate its own children; now the state educates them. Once every man went armed to protect himself. Now the city protects him by its armed police. These hints must be followed out. The city of the future must furnish doctors for all; lawyers for all; entertainments for all; business guidance for all. It will see to it that no man is plundered, and no man starved, who is willing to work."

ADDITIONAL READINGS

The best recent work for general background in this subject is *Farmer's Age: Agriculture, 1815–1860* by Paul Wallace Gates (New York, 1960). The standard treatments of the public domain are Roy M. Robbins's *Our Landed Heritage* (Princeton, 1942) and Benjamin H. Hibbard's *A History of the Public Land Policies* (New York, 1924). Shaw Livermore, in *Early American Land Companies* (New York, 1939), does not deal with the trans-Mississippi West, but the prototypes are there. For introductions to the life of squatters, see Joseph Shafer, *Social History of American Agriculture* (New York, 1936); and Fred A. Shannon, *The Farmer's Last Frontier* (New York, 1945). For an analysis of Walter Prescott Webb's classic *Great Plains,* excerpted above, see Fred A. Shannon, "An Appraisal of Walter Prescott Webb's The Great Plains," *Critique of Research in the Social Sciences* (New York, 1940). Vivid descriptions of plains settlement may be found in Everett Dick, *The Sod-House Frontier, 1854–1900* (New York, 1937). For an unusual appreciation of the beauties of the plains, see John Muir, *Story of My Boyhood and Youth* (Boston, 1913). Those who wish to read further in the story of later agrarian discontent should begin with John D. Hicks, *The Populist Revolt* (Minneapolis, 1931).

15

CULTURE AND
THE FRONTIER

Though it may be surprising to some, culture in the sense of education, the arts, and the sciences is highly important as an aspect of frontier
development. The number of artists and scientists who pushed into the
West in the frontier period is admittedly small compared with farmers
or miners, but their percentage is likewise small in any society, and to ignore them is to ignore the tremendous impact of the West in these fields.

George Catlin, a western painter of the 1830s, compared American
Indians to Grecian youths at the first Olympic Games, and in so doing he
was engaging in that most typical of nineteenth-century pastimes, the
romanticizing and exoticizing of the West. Later in the century a whole
school of painters, led by Albert Bierstadt and Thomas Moran, came to
be known as the Rocky Mountain School because they used Western
peaks as their chief motif just as an earlier romantic group of painters had
used the Hudson River. To artists of this kind, and often to groups of
their colleagues in the East and Europe, the little-known West was an
absorbing fascination and an important influence.

The scientists in the early West characteristically represented Eastern
or European academies and institutions. Such organizations as the
Academy of Natural Sciences in Philadelphia or the Smithsonian Institution in Washington actively sponsored Western expeditions or assembled
the boxes of specimens that poured in from the Western field. One great
aim of nineteenth-century botany and zoology was the completion of the

cataloguing of all the earth's plants and animals; and a vast tract of unknown land, like the American West, was thus a tremendous challenge. Likewise, the geologists and the geographers looked to a more comprehensive understanding of the earth's surface. Many of these enterprises in pure science had their more practical aspects. John Charles Frémont, for example, was a scientist; but since his intellectual exploits became a tool for political expansion, he has been considered elsewhere. Similarly, scientific work accompanied the assessment of routes for the transcontinental railroad. Here, however, we are concerned with those scientists, like John Townsend, whose excitement over the West stemmed from the joy of more abstract learned pursuits.

After the Civil War the West continued to feel the impact of scientific surveys, and some of the great names of Western exploration were stamped on the land as late as the 1860s and 1870s. Clarence King, Josiah Whitney, William Brewer, Ferdinand V. Hayden, and a host of others worked over the West with painstaking care in these decades, analyzing and documenting as they went. They were supported either by endowed scientific societies of the East or by the United States government, chiefly the United States Geologic Survey. But the greatest mind of them all was John Wesley Powell, because he understood the peculiar needs and problems of the West perhaps better than any man before or since. Powell's voice cried from the wilderness that water was the key to development of the West, that institutions had to be developed on regional rather than state or county lines, that laws of land and water had to be completely rewritten for these regions. Only in the twentieth century are we coming to realize the sound and at the same time prophetic nature of Powell's vision.

Culture is carried in many ways. As tradition, the inner core of a society, it can be carried unconsciously into a new land. We have seen how ideas of government and order, whether to mining camps or to new cities, are unavoidably transposed. But two great carriers of culture—books and schools—have not yet been surveyed. What did the frontiersman read, and what books did he consider important enough to bring with him over the long, dreary miles? He was forced to ponder the age-old gamester's question of choosing the books with which to be stranded. And as soon as he settled, he sought means to educate his children.

Hence the little red schoolhouse with its respect for the three R's moved West like the men; it was an institution that, in Henry Beecher's words, went "lowing along the western plains as Jacob's herds lowed along the Syrian hills." But what is more surprising is the great incentive to the founding of colleges in the West. Eastern schools like Yale and Princeton and religious bodies like the Presbyterians and Methodists prided themselves on being the "mothers" of Western institutions. And they fructified abundantly. By the end of the nineteenth century, for example, California already boasted no fewer than twelve institutions of higher learning.

In education, as in so much of tradition, the West did not innovate as much as it selected and emphasized. The nature of education was an unsettled question for America at large; the worship of practicality and consequent distrust of theory and classical learning had an effect everywhere. The West was only more emphatic. Frederick Jackson Turner once quoted a frontiersman as saying, "if you can't stand seeing your old New England ideas, ways of doing, and living and in fact, all of the good old Yankee fashions knocked out of shape and altered, or thrown by as unsuited to the climate, don't be caught out here." Classical education, then, was "knocked out of shape"; but in delivering such blows, the frontier only accentuated what had already begun elsewhere.

The selections that follow show the force of individualistic innovation balanced by the old and the known. The artist as a romanticist tended to look for the exotic and the unknown, and he may even have brought with him vague, visionary hopes of finding unicorns and dragons. The scientist, on the other hand, may not have expected dragons, but the thrill he received at the sight of a new, strange bird came from its filling a gap in a catalogue which generations of scientists before him had compiled. In short, although the bird was new, it was soon captured in a listing which might symbolize tradition. Powell studied unknown stretches of a river, but by means of an instrument whose design was centuries old. Educators were faced with demands for practical training while they preached classical studies as the essential ingredient of the free mind. The West was an epitome of the eternal confrontation of the old and the new, of the freedom gained through tradition (or "association," as Beecher called it) with the freedom of loneliness, novelty, and innovation.

Rudolph Friedrich Kurz

The Swiss artist Rudolph Friedrich Kurz (1818–1871) spent the years from 1846 to 1852 at various Western trading posts on the Mississippi and upper Missouri rivers. He was particularly interested in the Indians, with whom he was deeply sympathetic. The following selections from his journal give some insight into the problems and status of the artist on the frontier.

A Painter's Journal*

From my earliest youth primeval forest and Indians had an indescribable charm for me. In spare hours I read only those books that included descriptions and adventures of the new world; even my own beautiful homeland pleased me best in its records of primitive times, when sturdy shepherds and huntsmen, with their noble forms unconcealed—like the "woodmen" in heraldry or the Germans of Tacitus—roamed freely in the virgin woods where dwelt the aurochs and the stag, the bison and the gazelle, the wild boar and the unicorn, the chamois and, what is more, the dragon. Now primeval forests exist only in inaccessible mountain fastnesses; cultivation extends even to the snow-capped peaks. Man's habitations spread over the whole earth; there are churches and schoolhouses without number; yet where are men found dwelling together in unity? Where does sober living prevail? Or contentment? I longed for unknown lands, where no demands of citizenship would involve me in the vortex of political agitations. I longed for the quietude of immemorial woods where no paupers mar one's delight in beauty, where neither climate, false modesty, nor fashion compels concealment of the noblest form in God's creation; where there is neither overlordship of the bourgeois nor the selfishness of the rich who treasure their wealth in splendid idleness, while the fine arts languish.

When I was allowed to devote myself to painting, those longings became all the more intense for the reason that, from the moment I determined to become an artist, my life purpose was fixed: I would devote my talents to the portrayal of the aboriginal forests, the wild animals that inhabited them, and to the Indians. From that moment I had an ideal—a definite purpose in life to the attainment of which I might dedicate all my powers. To depict with my brush the romantic life of the American Indian seemed to me a subject worthy of the manifold studies I was to undertake. In fact, the comprehensiveness of the plan proved my greatest difficulty, because, in the study of art, landscape and animals require each a special training that is only little less important than that demanded for the representation of human beings. Many years would be required of me, if I was to attain to mastery in a single one of these subjects. Nevertheless, my enthusiasm for art, my perseverance and untiring patience—self-will, as this trait is often named—gave me fair hopes of realizing my aims. . . .

---

* From Rudolph Friedrich Kurz, *Journal* (Washington, D.C.: Government Printing Office, 1937), Bureau of American Ethnology, Bulletin 115, pp. 1–342 *passim*. Courtesy of the Smithsonian Institution.

As the purpose of my stay in America was to accomplish certain aims in the study of art, all plans for employment in other directions for the sake of earning my bread (my supply of funds was already low) had to be subordinated, necessarily, to that purpose. I found out soon enough that I could never do anything so antagonistic to my true nature as to go into business, even for the length of time required to earn enough money to get forward independently as an artist. That a man cannot serve two masters was never more truly verified than in me. If my penchant for portraying aboriginal nature in art had made me dissatisfied with what my own beautiful country could offer, now that I had actually seen primeval woods and the wild beasts, Nature's true children, that desire of earlier years had become a passion. I was so happy not to have been disappointed in the woodlands and forests: they were, I found, far more rich, included more that was original, and the Indians were of a more noble type than I had ever dreamed.

I had already accomplished something in the pursuit of my aims: primeval woods, prairies, and river I had observed at every season of the year—torpid under the benumbing influence of frost, brimming with life under the influence of warmth. Now I longed to study Indians and wild animals. . . . I am not conscious of the least yearning for so-called cultured societies, for I am not urged on to this work by ambition to contemplate the most beautiful objects and reproduce them on canvas but I am inspired by my ideal—my adoration of beauty. Here one lives much more at ease, is more free than in the civilized States; the so-called savage is not always disputing about the teachings of religion, about political matters[,] the rights of man, etc., principles concerning which men should have reached some uniform understanding long ago. With the savage, the sound sense with which Nature endowed him has settled all such matters. Cursing, quarreling, such as one hears constantly among us, is never heard among the Indians. Let one but look on when they are playing billiards; the strokes are so nearly equal, the game so close, that the players themselves cannot easily decide which one wins (and they always play for a stake, oftentimes quite high). They then appeal at once to the bystanders as arbiters. There is no swearing, no contention—they lack even expressions for such. Furthermore, insult would inevitably bring definite results; deadly revenge from the person insulted, involving even bloodshed and death. . . .

Mr. Denig [one of the chief fur traders] came upon me while I was working on a sketch of my feminine beau ideal. He was extraordinarily pleased with the form and wished to have it painted at once, so that he might hang the picture on the wall in the reception room. He could not forbear his bad jest, however, concerning my hard task in attempting to portray a naked human figure so divine, so exalted, that it would make no appeal to the sensual. He made me feel sick; I was, therefore, not willing to expose my ideal to further remark. But I know that I must accustom myself to this conclusion: There will always be ordinary people who see in the nude only physical attraction, not spirit. A moi mon ideal!...

As I now dare assume that my studies are sufficiently thorough and comprehensive to justify my executing paintings true to life, yet in aesthetic manner, representing scenes in the Far West (characteristic of life there in former days rather than at present), and as I am offered no better outlook for earning my bread as artist in St. Louis than in any of the other new States, owing to the prevailing lack of interest in painting, I must, though with heavy heart, dispose of a large part of my Indian collection in order to get money enough to travel to New York or to Paris, where I hope to find more encouraging prospects.

To force myself to abandon art merely for the sake of making a longer stay in this region possible by earning my living painting houses, ships, and mural decorations, or by undertaking once more the duties of merchant's clerk, is an outlook I cannot contemplate; my harsh experience in business transactions, heretofore, make such a plan all the more distasteful. Furthermore, my chances for success are better in Europe than in this country and, finally, I regard my collection of studies sufficiently comprehensive to render a longer stay, in straitened circumstances, unnecessary. After severe mental conflict I decided to part with a large portion of my valuable collection in order to get funds to travel east. Before I let it go out of my possession I made copies of the objects included, so that I might rescue at least that much for myself. It was extremely painful to give up my Indian relics; my heart was so set upon them; I had submitted to so many deprivations for the sake of possessing a collection, as complete as possible, of Indian apparel, weapons, and ornaments. But this is my fatal destiny: I have only to set my heart upon something and, straightway, I am destined to loss. So it was with my collection of engravings, with my love affairs, with my horses.

John Kirk Townsend

John Kirk Townsend (1809–1851) was a Philadelphia Quaker who, with Audubon, became one of the nation's leading ornithologists. In 1834, when he was only twenty-five years old, he joined the naturalist Thomas Nuttall on the Nathaniel Wyeth expedition from Independence, Missouri to Fort Vancouver on the Columbia River. His narrative of this journey is full of the excitement of the pure scientist in his first contacts with the West.

Journey to the Columbia River*

The birds thus far have been very abundant. There is a considerable variety, and many of them have not before been seen by naturalists. As to the plants, there seems to be no end to them, and Mr. N[uttall] is finding dozens of new species daily. In the other branches of science, our success has not been so great, partly on account of the rapidity and steadiness with which we travel, but chiefly from the difficulty, and almost impossibility, of carrying the subjects. Already we have cast away all our useless and super-fluous clothing, and have been content to mortify our natural pride, to make room for our specimens. Such things as spare waistcoats, shaving boxes, soap, and stockings, have been ejected from our trunks, and we are content to dress, as we live, in a style of primitive simplicity. In fact, the whole appearance of our party is sufficiently primitive; many of the men are dressed entirely in deerskins, without a single article of civilized manufac-ture about them; the old trappers and hunters wear their hair flowing on their shoulders, and their large grizzled beards would scarcely disgrace a Bedouin of the desert.

The next morning the whole camp was suddenly aroused by the falling of all the tents. A tremendous blast swept as from a funnel over the sandy plain, and in an instant precipitated our frail habitations like webs of gos-samer. The men crawled out from under the ruins, rubbing their eyes, and, as usual, muttering imprecations against the country and all that therein was; it was unusually early for a start, but we did not choose to pitch the tents again, and to sleep without them here was next to impossible; so we took our breakfast in the open air, devouring our well sanded provisions as quickly as possible, and immediately took to the road. . . .

In the afternoon, I committed an act of cruelty and wantonness, which distressed and troubled me beyond measure, and which I have ever since recollected with sorrow and compunction. A beautiful doe antelope came running and bleating after us, as though she wished to overtake the party; she continued following us for nearly an hour, at times approaching within thirty [or] forty yards, and standing to gaze at us as we moved slowly on our way. I several times raised my gun to fire at her, but my better nature

---

* From John K. Townsend, *Narrative of a Journey across the Rocky Mountains to the Columbia River* (Philadelphia: Henry Perkins, 1839), pp. 59–65 *passim,* 163.

as often gained the ascendency, and I at last rode into the midst of the party to escape the temptation. Still the doe followed us, and I finally fell into the rear, but without intending it, and again looked at her as she trotted behind us. At that moment, my evil genius and love of sport triumphed; I slid down from my horse, aimed at the poor antelope, and shot a ball through her side. Under other circumstances, there would have been no cruelty in this; but here, where better meat was so abundant, and the camp was so plentifully supplied, it was unfeeling, heartless murder. It was under the influence of this too late impression, that I approached my poor victim. She was writhing in agony upon the ground, and exerting herself in vain efforts to draw her mangled body farther from her destroyer; and as I stood over her, and saw her cast her large, soft, black eyes upon me with an expression of the most touching sadness, while the great tears rolled over her face, I felt myself the meanest and most abhorrent thing in creation. But now a finishing blow would be mercy to her, and I threw my arm around her neck, averted my face, and drove my long knife through her bosom to the heart. I did not trust myself to look upon her afterwards, but mounted my horse, and galloped off to the party, with feelings such as I hope never to experience again. For several days the poor antelope haunted me, and I shall never forget its last look of pain and upbraiding. . . .

On the afternoon of the 31st [May], we came to green trees and bushes again, and the sight of them was more cheering than can be conceived, except by persons who have travelled for weeks without beholding a green thing, save the grass under their feet. We encamped in the evening in a beautiful grove of cottonwood trees, along the edge of which ran the Platte, dotted as usual with numerous islands.

In the morning, Mr. N. and myself were up before the dawn, strolling through the umbrageous forest, inhaling the fresh, bracing air, and making the echoes ring with the report of our gun, as the lovely tenants of the grove flew by dozens before us. I think I never before saw so great a variety of birds within the same space. All were beautiful, and many of them quite new to me; and after we had spent an hour amongst them, and my game bag was teeming with its precious freight, I was still loath to leave the place, lest I should not have procured specimens of the whole.

None but a naturalist can appreciate a naturalist's feelings—his delight amounting to ecstacy—when a specimen such as he has never before seen, meets his eye, and the sorrow and grief which he feels when he is compelled to tear himself from a spot abounding with all that he has anxiously and unremittingly sought for.

This was peculiarly my case upon this occasion. We had been long travelling over a sterile and barren tract, where the lovely denizens of the forest could not exist, and I had been daily scanning the great extent of the desert, for some little *oasis* such as I had now found; here was my wish at length gratified, and yet the caravan would not halt for me; I must turn my back upon the *El Dorado* of my fond anticipations, and hurry forward over the dreary wilderness which lay beyond.

What valuable and highly interesting accessions to science might not be made by a party, composed exclusively of naturalists, on a journey through this rich and unexplored region! The botanist, the geologist, the mamalogist, the ornithologist, and the entomologist, would find a rich and almost inexhaustible field for the prosecution of their inquiries, and the result of such an expedition would be to add most materially to our knowledge of the wealth and resources of our country, to furnish us with new and important facts relative to its structure, organization, and natural productions, and to complete the fine native collections in our already extensive museums. . . .

The gale continues with the same violence as yesterday, and we do not therefore think it expedient to leave our camp. Mr. N.'s large and beautiful collection of new and rare plants was considerably injured by the wetting it received; he has been constantly engaged since we landed yesterday, in opening and drying them. In this task he exhibits a degree of patience and perseverance which is truly astonishing; sitting on the ground, and steaming over the enormous fire, for hours together, drying the papers, and rearranging the whole collection, specimen by specimen, while the great drops of perspiration roll unheeded from his brow. Throughout the whole of our long journey, I have had constantly to admire the ardor and perfect indefatigability with which he has devoted himself to the grand object of his tour. No difficulty, no danger, no fatigue has ever daunted him, and he finds his rich reward in the addition of nearly *a thousand* new species of American plants, which he has been enabled to make to the already teeming flora of our vast continent. My bale of birds, which was equally exposed to the action of the water, escaped without any material injury.

John Wesley Powell

The writings of John Wesley Powell (1834–1902) have provided inspiration for many twentieth-century historians. Walter Prescott Webb, for example (see Chapter 1), builds firmly on the ideas of Powell, especially on Powell's classic Report on the Lands of the Arid Regions of the United States *(1879). But though Powell's work, like that of Frémont, had numerous political ramifications, he roamed the West primarily as a scientist and an adventurer; and in this respect none of his writing equals his* Exploration of the Colorado River *for sheer joy in scientific discovery, coupled with nerve and devotion. On this Colorado River voyage in 1869 he was a one-armed man in a small group facing the unknown with scientific senses quivering at the task.*

Exploration of the Colorado*

August 13.—We are now ready to start on our way down the Great Unknown. Our boats, tied to a common stake, are chafing each other, as they are tossed by the fretful river. They ride high and buoyant, for their loads are lighter than we could desire. We have but a month's rations remaining. The flour has been resifted through the mosquito-net sieve; the spoiled bacon has been dried, and the worst of it boiled; the few pounds of dried apples have been spread in the sun, and reshrunken to their normal bulk; the sugar has all melted, and gone on its way down the river; but we have a large sack of coffee. The lighting of the boats has this advantage; they will ride the waves better, and we shall have but little to carry when we make a portage.

We are three quarters of a mile in the depths of the earth, and the great river shrinks into insignificance, as it dashes its angry waves against the walls and cliffs, that rise to the world above; they are but puny ripples, and we but pigmies, running up and down the sands, or lost among the boulders.

We have an unknown distance yet to run; an unknown river yet to explore. What falls there are, we know not; what rocks beset the channel, we know not; what walls rise over the river, we know not. Ah, well! we may conjecture many things. The men talk as cheerfully as ever; jests are bandied about freely this morning; but to me the cheer is somber and the jests are ghastly.

With some eagerness, and some anxiety, and some misgiving, we enter the canyon below, and are carried along by the swift water through walls which rise from its very edge. . . .

With great care, and constant watchfulness, we proceed, making about four miles this afternoon, and camp in a cave.

August 14.—At daybreak we walk down the bank of the river, on a little sandy beach, to take a view of a new feature in the canyon. Heretofore, hard rocks have given us bad river; soft rocks, smooth water; and a

---

* From John Wesley Powell, *Exploration of the Colorado River of the West and Its Tributaries* (Washington, D.C.: Government Printing Office, 1915), pp. 198–246 *passim.*

series of rocks harder than any we have experienced sets in. The river enters the granite!*

We can see but a little way into the granite gorge, but it looks threatening.

After breakfast we enter on the waves. At the very introduction, it inspires awe. The canyon is narrower than we have ever before seen it; the water is swifter; there are but few broken rocks in the channel; but the walls are set, on either side, with pinnacles and crags; and sharp, angular buttresses, bristling with wind and wave-polished spires, extend far out into the river. . . .

About eleven o'clock we hear a great roar ahead, and approach it very cautiously. The sound grows louder and louder as we run, and at last we find ourselves above a long, broken fall, with ledges and pinnacles of rock obstructing the river. There is a descent of, perhaps, seventy-five or eighty feet in a third of a mile, and the rushing waters break into great waves on the rocks, and lash themselves into a mad, white foam. We can land just above, but there is no foothold on either side by which we can make a portage. It is nearly a thousand feet to the top of the granite, so it will be impossible to carry our boats around, though we can climb to the summit up a side gulch, and, passing along a mile or two, can descend to the river. This we find on examination; but such a portage would be impracticable for us, and we must run the rapid, or abandon the river. There is no hesitation. We step into our boats, push off and away we go, first on smooth but swift water, then we strike a glassy wave, and ride to its top, down again into the trough, up again on a higher wave, and down and up on waves higher and still higher, until we strike one just as it curls back, and a breaker rolls over our little boat. Still, on we speed, shooting past projecting rocks, till the little boat is caught in a whirlpool, and spun around several times. At last we pull out again into the stream, and now the other boats have passed us. The open compartment of the "Emma Dean" is filled with water, and every breaker rolls over us. Hurled back from a rock, now on this side, now on that, we are carried into an eddy, in which we struggle for a few minutes, and are then out again, the breakers still rolling over us. Our boat is unmanageable, but she cannot sink, and we drift down another hundred yards, through breakers; how, we scarcely know. We find the other boats have turned into an eddy at the foot of the fall, and are waiting to catch us as we come, for the men have seen that our boat is swamped. They push out as we come near, and pull us in against the wall. We bail our boat, and on we go again. . . .

---

* Geologists would call these rocks metamorphic crystalline schists, with dikes and beds of granite; but we will use the popular name for the whole series—granite. [Powell's note.]

It is not easy to describe the labor of such navigation. We must prevent the waves from dashing the boats against the cliffs. Sometimes, where the river is swift, we must put a bight of rope about a rock, to prevent her being snatched from us by a wave; but where the plunge is too great, or the chute too swift, we must let her leap, and catch her below, or the undertow will drag her under the falling water, and she sinks. Where we wish to run her out a little way from shore, through a channel between rocks, we first throw in little sticks of driftwood, and watch their course, to see where we must steer, so that she will pass the channel in safety. And so we hold, and let go, and pull, and lift, and ward, among rocks, around rocks, and over rocks.

And now we go on through this solemn, mysterious way. The river is very deep, the canyon very narrow, and still obstructed, so that there is no steady flow of the stream; but the waters wheel, and roll, and boil, and we are scarcely able to determine where we can go. Now, the boat is carried to the right, perhaps close to the wall; again, she is shot into the stream, and perhaps is dragged over to the other side, where, caught in a whirlpool, she spins about. We can neither land nor run as we please. The boats are entirely unmanageable; no order in their running can be preserved; now one, now another, is ahead, each crew laboring for its own preservation. In such a place we come to another rapid. Two of the boats run it perforce. One succeeds in landing, but there is no foothold by which to make a portage, and she is pushed out again into the stream. The next minute a great reflex wave fills the open compartment; she is waterlogged, and drifts unmanageable. Breaker after breaker rolls over her, and one capsizes her. The men are thrown out; but they cling to the boat, and she drifts down some distance, alongside of us, and we are able to catch her. She is soon bailed out, and the men are aboard once more; but the oars are lost, so a pair from the "Emma Dean" is spared. Then for two miles we find smooth water. . . .

August 27. . . . For the last two days, our course has not been plotted. I sit down and do this now, for the purpose of finding where we are by dead reckoning. It is a clear night, and I take out the sextant to make observation for latitude, and find that the astronomic determination agrees very nearly with that of the plot—quite as closely as might be expected, from a meridian observation on a planet. In a direct line, we must be about forty-five miles from the mouth of the Rio Virgen. If we can reach that point, we know that there are settlements up that river about twenty miles. This forty-five miles, in a direct line, will probably be eighty or ninety in the meandering line of the river. But then we know that there is comparatively open country for many miles above the mouth of the Virgen, which is our point of destination.

As soon as I determine all this, I spread my plot on the sand, and wake Howland, who is sleeping down by the river, and show him where I suppose we are, and where several Mormon settlements are situated.

We have another short talk about the morrow, and he lies down again; but for me there is no sleep. All night long, I pace up and down a little path, on a few yards of sand beach, along by the river. Is it wise to go on? I go to the boats again, to look at our rations. I feel satisfied that we can get over the danger immediately before us; what there may be below I know not. From our outlook yesterday, on the cliffs, the canyon seemed to make another great bend to the south, and this, from our experience heretofore, means more and higher granite walls. I am not sure that we can climb out of the canyon here, and, when at the top of the wall, I know enough of the country to be certain that it is a desert of rock and sand, between this and the nearest Mormon town, which, on the most direct line, must be seventy-five miles away. True, the late rains have been favorable to us, should we go out, for the probabilities are that we shall find water still standing in holes, and, at one time, I almost conclude to leave the river. But for years I have been contemplating this trip. To leave the exploration unfinished, to say that there is a part of the canyon which I cannot explore, having already almost accomplished it, is more than I am willing to acknowledge, and I determine to go on.

I wake my brother, and tell him of Howland's determination, and he promises to stay with me; then I call up Lawkins, the cook, and he makes a like promise; then Sumner, and Bradley, and Hall, and they all agree to go on.

August 28.—At last daylight comes, and we have breakfast, without a word being said about the future. The meal is as solemn as a funeral. After breakfast, I ask the three men if they still think it best to leave us. The elder Howland thinks it is, and Dunn agrees with him. The younger Howland tries to persuade them to go on with the party, failing in which, he decides to go with his brother.

Then we cross the river. The small boat is very much disabled, and unseaworthy. With the loss of hands, consequent on the departure of the three men, we shall not be able to run all of the boats, so I decide to leave my "Emma Dean."

Two rifles and a shotgun are given to the men who are going out. I ask them to help themselves to the rations, and take what they think to be a fair share. This they refuse to do, saying they have no fear but that they can get something to eat; but Billy, the cook, has a pan of biscuits prepared for dinner, and these he leaves on a rock.

Before starting, we take our barometers, fossils, the minerals, and some ammunition from the boat, and leave them on the rocks. We are going over this place as light as possible. The three men help us lift our boats over a rock twenty-five or thirty feet high, and let them down again over the first fall, and now we are all ready to start. The last thing before leaving, I write a letter to my wife, and give it to Howland. Sumner gives him his watch, directing that it be sent to his sister, should he not be heard from again. The records of the expedition have been kept in duplicate. One set of these is given to Howland, and now we are ready. For the last time, they entreat us not to go on, and tell us that it is madness to set out in this place; that we can never get safely through it; and, further, that the river turns again to the south into the granite, and a few miles of such rapids and falls will exhaust our entire stock of rations, and then it will be too late to climb out. Some tears are shed; it is rather a solemn parting; each party thinks the other is taking the dangerous course.

My old boat left, I go on board of the "Maid of the Canon." The three men climb a crag, that overhangs the river, to watch us off. The "Maid of the Canon" pushes out. We glide rapidly along the foot of the wall, just grazing one great rock, then pull out a little into the chute of the second fall, and plunge over it. The open compartment is filled when we strike the first wave below, but we cut through it, and then the men pull with all their power toward the left wall, and swing clear of the dangerous rock below all right. We are scarcely a minute in running it, and find that, although it looked bad from above, we have passed many places that were worse.

The other boat follows without more difficulty. We land at the first practicable point below and fire our guns, as a signal to the men above that we have come over in safety. Here we remain a couple of hours, hoping that they will take the smaller boat and follow us. We are behind a curve in the canyon, and cannot see up to where we left them, and so we wait until their coming seems hopeless, and push on.

John Walton Caughey

If the Western scientist, like any educated migrant, carried germs of culture with him, it was nevertheless not easy to institutionalize cultural yearnings. The theater, one such cultural institution, had a remarkable growth, however, in Western mining camps. In the following selection, Professor John Caughey of the University of California at Los Angeles describes and explains this phenomenon.

The Gold Rush Theater*

By general observation, if not by definition, frontier communities are characterized by cultural poverty. That such a condition should exist is natural and almost inevitable. At the edge of settlement population is sparse. The few who are present have their hands full with such elemental tasks as clearing the land, breaking the sod, erecting shelter, and gathering food. Problems of defense and those of shaping a government usually demand attention, leaving little energy for such luxuries as art and letters. Usually, too, the material resources necessary to cultural development are lacking. . . .

Yet, whereas gold dealt roughly with the rudimentary beginnings of culture in California, it soon redressed the damage. The golden alchemy that caused stage and steamer lines, banks and business houses, farms and factories, courts and legislatures to blossom where had been a desert, performed like miracles in the realm of things cultural. Letters, the creative and ornamental arts, the schools, and even the churches put forth vigorous new growth and fruited precociously. . . .

The theater, as must readily appear, was a culture form that could respond . . . buoyantly to the stimulation of gold. A rolypoly little Englishman, Stephen C. Massett, who liked to bill himself as Jeems Pipes of Pipesville, apparently was the first professional to take a turn. On a June night in 1849 he put on a one-man show at San Francisco. In a rich baritone he sang several of his own compositions. Shifting to a clear falsetto, he mimicked an operatic diva. Then he did a series of monologues, imitating Yankee characters, and ended up with a seven-part reproduction of a New England town meeting. Here in miniature was a foretaste of Gold Coast theater: a variety show, with a touch of sentiment, a vein of broader humor, some burlesque, and a demonstration of versatility. . . .

Sacramento was a long step in advance. In a large tent labeled Eagle Theater a company opened a dramatic season with "The Bandit Chief; or, The Forest Spectre." Such plays as "The Wife," "Dead Shot," "Othello," "Bachelor Buttons," "William Tell," "Rent Day," and "Charles II" also adorned their repertoire. Night performances were the invariable rule, with a nightly change of bill and an afterpiece almost always added to the more ambitious drama with which the show began. . . .

Although their critical faculties may have been dulled by a feeling of starvation for entertainment, the mining-camp playgoers were exacting.

* From John Walton Caughey, *Gold Is the Cornerstone* (Berkeley: University of California Press, 1948), pp. 269, 272, 278–283. Reprinted by permission.

Like their San Francisco counterparts, they had a habit of protesting when lines were cut, forgotten, or poorly delivered. Of his first recital Massett reports that when his melodeon wheezed to a stop in the middle of his first number, a voice from the pit advised him to "dry up." Other artists had their anxious moments and turned gingerly to the outspoken dramatic criticism of the local press. . . .

Nevertheless, the tidings of flush days on the coast intrigued artists and their managers, and ere long topflight stars were staging a gold rush of their own. Included were Ed Christy and minstrel headliners such as Eph Horn the end man, Dan Bryant the soft-shoe expert, and Thomas F. Briggs the banjo virtuoso. Songsters such as Elisa Biscaccianti and Kate Hayes joined the trek. So did a host of noble actors, including the Booths, father and son, the Chapmans, Edwin Forrest and Catherine Sinclair, and, a bit later, Lola Montez, Adah Isaacs Menken, and Matilda Heron.

Of these the most noteworthy was perhaps Edwin Booth, because he arrived an unknown, introduced almost contemptuously by his father as a good banjo player. When he left the state a few years later, Edwin had come into his own as a Shakespearean actor. The wildly enthusiastic reception accorded Biscaccianti is most significant in its demonstration that the rough-hewn men of the mines would sit enthralled by a strictly classical program—at least from one possessed of winsome face and graceful figure.

Lola Montez' fame ensured a first-night sell-out. Her beauty did not disappoint, nor did her skill at repartee, but, quickly exposed as neither actress nor dancer, Lola wisely retired to a cottage salon at Grass Valley. Her most notable effect upon the California theater, aside from becoming a legend in it, was the inspiration of burlesques written by guitarist Robinson, M.D., and romped through by the irrepressible Caroline Chapman.

After all else is said, it may be that Lotta Crabtree is the best exemplar of the gold-rush theater. Her debut was at a tiny log theater at Rabbit Creek. Dressed in long-tailed green coat, knee breeches, and tall hat, she tossed aside a shillelagh and danced a vigorous Irish jig and reel, laughing infectiously the while. After many encores she came back on stage looking angelic in white dress with round neck and puffed sleeves and sang a plaintive ballad. The hardened miners went wild, showering the stage with coins, nuggets, and a fifty-dollar slug. Black-eyed, red-haired Lotta, all of eight but looking no more than six, was their darling.

Under the tutelage of her ambitious mother, versatile Mart Taylor, and other willing helpers, Lotta embarked on a rapid tour of the mining camps. She learned new songs and steps. At Placerville a Negro minstrel taught her how to do a soft-shoe breakdown. Lola Montez introduced her to Spanish dancing. From others she picked up hornpipes, buck and wing, new bits of pantomime, and a comic way of picking up the largess of coins and nuggets, while from Jake Wallace she learned how to make a banjo ring.

Thus equipped, she could have emulated Massett's early example of putting on a whole show. By the middle 'fifties, however, talent had become abundant and the real problem was to get a chance to perform. But with barrel-top numbers at auctions, with variety-show billings in the mines and at San Francisco, with bits in the regular plays, and with specialities between their acts, Lotta had as busy a childhood as one could ask. In one little bundle vibrant with energy, she represents the contradictory elements that the miners most prized: humor and pathos, high skill and less high buffoonery, mastery of the traditional forms and indulgence in individual pyrotechnics.

Lusty, opulent, wonderfully diversified, star-studded, attracting the best from the boards in the States, and remolding actors and vehicles to fit the less trammeled milieu of the Gold Coast, this chapter of theatrical history is one of the most distinctive features of the Argonaut generation. Without the gold of California only the merest fragment of its pageantry could have existed. To what extent it influenced the future is less patent, but the heritage of passionate interest in the theater is readily discernible.

Henry Ward Beecher

Henry Ward Beecher (1813–1887) was the influential pastor of the Plymouth Church in Brooklyn, New York, and brother of Harriet Beecher Stowe. Beecher espoused a variety of moral crusades, and on the occasion of the following address (1856) he was engaged in fund raising for Western schools. In the speech he suggests some of the forces behind the founding of Western colleges.

The Transplanting of Schools*

The first want of society is the fullness, the liberty, the vivacity and freshness of its individual citizens. No state is permanently strong which absorbs the liberty of the individual into the body politic. If the *state* is the

---

* From Henry Ward Beecher, *Man and His Institutions: An Address before the Society for the Promotion of Collegiate and Theological Education at the West* (New York: Calkins & Stiles, 1856), pp. 1–14 *passim*.

great value; if men are only bricks, separately worthless, and good only
when laid in orderly rows and held by the cement of laws, then it will come
to pass that, in a little time, men will begin to shrink, to dry up, to wither
away. A state whose citizens are but the pabulum of the state, will soon
have nothing to feed on, and will be no better than a pyramid enormously
built for the pitiful purpose of holding dead men's dust through worthless
ages! Men are the roots and leaves—society is the tree which they make.
The trunk and branches are but the frame. The life lies in the extremities.

But individualism needs help. Men are stronger to conceive than to
execute, and one man may devise what only a hundred can achieve. Common good requires *association*. This is the first step toward Institution. Association is simply combination. It does not yet incarnate a principle so that
it shall work by physical instruments, and continue by its own enduring
nature. Men are short-lived; they drop the thread before the pattern is half
done. The shuttle moves slower and slower after sixty, and the loom stops
often at half that number of years. How shall the threads be taken up
again? What shall unite men to carry forward common enterprises? How
shall the variableness of the individual, crippled by sickness sometimes, and
sometimes swayed by casual attractions—wearied often, and sometimes
quite cast down, daunted, or cajoled—pushed too hard, or held back too
far by all the influences which throng life—how shall we give continuity to
the force of the individual—concentrate it and carry it forward over long
periods of time—except by supplementing one man by another, and, as the
unequal expansion of metals works steadiness for the pendulum, so, by the
inequality of dispositions, work a symmetrical whole for the individual?
Setting a fresh man over against one man's weariness, a strong man over
against his weakness, a wise man, where he is unskilled, thus using one man
to fill up another with, and by succession, as a kind of splicing, draw out
the life of a design, through many men's natural lives, giving immortality
to our purposes! . . .

That which the West needs is not so much the educated men of the
East, as the Institutions by which to educate her own men. These are the
suns that spread the East with harvests, and fill the hands with bounty, that
were held out for supply!

Colleges stimulate society through every nerve. They give power to
the liberal professions. They foster industry by giving intelligence to the
citizen. Colleges civilize the hand and put brains into its palm. The hand of
an intelligent freeman thinks more than the head of a slave. Give colleges,
and you give necessarily every thing which manhood can perform. You
give that which arouses manhood within men—which inspires them to become inspirers! Institutions which develop men are the bosoms of God,
from which society draws its life! . . .

Since the world began, I know of nothing so remarkable as the formation of society along our western border. Old nations have abandoned their

former seats, and overrun new lands, carrying with them their flocks, their arms, and those personal habits which no man can leave behind. But they have carried no constitutions, no systems of law, no circles of schools, no colleges or universities, no institutions as a moral artillery, through which the zeal of the people should utter itself!

But our own people, scarcely less nomadic than the tented Arab, scarcely less impetuous than the Goth and Hun, pour abroad along the western wilderness in swarming millions, countless, with implements, with wealth of flocks and herds, and with a breadth and depth of civilization such as never emigrated before. They drive schools along with them, as shepherds drive flocks. They have herds of churches, academies, lyceums; and their religious and educational institutions go lowing along the western plains as Jacob's herds lowed along the Syrian hills.

You can not inoculate a nation with institutions whose animating ideas are foreign. Institutions must be indigenous. They are so with us. Nothing expresses the very American spirit so much as the fourfold forms of institutions, *Commercial, Civil, Religious,* and *Educational.* The *Family* is a *natural* institution, and is the mother and nurse of all others.

It is this very wealth of institutions that brings from the West such an appeal for help. We have sent to the fairest fields that the sun ever lightened, or showers enriched, our sons and daughters, who know nothing but to rear along the vast intervales and valleys of the West a civilization as deep, as wide, as compact of social refinement, of intellectual culture, of moral richness, as that which hovers in their memory of dear old New England. But it is not possible for youthful States to lift up society in its whole breadth and depth at one lift. The *spirit* of institutions quickens their hearts, but how to give them bodies is their exceeding great task! It is enough to say of their willingness, that it is worthy of their parentage. To perform the duties of life, it is necessary first *to live.* A *living* is the first duty and necessity of emigrants. But with the burden of all the material tasks which underlay society, suddenly upon them, they are called to upheave, in gigantic proportions, the forms of higher institutions. *Ships* are first built, and then, sent on voyages. But Western States are as if men were rafted to sea with materials, and were obliged to build the ship under them while they sailed. Yea, and to grapple in desperate conflict with piratical errors and Red Rovers of ignorance, while yet they are laying down the decks, and setting up the rigging.

Baynard Rush Hall

In 1824 Baynard Rush Hall, Presbyterian clergyman and graduate of Princeton, was appointed the first principal of the Indiana State Seminary, which would become the state university. He received a salary of $250 a year, which hardly betokened the difficulties he faced, some of them detailed in the following selection. His book The New Purchase *contains a good deal of autobiographical material, only slightly concealed by his calling himself Clarence in the story. Indiana is admittedly not the trans-Mississippi West, but Hall's experience may be taken as the prototype of a hundred later efforts.*

A Western School*

Our fourth year introduces an epoch, the Augustan age of the New Purchase—the opening of the State College!

And now comes on the stage, as one principal actor, my friend, the Reverend Charles Clarence, A.M., Principal and Professor of Ancient Languages. This gentleman had accepted our appointment, not for the paltry stipend paid as his salary, but wholly because he longed to be in the romantic West, and among its earliest literary pioneers; and hence, early this spring, he was with us, and not merely ready, but even enthusiastically impatient to commence his labours. . . .

Here was a sad waking from day-dreaming! and Clarence was with us, having altered views of life, and seeing that we have something to do in it, besides to amuse or be amused. Happy chastisement our friend afterwards deemed it, when encountering sore disappointments and many, in his professional career: ay! he was destined to endure the utter crushing of all his high hopes and purposes. For, if ever man was influenced by disinterested motives, and fired with enthusiasm for advancing solid learning,—if ever one desirous of seeing Western institutions rival if not excel others,— if ever a person came willing to live and die with us, and to sacrifice eastern tastes and prejudices, and become, in every proper way, a Western Man, my friend Clarence was he.

His labours and actions proved this. Look for instance at his daily

---

* From Baynard Rush Hall [pseud., Robert Carlton], *The New Purchase* (2 vols., New York: D. Appleton & Co., 1843), II, 77–78, 80–86.

teaching—his five and six hours usually spent in the recitation room; at his preaching, always twice on the Sabbath, and commonly several times during the week; at his visits to the sick and the dying, and his attendance on funerals! And these things extended beyond his own denomination—when requested, and that was often; for rarely, even in his own sicknesses and melancholy hours, did he refuse what seemed his duty to others. When too feeble to leave his house, he heard the recitations in his bed; and when unable to stand, he sat in his congregation and preached, his person emaciated and his face death-like. Nor did he confine his teaching to the routine himself had followed, but he introduced other branches, and also a course of Greek, unknown then in western colleges, and not common in eastern ones; and this, although it added to the severity of his private studies, and for many months kept his lamp burning even till two o'clock! His only inquiry was, how can I best promote the interests of the institution? In short, therefore, all his learning, his talents, his experience, his accomplishments, were freely and heartily employed and given, in season and out of season;—and a knowledge of all the music he possessed, vocal and instrumental, was imparted, *gratuitously*, to the students—and also grammar, moral philosophy, and the like, *gratuitously*, and at *extra* hours, to certain teachers of ordinary schools, and some of these his former opponents! . . .

Be it remembered, as was intimated in the early part of volume first, that Uncle Sam is an undoubted friend of *public* education, and that, although so sadly deficient in his own; and hence, in the liberal distribution of other folk's land, he bestowed on us several entire townships for a college or university. It was, therefore, democratically believed, and loudly insisted on, that as the State had freely received, it should freely give; and that "larnin, even the most powerfullest highest larnin," should at once be bestowed on every body! and without a farthing's expense! Indeed, some gravely said and argued that teachers and professors in the "people's college ought to sarve for the honour!" or at least be content with "a dollar a day, which was more nor double what a feller got for mauling rails!" The popular wrath therefore was at once excited almost to fury when necessity compelled us to fix our tuition fee at ten dollars a year; and the greatest indignation was felt and expressed towards Clarence "as the feller what tuk hire for teaching and preaching, and was gettin to be a big-bug on the poor people's edicashin money."

Be it recollected too, that both big and little colleges were erected by persons who, with reverence be it spoken, in all matters pertaining to "high larnin," had not sufficient discrimination to know the second letter of an alphabet from a buffalo's foot. Nothing, we incline to believe, can ever make State schools and colleges very good ones; but nothing can make them *so* bad, we repeat, as for Uncle Sam to leave every point open to debate, especially among ignorant, prejudiced, and selfish folks in a New Purchase. For while trustees may be ninnies, nincompoops, or even ninnyhammers as to proper plans and buildings, yet are such when masons, bricklayers and carpenters, keen-sighted enough to secure the building contracts for themselves and their friends, and curiously exorbitant in their demands on the sub-treasurers for their silly work. The mean-looking and ridiculous arrangements at Woodville cost as much, perhaps more, than *suitable* things would have cost; so that when a college is to be commenced it ought to be done, not only by honest but by wise, learned, classical men; but as such are not abundant in very new settlements, let such men at Washington—(and such *are* at Uncle Sam's bureau)—let them prescribe when, and how, and where, our new western institutions are to be; and if rebellious democrats refuse the gift so encumbered, let it thus be given to more modest and quiet democrats.

Proceed we, however, to open the college. And my narration may be depended on, as Clarence has reviewed the whole and says it is substantially correct,—indeed, in some respect I was a *quorum-pars*.

The institution was opened the first day of May, at 9½ o'clock, A.M., anno Domini 1800 and so forth. And, some floors being unlaid, and the sashes all being without glass, the opening was as complete as possible—nearly like that of an Irish hedge school! When the Principal—(so named in our minutes and papers, but by the vulgar called *master,* and by the middle sort, *teacher,*)—appeared, a clever sprinkle of *boy* was in waiting; most of which firmly believed that, by some magic art, our hero *could,* and being paid by government, *should,* and without putting any body to the expense of books and implements, touch and transmute all, and in less than no time, into great scholars.

"Boys and *young gentlemen,*" said Mr. C. compounding the styles of a pedagogue and professor, "I am happy to see you; and we are now about to commence our State College, or, as some call it, the Seminary. I hope all feel what an honour attends being the first students in an institution so well endowed; and which, therefore, by proper exertions on our parts, may eventually rise to the level of eastern colleges, and become a blessing to our State and country. You have all, I suppose, procured the necessary books, of which notice was given at meeting, and in several other ways, for the last four weeks."

"I've got 'em—"

"Me too—"

"I've brung most on 'em—"

"Master—Uncle Billy's to fetch mine out in his wagin about Monday next—"

"Father says he couldn't mind the names and wants them on a paper—"

"Books!—I never heern tell of any books—wont these here ones do, Master?—this here's the Western Spellin one—and this one's the Western Kalkelatur?"

"Mr. Clarinse—I fotch'd my copy-book and a bottle of red-ink to sit down siferin in—and daddy wants me to larn book-keepin and surveyin."

"Order boys—order!"—(hem!)—"let all take seats in front. There is a misunderstanding with some, both as to the books and the whole design and plan of the school, I perceive. This is a Classical and Mathematical School; and that fact is stated and fully explained in the trustees' public advertisements; and no person can be admitted unless one intending to enter upon and pursue the prescribed course; and that includes even at the start Latin, Greek, and Algebra. Now, first, let us see who are to study the dead languages—"

"I do—I do—me to—me to," &c., &c.

"Do you, then, sit there. Well—now let me have your names for the roll—A. Berry—S. Smith—C. D. &c., &c.—ten names—I will attend to you ten directly, so soon as I have dismissed the others. I regret, my young friends, that you are disappointed—but I am only doing my duty; indeed, if I wished I have no power to admit you, unless to the course of studies —nay, even the trustees have power to do only what they have done. I hope, therefore, you will now go home, and explain the matter to your friends—"

By several—

"Daddy says he doesen't see no sort a use in the high larn'd things— and he wants me to larn Inglish only, and bookkeepin, and surveyin, so as to tend store and run a line."

"I allow, Mister, we've near on about as good a right to be larn'd what we wants, as them tother fellers on that bench;—it's a free school for all."

"I am sorry, boys, for this misunderstanding; but we cannot argue the subject here. And yet every one must see one matter plainly; for instance, any man has a right to be governor, or judge, or congressman; yet none of you can be elected before the legal age, and before having some other qualifications. It is so here, you all have a right to what we have to bestow; but you must be qualified to enter; and must be content to receive the gift of the State in the way the law provides and orders. You will please go home now."

The disappointed youngsters accordingly withdrew; and with no greater rudeness than was to be expected from undisciplined chaps, full of false notions of rights, and possessed by a wild spirit of independence. Hence, Mr. C. heard some very flattering sentiments growled at him by the retiring young democrats; but which, when they had fairly reached the entry, were bawled and shouted out frankly and fearlessly. And naturally after this he was honoured with some high sounding epithets by certain hypocritical demagogues in rabble-rousing speeches—sneaking gentlemen, who aimed to get office and power by endless slanders on the college, and most pitiful and malicious slang about "liberty and equality, and rights, and tyranny, and big-bugs, and poor people, and popular education," *et id omne genus!*

Ay! certain small-potato-patriots publicly on the stump avowed "it was a right smart chance better to have no collidge no how, if all folks hadn't equal right to larn what they most liked best." And two second-rate pettifoggers electioneered on this principle; "that it was most consistent with the republicanism taught by the immortal Jefferson, and with the genius of our institutions, to use the college funds to establish common schools for rich and poor alike, and make the blessings of education like air, sunshine, and water!"

Clarence, therefore, was now hated and villified, as the supposed instrument of pride and aristocracy, in drawing a line between rich and poor; and for a while his person, his family, his very house was abominated. On one occasion he was in Woodville when a half drunken brute thus halloed against him—"Thare goes that darn'd high larn'd bug what gits nine hundred and ninety-nine dollars and ninety-nine cents of the people's eddekashin money for larnin ristekrats sons high flown words—gimme that 'are stone and I'll do for him." Whether this was fun or earnest, Clarence did not care to ascertain; for hearing the sneers and derision of the bystanders, and fearing it might become earnest, he took shelter in my store.

At another time walking with Professor Harwood in the outskirts of the village, they heard a cry in their rear—"knock 'em down"—when suddenly turning, there stood a stout chap flourishing a bludgeon over their heads, evidently, indeed, in a *sort* of fun, which was, however, an index of the popular ill-will and spite.

When persons rode by his dwelling, remarks like the following would be shouted forth:—

"Well—thar's whar the grammur man lives that larns 'em Latin and grand-like things—allow we'll oust him yet—he dosen't own little college any how; he's poor as Job's turkey, if it want for that powerful sallury the trustees give him."

Clarence's salary was four hundred dollars per annum!

"Well," bawled out one fellow—"dog my hide if that ain't the furst time I ever seed that big man's door open!—hem!—powerful fine carpet! —(a beautiful rag carpet made by Mrs. C.)—allow, people's eddekashin money *bought* that!"

Even Mr. C.'s gratuitous preaching could not secure him from ill-natured remarks. "Well," said an occasional hearer to another once—"how do y'like that sort a preachin?" "Foo!" was the reply. "I don't want no more sich! I like a man that kin jist read, and then I know it comes from the sperit! he tuk out his goold watch twice to show it, and was so d—mnation proud he wouldn't kneel down to pray!"

But the reader may wish to know how Mr. Clarence got along with "the Few." Well, as the warm weather approached, the "boys and young

gentlemen" came to recitation without coats ; and, as the thermometer arose,
they came without *shoes*—

"What ! in the State college ? Could your Mr. Clarence not have things
ordered with more decency ?"

Softly, Mr. Dignity—in a world where our presiding judge, a man of
worth and great abilities, presided in court without his coat and cravat,
and with his feet modestly reposed on the upper rostrum, thus showing his
boot-soles to by-standers and lawyers; where lawyers were stripped and in
shirt-sleeves; and where even Governor Sunbeam, in a stump speech, gave
blast to his nose pinched between a thumb and finger, and wiped said
pinchers afterwards on the hinder regions of his inexpressibles; do you,
sir, think our Mr. C., or all eastern dignitaries combined, could have compelled young bushwhackers to wear coats and shoes in recitation rooms?
He indeed ventured once as follows :—

"Young *gentlemen*"—(hem !)—"why do you attend recitations without
coats and shoes ?"

" 'Tis cooler, sir !"—with surprise.

"Ay! so it is—perhaps it would be still cooler if you came without
your *pantaloons*."

Haw ! haw !—by the whole ten.

"And *did* they, Mr. Carlton, come without their indispensables ?"

Oh! dear me! no; on the contrary, the young gentlemen were so
tickled at our professor's pleasant hint direct, that next day they not only
come in their breeches, but also with shoes and coats on! But still, many
proper regulations of our friend were distasteful to scholars and parents
equally—for instance, the requirement of a written excuse for certain ab-
sences. One parent, an upper class Thompsonian doctor, did, indeed, once
send a note—but that was an insolent and peremptory order to Clarence to
believe in future his son, without a written excuse! And another person, a
captain in the *late* war, not only refused to write a note, but he sent a
verbal message by his son to the master, viz.—"Charley Clarence, you
needn't think of introducing your d—n Yankee tricks out here !"

Louis B. Wright

*Louis Booker Wright, director of the Folger Shakespeare Library in
Washington, has long been a student of Anglo-American civilization. In
recent lectures at the University of Indiana, the school founded by Baynard
Hall, he remarked judiciously on the carriers of culture in the West.*

Religion and the Frontier*

The freedom, the lack of restraint, and the lawlessness of the American frontier have received such dramatic emphasis in the literature describing the movement of settlers across this continent that we are prone to forget other more significant characteristics. We are likely to overlook the unspectacular efforts of godly and law-abiding folk to establish old patterns of behavior. Yet on every frontier, as the American continent was settled, a group who sometimes described themselves self-consciously as the "better element" waged a persistent warfare against the disintegrating forces which the liberty of a wild country unloosed. This group were the conservators of traditional conduct, traditional ways of doing things, traditional manners and morals, and they sought to preserve and perpetuate the ancient inheritance of things of the mind and spirit. In short, they tried to reproduce in the new environment the best of the civilized way of life they had previously known. Sometimes this better element was a minority, but a potent minority who, if they lost an occasional battle, usually managed in some fashion to win the war against the powers of darkness. The conservation and perpetuation of traditional civilization in each newly settled region of the country have not received dramatic acclaim; they are not the subjects for stirring novels or sensational movies; but few characteristics have had a greater importance in the development of American society as we know it today. . . .

Puritanism in its various manifestations in New England had been a way of life, a part of the everyday existence of men, and not something put on on Sunday. New England towns in the earlier days had often grown by congregations splitting off and migrating with their ministers to new sites. The strict moral code of the Puritans implied an active concern of the churches for the behavior and welfare of their members and indeed for the whole community, whether within the bosom of the church or outside. And the welfare of the community also implied a concern for education which became a characteristic of New Englanders wherever they went.

Few of the Dissenting sects exceeded the Presbyterians in evangelical zeal during the late years of the eighteenth century and the first half of the nineteenth. Presbyterianism was the religion of the Scotch-Irish frontiersmen who pushed westward from Pennsylvania and from the highlands of Virginia and the Carolinas. They were among the hardiest of the pioneers, and the religious leaders were men of learning, many of whom had degrees

---

*From Louis B. Wright, *Culture on the Moving Frontier* (Bloomington: Indiana University Press, 1955), pp. 12, 168–193 *passim.*

from Scottish universities. They were as convinced of the civilizing value
of Greek and Latin as they were of the truth of Holy Writ and when they
combined the classics and the Bible in their educational efforts, they were
certain that they had found the way to cultural and spiritual salvation.
After the Act of Union in 1801 which brought Congregationalists and
Presbyterians together as joint agents in the missionary enterprise in the
West, their influence was even greater. The Congregationalists feared that
their form of church polity, suited though it was to the compact towns of
New England, would not provide an effective organization for the sparsely
settled regions of the West. Since the Congregationalists of western Massachusetts and Connecticut retained a greater degree of doctrinal conser-
vatism than the more liberal churches in the urban areas in the East, it was
easy for them to affiliate with the Presbyterians who were equally conservative in matters of doctrine. Their alliance for the spiritual conquest of the
West proved an excellent arrangement, though some Congregationalists
declared that the Presbyterians swallowed them up. "Congregationalism,"
observes an historian of American home missions, "was likened to a river
which took its origin in New England and flowed into a Presbyterian ocean
in the West." Presbyterian or Congregationalist as they might be, hundreds
of devoted preachers carried the light of religion and learning to raw communities throughout the West.

Beginning in 1797 with a revival conducted in Logan County, Kentucky, by James McGready, a Presbyterian preacher, a wave of religious
excitement swept the West for the next decade. This period, called the
Second Awakening by analogy with the Great Awakening in the eighteenth
century, or sometimes the Great Revival, was marked by the development
of the camp meeting as a means of reaching the great masses of the people.
These meetings, providing drama, excitement, and social contacts to a
people living isolated in scattered settlements, attracted everybody, good
and bad. Under the lash of clerical oratory, congregations sometimes broke
into wild hysteria, but the excesses have been greatly exaggerated by sensational writers. Camp meetings could also be as solemn and decorous as a
service in a New England meeting house. Started by the Presbyterians,
they became a characteristic feature of Methodist revivalism in the West,
though they were never officially recognized by the Methodist church con-
ferences. Nevertheless they helped to win thousands of converts to Methodism which by the second decade of the nineteenth century had overtaken
Presbyterianism as the most dynamic of the frontier faiths.

Much nonsense has been written about the emotionalism of the Methodist preachers. The Methodists, as their name suggests, believed in an
orderly system of worship, and many of their leaders, including Bishop
Francis Asbury, frowned on too much "enthusiasm" or emotionalism. Like
the Jesuits, they had a system almost military in its organization which
suited conditions of Western society. Circuit riders received appointments

from the bishop of the church conference having jurisdiction over a particular territory, and these itinerant preachers, riding through the wilderness, carried the gospel to the most distant settlements. At first the Methodists did not try to build churches but preached in homes, barns, or the open fields wherever they could gather a congregation. In their saddlebags they also carried books, pamphlets, and magazines which often constituted the only reading matter that ever reached many pioneers. Though not every preacher lived up to the high ideals of John Wesley, prevailingly the Methodist preachers were a self-sacrificing and devoted group who did much to civilize the West. The integrity, courage, and common sense of circuit riders like Peter Cartwright won respect wherever they went. The hardihood of the circuit riders gave currency to a saying when the weather was too bitterly cold for most mortals to stir abroad that "there is nothing out today but crows and Methodist preachers."

The civilizing influence of the itinerant Methodist preacher and the literature that he distributed is incalculable, but it is a subject that deserves further investigation. Certainly he did much to bring a notion of learning and letters to people whom not even the Presbyterians could reach. John Wesley, the founder of Methodism, had edited a sort of "Great Books" series called the "Christian Library" in fifty volumes for the instruction of the faithful; and he had insisted upon his preachers reading. Self-education through reading became a definite part of Methodist teaching. When the Methodists had transferred their evangelical zeal to the Western frontier, they were still concerned with edification as well as salvation. "Frontier Methodism," remarks one historian, "was far more solidly based than is usually pictured. It was by no means all froth. The long lists of books, Bibles, hymn books, Disciplines, and church periodicals sold to the people by the circuit riders, all of whom were agents for the Methodist Book Concern, are evidence that the amount of religious instruction afforded the people of the frontier was not inconsiderable." The circuit rider as book agent, as a carrier of letters and learning, even on the modest level that his own background and the capacity of his saddlebags could provide, is a theme worthy of our respect—and our study. The dissemination of books in the West became a particular preoccupation of the Methodists. The General Conference of 1800 declared that "it shall be the duty of every preacher who has charge of a circuit to see that his circuit is supplied with books" and two investigators for the Massachusetts Missionary Society reported after a trip through the West in 1814 that the activity of the Methodists in distributing books "puts to blush all other charitable institutions in the United States." . . .

Sectarian competition, indeed, helped to generate activity and spur religious groups to extraordinary efforts in establishing churches and schools. Nearly all of the frontier colleges which sprang up like mushrooms in the nineteenth century were religious in origin. Each denomination felt that it must have a college if it expected to keep pace with its rivals. Even the Baptists joined in the educational race. "Nearly all our colleges are ... the creations of the different religious denominations which divide our people," declared President F. A. P. Barnard of the University of Mississippi in 1856. "They are regarded as important instrumentalities, through which the peculiarities of doctrine which distinguish its founders are to be maintained, propagated, or defended. It is this which has led to the great multiplication of collegiate institutions in our country, and which is daily adding to their number." The multiplication of colleges did not receive unalloyed praise from all observers. Concerning the crop of colleges which germinated in Illinois in the 1830's, one commentator remarked that "a settler could hardly encamp on the prairies but a college would spring up beside his wagon." These institutions, often colleges in name only, with a clergyman and his wife composing the academic staff, obviously sought to emphasize the dogmas of their sects, but they also provided a surprising amount of cultural training. Many an intellectual leader in the West owed his education to some college which flourished a few years and died. . . .

Far from being radical, the Western colleges founded by religious groups were more conservative ideologically than many of the older Eastern institutions. Socially the Western college might be democratic; it might open its doors to women on an equal footing with men; it might not condone the snobbery of exclusive clubs and fraternities; but ideologically, Western colleges were rarely given to experimentation or speculative thinking. Even today in the West boards of trustees worry about radicalism in a way that seems ridiculous to many of their counterparts in the East. The typical frontier college wanted to reproduce both the religion and the culture which their founders had regarded as orthodox, and most of these colleges were determined to have no traffic with uncertified notions and beliefs. . . .

When we talk of the poverty of reading matter on any of our frontiers from the seventeenth to the mid-nineteenth century, we are prone to think in quantitative terms. We are likely to forget that one book well read may have a far greater impact than dozens skimmed and tossed aside. No one can say that the Bible was not earnestly read by thousands. In pious households it was read aloud at family worship and children were accustomed from infancy to its sonorous music. Unconsciously it became a part of an esthetic experience in addition to whatever religious effect it may have had. One of the works which most influenced the style and thinking of Abraham Lincoln was the Bible. Though some of his friends described him as a freethinker if not an infidel, others who heard him quote Scripture with respect thought him a religious man. Before he had learned to read, he had heard his mother quoting Bible verses as she worked and he had learned many of these verses by heart. "Lincoln read the Bible closely," Carl Sandburg asserts, "read it from cover to cover, was familiar with its stories and its poetry, quoted from it in his talks to juries, in political campaigns, in his speeches, and in his letters." Lincoln's acquaintance with the Bible was not unusual, for the Bible was a part of the general education of every citizen. If a backwoods lawyer had to choose between Blackstone and the Bible, he was better advised to stick to citations from the Bible because jurors were more familiar with it and could be persuaded by its dramatic connotations no less than by the weight of its authority as revealed truth. In the Bible, the frontiersman had a whole library of poetry, drama, historical narrative, folk tales, didactic exposition, and practically anything else his taste might require, all available in a diction and a style that have rarely been equaled in any language. The concentration upon this volume which poverty forced upon many a household was not without benefits which the modern reader might envy.

ADDITIONAL READINGS

A complete reading of Louis B. Wright's *Culture on the Moving Frontier* (Bloomington, 1955) should precede anything else on this subject. *Virgin Land,* by Henry Nash Smith (Cambridge, Mass., 1950), is an indispensable study for the area of literature. The chapter on the West in Constance Rourke's *American Humor: a Study of the National Character* (New York, 1931) is delightful. Oliver Larkin, in *Art and Life in America* (rev. ed., New York, 1960), deals occasionally with the effects of the West on art.

Index

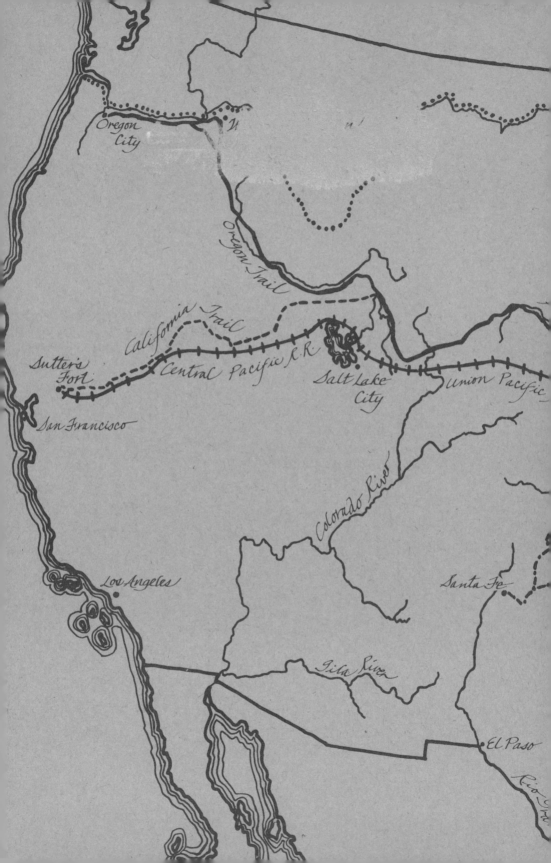